The Methods and Uses of Anthropological Demography

The International Union for the Scientific Study of Population Problems was founded in 1928, with Dr Raymond Pearl as President. At that time the Union's main purpose was to promote international scientific cooperation in the study of various aspects of population problems, through national committees and by its members. In 1947 the International Union for the Scientific Study of Population (IUSSP) was reconstituted into its present form. It expanded its activities to:

- stimulate research on population
- develop interest in demographic matters among governments, national and international organizations, scientific bodies, and the general public
- foster relations between people involved in population studies
- disseminate scientific knowledge on population.

The principal ways through which the IUSSP currently achieves its aims are:

- organization of worldwide or regional conferences
- operations of Scientific Committees under the auspices of the Council
- organization of training courses
- publication of conference proceedings and committee reports.

Demography can be defined by its field of study and its analytical methods. Accordingly, it can be regarded as the scientific study of human populations primarily with respect to their size, their structure, and their development. For reasons which are related to the history of the discipline, the demographic method is essentially inductive: progress in knowledge results from the improvement of observation, the sophistication of measurement methods, and the search for regularities and stable factors leading to the formulation of explanatory models. In conclusion, the three objectives of demographic analysis are to describe, measure, and analyse.

International Studies in Demography is the outcome of an agreement concluded by the IUSSP and Oxford University Press. The joint series is expected to reflect the broad range of the Union's activities and, in the first instance, will be based on the seminars organized by the Union. The Editorial Board of the series is comprised of:

The Methods and Uses of Anthropological Demography

Edited by

Alaka Malwade Basu
Peter Aaby

CLARENDON PRESS · OXFORD

*This book has been printed digitally and produced in a standard specification
in order to ensure its continuing availability*

OXFORD
UNIVERSITY PRESS

Great Clarendon Street, Oxford OX2 6DP

Oxford University Press is a department of the University of Oxford.
It furthers the University's objective of excellence in research, scholarship,
and education by publishing worldwide in

Oxford New York

Auckland Bangkok Buenos Aires Cape Town Chennai
Dar es Salaam Delhi Hong Kong Istanbul Karachi Kolkata
Kuala Lumpur Madrid Melbourne Mexico City Mumbai Nairobi
São Paulo Shanghai Taipei Tokyo Toronto

Oxford is a registered trade mark of Oxford University Press
in the UK and in certain other countries

Published in the United States
by Oxford University Press Inc., New York

ISBN 0-19-829337-2

Preface

This book is an outcome of a workshop organized by the Scientific Committee on Anthropological Demography of the International Union for the Scientific Study of Population. When the committee began its term in 1992, it felt that it needed to first make some formal attempt to define the scope of anthropological demography and develop not so much a manual as a guiding text to attract more demographers to this relatively new but potentially rich sub-discipline. This was especially necessary because interested demographers have nowhere to turn to for an exposition of the *methods* of anthropological demography; and even the kind of substantive research that is discussed in this volume and that will surely provoke further research, has until recently been unavailable in the standard demography journals, which have traditionally been biased towards more quantitative analyses.

Accordingly, the Committee decided to begin its activities with a workshop which invited mainstream demographers and anthropologists to discuss, debate, and reflect on the possibilities inherent in anthropological demography and to describe in usable terms the ways in which it can contribute to better demographic understanding. The workshop was held in Barcelona in November 1993 and several individuals and institutions deserve mention for its success.

To begin with, we would like to thank all seven members of the Committee on Anthropological Demography, even those whose names are missing from the formal contributions. The members are: Peter Aaby, John Anarfi, Alaka Basu, Caroline Bledsoe, Gilbert Herdt, Susana Lerner, and Kim Streatfield. The workshop and the book which follows was a joint endeavour at all times. In addition, the Committee was for all practical purposes made up of nine members, because Bruno Remiche and Irene Grignac from the IUSSP Secretariat were an integral part of all deliberations, academic as well as organizational. Bruno Remiche has since passed away and the Committee would like to record its special thanks for all his generous help and advice.

The workshop was made possible by funding from the Mellon Foundation and we are very grateful for this support. In addition, we have to thank the local organizers in Barcelona, the Centre d'Estudis Demografics and the Institut Catala d'Estudis Mediterranis. Not only did these organizations meet the local expenses of the workshop, they handled the administrative arrangements in a way that left a lasting impression. The workshop proceeded smoothly because of their efforts and the city of Barcelona came alive and exciting to participants because of their own excitement about their wonderful city. In particular, we must thank personally Anna Cabre as the chief representative of the local organizers.

An initial round of copy-editing and general tidying up of the chapters by Richard Hankinson greatly smoothed the progress of the manuscript. The two anonymous reviewers of the IUSSP did an excellent job of reading and commenting on the individual papers; we thank them for their thoughtful suggestions and enthusiasm for the project. Their support has since been augmented by the support of the staff of Oxford University Press dealing with the manuscript and we would like to record our appreciation of this.

Alaka M. Basu
Peter Aaby

Contents

List of Contributors

PETER AABY — Department of Epidemiology, University of Copenhagen, Copenhagen, Denmark

JOHN KWASI ANARFI — Institute of Statistical, Social, and Economic Research, University of Ghana, Legon, Ghana

ALAKA M. BASU — Division of Nutritional Sciences, Cornell University, Ithaca, NY, USA

SUKUMARI BHATTACHARJI — Jadavpur University, Calcutta, India

CAROLINE BLEDSOE — Department of Anthropology, Northwestern University, Evanston, IL, USA

JOHN C. CALDWELL — National Centre for Epidemiology and Population Health, Australian National University, Canberra, Australia

PAT CALDWELL — National Centre for Epidemiology and Population Health, Australian National University, Canberra, Australia

ANTHONY T. CARTER — Department of Anthropology, University of Rochester, Rochester, NY, USA

JOHN CLELAND — Centre for Population Studies, London School of Hygiene and Tropical Medicine, London, UK

ALLAN HILL — Harvard University, Cambridge, MA, USA

GEORGIA KAUFMANN — Institute of Development Studies, University of Sussex, Brighton, Sussex, UK

JOHN KNODEL — Population Studies Center, University of Michigan, Ann Arbor, MI, USA

PHILIP KREAGER   Pauling Centre for Human Sciences, University of Oxford, Oxford, UK

I. O. ORUBOLOYE   Faculty of Social Sciences, Ondo State University, Ado-Ekitim, Ondo State, Nigeria

JANE SCHNEIDER   Department of Anthropology, The City University of New York, New York, NY, USA

PETER SCHNEIDER   Division of Social Sciences, Fordham University, Bronx, NY, USA

SJAAK VAN DER GEEST   Anthropological Sociological Centre, University of Amsterdam, Amsterdam, Netherlands

Introduction:
Approaches to Anthropological Demography

ALAKA MALWADE BASU AND PETER AABY

The discipline of demography has generally been tolerant of intervention by outsiders, and has welcomed their contribution to the study of its primary concerns—births, deaths, and population movements. Thus, economists continue to have their say on these matters, along with epidemiologists, statisticians, and sociologists. But one of the disciplines most intimately interested in questions of life and death, namely anthropology, was until recently curiously disinclined to go the next step and attach a wider demographic component to its deliberations. At the same time, demographers, with their unstinting loyalty to field and analytical methods antithetical to the traditional field and analytical techniques of anthropology, did not seem to find this at all curious.

All that has now changed with a vengeance. Since the 1980s, demography has branched into what may be called a new sub-discipline, anthropological demography,[1] which in its infant stages consisted of a combination of quantitative and qualitative data collection by researchers personally involved in their study sites. This was a big jump indeed from the demographic tradition of relying solely on second-and third-hand data sets compiled by an army of field investigators. Once started, demographic research has been deluged with demographers trying to do 'micro-research', which unfortunately has often meant little more than repeating with much smaller samples the traditional techniques of data collection and analysis of standard demography.

This too is now changing, albeit slowly. Anthropological demography is now well out of its infancy and has in recent years demonstrated its right to sub-disciplinary status through a combination of anthropology and demography in much more than field procedures. Today, some demographers at least refer to ethnographies, study culture, and kinship, and even come perilously close to using some of the theories and concepts of traditional anthropology. Anthropological demographers also are realizing that their efforts are greatly helped by coopting mainstream anthropologists into the task of demographic research, thus taking the latter one step further into the sub-discipline of 'demographic anthropology'.

This volume is the product of an attempt to take stock of the current status of anthropological demography and to examine its major methods, its main strengths, and its main limitations. To this end, the Committee on Anthropological Demography of the International Union for the Scientific Study of Population (IUSSP) organized a workshop with the somewhat unimaginative title of 'New Approaches to Anthropological Demography' in Barcelona, Spain, in November 1993, to which it invited a number of mainstream anthropologists and demographers who had demonstrated interest in or potential for straddling both disciplines. The result of the workshop and the long discussions that it stimulated is this monograph, which it is hoped will inspire and guide further research in anthropological demography and a better understanding of not only demographic events but also demographic processes.

The next few sections trace the ways in which anthropological demography can enhance demographic understanding, as well as some of the problems associated with this branch of research in practice (even if these problems are surmountable in principle). Both the strengths of this approach and its limitations are illustrated in the papers that follow. At the outset, it is worth stressing that all the contributors to this volume continue to value the traditional demographer's armoury of field methods, analytical techniques, and conceptual frameworks and recommend anthropological input as a means to supplement or complement this armoury, not to supplant it. This consensus is not the result of design; it is a natural outcome of the increasing awareness in other disciplines of the great potential of demography realistically to illuminate many of life's problems.[2] It is also clear that not all the interesting questions in demography need an anthropological input to improve the quality of the answers provided.

This volume is also an attempt to seduce more mainstream demographers into anthropological demography and to support as well as caution those who have already converted. While mainstream anthropologists and demographic anthropologists contribute seminally to this task in several chapters, the book as a whole tries less to draw anthropologists into demographic research than to find common ground in new forms of enquiry. If in the process some anthropologists also discover the attractions of demography, it will have been doubly successful.

The Field Methods of Anthropological Demography

As already mentioned, the sub-discipline of anthropological demography began as, and largely continues to be, a field procedure. Two features of traditional anthropology were coopted by demographers and adapted to suit their own inclinations and techniques. The first of these was a greater emphasis on open-ended questions in the traditional survey. This meant that a set of precoded answers were not appended to such questionnaires by statistical demographers confident of obtaining valid field responses. Instead, respondents were increasingly allowed to speak in their own words, these words were recorded, and the data thus collected was used in a qualitative way in addition to being collapsed into coded categories for quantitative analysis.

In this scheme, categories such as 'Other', 'Don't know', and 'Non-response' become important responses in their own right and demand further scrutiny instead of merely being recorded as such or, even worse, being excluded from the denominator of calculated rates. This category of answer has been the demographer's nightmare for a range of survey questions, especially those requiring a numerical response from the respondent. The reporting of age is an important example, on which standard demography has produced reams of discussion and advice. But until the advent of anthropological demography, the kernel of this advice usually consisted of ingenuous ways of determining age in the field or imputing it during the editing of questionnaires. It was only when qualitative responses came to be legitimate that answers such as 'How old do I look?' (see Basu 1992) and visibly contradictory answers (such as young women referring to themselves as 'very old' and vice versa) deepened the appreciation that social age is as valid a determinant of behaviour as chronological age and that its incorporation in tables can do wonders for demographic understanding.

Similar frustration faced the traditional demographer interested in questions of ideal family size. World Fertility Survey (WFS) interviewers, for instance, who were trained to insist on numerical responses to this question (see the WFS 'Interviewers' Instructions' and Lightbourne and MacDonald 1982), even felt that such insistence was justified by the results. But how wise is such insistence? The fact that in the Bangladesh WFS for example, there was still a stunning 29% non-numerical response rate to this question calls for serious rethinking on the value of excluding these cases in calculations of the demand for family planning.

The second major feature of anthropological demography was a greater field involvement by demographers themselves. While such involvement sometimes deteriorated into the policing of the field team's work, it soon became obvious that curious demographers had much to gain by becoming a part of the field team in a much more anthropological way—by living in the field, talking to people other than survey respondents, and observing behaviour that might initially seem to have little ostensible demographic significance. While this form of data collection quite rightly did not lead to the abandonment of the quantitative survey instrument, it did let its qualitative findings feed into the survey and let the survey findings throw up issues for more intense qualitative investigation.

The paper by Caldwell, Orubuloye, and Caldwell (Chapter 1) documents the authors' experience of conducting such research in the very complicated area of sexual networking. Understanding fertility and contraceptive behaviour through impersonal large-scale surveys in a traditional society is difficult enough; when it comes to exploring sexual behaviour in the kind of detail needed to establish sexual networks and predict the risk of AIDS, the standard survey becomes almost useless if it is not complemented with and greatly assisted by qualitative procedures, by greater interviewer–respondent rapport, and by an ability to change the research procedure rapidly as new findings and problems present themselves. This paper is an excellent example of both the great charms and the great challenges of good anthropological demography. Field anthropological demographers need the professional and personal skills and confidence to design their own research agenda in an innovative and flexible way and to have eyes at the back of their heads so that they can, as Aaby (1987) puts it, 'observe the unexpected'.

Out of this increased interest in letting reality speak for itself through open-ended questions and greater field involvement have come most of the papers in this collection. Several of them employ this mix of qualitative and quantitative, and micro-level and macro-level, approaches in their own research, although they do not offer us the same kind of methodological detail as the paper by Caldwell *et al.* Instead, they use this mix to tell us their findings on a range of issues that concern the anthropological demographer, as is discussed in later sections of this Introduction. These include the papers by Bledsoe and Hill (Chapter 12), Aaby (Chapter 10), Schneider and Schneider (Chapter 8), and Kaufmann (Chapter 5).

At the same time, this volume cautions that anthropological demography may have given itself a deceptive reputation for simplicity. It is almost as if this kind of work is easy to do, requires few special skills, and is a good alternative for those of us uncomfortable with large numbers or complex numerical calculations. Of course this is far from being the case. A truly useful contribution in anthropological demography is much more the result of good training and intrinsic skills than of discomfort with pure numbers. Such skills and training are unfortunately rarer than the outpouring of research in the area of anthropological demography would suggest. Much current work is shoddy, equates merely small sample size with anthropological demography, and equates superficial description with real understanding of the complexities of demographic behaviour.

Several questions may be asked. Does one need skills in demography as well as anthropology to do good work in anthropological demography? Indeed, is it possible for such dual skills to reside in many individuals? Or is the purpose of anthropological demography better served by the team method of research? That is, can mainstream demographers and anthropologists be sufficiently sensitized to each other's disciplines that they can work in tandem to exploit their comparative skills? Such teamwork is of course more often anathema to the mainstream anthropologist than to the mainstream demographer, who often cannot survive without an army of field investigators. In addition, mainstream anthropologists have tended to be uninterested in demographic outcomes even though they have so much interest in the cultural determinants of these outcomes. This disinterest has been especially large in the area of mortality, and the result is that most anthropological demographic research on mortality tends to be done by demographers with little training in culture theory or in methods such as participant observation. It thus more often ends up being a replication of traditional demographic research on mortality with a smaller sample, thereby losing even the saving grace of robust statistical analysis.

One possibility that has been insufficiently explored is that of training local demographers better to use their own implicit cultural knowledge to improve both the context and the interpretation of findings. This is not to denigrate the importance of formal anthropological training: it is only to suggest that simple information on matters such as potentially harmful health behaviours (like unhygienic methods of umbilical cord cutting, or the discarding of colostrum) and immediate, as opposed to long-term, economic reasons for high fertility (such as an inability to dispose of condoms) can be identified better through the knowledge of the local culture than by the trial- and-error methods available to the 'foreign' demographer. Information on such constraints by local demographers can have great value.

Similarly, the curious and ingenious local demographer has only to sit down and think about the proximate determinants of child mortality to realize that his or her own culture may be affected by factors such as an awkwardness in taking girls to a male doctor or the practice of some women having their first births in their husbands' rather than their parental homes. A South Asian demographer, for example, would not be surprised by the statistical finding that such births are associated with higher maternal and child mortality (see e.g. Prathinidhi *et al.* 1989). Indeed, it should occur to the good South Asian demographer to look for such associations. Gursoy-Tezcan (1992) has used precisely this kind of local insight to demonstrate the high infant mortality experienced by Turkish women living in extended, patrilocal households, either currently or at the time of delivery. She suggests that this is because the nurturing capabilities of the mother are allowed less expression when the relationship between a woman and her mother-in-law is rigidly hierarchical.

Such caveats notwithstanding, there is no doubt that to most non-anthropologists, native or foreign, the first words that spring to mind when confronted with the word 'anthropology' are 'participant observation'. This cornerstone of anthropological research, whereby one becomes a part of the community one studies, is one of its greatest attractions, and it is not surprising that mainstream anthropologists are often fiercely possessive of their territories and their findings (see e.g. Gupta 1995). Van der Geest's paper (Chapter 2) suggests that this attraction can be legitimately enjoyed by the demographer as well, because the scope for better and deeper demographic understanding is often increased by participant observation. His paper is rich with descriptions of this style of research, the special insights it can generate, and, just as importantly, the intense personal gratifications it affords, not only at the emotional level that van der Geest himself experienced in the field, but also at the intellectual and social levels.

From the demographer's perspective, this method has three major assets. First, as the term itself specifies, there is the visual part of participant observation; the researcher 'observes' as well as asks and listens. In particular, the context in which the events of interest occur can be noted. Second, as van der Geest stresses, through the process of introspection that such close communion with the studied society generates, participant observation forces a re-evaluation of the different cultural meanings of terms that the armchair demographer takes so much for granted. (Van der Geest refers to the 'false exactitude' of key terms used in demography.) The precoded interview is often too hasty in assuming that words like 'marriage', 'the family', and 'ideal family size' mean the same thing to the respondent, the interviewer, and the data analyst and interpreter.

The third major advantage of such field research is also referred to in the paper by Caldwell *et al.* This is the greater ability to *verify* information. While a lot of misinformation may be the result of misunderstanding, there also definitely exist what Bleek (1987) calls 'lying informants'; respondents who rationally give incorrect answers to awkward questions. This tendency is much greater and easier to indulge in in the impersonal one-shot survey. Van der Geest's example of such mismatch between survey responses and reality throws cold water on the demographer's often blind faith in the data.

The more harried demographer, the money-strapped demographer, or simply the demographer interested in more specific and often more immediately policy-relevant issues can still go far by choosing something in between the standard large survey and the relatively long-term process of participant observation. The focus group discussion is one such method that has attracted much interest, precisely because it combines the specific focus of the demographic enquiry with allowing reality to contradict the investigator's assumptions where appropriate through the process of group discussion (Manderson and Aaby 1992). Knodel's paper (Chapter 3) discusses one such alternative—the use of focus groups—and illustrates the value of this method in a study of the old-age security motive for high fertility. The detailed conversations with respondents in groups that this method involves may strike some researchers as not being very well suited to exploring questions of sexual behaviour, or of deviance between norms and behaviour and other such probably private matters, but they definitely seem to yield very plausible explanations for the apparently vexing contradiction between families continuing to rely on children for security in their old age while rushing through a demographic transition of the kind currently being experienced in Thailand. Once these respondents sit down to actually think aloud, as it were, it soon seems quite consistent to both want fewer children and still not shed any dependency on them in old age. Knodel's paper is also an excellent example of the complementarity of survey and anthropological methods of enquiry; the author goes back and forth between his survey results and his focus group findings and ends up significantly strengthening both sets of results.

There is one other kind of field anthropological demography that deserves specific mention. This is the method of longitudinal population studies. The IUSSP Committee on Anthropological Demography devoted a whole seminar to the contribution and problems of such studies within the health field (Das Gupta *et al.* forthcoming), and therefore this approach is not described specifically in this volume. However, it should be emphasized that longitudinal population studies are eminently suited to uniting the two central features of the anthropological demographic approach, namely the need to combine large 'numerical' data sets with an understanding of demographic processes in terms of cultural ideas and behaviour patterns. Several communities in Haiti, Senegal, Guinea-Bissau, Kenya, Tanzania, Zaire, South Africa, India, and Bangladesh have been followed over many years with a routine registration of basic demographic events such as marriage, family formation, pregnancies, births, growth, infections, immunizations, deaths, and migrations. While the populations covered by these studies vary considerably in size (from between 5 and 1,000 persons to more than 200,000, depending on the specific purposes of the study), they are usually concerned with establishing demographic patterns and processes with greater certainty than is customary in the normal anthropological field study.

Longitudinal studies usually begin with a few specific issues on which it is possible to situate the research questions in a wider context and with a stronger emphasis on process than is possible in a one-shot survey. But such longitudinal studies often generate their own new research issues as investigators have their ideas questioned or contradicted through increasing knowledge of local conditions and ongoing demographic trends (Aaby forthcoming). This aspect of longitudinal studies is similar to the experience of anthropological fieldwork, where cultural reality often contradicts the researcher's assumptions until a new interpretation emerges. The method of longitudinal population studies has been used mostly by social scientists with an interest in health and mortality (Das Gupta *et al.* forthcoming), but could be used equally well in studies of marriage, fertility, and migration.

The Potential Contribution of Anthropological Knowledge

It is worth re-asking if it is really necessary for the anthropological demographer to become a field anthropologist. An important element of anthropological demography should surely be the exploitation of existing information and theory from anthropology to understand better large-scale demographic findings, rather than settling down in the field oneself. The lack of attention to existing information, whether in the form of ethnographies or theories about behaviour and change, is still an important shortcoming of anthropological demography as currently practised, and the next section describes the great potential for improvement in this area. It first considers the potential usefulness of existing anthropological information, and then goes on to discuss the ways in which primary data from the field, both quantitative and qualitative, can be better interpreted using the theoretical and conceptual frameworks of formal anthropology.

The Cultural Context

It is true that the second-hand use of anthropological information is often a difficult undertaking and requires an understanding of qualitative research techniques (including the ability to sift the representative from the unique and the ideal from the actual) and a familiarity with anthropological concepts which conventional demographic training does not usually provide. But the interested demographer can begin with the relatively easier method of using empirical *descriptions* from anthropological research to throw light on the mechanisms behind several demographic findings.

This is explained best with a personal example. In (Basu 1993), the author was struck by evidence in several data sets from North India that showed an unduly long interval between effective marriage and the first birth, contradicting all theories about the value of reproduction in this culture and accepted wisdom about early marriage being a proxy for an early start of childbearing. The explanation emerged not from standard demographic or socioeconomic surveys, but from reading in the anthropological literature about the institutionalized practice of young brides in North India going to visit their natal homes for several months at a time. Anthropologists have discussed this practice in terms of the economic roles of women, the formal relations between the woman's parental and marital homes, and the geographical distance between these two homes. But to the demographer aware of 'exposure to pregnancy' variables, it becomes immediately obvious that such extended trips preclude intercourse and thus greatly reduce the overall risk of pregnancy in this culture.

Basu's paper is this book turns to anthropological descriptions of marriage and kinship in India to search for more general relationships between what is called the 'status of women' in the demographic literature and standard demographic outcomes. The special value of anthropology for understanding cultural or community influences on women's status, especially as these in turn impinge on demographic outcomes, is illustrated with the anthropological discussion of two aspects of marriage—hypergamy and territorial exogamy—in North India. These two practices are relatively rare in South India and the paper relates this regional difference to North India–South India differences in reproductive behaviour, child mortality, and the gender gap in survival.

The paper by Basu also illustrates the use of the comparative method, an important and long-established technique (see e.g. Radcliffe-Brown 1951; Evans-Pritchard 1965) of social anthropology, and one that demographers also implicitly use in much of their large-scale analyses. For example, the World Fertility Survey and the Demographic and Health Surveys have been especially adept at what they call 'comparative studies' and 'cross-cultural studies'. Since most of these statistical comparisons do not go into questions of what it is that defines the different societies they compare (besides geographic location of course), adding an element of anthropological comparison of these societies would aid greatly in the interpretation of regional or cultural differentials.

Kinship and marriage systems in South Asia are relatively stable and allow the continued use of conventional categories to define them. In many other parts of the world, as the paper by Kaufmann (Chapter 5) discusses, there is much greater variation between norms and behaviour, and the definition of marriage itself varies greatly across societies and over time. Thus, in some cultures and under some circumstances, marriage may legitimize pregnancy and childbearing, while in others pregnancy and childbearing may legitimize a sexual union into marriage. In the latter case, there may be a very fluid definition of what constitutes marriage, with individuals becoming more or less married with time and changing circumstances. (This situation is posited to exist especially strongly in sub-Saharan Africa; see for example the report of the National Academy of Sciences 1993; Bledsoe and Pison 1994.)

In Kaufmann's Brazilian study, on the other hand, there is very little of such ambiguity, and childbearing during singlehood, cohabitation, or marriage does not represent different stages of a life course. Instead, marriage and cohabitation are mutually exclusive alternatives, with marriage reserved for those more fortunate to begin with. Family types as well go against traditional modernization theory in Kaufmann's *favela*. The neolocal conjugal unit is usually the least advantaged of all family types, because it is the family form thrust upon individuals originally from rural areas, having few material resources in the city and few extended kin to live with and rely upon. This kind of finding calls into serious question the assumption in modernization theory that a universal convergence to the nuclear family is a positive feature of development or modernization. Indeed, family type is so much an outcome of material circumstances in this area that it has little bearing on indicators of fertility; it is marital status that confers the values and abilities related to fertility outcomes.

This volume also tries throughout to maintain a balance in its endorsement of anthropological demography for demographers. It recognizes that not only is the traditional demographic approach essential for demographic understanding, but also, some aspects of anthropology may have little to offer the mainstream demographer. For example, the paper by Basu (Chapter 4) highlights some of the ways in which different stages of the intellectual development of feminist anthropology have different things to offer to the demographer. In addition, it discusses some of the shortcomings of feminist anthropology for demographers interested in women's status and demographic behaviour interrelationships. In particular, it criticizes the tendency to confuse the women's status question with the gender question. From the demographer's perspective at least, low female status during the reproductive ages is often a result of power asymmetries among different women in a household as much as a reflection of male–female hierarchies.

The limitations of anthropological demography in its current form become more apparent in Cleland and Kaufmann's attempt to scour the anthropological literature to try to throw more light on the well documented but still little understood near-universal relationship between maternal education and demographic outcomes (Chapter 6). Why do educated women have fewer children and experience lower child mortality, even when statistical rigour controls for the possible confounding variables of income and occupation? What is it about their education that gives them these special skills or attitudes? Cleland and Kaufmann conclude from their review of the anthropology of education that education is as contextual a variable as fertility, and thus they marvel at the near universality of the education–fertility relationship. But, while they are able to unearth much material on the *meaning* of education, they come up with surprisingly little on the *impact* of education on social behaviour. On the surface, this would appear a ripe subject for anthropological investigation, and when it is turned to it probably will yield much of demographic value. But the current anthropology of education—that is, anthropological research on education not directly connected to demographic concerns—gives up few secrets that are useful to the demographer. Indeed, at the moment this appears to be an area in which anthropology could get more out of demography than the other way around. The demonstration of a near-universal relationship between maternal education and fertility and mortality is one of the key contributions of contemporary demography, both as a research finding that seems to defy context and as a policy tool with few negative implications.

The Wider Context

Anthropological demography (or the micro-level research that passes for much anthropological demography) limits itself greatly by focusing exclusively on only one determinant of behaviour when it moves away from the conventional demographer's perspective of the individual with personal characteristics. This variable is called 'culture', defined as a broad umbrella that covers several related markers such as language, religion, and geographical location. The Princeton Fertility Project was, of course, a major impetus in the recognition of culture and of increased awareness among demographers that anthropology might have valuable insights into demographic behaviour because of its traditional concern with cultural matters. But cultural anthropology is only one, however important, component of anthropology. There are other components that are alive and thriving, and that have almost as much to offer demography, as some of the papers in this volume demonstrate. In particular, there is much to be learnt from history and from political anthropology.

Historical materials in themselves, as opposed to a study of historical processes, have been inadequately exploited as a source of information on the past, even if they do not very directly or obviously inform the present. Bhattacharji's paper (Chapter 7) rereads the ancient Indian texts to throw fresh and iconoclastic light on the generally accepted view that all the troubles associated with women's status in the region are a modern invention and that the glorious past was indeed glorious. If one agrees with her that prescriptive texts cannot be read purely as descriptive texts, one also comes closer to agreeing with her that the very existence of normative and prescriptive texts delineating ways of dealing with women suggests that there existed problems which called for these texts to be written and passed on. This paper illustrates the many different forms of demographically relevant material that can be gleaned from these texts—from norms about the age at marriage and ideal family size to societal attitudes towards women. In particular, she highlights an innovative indirect way of inferring the position of women in ancient India by scanning the metaphors and similes used in talking about life in general. For instance, in the earliest Vedic scriptures the sun is frequently depicted as following the dawn (mythologically, Veda's wife), a metaphor that soon disappears from popular and literary usage. Bhattacharji's paper also makes good reading for the modern conscience because it suggests that many of our ills are inherited and not created out of thin air.

Historical processes play an even more irrefutable role in Schneider and Schneider's depiction of fertility decline among the artisans of inter-war Sicily (Chapter 8). Firmly eschewing the kind of compartmentalized conception of fertility determinants implicit in the ideology-versus-structure debates in demography, at one level their paper reinstates traditional demographic transition theory by looking at the broader sweep of socioeconomic changes accompanying fertility decline. But this traditional approach is modified by them to take time and place into account as well as to accommodate the cultural processes stressed by the neo-Princeton Fertility Project school of thought.

Schneider and Schneider empirically demonstrate that in the real world many things often happen together, and that one's responses to events bearing on one aspect of life—the economy, for instance—are greatly conditioned by what has simultaneously happened on other fronts. Villamaura artisans adopted fertility control as their material conditions became more pressing at the same time as their educated status did not allow them the luxury of having ill-trained and impoverished children and their political and intellectual connections with the wider world of Europe exposed them to withdrawal as a legitimate means of contraception.[3] This legitimacy was strengthened by the close conjugal bond in artisan families as well as by an ability to defy the church on matters of sex and procreation. All in all, a host of factors combined to make it inevitable that fertility would fall. Schneider and Schneider's explanations may seem in principle too messy to have much predictive value, but the reader will be struck by how much intuitive sense they make and by the diverse forms of empirical evidence that they have marshalled to state their case. Anthropological demography has much to gain by aspiring to the holistic method of research described in this paper, such holism in research methodology flowing naturally into a holism in explanations of changing behaviour. Such holism can also temper the demographer's enthusiasm for single-sector interventions designed to change demographic behaviour.

This notion of a wider context is also applied very strongly in Anarfi's paper on migration (Chapter 9). Anarfi dips into anthropological demography to argue that African migration is even more complex than migration in other parts of the world, which is complicated enough. Anthropological techniques to understand the implications of migration become even more salient in the face of the rapidly changing microeconomics of migration. While the poverty–migration nexus is not doing much to help men, its negative implications today seem to affect women particularly, both as migrants themselves and as non-migrants left behind when the men leave. Their economic predicament is one thing; even more devastating seems to be the possible adverse health consequences that they experience in the changing sexual climate that characterizes large-scale movements into the cities. Such changing behaviour may take many forms, including a loosening of sexual restraints in the village, a growing need to sell sexual services, and, in the case of the women left behind, sex with a potentially infected returning migrant partner. All these new kinds of sexual behaviour become more dangerous in the current situation of a high prevalence of HIV/AIDS in Africa, and it is research of the anthropological demographic type that can best tease out the finer nuances of the new health implications of migration. In addition, Anarfi calls for more micro-level research on the economic, political, and historical basis of contemporary migration so that migrants are placed in their larger circumstances and their constraints are given a larger perspective.

Historical and political factors need to be figured even more forcefully into the analysis of the determinants of health and mortality. The demographer and anthropological demographer's emphasis on the individual, and especially the mother, can divert crucial attention from matters such as the role of poverty, of inequality, and of the state in determining poor health and survival for a vast majority of the world's people. This inattention to what might be called the 'extra-cultural macro environment' of health can backfire by increasing the responsibilities and burdens of the very people that population policy seeks to help (Basu 1995). If intra-household inequalities and power imbalances are worth addressing in the interests of individual rights, as well as of household welfare on matters such as child survival, then inter-household and inter-regional inequalities surely need mitigation on the same grounds. As Cleland and Kaufmann point out in Chapter 6, as much as one-third to one-half of the much heralded negative relationship between maternal education and child mortality can be explained by the higher incomes associated with maternal education. Furthermore, cultural constraints surely should not cloud acknowledgement of the constraints imposed by scarce material resources, and if anything the latter should be more amenable to manipulation and change than the former.

Indeed, even when it eschews the larger political context (which it should not), health and mortality research in demography has more common ground with anthropology than a superficial look at differences between the two disciplines would suggest. The bridge is provided by the epidemiological nature of most such research in demography, research that is increasingly concerned much more with the social, economic, and cultural concomitants of poor health and its outcomes than with its biomedical aspects. Although it appears that the disciplines of epidemiology and medical anthropology are themselves far from agreed that they do have a convergence of interests and strategies, a closer look at these interests and strategies suggests that such an agreement is reasonable (see e.g. Inhorn 1995). A major source of the perceived difference—the tendency for epidemiology to be concerned with *disease*, a biomedical construct, while anthropology looks at *illness*, a social and cultural construct—seems not really to be a bone of contention at all. One is struck, even in a casual perusal of some of the more obvious journals interested in the results from demography, epidemiology, and medical anthropology (*Health Transition Review* and *Social Science and Medicine* spring immediately to mind), by the overwhelming attention to the non-clinical aspects of health and mortality.

It is also true that this was not always the case. Traditional, large-scale demography was for a long time concerned primarily with the 'bio-demographic' determinants of poor health. In the specific case of child mortality, for example, characteristics such as the age and sex of the child, its birth order, the length of its preceding and succeeding birth interval, the age of its mother at its birth, and so on were all identified as major

determinants of the 'risk' of death. Interventions were (and still are) therefore sought to reduce the incidence of high-risk births rather than to try and
change the circumstances surrounding these high-risk individuals, because it
was believed that such high-risk characteristics were risky for largely biological reasons, even if their incidence itself was determined by socio-cultural
factors. This belief was strengthened by the sense that the relationships
between high-risk factors and poor health could be explained by biomedical
and clinical conditions such as the maternal depletion syndrome.

   Anthropological demography and medical anthropology have made a
major contribution by demonstrating that many of these biological predis-
positions to death are in fact only partly biological (see Basu 1995). Much of
their lethal impact can be traced to behavioural and environmental factors
associated with them, and large-scale statistical associations may unduly
inflate their biological vulnerability. Take the question of the higher infant
mortality associated with very young mothers which has been repeatedly
documented in the demographic literature and has also been used to legitimize the call for delayed childbearing. Is there really such a large time gap
between puberty and good reproductive performance? Or is there something
in the anthropological literature which suggests that young mothers are also
handicapped by the circumstances of their pregnancies? In sub-Saharan
Africa for example, the age of the mother may be much less important in
determining pregnancy outcome than the social status associated with her
pregnancy and the social support she can claim for her childbearing and
childrearing experience (National Academy of Sciences 1993). It may well be
that this statistical finding is biased by the over-representation in data sets of
women who socially rather than biologically are not ready to have children.
At the same time, biological explanations do not disappear, and in Africa at
least it does appear that a part of the marked birth-weight and survival
disadvantage of first-born children may be related to the much stronger
impact of malaria during the first pregnancy (Brabin 1991; Greenwood *et
al.* 1994): the uterus apparently acquires local immunity to malaria only
during the first pregnancy.

   Aaby's paper in this volume (Chapter 10) and several other pieces of his
research in this area provide another example of the ways in which even
differences in supposedly neutral practices (that is, not based on socioeconomic differentiation as in the young–mother case above) can also mask,
accentuate, or even create what appear to be major biological differences.
The sex differential in child mortality which seems to have such a clear
regional pattern in the world has now received much attention in the context
of the greater disadvantage of girls in many parts of Asia and the Middle
East. Since the Western pattern of higher male-child mortality is believed to
be the normal or biologically conferred pattern, this deviation has been
attributed in the literature to intentional neglect of girls in the matter of
food or health care and sometimes, more generously, to unintentional

neglect occasioned by norms about health-seeking behaviour for girls. Aaby identifies yet another marker of risk, which is culturally or socially constructed but has no ostensible relation to health outcomes either from the parents' perspective or, until recently, from the perspective of researchers themselves. This is the risk associated with the transmission pattern of potentially fatal infections like measles and whooping cough. These infections are more severe when they are contracted from someone at home rather than from someone outside, presumably because prolonged contact at home leads to more intense exposure and a higher dose of infection. In the European experience, on which much of the assumptions of scientific immunology are based, girls were more likely to contract infection outside the home and infect their brothers at home, thus contributing to higher mortality among boys. On the other hand, in cultures with a partial seclusion or isolation of girls (a common attribute of societies with higher female mortality), boys are more likely to contract an infection outside the home and then to pass it on to their sisters at home.

At the same time, it is anthropology and anthropological demography that have also raised uncomfortable policy questions about the way to deal with *intentional* high mortality, whether of girls, high-parity children, or children with other kinds of unwanted characteristics. In such cases, where neglect is deliberate, it does not make much sense to advocate more health services or even more user-friendly health services. The issues go well beyond such simple interventions and raise questions of ethics which mainstream demography has always felt uncomfortable confronting but anthropological demography faces head on. These questions are only going to increase as medical technology rises to ever greater heights and forces a rethinking of the current acceptance of support for preventing pregnancies or births that are unwanted for parity or timing reasons, while actively condemning attempts to prevent or deal with pregnancies or births that are unwanted for other reasons.

There are other questions of ethics and politics which concern the nature of social science research itself, as opposed to the policy implications of social science research mentioned previously. The present volume does not enter into these debates, not because they are not important, but because they are currently not sufficiently part of the demographer's agenda. But it is worth mentioning, however briefly, that many of the current criticisms of anthropology and social science in general apply to demographers as well; the fact that demographers tend to be well-meaning people politically, or that they do not feel equipped to question the larger implications of some of their work, is not a valid ground for exonerating them from the introspection that is sweeping field-based research in general. There is much academic debate on what has been called the colonizing nature of social science research, the power asymmetries inherent in it, its exploitative tendencies and so on. Such debate will undoubtedly enter the demographer's consciousness more rapidly as more of the methods and findings of other more self-critical disciplines are absorbed, and this may indeed be a crucial by-product of the development of anthropological demography.

This volume also does not enter the modern and post-modern debates *within* current anthropology; instead, it contents itself with the potential contribution of more conventional anthropological demography. This is because demographers are on the whole still ill-equipped to handle this information; the debates are vociferous and contentious enough in anthropology itself, making it difficult for the outsider to sift the arguments. In any case, for the moment these debates are interesting to the demographer primarily for academic reasons and not for the policy considerations that guide so much demographic research. These policy considerations, as mentioned several times above, can be much more effectively, sensitively, and ethically channelled if they incorporate the research methods and findings of traditional anthropology.

The Limits of the Cultural and Wider Contexts

As stated earlier, anthropology tells demography that the larger context is important, and also that the larger context means more than culture, however defined. This approach does not deny that individuals' immediate and personal circumstances are also major constraints on their demographic behaviour, as many large-scale conventional demographic surveys ably demonstrate when they find differentials by variables such as education, income, and occupation. But innovative anthropology (which is what anthropological demography should most readily exploit) also cautions us that people are more than the sum of their constraints. An important theme running through many of the papers in this volume is that attention to the larger context of people's lives, as an important determinant of their behaviour, by no means implies that individuals are passive victims of their circumstances, whether cultural, socioeconomic, political, or legal.

Not only are the constraints imposed by structural or cultural circumstances often actively resisted, but often such resistance is not even necessary; instead, these constraints can be peacefully negotiated, reinterpreted, and even manipulated. Three of the papers take on this theme directly and challenge the demographer's tendency to treat contextual variables in a static and deterministic way. Demographers taking concepts from anthropology too easily assume that structural factors determine norms and norms determine behaviour, all in a relatively straightforward way, while anthropology itself has made rapid advances away from this simplistic position (Lockwood, 1995).

Carter, in Chapter 11, addresses the thorny issue of culture versus agency. He rebuts the assumption implicit in much 'culture-conscious' demography that culture is an attribute of pretransition societies, and makes itself felt primarily through its effect, together with biology, on natural fertility, or (to use the economist's term) on the supply of children. The further implicit assumption in such cultural demography is that the concept of demand rears its head only when societies begin to move away from their pretransition high-fertility states, so that agency begins to replace culture as the major determinant of fertility. Carter demonstrates, with a range of examples from anthropology and anthropological demography, that agency is alive and well in pretransition populations and that high-fertility outcomes can be the result of very different attitudes towards reproduction and very different reproductive regimes, and that the superficial absence of parity-specific behaviour can be misleadingly equated with passivity. Indeed, the absence of fertility-stopping behaviour by no means implies uncontrolled fertility; as Santow (1995) demonstrates, conscious spacing behaviour (mainly through coitus interruptus) characterized many pretransition populations that ostensibly did not practise birth control in the sense of controlling the completion of reproduction.

At the same time, such active intervention in issues impinging on reproduction does not imply that individuals are driven by conscious motives alone. If all actions were to be the result of rational decision-making, there would be little time for the actions themselves, and Carter does well to remind readers that it is the continuous interaction between culture and agency rather than either of these alone that determines most forms of behaviour, including reproduction.

Bledsoe and Hill (Chapter 12) use Gambian data to illustrate the most extreme form of the accommodation by individuals to larger constraints by making allies of these constraints through judicious recourse to them. Their paper focuses on norms about post-partum abstinence and how these norms can be exploited by women and by men to meet their individual interests in the areas of sexual relations and healthy birth intervals. Such exploitation is greatly facilitated by the existence of many different sets of norms, which are sometimes consistent but often mutually conflicting, so that they can be selectively used to legitimize behaviour rather than to constrain it. The emergence of the state as a major player in the setting of norms and rules makes the task of doing what one wants even easier for the intelligent actor. Thus, women can resist unwanted sexual advances from their husbands by invoking norms about abstinence during breastfeeding (Bledsoe and Hill use the very fitting phrase 'norms as excuses' to describe such strategic recourse to norms), while husbands can seek sexual favours by turning the Muslim proscription on sexual activity within the first forty days of a delivery on its head and demanding such activity immediately after this forty-day period. Similarly, the normative legitimacy of a concern with child health can be exploited by women who visit a health centre to seek discreetly the contraception which ensures that sexual activity does not get compounded into unwanted pregnancies and births as well. Indeed, this sometimes discreet and more often overt collaboration by the state in the subversion of many forms of intra-household control should be a recurring theme in studies of contemporary developing societies. Watkins's (1997) description of the role of an aggressive family planning programme in increasing women's reproductive autonomy and ability to challenge male authority in Kenya can be extended to many other populations in which family planning programmes tend to be analysed only in terms of their antagonistic elements.

Bledsoe and Hill's framework is particularly useful because it cautions demographers not only against assuming that norms are a proxy for behaviour, but also against assuming that when behaviour is consistent with norms it is entirely determined by these norms. In the process, the authors also distinguish between the value of particular norms to the society that formulates them (the staple of much traditional anthropology) and their meaning to the individuals who do or do not observe them.

Bledsoe and Hill do not expand beyond the household the question of *why* there should be the observed spousal differences in attitudes to post-partum abstinence. In a recent paper, Lockwood (1995) extends their analysis by speculating about the larger political economy of these changes in male–female differences in the observance of abstinence norms. The spirit of this speculation is similar to that of the anthropological demography of Schneider and Schneider in Chapter 8, where fieldwork is combined with the use of a number of other sources of information—history, economics, and politics in particular.

Kreager's paper (Chapter 13) similarly highlights the problems of traditional diffusion theory, which so much of demographic transition theory since the Princeton Fertility Project rests on. It challenges the evolutionary and linear conception of diffusion that is implicit in much demographic writing on the subject and cites Malinowski (1928) that, 'whenever one culture "borrows" from another, it always transforms and readapts the objects or customs borrowed...' to underscore the complex nature of diffusion. This perspective, although current in anthropology, is still somewhat alien to demographic models of modernization and Westernization which bow to Goode's (1963) thesis of the evolutionary global convergence to Western nuclear family values and institutions.

Kreager uses the example of changes in African marriage systems to illustrate the great openendedness of diffusion outcomes and to underline that diffusion does not mean merely imitation or adoption, or even rejection. He also uses this example to highlight the great potential for anthropological demography to contribute to a new diffusion theory more suited to understanding demographic change. Such an approach would focus on the ways in which larger factors constrain the diffusion process as well as the ways in which these constraints themselves are bent or circumvented, with the result that outcomes cannot be comfortably predicted in any generalized way.

These three papers in particular, and the entire body of this book in general, document what may be the largest contribution of anthropological demography: its stress on the interconnectedness of various aspects of life and, especially, the two-way flows between any two sets of variables, so that it is difficult to say where determinants end and consequences begin. An appreciation of this interconnectedness is also important for an appreciation of the possible side-effects of potentially valuable interventions, and thus for an identification of those facets of human behaviour that are more amicably amenable to change.

Traditional demography, on the other hand, has a fascination with single variables. It is true that it makes much statistical sense to conceive of fertility as either natural or controlled, or as determined by either structural or ideological factors, or as determined by either culture or agency; and to conceive of births as either wanted or unwanted. But real life is unfortunately much more mixed up than these straightforward classifications imply, and while a constant awareness of these complications can serve merely to legitimize inaction, a recognition of the greys is essential to prevent policy prescriptions that may turn out to be foolhardy or even counter-productive.

Notes

1. As opposed to demographic anthropology, which mainstream anthropologists are in turn trying to develop in a complementary move (see, in particular, Greenhalgh, 1995; Kertzer and Fricke, 1997). It should also be mentioned that the concept of a 'sub-discipline' of anthropological demography is not yet unanimously accepted. Many demographers would prefer to subscribe to the more limited view that demography can be enriched by borrowing from the methods and findings of anthropology rather than by branching out into a new sub-discipline.
2. The new and internationally endorsed interest in development research to define human welfare in less obviously material terms and to resort instead to measures such as infant mortality and literacy, both active interests of conventional demography, has in fact led to a massive appropriation of demography by social scientists of various hues.
3. At this point, it may be worth adding something about the ways in which these connections between small communities and the larger world operate. Anthropological demography is very well suited to exploring some of the routes taken by the message as it flows from the latter to the former. Agents such as the mass media may be very important today, but, even in the absence of television and radio, other powerful informal networks of communication can develop and help to change mind-sets. Watkins (1990), for example, refers to the impressive ability of women's gossip networks to spread new ideas.

References

Aaby, P. (1987), 'Observing the unexpected', in A. Hill and J. Caldwell (eds.), *Microapproaches to Demographic Research*, London: Kegan Paul.

Aaby, P. (1997), 'Bandim: an unplanned longitudinal study', in Das Gupta *et al.* (eds.) (1997).

Basu, A. M. (1992), *Culture, the Status of Women, and Demographic Behaviour*, Oxford: Clarendon Press.

—— (1993), 'Cultural influences on the timing of births in India: large differences that add up to little difference', *Population Studies*, 47(1): 85–95.

—— (1995), 'Anthropological demography in the understanding of child mortality: the underinvestment framework and some misapplications', Paper presented at the seminar in honour of J. C. Caldwell, Canberra: Australian National University.

Bledsoe, C. and Pison, G. (1994), *Nuptiality in Sub-Saharan Africa: Contemporary Anthropological and Demographic Perspectives*, Oxford: Clarendon Press.

Bleek, W. (1987), 'Lying informants: a fieldwork experience from Ghana', *Population and Development Review*, 13(2): 314–22.

Brabin, B. (1991), 'An assessment of low birthweight risk in primaparae as an indicator of malaria control in pregnancy', *International Journal of Epidemiology*, 20: 276–83.

Das Gupta, M., Aaby, P., Pison, G., and Garenne, M. (eds.) (1997), *Prospective Community Studies in Developing Countries*, Oxford: Clarendon Press.

Evans-Pritchard, E. E. (1965), 'The comparative method in social anthropology', in E. E. Evans-Pritchard, *The Position of Women in Primitive Societies and Other Essays in Social Anthropology*, London: Faber & Faber.

Goode, W. (1963), *World Revolution and Family Patterns*, New York: Free Press.

Greenhalgh, S. (ed.), (1995), *Situating Fertility*, Cambridge: Cambridge University Press.

Greenwood, A. M., Memendez, C., Todd, J., and Greenwood, B. M. (1994), 'The distribution of birthweights in Gambian women who received malaria chemoprophylaxis during their first pregnancy and in control women', *Transactions of the Royal Society of Tropical Medicine and Hygiene*, 88: 811–12.

Gupta, D. (1995), 'Feminification of theory', *Economic and Political Weekly*, 30(12): 617–20.

Gursoy-Tezcan, A. (1992), 'Infant mortality: a Turkish puzzle?' *Health Transition Review*, 2(2): 131–49.

Inhorn, M. C. (1995), 'Medical anthropology and epidemiology: divergences of convergences?' *Social Science and Medicine*, 40(3): 285–90.

Kertzer, D. I. and Fricke, T. E. (eds.) (1997), *Anthropological Demography: Towards a New Synthesis*, Chicago: University of Chicago Press.

Lightbourne, R. E. and MacDonald, A. L. (1982), *Family Size Preferences*, World Fertility Survey Comparative Studies No. 14, Geneva: World Fertility Survey.

Lockwood, M. (1995), 'Structure and behaviour in the social demography of Africa', *Population and Development Review*, 21(1): 1–32.

Malinowski, B. (1928), 'The life of culture', in G. E. Smith *et al.*, *Culture: The Diffusion Controversy*, New York: W.W. Norton.

Manderson, L. and Aaby, P. (1992), 'An epidemic in the field? Rapid assessment procedures and health', *Social Science and Medicine*, 35: 839–85.

National Academy of Sciences (1993), *Social Dynamics of Adolescent Fertility in Sub-Saharan Africa*, Washington, DC: National Academy of Sciences.

Pratinidhi, A. *et al.* (1989), 'Effect of social custom of migration for delivery on perinatal mortality', *Demography India*, 18: 171–6.

Radcliffe-Brown, A. R. (1951), 'The comparative method in social anthropology', *Journal of the Royal Anthropological Institute*, 81: 15–22.

Santow, G, (1995), '*Coitus interruptus* and the control of natural fertility', *Population Studies*, 49(1): 19–43.

Watkins, S. C. (1990), 'From local to national communities: the transformation of demographic regimes in western Europe 1870–1960', *Population and Development Review*, 16(2): 241–72.

——, Rutenberg, N., and Wilkinson, D. (1997), 'Orderly Theories, Disorderly Women', in G. W. Jones, R. M. Douglas, J. C. Caldwell, and R. M. D'Souza (eds), *The Continuing Demographic Transition*, Oxford: Clarendon Press.

1 Methodological Advances in Studying the Social Context of AIDS in West Africa

JOHN C. CALDWELL, I. O. ORUBULOYE, AND PAT CALDWELL

The African AIDS epidemic has given rise to a need for both anthropological and survey methods of research and for modifications to existing methods because of the great sensitivity of the subject. Only very limited research on sexuality and sexual relations has ever been undertaken in sub-Saharan Africa even by anthropologists.[1] This can hardly be explained by the fact that anthropologists looked upon it as a matter of trivial social importance or as having no significant bearing on other social relationships and behaviour. There are two possible explanations. The first is that they regarded the topic as so sensitive, and perhaps so central, that they believed its investigation would distort their relations with their respondents and hence would be damaging to their other inquiries. The second is that, arising from the nature of their own societies, they had difficulty in coming to terms with research on sexual relations as a serious, and even respectable, study.

The most closely related field of research was that on fertility, infertility, and family planning. Most of the published research in this area had been undertaken by demographers, although special inquiries among anthropologists showed that they knew more than they had usually included in their writings (Molnos 1973). The lack of attention to the subject in sub-Saharan Africa is shown by the fact that, even after decades of medical research into sexually transmitted diseases (STDs) in the region, and even though STDs have long been conceded to be a major problem, there is almost no published research on the social context of the transmission of these diseases. If there had been, researchers would have possessed a greater armoury of methodologies and a more substantial body of knowledge when the AIDS epidemic struck.

Information has been provided by Dr John Anarfi (Institute of Statistical, Social and Economic Research, University of Ghana) to supplement that drawn from the report of Kofi Awusabo-Asare and D. K. Agyeman (listed below) in the preparation of the section of AIDS in Ghana. Assistance has been provided by Modupe Orubuloye, Jacob Oni, Folakemi Oguntimehin, Oluwatoyin Akinwande, Wendy Cosford, and Pat Goodall. This research has been funded in chronological order by the Australian National University, the Rockefeller Foundation, and SAREC (the Swedish Agency for Research Cooperation with Developing Countries). It has employed the facilities of Ondo State University, Ado-Ekiti, Nigeria; and the University of Ghana and University of Cape Coast, Ghana. It has also drawn on the experience of the West African Research Group on Sexual Networking

Although the researchers best equipped to undertake investigations of the social context of AIDS were those who had been working in the fertility and family planning field, there were still problems. The first was that such researchers had been very reluctant to investigate sexual relations even when involved in what became a major area of research, the study of premarital pregnancy. The second is that family planning research had placed a major emphasis on national sample surveys such as the Knowledge, Attitude, and Practice (KAP), World Fertility Survey (WFS), and Demographic and Health Survey (DHS) programmes. These programmes had done well in devising questions which got reliable answers in an area that had originally been both sensitive and largely beyond the experience of the African societies under investigation. It seemed obvious at first to many demographers that national surveys were needed in order to be able to present governments with the evidence they required for formulating policies for entire countries. Accordingly, the WHO Global Programme on AIDS (GPA) supported national surveys in a range of sub-Saharan African countries. It is doubtful whether any of these surveys has yielded usable data on the more intimate and important aspects of their inquiries. Subsequently, the GPA pulled back and placed greater emphasis on funding intensive small-scale research of an anthropological–demographic type. The third point is that AIDS research has proved in practice to differ more from fertility research than was at first appreciated. In the next section we will briefly outline the nature of existing African fertility research, to demonstrate the changes that have to be made to fertility research methodology before it can get satisfactory information about the social context of AIDS.

First, however, it is necessary to address the central issue of sensitivity to providing information on sexual relations outside marriage. There is substantial premarital and extramarital sexual activity in West Africa, especially on the part of males among whom it is general. Yet this matter is usually not widely discussed, and interviewers may be misinformed or refused information. The knowledge that an investigation is seeking information within a community on non-marital, and especially multiple, sexual relations can cause excitement and a curiosity about which person is being interviewed. Nevertheless, West Africa is not the Middle East. The spread of knowledge that a married woman has had relations with a man who is not her husband is unlikely to lead to death and usually not even to divorce, although it can lead to grievance and unpleasantness. At the same time, the AIDS epidemic has led to an apprehension of infection and, on the part of many people who feel they may be in danger, to a desire to discuss modes of transmission and risks even if it does mean divulging why they feel they are at risk and the nature of that risk.

Researching the social context of AIDS is probably easier in West Africa than in East or Southern Africa or most of the Third World. Non-marital female sexual activity is not equated with sin to the extent that it is in most of

Africa. West African women remain attached to an appreciable extent to their families of origin and hence are less subject to patriarchial power than in East and Southern Africa. In addition, the low level of AIDS in most of West Africa means that there is little paranoia about discussing African sexual patterns. Yet interviewing is still difficult because of the sensitivity of the topic of sexual relations. One reason is that traditional society attempted to ensure that betrothed girls went to their husbands as virgins and that wives remained sexually faithful. Such behaviour was believed to be controlled by punishments, often by extra-human agencies. Thus, an adulterous woman would be detected by sustaining a difficult childbirth or even dying during the birth. Admittedly, this was not always as frightening and prohibiting as it might seem, for there were substances, rites, or courses of action that could nullify these punishments. A woman in difficulty during childbirth could overcome the problem by whispering the names of her paramours to her mother or some other female relative. Men were not in equal danger, but discretion was often the best policy because their female partners might be in danger or might present a danger to the men if their husbands learnt of the relationship and had employed magic arts to ensure that their relations with others would cause harm. Perhaps related to this is an extreme reluctance to discuss sexual activity even within groups where it is widely practised. This is less so among peer groups of the same sex and age, but discussion is rare and difficult between spouses—as family planning programmes learnt—and especially between the generations. This is why the oral tradition is so silent on actual, in contrast to normative, sexual activities in the society.

Another reason for sensitivity about non-marital sexual relations is the missionary activity of Christianity and Islam. Missionaries have consistently inveighed against non-marital sexual activity and have sometimes argued that such activity was reinforcing older ideals. They have not always been successful in changing behaviour, but they have helped reinforce sensitivity and silence about such matters. In Ghana, AIDS appears to have been brought to the country by commercial sex workers returning from Abidjan in the Ivory Coast, and when research began there were six infected women for every infected man; the ratio is still two to one. The identification of a woman infected with AIDS is still taken to be an accusation of prostitution and a suggestion that the family is living off its proceeds.

An Anthropological–Demographic Approach to the Study of Fertility and Fertility Control

In our fertility studies in Ghana and Nigeria in the 1960s and 1970s, we employed an approach which we then planned to follow in other areas of behavioural studies. We began by locating all the relevant material we could identify in the literature. Then we embarked upon a series of small-scale anthropological investigations in different parts of the country to explore aspects of fertility behaviour, to modify the picture we had obtained from the literature and to identify issues that could be investigated satisfactorily by a survey approach. We subsequently built up a questionnaire, and translated it into the languages of the areas to be surveyed, placing much greater emphasis on getting the meaning right than on providing a literal translation. This questionnaire was tested and simplified until there were no great differences in non-response or apparent comprehension of the questions by education, urban–rural residence, or other socioeconomic measures.

The survey was not carried out in each location until extensive approaches had been made to the community leadership, and, by such mechanisms as village meetings, to the people themselves. At these meetings we explained the need for the research, solicited the villagers' agreement, and usually read out the whole questionnaire explaining the meaning of questions as we went. What may have been lost by people subsequently discussing the matter and influencing each other was certainly outweighed by the gain in comprehension of what was often a new and difficult subject area. Because of the difficulties in sampling rural areas, the final sampling unit was often a cluster in the form of a small area of land where all residents were interviewed.

The interviewer was recognized when visiting a household and all its members and neighbours were aware of just what was taking place. We employed a high ratio of supervisors to interviewers with a large fraction of interviews subject to reinterview, partly to test the interviewers and maintain standards and partly to be able to estimate the variability in answers and the extent to which respondents had a firm answer to give to each question.

The interviewers were usually from the same sub-ethnic group but not from the immediate area. Trustworthy people were employed for coding and other data processing and analysis, but no very strict arrangements were made to safeguard confidentiality (although no leaks ever seem to have occurred).

Experience in the investigation of AIDS demonstrated just how many of these apparently universal social science research guidelines had to be changed.

Researching Sexual Networking in Nigeria

The original research aimed at finding how many different sexual partners respondents had both inside and outside marriage and how such relationships were distributed over time. Descriptive data were collected both on the respondent and on the different sexual partners. However, these partners were not personally identified in the sense of their names and addresses being provided, partly because we believed that this might damage the interview by leading to refusals and devious answers, but mostly because we believed that it was an unwarranted invasion of the privacy of the partners. After it was decided that successive interviews along chains of persons involved in sexual relations was not ethical, field testing was not undertaken.

We soon discovered that there was very little relevant literature to draw upon, and that studies done elsewhere, predominantly of the AIDS epidemic in the homosexual community in the West, were not very useful. Thus, the need for preliminary anthropological work was stronger than in traditional fertility studies.

We decided to keep community interest and excitement to a minimum by not taking the whole community into our confidence. Instead, we held confidential discussions with the chief, school headmasters, and the police to convince them of the importance and the need for the study. The measures taken to ensure the complete confidentiality of all the material gathered were also emphasized. The main reason for making these contacts was the expectation that any respondents who were worried, annoyed, or scandalized by the investigation would complain to one or other of these prominent people and could have their apprehensions allayed.

Other methods were also employed to reduce community interest in the study. At a somewhat greater cost, the sample was a dispersed one, so that when an interview took place in a household the neighbours were unlikely to have had a similar experience. In polygynous households, only one wife (chosen by lot) was interviewed in order to maintain the confidentiality of the survey questions. Care was taken that the other wives could not hear the interview and the women were assured that there would be no discussions with the others. Appropriate weightings were applied for the analysis.

More so than in fertility surveys, the critical ingredient for success proved to be the calibre of the interviewer, in terms of not merely intelligence, training, and competence, but also personality. Some interviewers can inspire trust and even the need to discuss sexual problems while others just cannot do this. The latter have to be withdrawn from interviewing, preferably to be put on to coding or some other survey tasks. Because no preliminary approach had been made to the whole community, the interviewer bore a much greater responsibility than in fertility surveys for explaining to the respondent why the research was so important, why their cooperation would be for the good of all, and just how confidential the information would be. These arguments had been emphasized when the interviewers were being trained.

The interviewers were also supported by a letter from the university. Rapport was strong because the research base was the local state university which had been established as a result of intense local pressure against federal suspicion and opposition. Even in small villages the university was trusted and aroused great loyalty. Experience showed that the respondents were convinced that no details of their sexual activity would reach the community. Where they needed assurance was in providing the promise that the university researchers would not identify the individuals or communities to the churches or the government, which they regarded as killjoys who had long sought to puritanize sexual relations and who would use any crisis to achieve this end.

Somewhat to our surprise, we found that the communities preferred to be interviewed by local interviewers who retained an understanding of the community even though they now worked outside and had progressed to university employment. They were satisfied that such persons would respect confidences in accordance with their education and new status. This meant employing a few good interviewers over a considerable period rather than a large research team, an approach that appeared to work well in all studies of sexual networking.

In the early sexual networking research, supervisors were employed mainly to check with the interviewers the location of the sampled household and their completed schedules, and to discuss problems as they arose and the need for further interviewing. We were reluctant to burden interviews by having an additional person present and to arouse hostility or embarrassment by arranging a reinterview by a different person.

These modifications of the practices adopted in fertility research raised questions of central importance with regard to the verification of the research. The fundamental problem was the decision that we could not identify the respondents' non-marital partners and interview them. Three different approaches have so far been employed regarding verification.

The first has been a cautious return to having different persons undertaking either complete reinterviews or reinterviews covering key parts of the questionnaire. Much of this work has confirmed that there is no great slippage in terms of the numbers of other partners or many of their characteristics. The real problem—and a very serious one, in terms of gauging the likely spread of sexually transmitted diseases—has been a misidentification by many males of partners, who were really commercial sex workers, as just friends. This partly reflects the actual situation and the degree of camaraderie and old acquaintanceship in bars and night spots. This misidentification leads to an underestimation of the number of other partners these women probably had.

The second method of verification, originally employed to correct data but increasingly built into the usual approach, was the addition of a series of questions to men about where they had met their partners, where sexual relations had taken place, the type of economic support provided, and the timing of transactions. Men who in our sense had misidentified relationships were able correctly to supply the answers to a battery of questions of this type, and so allowed the appropriate identifications to be made by the interviewers.

The third method of verification, aimed also at separating essentially commercial sex from less commercial relations—the difference is not always very clear—was done by a kind of 'balancing equations' approach. In addition to the individual interviews of men, interviewing was conducted with all women in places where commercial sex was arranged or took place about their numbers of partners over time, and the figures derived in this way were compared with estimates from the individual interviews of sexual relations arranged in these places. These compared fairly closely when the men had been subject to the battery of questions and when the nature of the relationship had been subsequently identified by the interviewers.

Such work indicated that there were other, but less serious, slippages. Women were more likely to understate their non-marital sexual relations than men and there was more understatement in rural than urban areas. This is why some of the subsequent, more difficult, research was restricted to men living in towns.

Studying Specific High-Risk Groups

The first research on commercial sex workers was undertaken by identifying bars, night-clubs (as used in the West African sense), and hotels where they worked. We found it necessary to persuade those males who acted as managers and contacts[2] to allow us access to the women. We also found it necessary to pay an amount that they calculated was the income lost by giving us their exclusive time. Later, when undertaking this work on a larger scale, we found that the sex workers were just as satisfied to be compensated by receiving trustworthy advice on AIDS, other sexually transmitted diseases, and the efficacy of condoms.

The earlier research in a smaller town provided some insights into why men had mis-stated the commercial nature of these relationships. The establishments also sell a range of entertainment, and most people who go there often drink and sometimes eat and dance too. The young women help serve the drinks and food and talk to the customers. Sex is not always a component of these relationships. Most of the customers are regulars. The men know the women and enjoy their company, and believe that they in turn are liked or even loved. The sex workers are not as open with most of their customers as the latter believe. Most men described their relationships as being with single women, but the research interviews disclosed that most of the women had been married and were separated or divorced and many had children. They were able to hide these facts because they came from elsewhere—usually from another ethnic group—and their children had invariably been left behind, often with their parents. Because these facts were not known to their male clients, the latter provided, if unwittingly, incorrect information to the interviewers not only on the commercial component of the relationship, but also on key characteristics of these partners.

Later research modified this picture in two ways, both with methodological implications. In a larger town, we found that a proportion of commercial sex workers operated from hotels where sex was the main transaction and where the customers were often not regulars but transients such as truck drivers. In these circumstances, the men know little about the characteristics of their partners. Further research work in the smaller town originally studied examined, with anthropological thoroughness, just where men did obtain commercial sex. The results showed that a significant proportion came from women who did not operate out of institutions and who had fewer customers: they were mostly housewives supplementing their other income. In many cases their activities were probably known to their husbands, who preferred these relationships to remain on a commercial basis. This means that the institutional approach to evaluating the levels of commercial sex is inadequate unless supplemented with other information.

A still later project, a study of commercial sex workers in the hotels, bars, and brothels of Lagos, differed again both methodologically and substantively. The number of listed institutions was so great that they had to be sampled, and then approximate weighting was achieved within the establishments by interviewing a fixed proportion of the young women working there. Even in the city, anonymity is achieved by coming from elsewhere. Only 24% were Yoruba, the indigenous people of the area, and only 30% had been born and raised anywhere in south-western Nigeria. Three-quarters were under 25 years of age, 82% claimed never to have been married, and a similar proportion claimed never to have had children. This may be true in Lagos, for ambitious young women go to the city to make money, most intending to stay only long enough to secure enough money to set themselves up in business back home and to secure a good marriage. Indeed, half had been in Lagos for two years or less, and five-sixths of the single ones intended to marry. This raises another survey methodological question, for most intended to go back home and make no mention of their Lagos trade to their families, future husbands, and, presumably, survey interviewers. Finally, it might be noted that questions about contraception, especially condom use and its relation to fears of STDs and HIV/AIDS and to customer reactions, were welcomed with a refusal rate of under 1%.

Everywhere in Africa, long-distance lorry (truck) drivers are a source of STD and HIV/AIDS infection, and levels of disease are consequently higher along the most densely trafficked routes. One research project aimed at finding and identifying those aspects of the drivers' behaviour and way of life that made them so dangerous. The problem in carrying out the research was their mobility. The solution was to interview them at a highway truck stop where they halt for a drink, rest, food, sex, or to have their trucks serviced and repaired. The drivers were busy, often rather self-important, men and were frequently impatient. It was discovered that successful interviewing could be carried out best by attractive young women to whom they were willing to give some attention and to talk either while eating or while overseeing the repair of their trucks. Even in these circumstances, the interviewers found that it was best to memorize the questionnaire and to intersperse their questions with a good deal of general light discussion. They also memorized the answers and completed the survey schedule later. The young women were given protection by placing hefty young men, often their boyfriends, in the crowd, but this precaution was largely unnecessary because the drivers recognized university-based researchers and rather enjoyed the game of wits, although seemingly providing accurate information.

Another project examined one of the most informal sectors of commercial sex: that provided by most, though not all, of the young itinerant female hawkers (vendors) who sell goods from a tray or a box which they carry on their heads in lorry parks or roadside truck stops. They are usually young and single and, when they marry or save up some capital, may acquire stalls in the main market adjacent to the lorry park. The girls quickly offer their produce to drivers and passengers as trucks, buses, and vans disgorge passengers or as people wait for transport. Most customers assume that the girls are willing to sell sex as well as merchandise.

Lorry parks are often tough and rough places, and are sometimes danger-ous. The hawkers are frequently apprehensive and even lonely. Because it was not thought desirable to have female interviewers apparently loitering in the lorry parks, most of the interviewing was done by males who found that a sympathetic and understanding approach elicited answers and even tales of woe. As it became clear just how ignorant most of these girls were about contraception and the transmission of coitally related disease, while being apprehensive of both pregnancy and infection, the project asked more ques-tions in these areas. The interviewers were also trained to provide, at the conclusion of the interview, some authoritative information on these matters.

A recent project has focused on prisoners in two urban gaols. The proper official approaches gained co-operation from the administration and warders, but at first it appeared that some of the prisoners would not be fully co-operative. The solution was arrived at by chance. The research team consisted of both social scientists and doctors because the latter were taking blood samples. The doctors noticed that a high proportion of prisoners were suffering from scabies and other minor but uncomfortable complaints; they obtained modest funding from the research programme to procure adequate medication, largely because they felt the need to help and not in order to effect cooperation. Yet the result was both a level of individual and group cooperation in providing information to an extent not commonly achieved.

More General Studies

One of the major aims of the research programme has been to learn about the sexual networks and how often they include as one link persons with a high chance of infection. In making the decision not to interview identified non-marital partners, we placed ourselves in a position where there was no alternative but to seek more information from the respondents about those partners. We decided that some degree of success was possible only if we chose the most auspicious circumstances. A town was selected where traditionally there had been an unusual level of openness about non-marital sexual relations.

The decision was also made to restrict the respondents to men, for two reasons. The first was that the research programme had already shown that men, especially urban men, were the respondents most likely to disclose fully their sexual activities. This is partly because, in a polygynous society, wives are not supposed to have sexual relations outside marriage, while men may merely be seeking another wife. In a polygynous society, too, it is assumed that men by nature need more than one woman and will certainly need other women while their wives are abstaining from sex during pregnancy and for long periods after childbirth. The second reason is that men actually know much more about their partners' partners than do women. This arises from the very strong cultural proscription of wives taking an interest in their husbands' other sexual activities or making inquiries about them. Women tend to behave exactly the same way with their extramarital partners. In contrast, men often take a suspicious interest in the relationships of their wives and other partners.

Nevertheless, even with all these precautions, the project showed that full networks could not be mapped in this way. Men were most likely to know about the existence and characteristics of their extramarital partners' husbands or partners in the most stable extramarital alliances, but not about more fleeting, or commercial, relations. Thus, they tended to underestimate the disease risks involved.

An increasingly important part of the research programme has been the study of women's control over their sexuality in conditions of risk, namely when their partners, especially their husbands, were infected with HIV/AIDS or other STDs, or when these partners pursued a high-risk sexual life-style. This research was meaningful among the Nigerian Yoruba population, where women are expected to refuse sex to even the most importunate of husbands when menstruating, pregnant, in the postpartum period (especially during breastfeeding), when they become grandmothers, or when they are post-menopausal. In a sense, these are looked upon as conditions of disability, and it has been easy to translate this to husbands' disabilities, such as drunkenness, in terms of emotional support from their relatives and not outraging accepted community standards when the women refuse sex.

Because we had no way of identifying the women most at risk, the starting point was a sample of all females over 17 years of age. This allowed us to ask general questions about attitudes to relations with partners under a range of conditions. Because HIV/AIDS levels are still very low in this population, it was necessary to focus attention on those women who had known their husbands to be infected with STDs—usually gonorrhoea, which is probably the most common and certainly the most frequently recognized STD in the society. The number in this group was smaller than had been predicted, because—and this was one of the most important findings of the study—most women with infected husbands do not realize their situation even in the presence of STDs, and this would be even more the case with asymptomatic HIV. The opportunity was also taken to investigate what happens in terms of both women's and men's control of their sexuality when either the female partner or both partners are known to be infected.

The project found that women had little control over their sexuality when their partners enjoyed a high-risk life-style but a high degree of control in the case of a known transient STD infection while the partner was being treated. The same may not be true with regard to untreatable infections like AIDS, but in this case the women would certainly be in a position to leave the husbands and would be supported in so doing by their families, although the wider community might be more ambivalent.

In the years immediately ahead, the major protection against AIDS will probably be changes in sexual behaviour. The most vociferous advocates of such changes in Nigeria, and elsewhere in sub-Saharan Africa, have long been the religious leaders. This is not an insignificant force, as nearly all Africans attend religious services, mostly either Christian or Muslim, and very considerable numbers of the Christians in Nigeria are likely to attend services of more than one persuasion, for instance Anglican and one of the Pentecostal sects. The issues are what is preached, whether that message has changed or intensified as a result of the AIDS epidemic, and how much the message influences the congregations.

It is no longer possible to set up a longitudinal study because one would need to have set up a baseline before AIDS was feared. We pursued our first objectives by listing and sampling religious leaders and getting their own evaluation of the context of their messages, the extent of change, and the reasons for change. In the absence of any registers of the leaders of the African Christian churches (also called syncretic), most being Pentecostal or millenarian and also faith-healing, the listings were built up in snowball fashion by asking all identified preachers about the names and locations of other preachers known to them. The interviewers belonged to their faiths, and in the case of the Muslims the interviewing was carried out by a very respected university Muslim theologian, because preliminary testing showed that there was resistance to interviewers who belonged to different religions. Lists of topics were used but the interviewers were also encouraged to explore the whole subject area thoroughly and to write up a general report.

Further research is planned to study the congregations' reactions to the preachers' messages about sexual behaviour and to changes in these messages. Because many preachers are thought to behave at variance with their messages, it will be necessary to distinguish between the impact of the message and that of the model. The message may be more influential because these are fundamentalist religions preaching not only wise behaviour but also God's commands.

Sources of Information on Societal Change

One obvious source of information about the older society would seem to be the oral tradition, which is said in traditional societies to preserve unwritten history for many generations. Work thirty years ago in remote areas of Ghana had suggested that this record might not extend much beyond the names of ancestors and rulers, because the attested descriptions of their societies were clearly wrong when they described the situation more than about one generation earlier than the oldest persons still living. The remembered record turned out to be much worse in the case of sexual behaviour because of the almost complete failure to discuss sexuality between generations let alone to transmit realistic descriptions of sexual behaviour. The result is that each generation believes that it is the deviant one from traditional norms. It was clear that the younger people had no real comprehension of the situation that had existed when persons still living, such as their grandparents, were young.

In the absence of any recourse to the oral tradition, we resorted to interviewing the remaining old people of the society. At first the strategy adopted was based on a wrong premises: we assumed that old persons would be sensitive about discussing their own younger sexual behaviour and that we should ask them about the behaviour of their friends. They proved to be very reluctant to reveal the secrets of those whom they pointed out were now dead and hence in the spirit world; in contrast, and to our surprise, most turned out to be quite willing to discuss their own past histories, especially as most of their spouses and other partners were long since dead. Many seemed to wish to discuss, in the legitimized research context, matters that were taboo subjects in their conversations with their only other audiences, their younger relatives. For instance, many of the older women had regarded themselves as married to the whole family, and had consequently accepted it as their duty to provide discreet sexual access to their husband's single brothers; but this was unknown to the younger generation who, in common with the Christian missionaries, regarded such behaviour as incestuous.

The richest source on sexual behaviour in the nineteenth and early twentieth centuries is provided by library and archival records from travellers, missionaries, government officials, doctors, and early anthropologists. Some of these sources devoted more attention to sexuality, admittedly often for culture-centred reasons, than did pre-AIDS contemporary social scientists.

Needed and Planned Research

Our inability until now to map sexual networks has prevented a real evaluation of the dangers of infection resulting from each linkage and the multiplicative dangers from the whole network, or a measure of the dangers resulting from older, more confined, networks increasingly overlapping with each other in a less traditional, more mobile, more urbanized, and more commercial society. The obvious way to undertake research of sexual networkings is by getting all respondents to list their sexual partners, then to interview those partners seeking information about the range of their relationships, and so on. This would serve two purposes. The first would be to map the networks more adequately and to enable us to evaluate the risk behaviour and even the health status of each person in the network. The second advantage would be that this would allow the best verification of information by ascertaining what proportion of respondents' partners named the respondents as among their own partners. Unfortunately, there are clearly ethical problems in that the respondents might become aware that the interviewing was based upon information already received. They might well become suspicious about why they had been chosen.

A possible solution to this dilemma would be to interview the partners by embedding them among the respondents selected for another study with a fairly dense sample where it would seem to all quite likely that they would be chosen. There are several problems even so. The first would be obtaining from the original respondents the names and addresses, or enough identifying information, of their partners without incurring suspicion about what was intended. The second would be the need to have very few people aware of the procedure and in charge of embedding the partners in the new survey and later extracting their data for separate analysis. The third would be the inability of the respondents to provide the required data, especially with regard to their least safe relationships. The fourth would be that some of the partners would be found outside the area where a survey could easily be mounted. The fifth, and greatest, problem would be the fact that even such an elaborate procedure would establish only one more link in the chain, and the investigation would be faced with the problem of mounting a large number of successive surveys in which to embed each successive wave of partners.

The most fundamental need for research on sexual networking is for establishing means for verifying information. The most likely means have all been discussed in the course of laying out the existing methodology. The most satisfactory means would be interviewing partners' partners, but this presents both ethical and operational difficulties. A macro method for looking at the commercial component of sex is the balancing method for getting information from both men and commercial sex workers. This will show whether the gross figures are approximately correct but will not identify inadequate individual respondents. Furthermore, it will work only if all types of commercial sex workers are identified. Clearly, more emphasis must be placed on reinterviewing, but the same omissions and mis-statements are only too likely to persist from one interview to the other.

There is also a need for collaborative work between social and medical scientists. For instance, we need to know what the proportion of women attempting to abstain from sex with their husbands, or attempting to insist on condoms, is of the actual number of women who *need* to behave in this way in order to reduce their risks. We need to know what fraction of persons with spouses infected with STDs or HIV/AIDS are actually aware of their situation.

There will also be an increasing need for longitudinal or successive studies to show how individual behaviour and whole sexual networks change as a result of government interventions aimed at altering sexual behaviour or encouraging the use of condoms.

Researching an Outbreak of AIDS in Ghana

The research group in Ghana,[3] in addition to researching sexual networking, found that they had to develop a methodology for locating and interviewing AIDS sufferers. They soon found that not all persons who had been diagnosed as having AIDS had told their families, and that some families who were aware of the situation had hidden this knowledge from their neighbours. Even when the community did know about the persons with AIDS, they did not always welcome the researcher or help to identify those afflicted. Clearly, in this situation there were also ethical problems in persisting with inquiries. This may be the situation with a new but rapidly developing epidemic, such as in Ghana, where the situation is more sensitive than it now appears to be in, say, Uganda.

In contrast, most of the AIDS sufferers were known to the AIDS counsellors at the government hospitals. This is because the victims or their families had felt the need to contact the hospital for diagnosis or treatment. A small minority had not even been recorded by this system, occasionally because some families do not take their sick to hospitals, but usually because the families had guessed what the sickness indicated and had hidden their shame from their neighbours by keeping the affected person inside the house and failing to seek treatment.

The AIDS counsellors in all hospitals in each district registered the AIDS cases with the government AIDS coordinator of the district. This, then, represented the only sampling frame available, and it was available only when the coordinator agreed to cooperate with the university researchers. Furthermore, even this framework was an imperfect coverage of those seen by the hospitals, because some families had hidden the patients from the system, in spite of their getting treatment, by giving the hospital fictitious names and addresses.

The social scientists prepared questionnaires and probing lists to explore the social context of AIDS, the treatment of AIDS victims, the relationships between those afflicted and their households and communities, and the costs and difficulties faced by the households. The first task was to train the AIDS counsellors on these schedules to convince them that the questions were relevant and important and to allow them to memorize the contents. The social scientists accompanied the AIDS counsellors on visits to those patients whose families knew of the condition and were introduced as part of an expert team.

Nevertheless, the interviewing was done mostly by the AIDS counsellors. Where it seemed appropriate, the social scientists supplemented these questions. The answers were remembered and recorded on schedules later. The reason for this was that the AIDS victims, and even more so their families, were sensitive to the stigma of the disease and apprehensive of the details of their households appearing in official records.

The social scientists felt freer to gather background social data. They talked to other members of the household. In particular, they noted how the AIDS patient appeared to be regarded and treated, where he or she slept, whether any degree of segregation seemed to be practised, what the eating arrangements were, whether the patient ever left the house, and what arrangements there were for the treatment of the adventitious complaints that accompany AIDS. They also explored and studied the surrounding community.

One of the investigators, John Anarfi (1993), possessed a separate body of data which also permitted the study of AIDS-afflicted persons. This was information from a study of migration from Ghana to Abidjan, Ivory Coast, about female migrants who had returned home. When these women were reinterviewed, a significant number were found to be suffering from AIDS, and this allowed their circumstances to be placed in the context of both their migration and that of households that send forth female migrants.

Future Research

Apart from improving the methodology that has been developed for studying sexual networking and the situation of AIDS victims, there is clearly a range of new matters to be researched. Much more work must be done on the economic impact of AIDS. The Ghanaian research suggests that the major impact is not on family incomes but on family expenditures because of the cost of obtaining treatment, whether effective or not in alleviating symptoms. Research has hardly begun on the demographic impact of AIDS. There are some studies of orphanhood, but nothing on such important matters as marriage and very little on marital disruption.

The major new field for investigation will probably be the impact of interventions. In Ghana, preliminary observational work has begun on the nature and efficacy of AIDS counselling. However, in the longer term the chief thrust must be to measure the impact of intervention programmes aimed at changing sexual behaviour. Such interventions have so far been limited to special groups, especially commercial sex workers. If community-wide programmes are attempted, then social scientists must be prepared to collect baseline data and periodic subsequent data on sexual behaviour. The opportunity already exists to attempt to measure change resulting from government information programmes and the publicity given to AIDS in the media.

Notes

1. In the case of two major synthesizing collections, one sought nuggets of information from across a mass of sources (Ford and Beech 1951) and the other encouraged anthropologists to write up what they knew but had not published (Molnos 1973).
2. Perhaps not surprisingly, the first male of this type located was also a driver.
3. John Anarfi at the University of Ghana, and Kofi Awusabo-Asare and Dominic Agyeman at the University of Cape Coast.

References

Anarfi, J. K. (1993), 'Sexuality, migration and AIDS in Ghana', in J. C. Caldwell, G. Santow, I. O. Orubuloye, P. Caldwell, and J. Anarfi (eds.), *Sexual Networking and HIV/AIDS in West Africa*. Supplement to *Health Transition Review*, **3**. Canberra: Australian National University.

Ford, C. S., and Beech, F. A. (1951), *Patterns of Sexual Behavior*. New York: Harper & Row.

Molnos, A. (ed.) (1973), *Cultural Source Material for Population Planning in East Africa*, iii, *Beliefs and Practices*. Nairobi: East African Publishing House.

Research publications reporting these methodologies

The following publications have emerged from the research programmes described here and contain descriptions of specific methodologies and findings resulting from the application of those methodologies.

Awusabo-Asare, K. and Agyeman, D. K. (1992), 'Social science research and the challenge of the AIDS epidemic', Paper presented to the Third National Seminar on AIDS, Accra, Ghana, 15–16 September.

Caldwell, J. C., Orubuloye, I. O., and Caldwell, P. (1991), 'The destabilization of the traditional Yoruba sexual system'. *Population and Development Review*, 17: 229–62.

——Caldwell, P., and Orubuloye, I. O. (1992*a*), 'The family and sexual networking in sub-Saharan Africa: historical regional differentials and present-day implications'. *Population Studies*, 46: 385–410.

——Orubuloye, I. O., and Caldwell, P. (1992*b*), 'Underreaction to AIDS in sub-Saharan Africa'. *Social Science and Medicine*, 34: 1169–82.

——Caldwell, P., Ankrah, E. M., Anarfi, J. K., Agyeman, D. K., Awusabo-Asare, K., and Orubuloye, I. O. (1993a), African families and AIDS: context, reactions and potential interventions', in Caldwell *et al.* (1993 *b*: 1–16).

——Santow, G., Orubuloye, I. O., Caldwell, P., and Anarfi, J. (eds.) (1993*b*), *Sexual Networking and HIV/AIDS in West Africa*. Supplement to *Health Transition Review*, 3. Canberra: Australian National University.

Dyson, T. (ed.) (1992), *Sexual Behaviour and Networking: Anthropological and Socio-Cultural Studies on the Transmission of HIV*. Liège: Derouaux-Ordina.

Orubuloye, I. O., Caldwell, J. C., and Caldwell, P. (1991), 'Sexual networking in the Ekiti District of Nigeria'. *Studies in Family Planning*, 22: 61–73.

——Caldwell, J. C., and Caldwell, P. (1992*a*), 'Sexual networking and the risk of AIDS in Southwest Nigeria', in T. Dyson (ed.), *Sexual Behaviour and Networking: Anthropological and Socio-Cultural Studies on the Transmission of HIV*. Liège: Derouaux-Ordina, pp. 283–301.

——Caldwell, J. C., and Caldwell, P. (1992*b*), 'Diffusion and focus in sexual networking: identifying partners and partners' partners'. *Studies in Family Planning*, 23: 343–51.

——Caldwell, J. C., and Caldwell, P. (1993*a*), 'The role of religious leaders in changing sexual behaviour in southwest Nigeria in an era of AIDS', in Caldwell *et al.* (1993*b*: 93–104).

——Caldwell, P. and Caldwell, J. C. (1993*b*), 'The role of high-risk occupations in the spread of AIDS: truck drivers and itinerant market women in Nigeria'. *International Family Planning Perspectives*, 19: 43–8.

——Caldwell, P. and Caldwell, J. C. (1993*c*), 'African women's control over their sexuality in an era of AIDS'. *Social Science and Medicine*, 37: 859–72.

2 Participant Observation in Demographic Research: Fieldwork Experiences in a Ghanaian Community

SJAAK VAN DER GEEST

The anthropologist engaging in demographic research risks getting lost in a forest of paradoxes. Nowhere are intimate personal feelings—let us call them love and passion—and national public interests so closely interwined as in the birth of children. Movements in the dark come to light nine months later and become hard data for policy-makers. The birth of a child is both a matter for cold statistics and a subject of human emotion. The same can be said about the end of a person's life. Death, the most devastating human experience one can think of, will eventually be transformed into demographic data. The shock of paradox reaches the level of absurdist theatre when the state attempts to break into the intimacy of lovers and publicly holds technical devices in front of them to persuade them to prevent the birth of another child.

The anthropologist working in demography faces these two extremes. In an attempt to 'make both ends meet', he or she sets out to prove that these paradoxes are only paradoxes and not irreconcilable contradictions. Love poetry as well as statistics will have to be dealt with, involving the use of both keyholes and keyboards.

The point of departure for this article is that the anthropological approach and the demographic survey complement one another, both in their methodology and in the type of information they produce. Even where the two seem to yield contradictory data, they should still be regarded as complementary, elucidating and nuancing one another. I subscribe to Kaufmann's conclusion that it is beneficial to combine the strengths of the two approaches:

Research and analysis of data were made possible by financial assistance from the Netherlands Foundation for the Advancement of Tropical Research (WOTRO). In the field I got valuable help, technical and personal, from many people. I would like to mention four of them by name: Kwasi Asante-Darko, Abena Henewaa, Kwasi Addae, and Nana Boateng. Useful comments on an earlier version of this chapter were received from Gilbert Herdt, John Knodel, Georgia Kaufmann, Jack Caldwell, and other participants of the Workshop on 'New Approaches to Anthropological Demography'. Earlier work on my Ghana research was published under the pseudonym of Wolf Bleek to preserve the anonymity of my informants. That pseudonym is no longer necessary.

Demographic data could be interpreted with the anthropological data, and the demographic data could be used to combat the specificity of the anthropological, extrapolating inferences from them with greater justification. (Kaufmann 1991: 55–6)

If this chapter extols the virtues of participant observation, it does not do so at the expense of quantitative methods. My objective is to demonstrate the need for qualitative research if we want to assess the meaning of quantitative data. The importance of quantification for an assessment of qualitative data is equally recognized but falls outside the scope of the present discussion. This chapter will show which methodological and mental tools the anthropologist in demographic research needs to do the job. They are: the ethnographic interview, participation, observation, and introspection.

I am an anthropologist who lived for almost two years in a West African village, in Ghana. I spent most of my time looking around and listening to people's stories, including their love stories, which mostly ended badly, as good stories should, as well as having my own personal love story. Being there, I became more and more surprised about the certainty with which demographers, economists, and politicians spoke about the 'population problem'. They refer to 'fathers', 'mothers', and 'children', but it is not always clear what they mean by these words. The confusion rises particularly when terms like 'marriage', 'fertility', and 'birth control' are used. My main purpose in this chapter will be to take away the false exactitude of such key terms in demographic parlance and to call for greater awareness of their cultural specificity. The conventional anthropological research approach will be useful to add meaning to statistical data. This should be done by asking, looking, and understanding what these words mean to people.

We should not expect too much clarity, however. People are inclined to conceal and deny what they cherish most. Some things are none of our business, so we have to guess at them. Other things we may not understand because we are never able to put ourselves completely in other people's places and to feel what they feel. Cultural analysis, writes Geertz (1973:23), 'is intrinsically incomplete' and 'essentially contestable'.

Asking Questions, Listening, Conversing

It would be a mistake to take the term for the anthropologist's favourite research technique, 'participant observation', literally and to think that it excludes interviewing. Listening is so much at the basis of every learning process that it is unnecessary to name it explicitly. Seeing a person's life and taking part in it, which are the two main ingredients of participant observation, makes sense only when they are accompanied by speaking and listening.

Spradley (1979) begins his book on the ethnographic interview with an example from the field. Elizabeth Marshall, an American anthropologist, meets a !Kung woman, Tsetchwe:

then after a moment's pause, Tsetchwe began to teach me a few words, the names of a few objects around us, grass, rock, bean shell, so that we could have a conversation later.

Spradley then comments:

'Tsetchwe began to teach me . . .' In order to discover the hidden principles of another way of life, the researcher must become a *student*. Tsetchwe, and those like her in every society, become *teachers*. Instead of studying the 'climate', the 'flora', and the 'fauna' which make up the Bushmen's environment, Elizabeth Marshall tried to discover how the Bushmen define and evaluate drought and rainstorm, *gemsbok* and giraffe, *torabe* root and *tsama* melon. She did not attempt to describe Bushmen social life in terms of what we know as 'marriage' or 'family'; instead she sought to discover how Bushmen identified relatives and the cultural meaning of their kinship relations.

And he concludes:

the naive realist assumes that love, rain, marriage, worship, trees, death, food, and hundreds of other things have essentially the same meaning to all human beings. Although there are few of us who would admit to such ethnocentrism, the assumption may unconsciously influence our research. Ethnography starts with a conscious attitude of almost complete ignorance. (Spradley 1979:4)

In my case, the ignorance was overwhelming. I spent almost six months in the village doing nothing other than learning the language. Some of my teachers were small children. They taught me the words for the things most physically present: table and chair, nose and eye, yam and rice. 'The stranger is a child', was one of the proverbs I learnt first. Another one was equally appropriate: 'The stranger does not break the law.' I was allowed to make mistakes, but I learnt they *were* mistakes.

The Demographic Approach

Naturally, one is inclined to think that the census and the survey questionnaire are the most suitable techniques for demographic research. There are however at least two reasons to treat that assumption with caution. In the first place, close-ended questions assume that the meaning of the question is clear, and that interviewer and respondent agree on that meaning, which may not always be the case. Second, questions may touch upon delicate and potentially embarrassing issues which people do not want to discuss.

Even simple questions such as 'Are you married?' or 'How many children do you have?' caused confusion in my own fieldwork. What did I mean by 'married'? There are different ways of having a partner. Formal customary marriage, which involved some flimsy rituals, was one of them. Christians could have a church wedding, which was a big thing, but it hardly occurred in the village although it was full of Christians. Rather, church weddings took place primarily among the urban élite. The same applied more or less to 'marriage by ordinance', the official state marriage.

On the 'illegal' side there were also various different shades of sexual union. *Mpena awadee* was a socially recognized but not customarily sanctioned relationship. Some people, after a couple of divorces, preferred *mpena awadee* because, as they said, they were 'tired of marriage'. Young people often engaged in a secret lover relationship, although that 'secret' was sometimes known to a large group of people. A married person—or, to be more precise, someone (usually a man) with a publicly known partner—could also have a secret love affair. And finally, there were a number of people who, for various reasons, opted for more casual relationships.

For example, a man of about 35, who rented a room in the compound where I was staying, told me that he had decided not to marry but to stick to lovers. 'Women', he explained, 'ask too much, so it is not advisable for a poor man to marry.' He had one child and said he gave the child one or two cedis each month (then about one-half of one British pound). He claimed he gave his girlfriends a cloth three times a year. 'That is cheaper than being married to them.'

I wonder what this man would answer to a poll-taker's question 'Are you married?' Depending on his mood, his impression of the poll-taker, etc., he could just as well answer yes or no. To him, either answer would be wrong anyway. For him, the right answer could never be one word; he would need a story to explain his position.

My main point, however, is not the ambiguity of the term 'marriage', but its emptiness. Even if it were clear what legal status and form of union the term refers to, we still would not know what 'marriage' means to the person interviewed. In the village where I did my fieldwork, some 'married' people hardly ever saw one another because they lived far apart. Even if a man and his wife were living in the same village, they usually did not cohabit. As a rule, each lived with his or her own lineage.[1] In the evening the wife would prepare a meal for her husband. She, or a child would bring the food to the man's lineage house where he would eat it together with his brothers and cousins and not with his wife.

In the late evening the wife may visit her husband and spend the night with him. (And while she is away her daughters may spend the night with their boyfriends and return home a little while before their mother returns.) There are also couples who do cohabit. A rich man is able to draw his wife away from her family because he can offer her financial and social security. Others live together because one of the couple, usually the woman, is from another village, which is too far away to practise a duo-local marriage.

It is not only the residence pattern, however, that varies from one marriage to another. Similar divergences exist with regard to care of children, division of tasks, and financial arrangements, to mention only three.

In summary, what do we really know if someone truthfully and correctly answers that he or she is married? What does this variable 'married' clarify with regard to the complex issue of fertility behaviour? In my research the answer was: Nothing. Asking the question 'Are you married?' was almost useless because the term itself had no meaning. Neither 'yes' nor 'no' carried the information I needed to understand what people were doing.

The irony of the survey question is that it conceals this lack of understanding. The 'closed' question (*nomen est omen*) does not lend itself to the complexity of the respondent's own ideas and experiences and thus escapes the correction of its wrong presumptions. The closed question is a 'safe' question, in that it allows the questioner to stick to his naïve realism (remember Spradley) without being aware of it, let alone being bothered by it.

Can social scientists really be so naïve? Am I not making a caricature of the survey approach? I think not: in addition, I believe that the naivité and false trust in statistical data are understandable from a cultural point of view. There are thoughts and practices that are self-evident only to those who are part of a specific culture. Things become unquestionnable in their 'natural environment' (i.e. their own culture). What to outsiders may seem a weird belief is respectable and rational knowledge (science) for the 'natives' of that culture. That is as true for beliefs about witchcraft among the Azande as for faith in quantitative data among certain Social Science tribes; thinking in terms of statistical data and not being bothered by what is outside those data is part of their culture, as is continuously evidenced by their publications.

Let us now, finally, look briefly at the second reason why the questionnaire approach may cause problems in demographic research. Some topics are too sensitive or embarrassing to be dealt with in a survey. A coincidence during my fieldwork demonstrated this in an almost disconcerting way (Bleek 1987).

I did my research in one extended family or lineage (*abusua*) and was able to have interviews and informal conversations with 42 of its adult members, nearly its total number. The conversations were about marriage and sexual relationships, having and not having children, and birth control, including the practice of induced abortion, to mention only the most important topics. My research supervisor judged the number of 42 too small for a research project with demographic implications. He advised me to carry out a survey among a larger sample of the village population. One of the steps I took to follow his advice was to interview mothers with young children during their visit to the local child welfare clinic. I had ascertained that these constituted a good representation of all mothers between 20 and 45 in the village. Six nurses from a nearby hospital carried out the interviews after receiving a brief period of training. All young, around the age of 20, they wore their uniforms during the interview to give the proceedings a medical air. I assumed that questions about sex and birth control would meet with the least resistance if put in an aseptic clinical environment. I kept out of sight as much as possible.

Examining the results, I soon realized that the quality of the research had not been improved by this survey. During my conversations with the women of the lineage, 63% of them (N = only 19) had told me that they had practised some type of birth control at some time, 21% of them said they had used three (or more) different types of birth control, and 53% confided to me that they had once (or more frequently) had an abortion. The corresponding percentages from the survey sample were 14%, 1%, and 4%. Clearly, that difference had to be explained by the research method and not by some exceptional characteristics of the particular lineage that I was studying. I became convinced that the respondents of the survey had tried to make a respectable impression on the nurses, something they had not been able to do with me, since I already knew 'too much' about them. I was sure, but could I prove it?

I was helped by a stroke of luck. I discovered that six women of the lineage I was studying had taken part in the survey. They had been interviewed without knowing that their responses would eventually come to my attention. When I compared their answers with what I knew about them, I made a both shocking and fascinating discovery. To put it plainly, they had lied lavishly; to put it in a more sympathetic light, they had construed their own 'truth', presenting themselves in terms that they expected would make the nurses respect them. Some of their answers were so far removed from the facts as I knew them that I was confounded. Some of the contradictory answers given by one individual, whom I have selected specifically to illustrate this point, are as follows:

Survey interview	*Anthropological research*
24 years old	31 years old
Divorced once	Divorced twice
Given birth to four children	Given birth to six children (two of which had died)
Has been pregnant four times	Has been pregnant at least nine times
Lives with husband in Accra	Lives with husband in village
Has never used any form of birth control	Has experience with many methods of birth control
Has never had an induced abortion	Has had at least three abortions

The conclusion is self-evident, old news: the questionnaire approach is unsuitable for eliciting information about intimate, potentially embarrassing thoughts and practices. If informants want to remain polite—and many do to an incredible degree—they have no other choice than to lie. These six did so profusely.

In conclusion, many issues in demographic research are too complicated, too ambiguous, and too intimate to be handled in a survey manner. Informants are likely to respond to closed or half-closed questions with true answers which do not make sense or with lies which do make sense, but a sense that is beyond the grasp of the poll-taker.

The Contribution of Anthropology

So far, this chapter has exposed some of the weaknesses of demographic research. How can it be made 'stronger'? How can the anthropological approach ameliorate the quality of demographic fieldwork? Some suggestions have already been implied in the above critique of conventional quantitative methods.

Conversation

Demographic research should begin with a qualitative reconnaissance in that specific setting of the meaning of words and practices to be used in the research. Such a reconnaissance becomes imperative when the researcher is not a member of the community or society under study and is unfamiliar with its culture. The most appropriate method of obtaining information is ordinary conversation, which is both informal and spontaneous. This method can slowly be developed into a more systematic and structured exchange of information. This is not the place to delve deeply into the methodological variations and details of qualitative research. Numerous introductions on qualitative methods exist, e.g. Spradley (1979); Burgess (1984); Hammersley and Atkinson (1995).

I have already referred to Spradley's plea for the anthropologist to see himself as a learner and the informant as a teacher. For an attentive researcher it is not difficult to 'play' that role in conversations and interviews. The comparison with a normal conversation in everyday life is the best guideline for effective qualitative research. One person listens to another. A question is asked and the questioner tries to understand what the respondent is saying. In the answer, the respondent is adding other pieces of information which may contribute to the context of the topic under study. New questions arise, and one soon realizes something can be learnt only by fully understanding its context.

Thus, a natural conversation consists of a flow of information which proceeds rather haphazardly. People think in an associative way, jumping from one topic to another; but the final result of that seemingly undirected communication is a gradual understanding of the initial topic. After the person who asked the questions has returned home, he or she may stumble upon an aspect which they forgot to discuss. The next day, on meeting the other person, the questioner will pick up the thread and a new conversation evolves, which will lead to new insights and a more complete comprehension. A definitive, perfect answer will of course never be achieved, either in real life or in anthropological research (cf. Geertz's remarks earlier on).

After a satisfactory level of general understanding has been reached with regard to the key issues of the research at hand, one will then be able to ask questions that will produce meaningful information. The question 'Are you married?' may have to be rephrased or combined with additional questions. Some questions must perhaps be cancelled, since they do not produce the type of information that can be quantified without losing all meaning. Qualitative and quantitative methods are shown in this way to be complementary, since qualitative research selects and steers the quantitative questions and is indispensable for interpreting the answers.

One of the disadvantages of the 'natural conversation' method is that it takes time. Another drawback, although to some extent also an attraction, is that it requires considerable psychological, and even emotional, investment. The latter is indeed an essential part of the anthropological approach. Without feeling there is no understanding. The personal engagement, an issue that will be discussed more fully later on, enables the researcher to assess what marriage and children, health and illness, youth and old age, and so on mean to the people themselves. The fieldworker is both the research tool and the unit of analysis, and involvement is a condition for intersubjectivity.

Observation

Malinowski, who is still revered by present-day anthropologists for his exemplary research among the Trobrianders, stressed the importance of direct observation time and again. The decisive difference between the fieldworker and the armchair anthropologist of his days was that the latter knew only from hearsay, while Malinowski, the fieldworker, *saw* things taking place 'under my very eyes, at my own doorstep' (1922: 8). Malinowski derived his great ethnographic authority from this personal presence at the spot. Geertz (1988: 73–101) has characterized him as an 'I-witness'.

There are two main reasons why Malinowski attaches so much importance to direct observation. In the first place, people usually do not speak about the most ordinary 'facts' of their lives. They are so familiar with them that they do not think of them. They are not worth mentioning and at the same time are hard to describe in words. Malinowski (1922: 18) calls them the 'imponderabilia of actual life'. For the anthropologist, however, they are not at all 'ordinary'. It is only by observation that he can learn about them.

Here belong such things as the routine of a man's working day, the details of his care of the body, of the manner of taking food and preparing it; the tone of conversational

and social life around the village fires, the existence of strong friendships or hostil-
ities, and of passing sympathies and dislikes between people; the subtle yet unmistak-
able manner in which personal vanities and ambitions are reflected in the behaviour
of the individual and in the emotional reactions of those who surround him. (Malinowski 1922: 18–19)

A second reason is extensively discussed in Malinowski's book on
sexual customs among the Trobrianders. Some information is not mentioned
during conversation or interview because the people are not willing to
reveal it. There can be a large discrepancy between statements and direct
observations:

The statements contain the ideal of tribal morality: observation shows us how far real
behaviour conforms to it. The statements show us the polished surface of custom
which is invariably presented to the inquisitive stranger; direct knowledge of native
life reveals the underlying strata of human conduct ... (Malinowski 1929: 425–6)

He is however quick to excuse the informants. They are not deceiving the
researcher. The latter is to blame for his naivité:

it must be made clear that no blame can be laid on native informants, but rather on
the ethnographer's whole-hearted reliance in the question-and-answer method. In
laying down the moral rule, in displaying its stringency and perfection, the native is
not trying really to deceive the stranger. He simply does what any self-respecting and
conventional member of a well-ordered society would do: he ignores the seamy and
ugly sides of human life, he overlooks his own shortcomings and even those of his
neighbours, he shuts his eyes to what he does not want to see. No gentleman wants to
acknowledge the existence of what is 'not done', what is universally considered bad,
and what is improper. The conventional mind ignores such things, above all when
speaking to a stranger—since dirty linen should not be washed in public. (Malinowski 1929:426)

But it is unlikely that Malinowski really got to *see* that dirty linen. His
most productive method of breaking through the wall of decorum was a
mixture of seeing and 'hearsay', let us call it gossip.

Indeed, most of what anthropologists write about they do not actually see,
since their ethnographic work is based mainly on what people have told
them. Ironically, moreover, the topics that interest anthropologists most are
things that people often do not want to talk about. The more things are
hidden, the more they rouse the anthropologist's curiosity. What can be seen
every day, and is known to everybody, is rarely the focus of anthropological
interest. Few anthropologists write about their own society, and if they do
they usually choose what is at the margin and virtually unknown to them.
One could almost say that an anthropological research topic by definition is
unobservable to the general public. This was certainly true for my research
topic, which concerned sexual relationships and birth control.

What then do anthropologists mean by participant *observation*? What
they do observe above all concerns the context in which the events that

interest them take place. And, as we just have seen, only by knowing the context do we begin to understand something about the events. The role of the eye in acquiring knowledge is so much taken for granted that we may forget its crucial importance. Seeing the houses in which people live, the land on which they work, their schools and churches, and their shops and their markets—all make a difference. I have seen how mothers bath and cuddle their babies, how children play, how older children take care of younger ones, how men and women move and do not move together, how people socialize and how they fight, and how they mourn their dead, Malinowski's *imponderabilia*. All these observations have helped me to describe and interpret what people do and think with regard to having and not having children.

Furthermore, observations produce questions. That effect too is so obvious that we hardly seem to be aware of it. The eyes pose questions continuously: Who is that person? Who lives in that big house? Whose children are playing together over there? Why does that woman beat her child? What food is this? Who uses this toilet and who cleans it? And so on.

Occasionally, an observation seems to contradict what we already know, or think we know. It may then lead to new questions about the same topic and possibly also to new insights. The previous information may have been untrue or too simple, revealing only 'one side of the coin'. Further observation enables us to correct our information or to reach a deeper level of understanding. In my journal I wrote:

My old landlord has two wives. In the evening they sit together, each in front of her own door, and have a lively conversation. The old man sits with them and takes part in the conversation. I see it every day: a homely scene, a harmonious polygamous marriage.

One night a loud noise wakes me up. Two women are shouting at one another. My crooked door leaves a big split. Through it I can see one of the two wives. The old man tries in vain to calm them down.

It is difficult for me to understand what they are saying. It goes too fast and there are many unfamiliar words in it. I hold the microphone of the cassette recorder in the split of the door and record their 'conversation'. The next morning my assistant translates it word by word: 'You with your crooked ass', 'You are black and dirty', 'You better take your bath in the afternoon rather than in the evening', 'You with your cracked heel', and so on.

The quarrel had causes and consequences which kept me busy the following days. I had to readjust my understanding of the old man's marriage and to change my somewhat romantic ideas about polygyny.

My diary is full of such observations which have enabled me gradually to get a clearer picture of the 'demography' of this village. One could say that such observations helped me to ask better questions, to check and interpret the answers, and to see new connections in my understanding of people's way of life.[2]

Participation

There is a Chinese proverb which translates roughly as meaning: 'I hear, I forget; I see, I remember; I do, I understand.' It succinctly captures the basic idea of participant observation, in that only by taking part in people's lives can we understand them. But what I previously said about observation also applies to participation. What interests us most are usually the things that are the least accessible and most difficult for us to participate in. In my research these included: marriage, death, witchcraft accusations, sexual relationships, and birth control. Getting involved in a sexual relationship for the sake of research would be a problematic kind of participation, not to speak of its ethical ambiguity. Any sort of participation for the sake of such research reeks of insincerity, and is inevitably both half-hearted and uncommitted. Such participation also produces feelings that are essentially different from those experienced by the people being studied, for whom it is a question not just of participation but of life itself. For the farmer working on the land, his work was a daily necessity, whereas for me the same work was an anthropological experience. The difference between real and artificial experience has been strikingly described by Orwell in his reminiscences of his life as a tramp in Paris and London:

my money oozed away—to eight francs, to four francs, to one franc, to twenty-five centimes; and twenty-five centimes is useless, for it will buy nothing except a newspaper. We went several days on dry bread, and then I was two and a half days with nothing to eat whatever. This was an ugly experience. There are people who do fasting cures of three weeks or more, and they say that fasting is quite pleasant after the fourth day: I do not know, never having gone beyond the third day. Probably it seems different when one is doing it voluntarily and is not underfed at the start. (Orwell 1933)

Having said all this, I still would like to defend participation as the most felicitous research method for anthropologists. It is true that participation is often limited to only a few aspects of life and that it is not 'real', but it is certainly better than nothing. To draw again a parallel with observation, the researcher participates in the context of the study, and by doing so gets closer to it. Sometimes, by chance, it may even prove possible to get in direct touch with it, as actually happened to me.

I fell in love with a girl from the village. It was both an awkward and an exciting experience. Her father was an important person related to the family I stayed with and we feared trouble. We met in secret, and I gradually realized that I was in the same situation as many others in the village. She came to my room in the night, after her mother had left the house. She knocked on my window and I softly opened the main gate of the compound to let her in. Before dawn she left me and joined her sisters in her mother's room. The sisters knew where she had been but kept the secret.

My love affair was never planned as 'participant observation', which is why it could become one. It taught me many things. We talked about ourselves, what we liked and disliked, about our parents, our brothers and sisters and other relatives, and about the past and the future. We also discussed how to prevent a pregnancy, and such matters as which contraceptives were the most effective. Actually getting the contraceptives was instructive. Buying oral contraceptives or condoms from a local store was risky if we wanted to keep our relationship secret. It was safer to buy them elsewhere. In solving these and other problems, I became more and more a participant in the everyday complications of a secret love affair. My relationship with her taught me more about sexual relationships and birth control in that community than the interviews I held.[3]

But the affair did more. Being involved in a secret relationship gave me a sense of belonging, and seemed to make me more one of them. I am convinced that most—if not all—of the people in my house knew what was going on, but they never referred to it directly. I would not be surprised if some of them watched us, peeping through the splits of their doors. I suspect that they 'secretly' enjoyed witnessing my affair. Three young people in the house were fully informed about our relationship and sometimes functioned as *postillons d'amour*. Even her father once made a remark which was probably a signal to me that he knew what his daughter was doing, but he never took any action.

My impression is that being in this somewhat awkward and vulnerable situation made me more accepted in the community. I compare this to an incident reported by Berreman (1962:10) during his fieldwork in a Himalayan village. When it became known that he, like many other inhabitants of the village, served clandestine alcoholic drinks in his house, his relationship with the people improved considerably. Geertz (1973: 412–17) in his essay on the Balinese cockfight makes a similar observation. During a police raid against the forbidden practice of cockfighting, Geertz and his wife had to run away together with the other spectators. The people appreciated their 'solidarity':

getting caught, or almost caught, in a vice raid is perhaps not a very generalizable recipe for achieving that mysterious necessity of anthropological field work, rapport, but for me it worked very well. It led to a sudden and unusually complete acceptance into a society extremely difficult for outsiders to penetrate. (Geertz 1973: 416)

In the same way, my love affair, which was less secret than I had hoped, helped to get me accepted as a member of the community, especially among the young. It made me seem a 'normal' human being.

I am not suggesting that anthropologists should have love affairs in order to do good research. As a matter of fact, such an affair may well jeopardize the entire research project. A less tolerant community may take offence at the visitor's behaviour and request him/her to leave. Deep emotional involvement with one person may also block good relationships with others. In some more conflictuous societies, a fieldworker is well advised to keep strict neutrality. I was fortunate, the people in 'my' village were relatively relaxed and liberal in sexual matters.

Good anthropological fieldwork is a question not so much of efficient planning as of flexibility and improvisation. Advances in the research are often strokes of luck, gifts of serendipity. Examples of such 'lucky strikes' can be found in many accounts of anthropological—but also in hard science—research.

What happened to me could be compared to Anja Krumeich's experience on the Caribbean island of Dominica. Her research was on mothers' ideas and practices during pregnancy and their care for young children. At first the mothers were friendly and helpful but somewhat reserved. They felt the anthropologist's questions were a kind of examination and they did their best to give the right answers. Then it was discovered that Anja was pregnant and that a Dominican man was responsible for it. From that moment onwards, the all-knowing anthropologist turned into a helpless young woman who, far from home, had been made pregnant by 'one of those men' and who needed their help and advice. Uninvited, they started to tell her what she should do to protect the pregnancy and have a safe delivery. And when the baby was born in the local hospital, they instructed her how to keep it healthy and how to bring it up in the proper way. Thus, the information she first tried to acquire with so little success was suddenly given to her in abundance (Krumeich 1994).

It was not only verbal information that was offered to her, however. Getting pregnant, having a baby, looking after a child, and fighting with its father enabled her to experience the emotions that are part of mother-hood in Dominica. She argued with others about her son's health, she was beaten up by the child's father, and was comforted by the mothers who had become her friends. Participation was no longer a methodological device alone; it had become a personal reality and was part of her own way of life.

Such participation, however, relates uneasily with a time-honoured principle of social research: non-intervention. Non-intervention makes sense in the laboratory concept of research. People are perceived as actors whose behaviour is observed in much the same way as one studies the reactions of mice in a particular situation. Intervention would thus spoil their 'normal' behaviour.

Personal involvement with the people one tries to understand necessarily leads to intervention. It is 'natural' that people exchange information, advise, and help each other. Refusing to do so for academic reasons shows that one is a false participant.

My own life in this Ghanaian community was a mixture of intervention and non-intervention. Looking back, I discern both pretence and sincerity, involving sham as well as true participation during my research. Sometimes I tried to help people, took part in family deliberations, and gave my opinion, whereas at other times I kept silent, waited, and watched. I seldom tried to influence young people's birth-control practices, even though I saw how dangerous and harmful they often were. In retrospect, I regret this and I am sure that I would have learnt more about these practices if I had tried to change them.

Being a full participant, I realized, was difficult (cf. Bleek 1979, 1980). Moreover, even full participants sometimes wait and watch. One cannot intervene all the time. And, of course, there are boundaries beyond which even local people are not supposed to intervene. What happens in another family, for example, may not be your concern.

Introspection

Anthropological research is bound to have an autobiographical side too. The researcher is likely to look for a part of himself or herself in the community studied and to achieve greater self-knowledge by understanding 'them'. Moreover, each fieldwork experience and each interpretation of data is filtered through the mind and heart of the researcher.

The unavoidable subjectivity of anthropological and much other research was suspect and disapproved of in the not-too-distant past. The researcher was urged to avoid it as much as possible. Nowadays, we tend to see it as an asset rather than an obstacle to good research. The implicit comparison between 'my' and 'their' experience is a prerequisite for understanding 'them'. If we do not recognize anything from ourselves in them, our data will tend to remain stale and meaningless. It would be like reading a novel about people and events which do not touch us in any way; if there is nothing we can share with the characters of the story, and we do not relate to their desires or anxieties, we will take little interest in them and understand them less. We will never finish the book.

Instead of suppressing personal views and feelings, the researcher should examine them carefully and try to use them in conversation, observation, and participation. Through exposure to an informant, a deeper level of mutual understanding and appreciation may be reached. When Desjarlais (1991: 394) asked an old man in Nepal what happens if one's heart is filled with grief, the man smiled and gave the best possible answer: 'You ask yourself.' During my research, I once had a conversation with an old woman and one other person. The topic arose of birth-control practices in the past and we asked her about coitus interruptus. She laughed loudly and asked me rhetorically: 'Can you do it?' I said nothing at the time and so missed a valuable opportunity. If I had said 'Yes', the conversation would probably have become much more enlightening.

Renato Rosaldo (1984) asked Ilongot people in the Philippines why they cut off other people's heads. They answered that the rage coming from sadness about someone's death impelled them to kill. Cutting off someone's head and throwing it away helped them to overcome their grief. They could not explain it any further. Either you understood, or you did not. Rosaldo admits he did not until he went through similar feelings when he lost his wife. Jackson (1989:4) relates this example in his book, which is one long plea for the recognition of subjectivity in fieldwork. Without subjectivity there is no intersubjectivity. I fully subscribe to the following remark by Lutz and White:

the youth of the typical ethnographer is a liability in the cross-cultural investigation of emotion insofar as limited life experience makes her or him unprepared to understand some things about the emotions of those met. (Lutz and White 1986: 415)

Freud, it seems, produced some of his most incisive comments on the human psyche by reflecting on his own experiences, including his dreams. It is significant, therefore, that his remarks about love are shallow and hardly insightful. He describes love almost as an aberration in which a person loses control of his mind: 'against all the evidence of his senses the man in love declares that he and his beloved are one'. The state of love 'represents at least a partial return to the primal state before the discrimination of self from mother'.[4] Freud's perception of love is one of an outsider: he admits that he himself never had that 'oceanic feeling', thus implicitly indicating that his understanding of love is incomplete (cf. Suttie 1988: 219–20).

People in the village I studied told me about their loves, about the blessings and frustrations of having children, about their fears of getting pregnant while at school, about the spectre of remaining without children, about their financial worries and concerns, and about their sadness when someone died. Looking back at my research, I realize that I was too young and unexperienced fully to grasp the meaning of their stories. I would have understood their worries better if I had lived through the same things myself. I could then have gauged much better the social and emotional significance of their information by comparing it with my own experience and knowledge.

When Lévi-Strauss suggests that people perceive and order the world by a mental act of binary opposition, I have no urge to check whether this applies to most societies about which anthropologists have written. Rather, when I am evaluating the responses to anthropological research questions, I close my eyes and ask myself: Does it apply to me? Do I use binary oppositions in my life? That is the first and, I think, the most effective way to assess the plausibility of any statement and I assume others do the same. I completely agree with Atwood and Tomkins's statement:

no theorist puts forward definitive statements on the meaning of being human unless he feels those statements constitute a framework within which he can comprehend his own experiences. (cited in Wengle 1987: 368)

Introspection, in summary, is a valuable quality in anthropological research. The researcher should explore his or her own ideas and feelings while listening to others and reflecting on their stories. The standard question to ask is: What would I do, think, or feel if this happened to me? The underlying assumption is that there is a similarity in the human experience all over the world (cf. Jackson 1989). Of course, that assumption sounds crude and simplistic when expressed in this way and borders on ethnocentrism, but it will take us further in the attempt to understand other cultures than will attitudes that involve distance and objectivity. I firmly maintain that introspection is an inherent part of the anthropological research approach.

Conclusion

My conclusion will appear as a truism to those who have ever practised demographic fieldwork. In the first place, I maintain that survey research alone cannot handle the delicate and complex issues involving people's ideas, desires, and practices with regard to sex and reproduction. More sensitive approaches and more subjective involvement are needed to analyse such issues in any depth.

In the second place, I suggest that the anthropological research approach is indispensible for the interpretation of quantitative data. My purpose in this paper has been to convince readers that there is no safety in numbers alone, and that any apparent safety found in statistics is in fact a mirage. I believe that quantitative and qualitative approaches are complementary. The information provided by the anthropologist is what the demographer needs to know to ask the appropriate, specific questions. Qualitative research helps demographers to count what they want to count. Most of the chapters included in this book illustrate these complementary virtues.

In this chapter I have presented and discussed four basic ingredients of the anthropological approach: conversation, observation, participation, and introspection. Most of the examples I described were derived from my own research on sexual relationships and birth control in a Ghanaian rural community.

By now, there is a long history of anthropologists writing about their fieldwork, but only few of them have included their own experiences with love and sex in their account. This apparent blind spot in methodological reflection was an additional reason for discussing such issues in the present chapter on participant observation.

Notes

1. One of the cultural repercussions of the absence of fathers is beautifully sketched by Bartle (1977: 239), who carried out fieldwork in a nearby town: 'in the compound where I

lived ... the girls would say, let's play *Mame ne mame* (mother and mother) or *Mame ne nana* (mother and grandmother). The adults these children emulated were their mothers and their mothers' sisters ... Their socialization took place in a matrilineal rather than bilateral kinship system.' Bartle's dissertation is available in only a few copies, most of which seem to be in Ghana. Bartle gave me his personal manuscript, from which I am quoting. It is possible that the quotation does not exactly agree with the final text of his dissertation.

2. By the way, this incident highlights the ethical aspect of participant observation. Several of my colleagues have criticised the secretive use of a microphone to record the exchange of words between the two women as unethical. I share their concern about the ethics of field-work. The direct confrontation between fieldworker and local people frequently results in ethical dilemmas which force the anthropologist to reflect on his or her position in the community. Unambiguous guidelines on how to behave correctly in anthropological research are difficult to formulate. Finding the correct way is very much part of the anthropological exploration itself. In this particular case, I allowed myself to record the shouting. Everybody in the compound heard and understood what the women were saying. I alone was left out, because my command of the language was too limited to grasp the meaning of the words. The cassette recorder was used in this case merely as a hearing aid, and it helped me to hear what everybody else had heard. My action would have been unethical if I had used the recording for another purpose which was against the interests of the people concerned.

3. My friendship with Kwasi Asante-Darko, a university student, who helped me during the research and shared almost every minute of my life in the community, was another invaluable source of learning. We stayed in one room and did nearly everything together. In our discussions, which sometimes continued late into the night, we talked about everything that had happened during the day. He explained people's reactions to our research, helped me to understand their stories, and showed me the mistakes I had made.

4. Freud's quotations from *Das Unbehagen in der Kultur* (1933) have been taken from Suttie (1988).

References

Bartle, P. F. W. (1977), 'Urban migration and rural identity: an ethnography of a Kwawu community, Obo'. Unpublished dissertation, University of Ghana, Legon.

Berreman, G. D. (1962), *Behind Many Masks*. Ithaca, NY: Society for Applied Anthropology.

Bleek, W. (1979), 'Envy and inequality in fieldwork: an example from Ghana'. *Human Organization*, 38: 200–5.

——(1980). 'Envy and inequality in fieldwork: a rejoinder'. *Human Organization*, 39: 291–3.

——(1987), 'Lying informants: a field experience from Ghana'. *Population and Development Review*, 13: 314–22.

Burgess, R. G. (1984), *In the Field: An Introduction in Field Research*. London: Allen & Unwin.

Desjarlais, R. R. (1991), 'Poetic transformations of Yolmo "sadness"'. *Culture, Medicine and Psychiatry*, 15: 387–420.

Geertz, C. (1973), *The Interpretation of Cultures*. New York: Basic Books.

——(1988), *Works and Lives: The Anthropologist as Author*. Cambridge: Polity Press.

Hammersley, M. and Atkinson, P. (1995), *Ethnography: Principles in Practice*. London: Routledge.

Jackson, M. (1989), *Paths towards a Clearing: Radical Empiricism and Ethnographic Inquiry*. Bloomington, Ind.: Indiana University Press.

Kaufmann, G. (1991), 'Family formation and fertility in a *favela* in Belo Horizonte, Brazil: an analysis of cultural and demographic influences'. Dissertation, Oxford University.

Krumeich, A. (1994), *The Blessings of Motherhood: Health, Pregnancy and Child Care in Dominica*. Amsterdam: Het Spinhuis.

Lutz, C. and White, G. M. (1986), 'The anthropology of emotions'. *Annual Review of Anthropology*, 15: 405–36.

Orwell, G. (1933), *Down and Out in Paris and London*. London: Victor Gollancz.

Malinowski, B. (1922), *Argonauts of the Western Pacific*. New York: Dutton.

——(1929), *The Sexual Life of Savages in North-Western Melanesia*. London: Routledge & Kegan Paul.

Rosaldo, R. I. (1984), 'Grief and a headhunter's rage: on the cultural force of emotions'. In E. M. Brunner (ed.), *Text, Play and Story: The Construction and Reconstruction of Self and Society*. Washington: American Ethnological Society, pp. 178–95.

Spradley, J. P. (1979), *The Ethnographic Interview*. New York: Holt, Rinehart & Winston.

Suttie, I. D. (1988), *The Origins of Love and Hate* (first published in 1935). London: Free Association Books.

Wengle, J. (1987), 'Death and rebirth in fieldwork: a case study'. *Culture, Medicine and Psychiatry*, 11: 357–85.

3 Using Qualitative Data for Understanding Old-Age Security and Fertility

JOHN KNODEL

Introduction

The reliance of parents on children for support and care during their elderly years is typically cited as a crucial prop of high fertility and a barrier to fertility transition by demographers (e.g. Caldwell 1977). In many societies where alternative forms of old-age support are lacking, adult children take on paramount importance for parents in their old age when physical health is impaired and the ability to perform economic activities is in decline. Two extensive reviews of the theoretical arguments and empirical research on the so-called 'old-age security motive' for having children exist, although both are written primarily from an economic perspective (Nugent 1985; Nugent and Anker 1990).

The extent to which the old-age security motive in fact exists and the way it operates is relatively understudied (Nugent 1985). As Nugent and Anker (1990) point out, most arguments postulating its importance have been made on the following prima facie evidence: responses to relatively simplistic survey questions; the (partially observed, partially presumed) lack of alternatives to children for the provision of old-age security; the observed heavy dependence of the elderly on children in high-fertility countries; and the inverse association between fertility level and existence of extensive old-age pension plans cross-nationally.

This paper considers the contribution that qualitative data generated from focus group discussions might contribute to our understanding of this issue. As Nugent and Anker (1990: 9) point out, 'what is important about the support of parents in their old age for fertility is not what actually happens— an objectively observable phenomenon—but rather expectations which are, of course, necessarily subjective.' This being the case, it would seem that such qualitative data might be of particular value.

This report is a revised version of a paper prepared for the IUSSP Seminar on New Approaches to Anthropological Demography, Barcelona, Spain, 10–13 November 1993. Special appreciation is expressed to Napaporn Havanon, Anthony Pramualratana, Chanpen Saengtienchai and Werasit Sittitrai, who collaborated in the collection and prior analyses of the focus group data that serve as the basis of much of this paper. Helpful comments on earlier drafts were provided by Anthony Pramualratana and Jeffrey Nugent.

The following analysis is based largely on my own research and thus concentrates on insights provided by data collected through focus group methodology in Thailand with only limited reference to other countries and other qualitative methodologies. Thailand is an unusually interesting case, however, as it is a leader in fertility decline among developing nations. Thus, understanding how the old-age security motive relates to reproductive behaviour there is a particularly fascinating exercise. Moreover, the focus group findings for Thailand can serve as a useful example of what qualitative data might contribute to furthering our understanding of these issues more generally.

Before proceeding to the main task at hand, I would like to make explicit my own conviction that neither quantitative nor qualitative data in isolation from each other provide sufficient information for a full understanding of most social demographic phenomena. Rather, I maintain that each type of data provides an incomplete picture on its own. As obvious as this may seem, in practice it is far more common among demographers to recognize that qualitative data provide an incomplete picture without suitable complementary quantitative data than vice versa. Only very recently have demographic researchers gone beyond the mere payment of lip service to the need for complementary qualitative data and actually begun to collect some. This is a healthy development to which a constructively critical exposition of qualitative methods suitable for demographic research may be useful.

The Focus Group Method

A variety of techniques for collecting qualitative data are available to social demographers. These include participant observation (often involving lengthy residence in a community), in-depth interviews (with key informants or representatives of some targeted subset of the population), case studies, and analyses of written textual material such as novels, letters, and diaries. Moreover, secondary sources of qualitative information such as ethnographic accounts can be drawn upon. Focus group discussions represent an additional technique.

The basic idea of a focus group is to generate a discussion on preselected topics of interest to the researcher among a small group of individuals. The group usually consists of six to ten participants recruited from a well-defined target population plus a trained moderator and note-taker. Following prepared guidelines, the moderator introduces the concepts to be discussed, asks open-ended questions to get the discussion underway, encourages participation, and guides the discussion to keep it on track. Interaction among participants is encouraged and is indeed a major advantage of the method compared with most other approaches to collecting qualitative data. The discussion is usually tape-recorded and transcribed and the transcripts serve as the data for analysis.[1] The group is 'focused' in the sense that the discussions concentrate on a relatively narrow set of topics. Moreover, the target populations from which participants are selected are usually circumscribed by specific characteristics of relevance to the research topic.

Despite origins in the social sciences at least half a century ago, focus groups became best known subsequently as a method of marketing research, used for quick assessment of consumers' impressions and feelings toward new products or advertisement concepts.[2] They have also been used with some frequency as a tool in evaluative and applied research projects including ones dealing with family planning programmes. More recently, however, focus groups have begun to be used by social scientists, including social demographers, to conduct basic research. As a result, the method continues to be refined and adapted to enhance its suitability for this purpose. A growing literature on the use of focus group methodology from a social science perspective is emerging.[3]

Probably the first use of focus group methodology in social demography (as opposed to family planning evaluation operations research) was in the study I conducted over ten years ago with Thai colleagues on the determinants of Thailand's fertility transition (Knodel *et al.* 1984). Since then, focus groups have been increasingly incorporated in social demographic research projects. This reflects, at least in my judgement, the combination of (1) the increasing recognition of the usefulness of qualitative data to complement more traditional quantitative data on demographic topics and (2) the greater compatibility of the focus approach (compared with most other qualitative techniques) with the research inclinations and abilities of many demographers.

With respect to the second point, I refer to the more structured nature of focus group methodology and the limited involvement required of the researcher compared with most typical anthropological approaches. Indeed, given the imposition of a fairly structured set of guidelines to be followed by the moderator of a focus group session and the systematic implementation of the guidelines across sessions, the data collected can be thought of as quasi-structured by the researcher rather than as more purely subject-generated, as would be the case in participant observation or other standard anthropological approaches (Fry and Keith, 1986). While a traditional anthropologist might see this as a drawback, it undoubtedly adds to the appeal of focus groups for many demographers who typically are trained in the sample survey tradition where structure and systematic data collection procedures are paramount.

Given the nature of focus group data, considerable subjective judgement is required of the analyst when examining and interpreting the transcripts. Often several alternative views are expressed within the same group and, even at times, by the same person. Moreover, different views often emerge among different groups. It thus helps to have some systematic way of summarizeing the content of the focus group discussions by topic and group to aid interpretation and to help minimize personal bias in drawing conclusions. For this purpose, I follow the practice of constructing overview grids (Knodel 1993). Such a grid has topic headings or particular views on one axis and focus group session identifiers on the other. The cells contain brief summaries of the discussion for each group concerning each topic. Other relevant information might also be indicated, such as the extent of elaboration or strength of opinion. The completed grid provides a good basis for determining, in a relatively systematic way, how common particular views are, as well as whether interpretable patterns of differences are evident along lines that demarcate the target populations from whom the participants are selected.[4]

Thailand as a Case Study

The Importance of Thailand as Case Study

Thailand's fertility decline is well documented. Total fertility fell virtually without interruption from levels between six and seven children per woman in the mid-1960s to approximately two at present. The latest official survey taken in 1991–2 indicated a total fertility rate (TFR) of 2.17 (corresponding to a net reproduction rate, NRR, of 0.99), which is just below the replacement level (Thailand National Statistical Office 1993). If anything, this estimate appears to err on the high side, at least in comparison with estimates derived from the 1990 census and the 1987 Thailand Demographic and Health Survey (Hirschman *et al.* undated).

Thailand is probably the first large, fairly typical developing country to achieve replacement fertility. Unlike the smaller but much richer newly industrialized countries such as South Korea, Taiwan, Singapore, and Hong Kong, Thailand's population is still predominantly rural and agrarian; only a minority in the reproductive ages have studied past primary school; and the average per capita income is mid-range for a developing country, although economic growth has been impressively rapid. Moreover, unlike China (where fertility also rapidly declined to low levels), the family planning programme never incorporated high-pressure campaigns or quasi-coercive methods to encourage small families. These features of the Thai demographic situation make the country a particularly interesting case in which to examine the role of the old-age security motive in fertility decision-making.

Data Sources

Fortunately, two fairly extensive bodies of focus group data are available which contain substantial material relevant to the issue of old-age security and fertility. In both cases I collaborated with Thai colleagues in the data collection and analyses. Here I draw from the previous reports and publications, modifying and supplementing the earlier analysis as appropriate.[5]

The first set of focus group data were collected through a project with the Institute for Population and Social Research, Mahidol University, to study the determinants of Thailand's fertility decline. This is the study mentioned above as being probably the first to employ focus group methodology in social demography. During late 1982 and early 1983, 23 sessions were conducted, divided between older-generation married participants (who were generally over age 50 and had at least five surviving children) and younger-generation married participants (who were generally in their 20s or early 30s and desired no more than three children). Separate groups of men and women were drawn from villages in all four major regions and from Bangkok construction workers.[6]

The second study was part of the University of Michigan Comparative Study of the Elderly in Asia. Researchers in four countries, including Thailand, conducted focus groups with both elderly people (aged 60 and over) and adult children of elderly parents. The topics discussed included expectations for support in old age from children and the relationship of these expectations to changing family size. The Thai fieldwork was conducted through the Institute of Population Studies, Chulalongkorn University, in 1990–1. The elderly participants typically had their children prior to the Thai fertility transition, while the adult children participants, mostly in their 30s and 40s, had small families. A total of 26 separate focus group sessions were conducted, divided evenly between elderly and adult children, in all four major regions as well as Bangkok. Groups were generally segregated by better and worse socioeconomic status. All 18 regional groups were from rural villages while the eight Bangkok groups represented the urban population. All groups included both men and women.

In what follows, I present a number of direct quotations from the focus groups. Implied words are included in parentheses to improve intelligibility. In addition, I sometimes extract comments from a longer discussion, leaving out the intervening statements for the sake of brevity. Each quotation is followed by an identification of the study and particular session from which it comes. For convenience, the first study will be referred to as the DOFT (for Determinants of Fertility in Thailand) and the second as CSEA (for Comparative Study of the Elderly in Asia).

Results

The importance of children for old-age security

The fact that the elderly actually co-reside with an adult child and receive a variety of services and material support from children has been commonly noted by anthropologists and ethnographers and is amply documented by survey and census data (Cowgill 1972; Lauro 1977; Keyes 1987; Tuchrello 1989; Pramualratana 1990; Caffrey 1992). Results of the 1980 and 1990 censuses, a 1986 national survey, and a 1990 quasi-national survey all show that the large majority of the Thai population aged 60 and over live with children (Chayovan *et al.* 1990; Knodel *et al.* 1992*a*; Andrews and Hennink 1992; Knodel *et al.* 1994). More to the point, there is considerable survey evidence that Thai parents generally feel that children have an obligation to support and care for them.

Three-fourths of a 1975 national sample of husbands of reproductive-aged women spontaneously mentioned children as a means of old-age support, representing a far larger percentage than for any other means mentioned. When probed specifically about help provided from children, 88% thought they would depend at least in part on children for economic assistance and 85% indicated they expected to live with children in their old age (Arnold and Pejaranonda 1977). In the Value of Children Survey conducted at about the same time, married men and women were asked if they expected their sons and daughters to support them financially when they (the parents) grow old. The proportion saying yes ranged from 75% of men answering with respect to daughters to 89% of women answering with respect to sons (Kagitcibasi 1982).

More recent survey results are similar. In a 1986 national survey of adults aged 15–44, 85% said that they themselves hoped to depend on children when they became elderly and 87% expected to live with a child (Chayovan 1992). In response to an open-ended question included in the 1988 Social Attitudes Towards Children Survey on what reproductive-aged women with at least one child expected from their children, over half (56%) explicitly mentioned old-age support or care. If other responses mentioning support from children or help in work or business without specific mention of old age are included, then 76% expect such help.[7] A 1991 survey conducted in two regions of rural couples in the mid-reproductive ages who had at least one child confirms similarly high percentages expecting support including co-residence during old age (Archavanitkul *et al.* 1992).

Qualitative evidence from both of the focus group studies confirm that the predominant view among Thais of both older and younger generations is to hope to have children stay with them when they are old and contribute to their material, physical, and psycho-social well-being. The perception that, as the situation now exists, there are really no alternative sources besides children of old-age support and care comes out clearly. This coincides with the fact that pension systems and old-age homes are indeed very limited in Thailand and virtually non-existent for the rural population sector (Reinecke 1993).

The children must do everything. It's the same as with our parents now. When they are sick and when we take care of them, it is like we are making them better again. If the children do not take care of you, the parent will lose heart. [DOFT: younger woman, central region]

When we are sick, when we are old, we expect our children to cook and find food for us, find water for us. We are not strong enough to fetch water, so we want to depend on them. If we have no strength to work, have no money, we will depend on them. [DOFT: older woman, central region]

Old people can't earn their own living so they must want children to support them. When we are old, we will want it the same way. [CSEA: adult woman, central region, low socioeconomic status]

In the future, if we can't manage anymore, we all hope that children will care for us. If children don't care for us, who is to do it? [CSEA: adult woman, south, high SES]

The focus groups also included a minority of participants who denied that they hoped or intended to depend on children in their old age. Probably the most common view in this category involved asserting that the parents are concerned primarily with their children's welfare and will be pleased if their children, when they are grown up, will be able to support themselves well.

We don't want them to care for us, just to be able to care for themselves. [CSEA: adult woman, Bangkok, high SES, group 2]

Even in such cases, however, it is not always clear that the participant is denying that he or she wants any kind of support (including non-material help or co-residence) but may instead be referring only to material support such as remittances.

The focus group discussions make clear that a sense of moral obligation for adult children to take care of their parents in old age is a pervasive cultural value and provides a strong normative basis for the prevailing support patterns. In both studies, participants across the whole spectrum of groups spontaneously mentioned that parents deserve to be taken care of in their old age as a form of repayment for bearing and raising the children. This includes an understanding that at least one adult child should live with the elderly parents.

Repaying parents is viewed as a continual obligation that starts when the children are old enough to provide meaningful help and typically begins long before parents reach old age. Thus, even young adult children whose parents are still middle-aged would be expected to assist their parents out of this same sense of debt. The care and support provided by children when their parents are too old to take care of themselves is viewed as the culmination of this process of repayment. The sense of moral obligation is shared by both generations and is found in all regions, largely transcending economic status or rural–urban residence.

Elders complain. They want us to take good care of them like when they took care of us when we were small. [DOFT: younger woman, north-east]

Mr. A: Children have to take care of their parents who brought them up...They must not forget parents' meritorious acts...

Mr. B: They can't complain about us living with them because we have looked after them since they are little. [CSEA: elderly, central region, high SES]

We are old. If we don't stay with our children, with whom can we stay? They have to take care of us as we have done for them. [CSEA: elderly man, north, high SES]

Mr. A: We raised them. If we can't work anymore, it is their duty to care for us.

Ms. B: We let children care for us. I brought them all up so I want them to care for me in return. I'm too old to care for myself...

Mr. C: Since we have children, we live with them. Otherwise we need to live by ourselves. They have to care for us since we are their parents and brought them up. They must be grateful... [CSEA: elderly, north-east, high SES]

Ms. A: They may blame us as being ungrateful if we don't let them live with us...

Mr. B: Parents cared for children since they were babies so children must care for parents in return...[CSEA: adult children, north-east, low SES]

The support and care that adult children are expected to provide parents covers a whole range of material and non-material needs. The particular mix will depend in part on the circumstances of the parents. For example, rural parents are likely to want labour assistance in farming and poorer families are especially likely to want remittances from children further away. One primary concern cutting across most social strata is that someone should be present to help in times of illness or disability.

Consistent with survey evidence, the predominant view among focus group participants is that old-age support should include co-residence (or living in adjacent dwellings). As the above quotations imply, this is indeed an important part of 'parent repayment'. Moreover, it is probably the most crucial aspect of the familial support system since no other arrangement is likely to meet better the diverse needs for care and support that many elderly experience as they approach their last years.

In making sense of the discussions about living arrangements, it is important to recognize that, as the elderly pass through the old-age span, the composition of the household is likely to evolve, with children leaving the household as they reach ages at which important life-course transitions are made. Single children may move out to find work outside of the home community, children who marry may move out to form their own households, and others may return to the parental household after a stint away.

Anthropological and ethnographic studies make clear that generally the goal of the elderly is to have one child remain as the designated care-giver. This final stem family arrangement often does not emerge until the elderly are at advanced ages. As a result, many parents start out their elderly years with several children co-resident. Over time, however, children leave until typically only one is left. Once this child marries and has children, a stem family structure results with the elderly parents, a married adult child with spouse, and the grandchildren living together. This is reflected in 1986 survey results which indicate that over 90% of co-resident elderly whose children have all married live with only one of their adult children (Knodel *et al.* 1992*b*). It also emerges in the focus group discussions, sometimes implicitly in connection with comments on other topics such as inheritance or migration.

Mr. A: The one who takes care of the parents will get [inherit] a lot [of land].
Mr. B: The child who takes care of the parents until they get old and die will get a lot [of land]. The one who goes to live with his wife's family and earns a living in other ways may get less. [DOFT: younger man, central region]

If there are many children, each goes to live separately but one of them must remain with the parents. It could be anyone. Usually the youngest daughter stays. However, if there is only one child, parents have no choice. [CSEA: elderly man, central region]

If there are few of them, we won't let them go. One must be with the parents. [CSEA: adult man, north-east, low SES]

It's normal that parents must be with one child. The children may all want parents to be with them but parents have to be with only one. [CSEA: elderly man, south, high SES]

Another feature of the familial system for care and support of the elderly in Thailand is the substantial flexibility with respect to who the eventual primary care-giver will be. To be sure, numerous anthropological studies indicate that the ethnic Thai majority prefer to co-reside with daughters, particularly the youngest one, and that such a preference is most pronounced in the north-east and upper north (Tuchrello 1989; Cowgill 1972; Keyes 1987). Overall, the focus group discussions also indicate that daughters and youngest children are most commonly favoured. However, they also reveal considerable flexibility whenever circumstances warrant it. The choice appears to be influenced by normative considerations regarding gender and birth order as well as practical and emotional considerations. Thus, despite normative preferences for a co-resident youngest daughter, individual families readily adapt to their particular situations.

Moderator: Usually with whom do old people want to be?
Ms. A: Most of them are with the youngest daughter . . . If there are no daughters, it's necessary for them to be with a son. [CSEA: adult children, north, high SES]

Moderator: Does it matter if you live with a son or a daughter?
Ms. A: You've to consider children's personality first. Maybe you can live with this one or that one. You can't live with one who doesn't take care of you, so you live with the other . . . [CSEA: elderly, south, low SES]

Quantitative data from a 1986 survey of the elderly confirm the impressions gained from the focus groups. The elderly are more likely to live with a daughter than a son, particularly when married children are considered and especially in the north-east and north. Nevertheless, substantial minorities tend to live with sons, and, most telling, elderly with sons only are as likely to co-reside with a son as those with daughters only are to co-reside with a daughter. This testifies to the ability to be flexible when options are limited (Knodel *et al.* 1992*a*).

Because of differences in questions and samples, it is difficult to reach any firm conclusion about trends in expectations for old-age support from the survey data cited above. Nevertheless, the general impression they provide is one of little major change. Significantly, the proportions of elderly actually co-resident with children remained unchanged between 1980 and 1990 (Knodel *et al.* 1994). The adult children groups in the CSEA study were explicitly asked if they thought the extent and type of assistance and care they would receive from their children when they were elderly would differ from that provided to the elderly today. It was a reasonably common view, especially among Bangkok groups, that the care they receive from their own children will be less than what the current elderly generation receives and that living arrangements will probably change with a reduction in co-residence likely. This contrasts somewhat with comments about the desire for old-age assistance from children and preferred living arrangements.

Interestingly, reduced family size was rarely mentioned spontaneously as a reason for the expected decline in old-age support. Rather, changes in the familial support system were seen as the likely outcome of a set of related social changes involving increased education, changing occupations, and work-related migration. These changes generally operate to increase the chance that the next generation of elderly will reside separately from adult children as children seek work elsewhere, leaving their parents in the home communities. In such situations, elderly parents may lose the services of a care-giver who is either co-resident or lives nearby, but this could be partially compensated for by monetary remittances or other forms of material support.

Moderator: Do you think your children will care for you when you are old as you did for your parents?
Mr. A: There will certainly be problems . . . .
Mr. B: They belong to the new generation . . . I don't expect any of my children to care for me. [Laughed]
Ms. C: We have to depend on ourselves first.
Mr. A: They just go away to continue their studies.
Mr. D: Then, they go to work somewhere away from home. [CSEA: adult children, central region, low SES]

Mr. A: We will have less support [than our parents].
Ms. B: Even now, it is beginning to change.
Mr. A: People tend to go away from home to earn a living. There are many who have already left . . .
Ms. B: Parents will have a more difficult time since children will not be with them. [CSEA: adult children, north-east, high SES]

There was not a clear consensus on this issue, however. Contrary opinions frequently arose in the same group. A number of participants believed that the tradition of having at least one child to co-reside with elderly parents would persist. Some see the obligation for children to repay parents by caring for them in their old age as so firmly ingrained in Thai culture that a radical reduction in co-residence in the foreseeable future is unimaginable. Elderly parents will have a child with them as long as children have developed a sense of gratitude.

Moderator: When people of your generation in this village become old, will they hope to depend on their children as their parents depend on them?
Mr. A: They have to care for the parents ...
Mr. B: They may not be with us, but they will send us things and money. Since they have to work elsewhere, they can't be with us or cook for us.
Mr. A: If they know the mother is by herself, they'll have the mother move to be with them. [CSEA: adult children, central region]

Mr. A: There will be a child who cares for the parents ... even in the future.
Mr. B: There must be. Old people won't be deserted ... There must be one in the family. [CSEA: adult children, north-east, low SES]

Old-age security concerns and fertility decline

The Value of Children Survey in the mid-1970s indicates that old-age security concerns are a frequently stated reason for having children. Among the Thai sample, 79% of women and 71% of men indicated that old-age support was a very important reason for having children, and only 3% of women and 6% of men said that it was not important (Kagitcibasi 1982). Since in neither focus group study were participants asked directly if couples are motivated by old-age security concerns when deciding to have children, direct statements to this effect rarely arose. One woman put the matter rather succinctly, however, as the following quote indicates:

If my children don't come back [to look after me] when I am old, I don't know why I had children. [DOFT: younger woman, north-east]

Even without direct statements on motives for childbearing, the importance of old-age security concerns in this respect seems obvious from the expressions about the importance of relying on children for a whole range of assistance later in life. Together with the abundance of survey evidence documenting continued parental expectations about relying on children in old age, the focus group data provide a further basis for concluding that the expectation of such help and support continues to be perceived as a fundamental reason in Thailand for having children. Despite the uncertainty expressed about whether adult children in the future will continue providing help to elderly parents to the extent they do at present and the explicit statements predicting that help would decline, the discussions leave the impression that children will remain the primary source of old-age security for the majority of Thai parents.

This persistence of the parent repayment ethic and hopes for assistance from children in old age raises a particularly challenging question. If parents in Thailand considered children as an important source of old-age security in the past and continue to consider them as one for the future, how can this be reconciled with the dramatic decline in family size that has taken place? The focus group data collected in the two projects mentioned above go a long way towards explaining how this comes about.

In both focus group studies, participants were explicitly asked about the effect of lower fertility on the familial support system of care for the elderly. A minority of older and younger-generation participants indicated that having few children threatened security in old age. Some viewed having many children as increasing the chance that at least one child will be dependable, as it allowed parents to have more choice with whom to live, and allowed children to share some of the responsibilities of care.

Right now, with few children, the probability that they will take care of you is low. [DOFT: younger woman, south]

If you have many children, you can choose to depend on this and that child. If you have only two, what persons can they depend on? [CSEA: elderly woman, central region, high SES]

In the next thirty years, suppose parents have two children; one goes to work in a far away place like a foreign country, the other works in the south. Then parents will go through hardship when they are old. [CSEA: adult man, Bangkok, low SES]

Opinions on the negative effects of small family size for the support and care of parents were often qualified by statements that couples can no longer afford to bring up large families. A relatively common view among this group of participants was that a trade-off is involved between maximizing the economic security and psychological comfort to be gained from having many children when elderly and minimizing the economic hardships and burdens of childrearing by keeping the family size small. Thai couples today opt for small families because they feel that the additional benefits to be gained later in life from having many children are not considered worth the hardships that raising a large family involve. Some simply feel there is in fact no choice to be made, since under current social and economic circumstances they could not possibly afford to raise many children.

In principle, having a lot of children will make you comfortable when you are old, but when they are young it will be difficult to find the money to raise them. [DOFT: younger man, north]

When children have grown up, the one who has many is more comfortable than the one who has few. But if the children are still small, the one with many children will not be as comfortable as the one with few. [DOFT: older man, north-east]

With a lot of them, we can't bring them all up. We have nothing to give them as a legacy. With few of them, if they don't care for us as we want them to, we've to let it be. [CSEA: adult male, north, high SES]

A more common view among participants, especially in the more recent CSEA study, is that family size is not a particularly important determinant of the care and support the elderly receive, including the crucial aspect of co-residence during the elderly years, and thus that smaller families are not a particular threat to the support system later in life. This view emerged across the full spectrum of groups regardless of whether participants were of the older or younger generation, of high or low socioeconomic status, or resided in rural or urban (Bangkok) settings.

In this respect, focus group discussions correspond well with findings of a 1986 national survey of adults aged 15–44. Almost two-thirds (64%) of respondents said it was not necessary to have many children to depend on in old age (Chayovan, 1992). Also consistent with the impression given by the focus group studies are results from the 1988 Social Attitudes towards Children Survey, in which the average preferred family size of married women in reproductive ages differs little between those who did and those who did not indicate that old-age assistance or support was one of their expectations for their children.[8]

One reason why having few children is not seen as jeopardizing old-age support is that such support is viewed as depending on the children's upbringing and character and not on their number, or that it depends on fate or luck with respect as to how the children turn out. A small number, if properly raised, would still be sufficient to provide parents with security later in life. Conversely, having many children is not necessarily a guarantee that they will provide the desired care and support. This view is expressed by both older and younger-generation participants.

[Support in old age] depends on how you raise and bring up your children. To have a small number of children but to raise them well is better than to have many children but not to raise them well. [DOFT: younger Muslim man, south]

Moderator: Do you think the number of children concerns the caring you may get when you are old?

Mr. A: We can't be certain. Some have a lot of children but no one is with them. Some have two children and both of them take care of parents. [CSEA: adult children, north, high SES]

If he is a good child, one is enough. If they are all bad, ten are useless. [CSEA: elderly man, Bangkok, low SES]

To understand the view that it is unnecessary to have many children to ensure old-age security, it is crucial to take into account the norm that only one child will reside permanently with the parents and hence carry the bulk of the burden of responsibility for parental care. For many participants, therefore, having a single reliable child was viewed as sufficient security for support in old age.

Either with many or few [children], there must be one left to care for parents... With only two of them, one will move out and have his own family and one lives with the parents. [CSEA: adult man, north-east, high SES]

Moderator: Will having fewer children affect the care received by parents in the future?
Mr. A: Yes. Still, there must be one with us. With two of them, one can go where he wants, the other must live with us. I won't let all go. [CSEA: adult children, north-east, low SES]

Interestingly, participants who stressed children's character rather than their number do not seem to feel that having more children increases the chance that one or more will have the desirable traits. This may stem from a conviction that few children can be raised better than many, permitting parents to better instil the sense of gratitude that leads to taking care of parents later in life. This view was rarely articulated in so many words, although some participants stated related opinions, implying that having few children has positive implications for the parents when they are elderly.

Results from a 1986 national survey of the elderly shed some light on the accuracy of the perception that old-age security is not strongly related to the number of children a couple has (Knodel *et al.* 1992*b*). Among the current generation of elderly parents, there is only a relatively weak association between the chances of co-residing and the number of living children. For example, elderly parents with two living children are only modestly less likely to co-reside with a child (71%) than those with larger families (82%). Even 62% of the elderly who have only one living child co-reside with that child. The probability of receiving contributions from children who do not co-reside, however, is more closely associated with numbers of children, but such help may not be considered by Thais to be as crucial as co-residence.

Some participants believe that the relationship between the number of children and economic support later in life has changed from the past. In today's social and economic environment, more highly educated children are better situated than ones with low education to obtain desirable non-agricultural jobs and thus to provide economic support to their parents, especially in terms of cash remittances. Since the cost of providing an adequate education for many children would be prohibitive, the economic prospects of both children and parents are improved by limiting family size to a few children who can be better educated.

[Parents will still be supported well] because education has progressed. Now children get a higher education. Repayment of parents will go according to the level of education. Before, not too many studied, but for those who got a high education, they repaid their parents well. The needs and expectations of parents with two or three children will be greater but the children will receive more care. Two children with education can repay parents better than ten [without]. [DOFT: older woman, north]

Moderator: Who is going to look after present-day parents assuming they have only two children?

Ms. A: They work to educate the children and to save some money. When they are old, the children care for them...

Mr. B: With a few children, parents can provide them with good education. If there are many of them, they can't. [CSEA: elderly, central, pre-test]

Ms. A: We have few children but we support them to the best education we can. They will have good means to settle themselves and support us in return. Moreover, we teach them about gratitude. So they should feel they've to treat us as we do our own parents.

Ms. B: With few, they have better chance of education. With better [education], they may be able to establish [themselves] well and may have more chance to care for parents in return... With one or two children, we don't have much expense and we can manage. [CSEA: adult children, Bangkok, high SES]

Not all participants agreed that providing children with education ensured care in old age. Often education was associated with work-related migration taking the children away from home. Nevertheless, a recognition of the increasing necessity to educate children for them to function in the modern economy is almost universal, and sometimes the trade-off of quality for quantity of children is perceived as an asset for the quality of future support to be expected from them.

One potential link between high-fertility and old-age security concerns that is mentioned frequently in the demographic literature is the need to have large numbers of children in order to insure against possible mortality of children prior to the time the parents reach old age. The issue of whether couples need to consider potential mortality risks when having children was explicitly addressed in the DOFT focus group guidelines. In general, younger-generation participants expressed only minimal concern about children dying and only a few agreed with the need to insure against potential mortality by having extra children. In the CSEA study which did not explicitly address this issue in the guidelines, mention of being left without children or with too few children because of potential mortality rarely surfaced. Undoubtedly, participants were aware of the substantial reduction in mortality that has taken place in Thailand, and thus see their own risks of losing children as low.

Nowadays there are few children who die. It is different from the earlier time when there were a lot. [DOFT: younger Muslim man, south]

I don't think children will die. I think they will grow up. I am not afraid of death due to disease but rather due to car accidents. [DOFT: younger woman, north-east]

If anyone has two children and one dies, it will be very surprising indeed. [DOFT: younger woman, north]

In brief, focus group discussions as well as surveys indicate that many younger couples still have expectations that their children will support them into old age even though they are having far fewer children. Old-age security concerns appear to be still an important force motivating Thai couples to have at least some children. However, there is much less agreement concerning a connection between the old-age security motive and the *numbers* of children that couples have.

Although some Thais believe that having many children maximizes support in old age, other considerations favouring small families override these concerns. Other Thais see no conflict since they believe that a few children are sufficient for such support. Some even argue that couples with small families will be better off, since they will be better able to educate their children and, given the social changes underway, more highly educated children will be in a more advantageous economic situation to meet the expected repayment to the parent.

These views go a long way in explaining how fertility could decline so sharply while expectations of assistance from children in later years remained intact, especially when interpreted in the specific context of modern-day Thailand. Particularly relevant features of this context include: (1) low mortality levels resulting in high survival chances for children, especially when past infancy; (2) a stem family system in which the bulk of responsibility for support and care of the elderly rests with one co-resident child; and (3) the absence of rigid rules with respect to the gender or birth order of the primary care-giver. Thus, for many modern Thai couples the modal preferred family size of two children appears sufficient for meeting their expectation of assistance later in life. Given the persistence of old-age security concerns, however, there may be some resistance to allowing fertility to fall much further below replacement level as experienced in a number of European countries, where reliance on children for old-age security is much weaker.

Discussion

The Value of Focus Group Data

In some cases the main value of focus group research is to confirm what other sources such as surveys or anthropological studies also indicate. The value of this function, as illustrated above, should not be understated. In the case of surveys, typically relatively simple closed-ended questions are posed. There is no guarantee that the questions are interpreted by respondents in the manner the researcher intends or that the responses actually mean what the often precoded answers seem to imply. The utility of additional confirmation from a more open-ended discussion in which meanings become clear is thus non-trivial.

In the case of anthropological studies, findings are often based on only one community or are stated in overviews that are vague with respect to where the supporting evidence originates for the broad generalizations they make. To be sure, in-depth community studies by anthropologists can ground attitudes and behaviour far more solidly in their socioeconomic context than can focus groups alone. However, the more systematic nature of focus group data collection and the fact that such group discussions can be conducted in a number of communities in the same study permit more assurance in differentiating what is a local peculiarity from what is more general in the society at large.

Another major value of focus groups is to provide a fuller understanding of what more restricted answers to survey questions mean. Often, survey questions force the respondents, or the interviewers recording responses, to condense answers to a limited set of precoded categories, or even to simple yes/no or agree/disagree responses, when in reality the respondents' thinking involves a number of contingencies or qualifications. Moreover, what was actually said by the interviewer to elicit an answer is not evident from the recorded response.

Focus groups permit—indeed, encourage—respondents to elaborate on their opinions or accounting of events. The data they produce (i.e. the transcripts) retain the complexity of the discussion of a topic intact, including the exact line of questioning. Thus, rather than having to read meaning into forced summary responses based on assumptions external to the data, the analyst can start with a fuller accounting of the study subjects' own perspective and how it was elicited. This does not mean that the researcher necessarily accepts the views expressed at face value, but at least interpretation can be based on more completely articulated viewpoints.

Perhaps the most important value of focus groups is the contribution they can make to explanations. Because focus groups allow more elaborate viewpoints to be expressed than the typical survey, they can provide more insights and thereby contribute significantly to the explanation of the phenomena under investigation. The type of explanation to which focus group data contribute is by necessity along intuitive lines, in contrast to the more 'rigorous' statistical testing of models to which quantitative data lend themselves. Without getting into the larger epistemological debates that this previous statement raises, it should be obvious that these two types of explanation can most profitably be viewed as complementary rather than as competing.[9]

Some Limitations of the Focus Group Method

While the primary purpose of this paper is to illustrate how qualitative data generated through focus group discussions can contribute to an understanding of demographic phenomena, some discussion of their limitations and liabilities is also in order. I concentrate here mainly on issues arising from the studies described above. Nevertheless, several of the major concerns that are commonly voiced about focus groups merit at least brief mention.

The typically small number of total participants and their purposive selection renders focus group data inappropriate for any quantitative analysis beyond merely distinguishing more commonly voiced views from those that are seldom mentioned. As with all qualitative methods, subjective judgements—and with them potential biases—are an inevitable part of data collection and interpretation. Moreover, the fact that the quality and perhaps even the validity of data generated from focus group sessions can be quite dependent on the personality and skills of the moderators is somewhat unsettling (Khan *et al.* 1991; Khan and Manderson 1992).

Less frequently recognized, and clearly a lesson we gained in the course of the two projects mentioned above, is that the amount of effort (and expense) involved in properly carrying out a focus group study for social science purposes is easy to underestimate by those attempting the task. This probably arises from the common, although mistaken, impression that the method is quick and simple to implement, engendered in part because of its rather different use (and misuse) in marketing research. In particular, the considerable effort and thought that is required for sound data collection and careful analysis of transcripts are often unanticipated. As a result, the quality of the data and findings often suffer accordingly.

Related to the above point, another prerequisite for successful focus group research within a social science context that is often not sufficiently recognized is the heavy involvement required of the principal investigators at many stages of the research process. There is no substitute for the analyst reading and re-reading the transcripts. Moreover, delegating tasks such as coding transcript segments or constructing overview grids to assistants can be done only at the expense of the quality of the analysis. It is exactly through these time-consuming (and somewhat tedious) tasks that the researcher comes to understand what the data are revealing.

In actual sessions, it often proves difficult to force participants to make the distinctions in their discussion that the researcher considers crucial from a social-theoretical point a view. For example, in the focus group discussions of old-age assistance, the distinction between preferred and actual situations was often blurred. It was not unusual, when the moderator attempted to determine the general normative ideal with respect to living arrangements, for participants to describe their own living arrangements without indicating if it was in fact their ideal. Conversely, 'posturing' to make oneself or one's group look favourable to the outsider is not always easy to overcome. Considerable subjective judgement is required at the analysis stage when attempting to sort out the ideal from the actual situation (both of which are of legitimate interest in their own right).

Although the designs of the two studies described above were intended to permit rough comparisons along several dimensions (e.g. generational and regional in both, religion in the DOFT study, and urban–rural and socio-economic status in CSEA), it often proved difficult to discern clear patterns in the analysis along these lines. This arose in part because each group had idiosyncratic aspects (the particular moderator and combination of particip-ants) that were unrelated to their position in the design scheme but influenced the flow and nature of the discussion. As a result, it is easier to have confidence in the generality of findings that are similar across groups than to be able to discern systematic differences attributable to generation, region, etc. Thus, including groups with different characteristics turned out in the end to be more valuable for helping determine what views are truly general in Thai society rather than how they differed among the major categories built into the study design.

As with virtually all qualitative research, no claim can be made that the results are representative of the target populations in any formal statistical sense. Nevertheless, we have no reason to believe that the participants or the views they expressed are atypical of either older or younger-generation Thais. Indeed, the fact that many common themes arose across the focus groups despite their being structured by design to vary by generation, region, etc., suggests that we were tapping fairly general attitudes and opinions, at least within the rural sector. I am less sanguine about the generality of the results for the urban sector, where life circumstances range more widely, resulting in a greater diversity of attitudes on a variety of subjects including old-age security and fertility. Targeting a sufficient range of urban particip-ants to capture the likely greater complexity of prevailing views is quite difficult.

While the primary material on which this paper is based is the transcripts of the focus group sessions described above, I have also drawn on other research of both a quantitative and qualitative nature that bears on the topic to help interpret the transcripts and in some cases to supplement the focus group findings. The subjective nature of focus group analysis often requires making sense of contradictions in the discussions and 'reading between the lines'. Drawing on external material such as surveys and ethnographic accounts can be particularly helpful in this task.

Other Countries, Other Methods

Attempts to explore the relationship between old-age security concerns and fertility using the focus group method have been made in at least two cross-national projects: the CSEA project involving Philippines, Singapore, Tai-wan, and Thailand; and, to a more modest degree, an ILO-sponsored project on 'Old-Age Security and Fertility' in Costa Rica and Thailand. I am unaware of other attempts.

It is interesting to note that the limited findings available for the Philippines directly relating to the perceptions of family size and old-age security bear a reasonable correspondence to those described for Thailand (Domingo *et al.* 1993). A concept remarkably similar to the Thai version of parent repayment appears to be deeply ingrained in Filipino culture, underlying persisting patterns of assistance provided by children to elderly parents. While large families may have been seen as a source of security in old age in the past, Filipino participants revealed doubts similar to those expressed by Thais that the number of children is crucial in the current situation. Emerging phenomena such as increased work-related migration, induced by both higher education and poverty, were more salient than declining family size as threats to future support. Moreover, some expressed the same thinking as emerged in the Thai groups, that having few children but educating them well was better than having many less well educated children in terms of consequences for support in later years.

The similarity between the focus group discussions in the two countries probably reflects certain broad South-east Asian cultural similarities which have been noted by a variety of observers (e.g. Mulder 1992). One notable feature of both countries is the lack of a strong son preference combined with considerable flexibility with respect to the gender and birth order of the child that eventually takes primary responsibility for the care of the elderly parents. It would be quite interesting to compare these results with those that would come from settings that differ in this and other crucial respects. Indeed, results from Taiwan are more ambiguous, but only those of the elderly generation are reported (Lee *et al.* 1993).

How does the focus group method for collecting qualitative data compare with other qualitative methods? As far as I am aware, there have been few attempts to examine this issue systematically and no effort to do so in the context of the relationship between old-age security and fertility. Nevertheless, it seems quite clear that focus groups leave considerable room for other qualitative techniques to make a contribution. In particular, in-depth case studies could be a particularly appropriate approach for collecting at least two types of qualitative information that would be difficult or inappropriate to elicit through focus groups.

The first would be more detailed *personal histories*, revealing how a respondent's present old-age support situation emerged and the interplay of this process with the family life course. Eliciting detailed and coherent accounts of the paths that lead to particular situations in old age could yield considerable insights into whether or not, as well as how, fertility decisions eventually translate into old-age support. Focus groups are a poor format for collecting such data. While some accounts of individual experiences inevitably arise during a session, it is usually inappropriate to probe the details of a particular individual's situation in the course of a group discussion. In-depth interviews conducted on a one-to-one basis would seem better suited for this purpose.

While focus groups are generally good at eliciting perceptions, opinions, and attitudes from participants, there are certain types of case where this may be better accomplished through *individual in-depth interviews*. The experience in the CSEA project suggests that persons whose circumstances deviate substantially from the modal or ideal situation may find it awkward to participate in a group whose members do not share a similar dilemma. For example, in Thailand, where the normal situation is for the elderly to be supported at least to some degree by adult children, persons who are not receiving such support may have little to say within a group context about these matters. Nevertheless, the views of such persons can be of interest to the researcher exactly because they deviate from the norm. Short of assembling a whole group of individuals with similar non-modal circumstances, it is probably more appropriate to use in-depth interviews to gather the equivalent qualitative data from them.

Conclusions

Social demographic research is most commonly associated with quantitative data and analysis. While censuses and vital registration systems have traditionally been the core source of such data, in the second half of the twentieth century medium or large-scale sample surveys have gained prominence. The survey approach provides valuable information on the characteristics, behaviour, and attitudes of the population with respect to social phenomena and can be tailored to investigate particular issues of interest such as the linkages between old-age security and fertility.

By themselves, however, surveys are often unable to provide the in-depth qualitative information necessary to understand the complexity of the behaviour, attitudes, and perceptions underlying the phenomena being studied. Moreover, the closed-ended questions used to elicit quantitative data, especially if not carefully framed and pre-tested, may be misunderstood by respondents and the answers subsequently misinterpreted by the analyst. Thus, it is often desirable to supplement quantitative data with qualitative research techniques, not only to help prepare better survey questions but even more to generate deeper understanding and explanations of the topics under investigation.

The foregoing analysis of old-age security and fertility in Thailand illustrates how useful qualitative data generated through focus groups can be in the pursuit of social demography objectives. It also hoped that it has made clear that the value of such data is considerably enhanced when other types of information are available for comparison. It would be naïve to assume that either qualitative or quantitative data are adequate in themselves.

Background knowledge on the part of the researcher, gleaned from the fullest variety of sources, can enhance the value of any data set, whether generated from surveys, in-depth interviews, or focus groups. Indeed, the need to look for converging evidence from other sources to substantiate conclusions is all the more compelling in the case of focus group research, given the purposive, non-representative nature of participant selection and the potential biases that could result from the group context of the discussions. Nevertheless, as qualitative methods become more common and acceptable in the realm of demographic research, their value as a research tool that can help to significantly expand the store of knowledge and understanding within the field will be increasingly recognized.

Notes

1. In cases where a 'quick' study is considered adequate, transcription and even tape-recording may be skipped and the detailed notes of a note-taker can serve as the basis for the analysis. Such short-cuts, however, are rarely suitable for serious social science research purposes.
2. The earliest description of a technique resembling focus groups of which I am aware is Bogardus (1926). More commonly cited is the work of Merton and associates in the 1940s (e.g. Merton and Kendall 1946) and particularly the book that emerged from their work (Merton et al. 1956).
3. A particularly up-to-date account is provided by the volume edited by David Morgan (1993). See also Morgan (1988); Knodel et al. (1988; 1990); Khan et al. (1991); and Khan and Manderson (1992).
4. Overview grids are only an aid to the analysis process, most of which involves reading and rereading the appropriate segments of the transcripts that deal with each sub-topic being addressed.
5. In particular, I will draw from Knodel et al. (1984 and 1992c).
6. The study design and the discussion guidelines used are provided in Knodel et al. (1987).
7. The 1988 Social Attitudes towards Children Survey results are based on original tabulations from the data tape and reflect exclusion of respondents classified as 'do not know, no answer, or did not think about it' from the calculation. Those who said they have no expectations are included in the base population.
8. Based on original tabulations from the data tape.
9. For an illustrative exposition of how focus group data can complement survey findings, see Wolff et al. (1993).

References

Andrews, G. and Hennink, M. (1992), 'The circumstances and contributions of older persons in three Asian countries: preliminary results of a cross-national study'. *Asia-Pacific Population Journal*, 7(3): 127–46.

Archavanitkul, K. Boonchalaksi, W., Chamratrithirong, A., Piriyathamwong, N., Pramualratana, A., Richter, K., and Thongthai, V. (1992), 'Parental expectation and experience of support from children in old age and its relationship with fertility'. *Journal of the National Research Council of Thailand*, 24(1): 1–30.

Arnold, F. and Pejaranonda, C. (1977), 'Economic factors in family size decisions in Thailand'. World Fertility Survey, Survey of Fertility in Thailand, Report No. 2, Institute of Population Studies, Chulalongkorn University, Bangkok.

Bogardus, E. M. (1926), 'The group interview'. *Journal of Applied Sociology*, 10: 372–82.

Caffrey, R. A. (1992), 'Family care of the elderly in Northeast Thailand: changing patterns'. *Journal of Cross-Cultural Gerontology*, 7(2): 105–116.

Caldwell, J. C. (ed.) (1977), *The Persistence of High Fertility*. Canberra: Australian National University.

Chayovan, N. (1992), 'Support of parents and attitudes towards the elderly among adults in Thailand'. Report 195/35, Institute of Population Studies, Chulalongkorn University, Bangkok (in Thai).

——Knodel, J., and Siriboon, S. (1990), 'Thailand's elderly population: a demographic and social profile based on official statistical sources'. Comparative Study of the Elderly in Asia, Research Report No. 90–2, Population Studies Center, University of Michigan, Ann Arbor, Michigan.

Cowgill, D. O. (1972), 'The role and status of the aged in Thailand', in D. O. Cowgill and L. D. Holmes (eds.), *Aging and Modernization*. New York: Appleton-Century-Crofts, pp. 91–101.

Domingo, L. Asis, M. M. B, Jose, M. C. P., Kabamalan, M. M. M. (1993), 'Living arrangements of elderly in the Philippines: qualitative evidence'. Comparative Study of the Elderly in Asia, Research Report No. 93–23, Population Studies Center, University of Michigan, Ann Arbor, Michigan.

Fry, C. and Keith, J. (1986), 'Introduction', in C. Fry and J. Keith (eds.), *New Methods for Old-Age Research*. South Hadley, Mass.: Bergin and Garvey.

Hirschman, C. Tan, J. E., Chamratrithirong, A., and Guest, P. (undated), 'The path to below-replacement-level fertility in Thailand'. Unpublished paper.

Kagitcibasi, C. (1982), 'Old-age security value of children: cross-national socio-economic evidence'. *Journal of Cross-Cultural Psychology*, 13(3): 29–42.

Keyes, C. F. (1987), *Thailand, Buddhist Kingdom as Modern Nation-State*. Boulder, Colo.: Westview Press.

Khan, M. E. and Manderson, L. (1992), 'Focus groups in tropical diseases research'. *Health Policy and Planning*, 7(1): 56–66.

——Anker, M., Patel, B., Barge, S., Sadhwani, H. and Kohle, R. (1991), 'The use of focus groups in social and behavioral research: some methodological issues'. *World Health Statistics Quarterly*, 44: 145–8.

Knodel, J. (1993), 'The design and analysis of focus group studies in social science research', in D. Morgan (ed.), *Successful Focus Groups: Advancing the State of the Art*. Newbury Park, Calif.: Sage, pp. 35–50.

——Havanon, N., and Pramualratana, A. (1984), 'Fertility transition in Thailand: a qualitative analysis'. *Population and Development Review*, 10(2): 297–328.

——Chamratrithirong, A., and Debavalya, N. (1987), *Thailand's Reproductive Revolution: Rapid Fertility Decline in a Third World Setting*. Madison, Wis.: University of Wisconsin Press.

——Pramualratana, A., and Havanon, N. (1988), 'Focus group research on fertility decline in Thailand: methodology and findings', in J. C. Caldwell, A. Hill, and V. Hull (eds.), *Micro Approaches to Demographic Research*. London: Kegan Paul International, ch. 3.

——Sittitrai, W., and Brown, T. (1990), 'Focus group discussions for social science research: a practical guide with an emphasis on the topic of ageing'. Comparative

Study of the Elderly in Asia, Research Report No. 90–3, Population Studies Center, University of Michigan, Ann Arbor, Michigan.

——Chayovan, N., and Siriboon, S. (1992*a*), 'The familial support system of Thai elderly: an overview'. *Asia-Pacific Population Journal*, 7(3): 105–26.

————(1992*b*), 'The impact of fertility decline on familial support for the elderly: an illustration from Thailand'. *Population and Development Review*, 18(1): 79–102.

——Saengtienchai, C., and Sittitrai, W. (1992*c*), 'The living arrangements of elderly in Thailand: views of the populace.' Comparative Study of the Elderly in Asia, Research Report No. 92–20, Population Studies Center, University of Michigan, Ann Arbor, Michigan.

——Chayovan, N., and Saengtienchai, C. (1994), 'Are Thais deserting their elderly parents? New evidence from the 1990 Census'. *Bold*, May 1994.

Lauro, D. (1977). 'A village perspective from two countries: some implications for differential fertility behavior', in J. C. Caldwell (ed.), *The Persistence of High Fertility*. Canberra: Australian National University.

Lee, M., Lin, H., and Chang, M. (1993). 'Living arrangements of the elderly in Taiwan: qualitative evidence'. Comparative Study of the Elderly in Asia, Research Report No. 93–26, Population Studies Center, University of Michigan, Ann Arbor, Michigan.

Merton, R. K. and Kendall, P. (1946). 'The focused interview'. *American Journal of Sociology*, 51: 541–57.

——Fiske, M., and Kendall, P., (1956). *The Focused Interview*. Glencoe, Ill.: Free Press.

Morgan, D. (1988). *Focus Groups as Qualitative Research*. Newbury Park, Calif.: Sage.

——(ed) (1993). *Successful Focus Groups: Advancing the State of the Art*. Newbury Park, Calif.: Sage.

Mulder, N. (1992). *Inside Southeast Asia*. Bangkok: D. K. Printing House.

Nugent, J. B. (1985). 'The old-age security motive for fertility'. *Population and Development Review*, 11: 75–97.

——and Anker, R. (1990). 'Old-age support and fertility'. Working Paper No. 172, World Employment Programme Research, International Labour Office, Geneva.

Pramualratana, A. (1990). 'Support systems of the old in a rural community in Thailand'. Ph.D. thesis, Australian National University, Canberra.

Reinecke, G. (1993). 'Social security in Thailand: political decisions and distributional impact'. Unpublished paper, report on the ASA project 'Social Security in Thailand'.

Thailand National Statistical Office (1993). *The Survey of Population Change 1991*. Bangkok: National Statistical Office.

Tuchrello, W. P. (1989). 'The society and its environment', in B. L. LePoer (ed.), *Thailand: A Country Study*, 6th edn. (Area Handbook Series). Washington: US Government Printing Office, pp. 55–120.

Wolff, B., Knodel, J., and Sittitrai, W. (1993). 'Analysis of concurrent focus groups and surveys: a case study', in David Morgan (ed.), *Successful Focus Groups: Advancing the State of the Art*. Newbury Park, Calif.: Sage.

4 Anthropological Insights into the Links between Women's Status and Demographic Behaviour, Illustrated with the Notions of Hypergamy and Territorial Exogamy

ALAKA M. BASU

While the field methods of anthropological demography are increasingly accepted as an important way to increase our understanding of the impact on demographic behaviour of a variable—the status of women[1]—which is today often considered an important key to sustained demographic change, the discipline of anthropology as a whole has much to offer in this understanding. In particular, its value lies in its ability to probe, define, and explain issues involving women's status, even those with no obvious demographic implications. These issues are captured extremely inadequately by conventional demographic techniques; the excessive quantitative concentration by demographers on the two variables of female education and employment is not at all surprising, given that so much of what constitutes female status (and gender issues in general) is non-quantifiable and often even intangible.

Demographic behaviour as an outcome of women's status, on the other hand, is best measured through traditional quantitative methods that demographers are comfortable with, a conclusion that mainstream anthropologists interested in demographic issues are only now begin to acknowledge.

This paper looks at the anthropology of South Asia (India in particular) to illustrate how the academic debate on issues of kinship and marriage in this region can throw much light on some of the motivations behind those demographic findings that the demographer has theoretically wondered about but rarely had the empirical support to substantiate with conventional tools of analysis. In particular, it looks at marriage systems in terms of the hypergamy and territorial exogamy that characterize much of North India

This is a revised version of the paper presented at the IUSSP workshop on 'New Approaches to Anthropological Demography', Barcelona, Spain, 10–13 November 1993. I am very grateful to Gitanjali Krishna for taking me through much of the anthropological literature used to develop this paper. I would also like to thank Patricia Uberoi and the participants at the Barcelona workshop for many helpful comments.

and tries to relate these to differences between North and South India in gender relations as well as in the demographic variables of interest.

But while the anthropological contribution to an assessment of women's status, and thus to demographic understanding, has some important and unique merits, there are also problems which the unwary demographer can fall foul of. In an attempt to describe some of the strengths and shortcomings of anthropological insights into women's status issues as they bear upon demographic behaviour, it is useful to begin with a consideration of the trends in anthropological research on the women's status question in general (that is, not limited to South Asia) and to try and relate each stage of this development to its potential for explaining demographic behaviour. The demographic variables considered, which are the most closely related to the question of women's status, are fertility, mortality (especially child mortality), and above all the sex differential in physical welfare, which is important in itself as well as an indicator of fertility.

Anthropology and Women's Status

My reading of the anthropological literature related to women's status issues suggests that there has been a steady and definite development in interests, priorities, and analytical tools. The trend thus far can be conveniently broken up into four parts, each with somewhat different implications for the demographer interested in applying anthropological methods or knowledge to the relationship between women's position and demographic behaviour.

Ethnocentric and Androcentric Social Anthropology

At one time or another, traditional social anthropology seems to have been called both these names and more. Born in a colonial environment, often obsessed with recording the customs and behaviours of exotic tribes and communities, tactlessly referring to its subjects of inquiry as 'primitive' and 'savage', the discipline took a hammering when it opened its doors to non-colonial or post-colonial researchers. But while this kind of criticism has been levelled most commonly against Western anthropologists studying Third World cultures, it can also legitimately be made about Third World anthropologists studying their own cultures. For the same kinds of reason that foreign[2] anthropologists are accused of misunderstanding and wrongly generalizing about alien cultures, one must in fairness (though perhaps less harshly) criticize local researchers who study their own culture. The main reasons for this are that (1) local researchers are usually trained in the same European–American tradition that they seek to decry, and (2) the societies they study are not homogeneous and can never be completely their own in all respects, so that they carry their own brand of ethnocentrism, except that this may more correctly be termed 'socioeconomiccentrism'.[3]

But from the perspective of women's studies, the androcentrism charge is more potent. This reproach is based on more than the fact that traditional anthropologists have been male for the most part, as have their respondents. The deeper problem is that the entire language of discourse is male determined and male oriented. Even when women are represented in this brand of ethnographic writing, the 'male bias' continues to intrude.

Moore (1992) identifies three levels of this bias. First, the androcentrism inherent in old anthropological theory defined the methods of data collection, interpretation, and presentation and thus carried into the field an androcentric deafness to female voices (or, as Ardener 1975 elaborates, to the voices of non-dominant groups in general). What is surprising is that even in marriage and kinship studies, which formed such a basic component of social anthropology, women were absent in any historical or ethnographic detail, in spite of being such a crucial part of the transactions involved. Second, there was the effect of male bias in the society being studied. With key informants being predominantly male, the male view of gender relations and women's status was the one transmitted to the researcher. Third, Moore mentions the male bias inherent in Western culture which led anthropologists of the old school, when they considered women as a separate category at all, to extrapolate the experience of gender inequality in the West to inform the interpretation of gender relations in other societies, even when the facts were clearly otherwise. In addition, one cannot completely ignore the problem of male access to women's lives in most traditional societies, which greatly limits any understanding of the female perspective.

Nevertheless, there is no denying that traditional anthropologists have left us a wealth of painstaking minutiae in their ethnographies and field descriptions, whatever their personal ideologies. While little of this material has an explicit focus on women as active participants in any aspect of life, the careful student can use much of this record, especially in a comparative way, to draw several not very far-fetched inferences about the status of women in different societies.

Anthropology of Women

This branch of inquiry was the first form of the revolt against the traditional absence of women as an identifiable and active category in anthropological research. By its very nature, this approach avoids labels such as 'androcentric' and 'ethnocentric' which the old school was stuck with, being concerned primarily with redressing the balance in the neutral area of pure description. At this stage in the development of the discipline, therefore, anthropologists interested in women's issues were busy setting down the female perspective in non-controversial, easily verifiable areas. The ethnographies of women were not very different from earlier ethnographies of other groups; in addition, they tended more often to be compiled by women anthropologists. The practical convenience of this has already been noted. This stage of research has been overwhelmingly useful in informing the theorizing by others, in anthropology as well as in other disciplines, as well as in explaining what might otherwise be curious findings. Especially important have been the findings of micro research, which have carefully recorded the important productive roles of those women that a census or survey would classify as unemployed.

Androcentric and Ethnocentric Feminist Anthropology

Obviously, this kind of theoretical and purely descriptive research could not engage the attention of the committed anthropologist for ever. Very soon, interest veered towards using the descriptions from field research to theorize about a range of women's issues. To quote Moore (1992), 'Feminist anthropology is more than the study of women. It is the study of gender, of the interrelations between women and men, and of the role of gender in structuring human societies, their histories, ideologies, economic systems and political structures' (p. 6).

The objective of feminist anthropology—to unravel some of these issues—is a laudable one. But the means employed were again inherently biased by the training and the personal origins of most feminist anthropologists, the former tending them towards androcentrism and the latter towards ethnocentrism. The careful demographer must be well aware of these pitfalls when seeking to use the product of research from feminist anthropology in scientific inquiries, or even when resorting to the methods of feminist anthropology to supplement a larger survey.

The androcentrism of early feminist anthropology is easy to understand, as has already been mentioned. Even with the ethnographer being female (and perhaps the respondent being female as well), the problem of using conceptual and analytical tools derived from male dominant models remains; only recently has anthropological training begun to incorporate specific courses on gender.

But ethnocentrism in feminist anthropology is something else, more invidious and easier to miss because it is often so well-meaning. In general, such ethnocentrism takes two forms, one relatively trivial (but nevertheless irritating) and related to attitudes, the other more serious and related to analytical techniques. The first, and far from uncommon, ethnocentric bias involves a 'looking down' upon one's subjects of inquiry, and a tendency to make value judgements about what constitutes high or low female status based upon what rankings of status are prevalent in one's own culture. Katherine Mayo's *Mother India* is but an extreme example; but even at a less hasty level, there has long been a tendency to view practices such as female seclusion or arranged marriages as indicators of the unhappy lot of the women concerned.[4] Similarly revealing about the yawning gap that might exist between emic and etic perceptions about welfare was the finding in Basu (1992) that, when poor women's perceptions about their own happiness were plotted against their family sizes, the relationship was uniformly positive.[5]

Fortunately, the demographer (often at the expense of social and cultural sensitivity) interested in anthropological inputs is less concerned about subjective or objective evaluations of intangibles such as welfare or happiness and more concerned with measures of status which rank women with respect to implications for fertility or mortality. In this narrow sense, the interest is in propositions of the if–then type; for example, if women work outside the home, they have fewer children, so if the aim is to reduce fertility, one intervention may involve increasing employment opportunities for women, regardless of whether this work makes them happy or unhappy, revered or despised. Only rarely does the need to step back and be concerned with the ideological basis of policy manifest itself.

The second kind of ethnocentrism in feminist anthropology (or feminist theory in general) is best described by the search for the 'universal woman'. Embodied in the definition of feminism are several implications.

First, it implies that, at some fundamental level, there exists a unitary body of women's interests, which should be and can be fought for. Secondly, it is clear that although feminism recognizes differences in feminist politics—socialist feminists, Marxist feminists, radical separatists, and so on—the underlying premise of feminist politics is that there is an actual, or potential, identity between women.... Thirdly, feminist politics depends for its cohesion—whether potential or actual—on women's shared oppression. The recognition of shared oppression is the basis for 'sexual politics' premised on the notion that women as a social group are dominated by men as a social group. (Moore 1992:10)

Such a formulation of the universal woman includes a search for universal panacea, of course, but, worse, it also includes a call for universal panacea based largely on Western needs and Western gender problems. To cite one brutally frank critic of this brand of feminist anthropology, 'these post-doctoral women anthropologists had not de-anthropologised themselves before embarking on their gigantic project of assessing women's condition in societies chosen haphazardly from all over the Third World' (Amadiume 1987). This ethnocentrism has deep implications for both social anthropology and demography. What constitutes 'welfare' for a white middle-class woman may be completely at odds with what the word means for a black woman of a different class. Hooks (1982) has very justifiably taken on the original feminists (such as de Beauvoir) for basing their ideologies entirely on the experience of Anglo-Saxon Protestant women and ignoring the diversity of female experience based on differences of class, colour, and nationality.

In the context of the definitions and determinants of women's status, such enthnocentrism has led to the development of several explanations for the 'universal' subordination of women by men, which again the policy-oriented demographer must be wary of adopting wholesale. These explanations no longer include the simple and obvious male–female dichotomy inherent in biology (which after all does unite women at a most basic level); instead, the emphasis is more on gender as a cultural construct, except that for a long time this cultural construction of gender was hypothesized to be the same across cultures. Thus, we have a supposed global gender hierarchy being explained through theories about a nature–culture dichotomy, except that these theories often had serious differences about which sex was associated with nature and which with culture. While the earlier emphasis was on man as nature, Ortner (1974) proposed that the symbolism was in fact reversed, woman being associated with the natural world of menstruation and child-bearing and men with the superior world of culture. Other dichotomies have focused on the domestic-versus-public domains of social life (Rosaldo 1974), and still others on the concept of the family as defining a woman's space more than a man's. The dichotomy is then expressed in terms of the mother–child unit versus the male (e.g. Barnes 1973).

To the demographer, what is interesting is that in this kind of feminist anthropology, the women's status–demographic behaviour relationship used by demographers to understand fertility and mortality is turned on its head. Instead of considering women's status effects on reproductive behaviour, all the above theories rest on some kind of notion of 'reproductive determinism' (Mukhopadhyay 1988), whereby the demands of childbearing and child-rearing are the basic determinants of the universal oppression of women. Fortunately for the demographer, the South Asia emphasis has been slightly different in this regard and has examined women's status in terms of pre-vailing systems of kinship, the family, and the economy, with any reproduct-ive determinism that there is being in the direction of increasing rather than decreasing the status of women, through the rewards of motherhood, as opposed to its costs to female status.

Non-androcentric and Non-ethnocentric Feminist Anthropology

The empirical nature of anthropology is one of its greatest strengths. Through the accumulated body of field knowledge about the range of the female experience, feminist anthropology soon became its own sternest critic and moved increasingly in the direction of emphasizing the differences between women as opposed to the similarities. Field experience generated too many counter-examples to standard theories about the determinants of women's status, as well as about the characterization of women's status as being globally similar, or even unchanging within the same culture over time. An excellent example is Boon's (1974) analysis of the crucial role of nannies and wet nurses in upper- and upper–middle-class Victorian households, which was so much at variance with the conventional picture of home life being centred around the mother caring for her young and forming a special domestic unit in which the father either did or did not play an active role. The 'nanny' phenomenon vitally affects the relationship between the culturally defined categories of woman and mother and questions many of our assumptions about what determines women's status.

Thus, while the individual anthropologist may still sometimes be as ethnocentric (or androcentric) as the armchair theorist, the range of the discipline has had a very important role to play in emphasizing the diversity of human experience and the futility of seeking universals. More importantly, this very range has in the long run called into question the discipline's ethnocentrism and androcentrism, as well as exposed the impossibility of making value judgements about the welfare levels of individuals or individual societies.

This is especially important in women's studies. Issues such as female subordination and repression have been placed much more in perspective by anthropologists' exposure to the work of their colleagues in different cultural settings and have often led to a complete turn-around on views such as what defines a high-status or a 'happy' (the two are not necessarily the same thing) woman (see e.g. Greer 1984). Even perceptive fiction writers such as Erica Jong (1985) have been struck by the very different meanings of liberation and autonomy in different cultures:

All the Russian ladies (many of whom were divorced) unburdened themselves to Isadora about the dire difficulties of being a woman in Russia. Of course they all had children (usually *one* cosseted child) that they had to raise alone, and they dreamed of a world in which women could stay home with their babies and be taken care of by men.... These women lusted for the dependency that Isadora's baby boom generation had been struggling *against* for twenty years! (Jong 1985)

Thus, an important role that the more recent feminist anthropological studies fulfils is that of highlighting the many-faceted nature of women's status and of evoking the cultural or institutional context of issues such as women's status and their bearing on demographic behaviour. We have enough evidence now that this context is important, and that data plucked and presented out of context, as survey analyses often do, can present a completely distorted picture of the reality of women's lives. For example, Basu's (1992) study of two (culturally distinct) groups of migrant women from Uttar Pradesh and Tamil Nadu found that an intervention such as education could have very different levels of effect on the fertility behaviour of the two groups. In addition, the base cultural differences were large— uneducated women from Tamil Nadu had significantly lower fertility even than educated women from Uttar Pradesh. Similarly, in the situation of high female labour force participation which characterized the Tamil women, even non-working women had more egalitarian norms about the treatment of sons and daughters.

Such micro-level findings are consistent with the view expressed by writers such as Cleland and Wilson (1987) that the spread of new ideas is often a more serious determinant of change than a structural change in the conditions of the actors, because it is the complement of the anthropological conclusion that culturally determined norms and values affect behaviour often much more strongly than do immediate socioeconomic conditions. The anthropologist's interest in cultural or community variables is also a refreshing and pragmatic change from the demographer, who is accustomed to moving from the individual to the community only in the direction of finding out how many schools, wells, or clinics a village has access to, as if all that is needed to change behaviour is the supply of such physical infrastructure.

Having said all this in its favour, it would still be in order to emphasize a few ways in which anthropology in general, and feminist anthropology in particular, may trap the unwary demographer. The most important trap lies in the difficulty in separating the anthropologist from the informant. While anthropology is theoretically aware of the emic–etic distinction, anthropologists themselves often do not distinguish clearly enough between the two in their writings, so that a third researcher is hard-placed to interpret their findings and to apply these to his or her own data. As stressed by Geertz (1973), ethnography provides a 'thick description', which means that it describes the ethnographer's construction of cultural categories as understood and interpreted by members of that culture; so that what we have are in effect 'interpretations of interpretations'. In contrast, the aim of the good ethnographer should be to try and look at cultural constructs as a native would look at them; it is only through this process that meaningful data can be gathered. In the demographer's hands, there is a real danger of these findings becoming interpretations of interpretations of interpretations, and it needs a seasoned anthropological demographer to distinguish between observer-based explanations of particular kinds of behaviour and what may be termed native rationales.

The second problem is the somewhat eccentric choice of study group. A number of factors determine which society or social group catches a particular anthropologist's fancy—physical accessibility (or, for the more adventurous, remoteness), exotic appeal, ease of communication, the availability of secondary material on the group, and so on. The demographer attempting to generalize from the reports of anthropologists or to make some cross-cultural comparisons needs to be keenly aware that the findings from a study may not even be representative of the whole social group to which they pertain. In the Indian anthropological tradition, for example, there has been an excessive emphasis on the behaviours of the upper caste and class groups; Miller's (1980) review of ethnographies from different parts of India and her classification of these findings for the propertied and unpropertied groups found too few entries in the latter category to be able to draw many definite conclusions.

Finally, it does need to be pointed out that feminist anthropology tends to see all women's problems in terms of gender relations. For the demographer's point of view, this is an incomplete characterization of the women's problem, because so much of intra-household decision-making is a function of hierarchies that are not necessarily gender based, at least not in an immediate everyday sense. Age and ritual position are often more important determinants of autonomy, and there is enough anthropological (but not enough feminist anthropological) evidence of the great power wielded by the senior female in the household, even in patriarchal societies, and especially in 'domestic' matters relevant to fertility and mortality.

I now propose to illustrate the role of anthropology in explicating the relationship between women's status and demographic behaviour, through a discussion of two of the more important topics in anthropological research on the Indian subcontinent with the potential to explain women's status as relevant to demographic behaviour. These two topics are hypergamy and territorial exogamy, and I discuss them in terms of the anthropologically generated knowledge of the norms governing behaviour on these matters as well as the conformity of behaviour with norms. The focus is on community or cultural norms, in an attempt to supplement the demographer's exclusive focus on individual characteristics, as already mentioned. The assumption is that individual characteristics like education may modify behaviour in small ways, but a real revolution requires the education to affect a longer-term change in the underlying norms prescribing behaviour for a group as a whole.

It is true that in general, in any patrilineal and patrilocal society, women are dependent on men because one of the characteristics of such societies is male control over the reproductive and productive activities of women. Here, I concentrate on some additional features of South Asian (or, more narrowly, Hindu) marriage and kinship as they are played out in North India and which place a further premium on high fertility as well as restricting the woman's ability to control mortality. Both these demographic impacts occur through the implications of these factors for the position of women. The hypothesis is that prevailing systems of hypergamy and geographical exogamy help us, in ways in which traditional survey research fails to do, to understand intra-household relationships, attitudes towards women, and son preference. In turn, the cultural ideologies and norms they promote may explain much that is observed in large data sets on fertility, mortality, and sex differences in health and mortality. That is, both my anthropological variables of interest influence women's status in ways that have a direct bearing on demographic outcomes.

The contribution of micro research in these two areas to demographic research becomes much more valuable in the hands of a third researcher (a demographer, one hopes) who takes on the task of (*a*) using these anthropological insights in a comparative way to look at socioeconomic or cross-cultural differences in these systems of hypergamy and exogamy, and (*b*) relating the differences in the two systems that emerge from such comparative studies to differences in large-scale demographic outcomes.[6]

This paper concentrates on a North India–South India comparison to illustrate these points. This is not to say that other levels of difference do not exist. In particular, perhaps a more accurate comparison would be between North India and the lower castes in South India; the upper castes in the South are in many ways similar to the North in their patterns of behaviour and values. But the overall regional comparison is a particularly neat way of illustrating how a larger universal (that is, all-India) prescriptive tradition can still act as an umbrella for clear variations in actual behaviour among different groups. My focus therefore is on local norms and behaviour rather than on Brahmanic or Sastric prescriptions.

I give the largest space to the discussion on hypergamy. Exogamy is covered relatively briefly because its implications for women's status and demographic behaviour are often similar to those for hypergamy and also because the purpose of this paper is to illustrate the ways in which anthropological and demographic approaches can be married rather than to attempt to say the last word on substantive results. This next section is also a good illustration of how seemingly non-demographic issues, such as the choice of a marriage partner and how often and for how long a married daughter visits her parental home, can have profound demographic implications.

The overall North–South demographic differentials are not in dispute and will not be described here, except to say that North India has been and continues to be characterized by significantly higher fertility, child mortality, and sex differences in health and mortality than the southern part of the country. This regional contrast has been very well recorded in the literature, and increasingly the academic debate is concerned with the reasons for its existence rather than with its extent. (For a review of the evidence, see Dyson and Moore 1983; Satia and Jejeebhoy 1991.)

Hypergamy

Hypergamy refers to the tendency for individual families and larger groups to 'negotiate a higher status for themselves by marrying their daughters "upwards" in the caste hierarchy'. The quote is from Uberoi (1993), and this motivation—the search for improved status through a socially desirable marriage alliance for one's daughter—is indeed attributed to hypergamous behaviour, by both anthropologists and their respondents. If one is in the (unhappy, it appears) position of being a woman, an anthropologist, and the daughter-in-law of a household in a hypergamous society, as Joyce Pettigrew was, one cannot but be starkly aware of the woman's position as 'a sister whom her brothers want to marry into a family that will raise their status' (Pettigrew 1981).

However, hypergamy in the caste hierarchy is but one (and the most conventional) feature of such marital alliances. More and more, the hierarchy is being defined by a variety of socially desirable characteristics such as wealth, social status, the professional qualifications of the groom, and so on. The general aim of a hypergamous marriage therefore is to marry one's daughter into a ritually or otherwise superior household, the expectation being that such an alliance also confers some superiority on the household of the bride-givers. As a corollary of this, while isogamous marriages may be tolerated (and indeed are increasingly the practice as opposed to the ideal) in many cases, a hypogamous marriage carries with it all the taint of defying convention as well as losing any return on the high cost of bearing and rearing a daughter.

The expectation of such a return on investment in a female child is also believed to be a relatively recent, practical innovation. As discussed by Trautmann (1979), while the practice of hypergamy itself does have religious sanction, the rewards it provides are not supposed to accrue in this world. The offering of a virgin daughter (*kanyadaan*) to a ritually superior family is meant to be in the nature of a religious gift; that is, it is marked by the absence of an obvious reciprocity. Any notion of exchange that exists is transcendental. This is also why the flow of gifts and deference too must always be one-way between the bride-givers and the bride-takers—accepting the smallest return, often even a glass of water in a married daughter's home, constitutes the acceptance of payment for one's daughter, therefore reducing the marriage to a commercial rather than divine transaction.

Enmeshed in the last few paragraphs are two somewhat separate notions of hypergamy with two overlapping sets of implications for women's status, as I will discuss shortly. To paraphrase Dumont (1964), the term 'hypergamy' is used in two ways in the literature:

1. more strictly, to describe a system of hierarchically ranked intermarrying groups (usually clans, but in the Indian context sometimes castes) where those who occupy a higher status receive women in marriage from those more lowly ranked;
2. in a general sense, to refer to any system of marriage where the wife-taker is regarded as 'superior' to the wife-giver.

In practice, as already mentioned, there is an increasing tendency towards ritual isogamy, with more worldly indicators of superiority gaining preference. But even when objective social or economic statuses converge, the one-way flow of daughters (and gifts) establishes a status differential between wife-givers and wife-takers which cannot be reversed for three generations at least, and certainly not as long as the memory of a previous marriage exists (Hershman 1981). That is, the marriage alliance itself confers a differential in the statuses of the two parties concerned. At the same time, this conferred inequality is strong enough to extend over some generations as already mentioned, even though, as pointed out for example by Vatuk (1975), the existence of such inequality between the two families does not say anything about inequalities between the larger clan or caste groups to which they belong. Nor is this situation of inequality confined to the immediate families of the bride and groom, as it usually extends to the localized kindred of each, agnates as well as affines. Thus, the bride's mother's brother, for example, is also respectful to the groom's mother's brother.

This enforced hierarchy is beautifully illustrated in Hershman's (1981) discussion of the abusive power of the word *sala*, Translated literally, the word merely means one's wife's brother, but it has become such an institutionalized term of abuse that it is not used even to denote a real relationship (which is referred to instead as one's child's mother's brother). Instead, the word is used to hurt, through the insult implied in being the one who gives his sister to be violated by the other. This is because 'to give a woman in marriage is to place oneself in a position of inferiority to the taker; and to take a woman is to assume a position of superiority to the giver' (Hershman 1981).

Implications of Hypergamy for Women's Status and Demographic Behaviour

What does the system of hypergamy offer to women themselves as opposed to their natal families? It should be remembered that we are concerned here only with those aspects of women's status relevant to demographic behaviour. In such a framework, one can think of the implications of hypergamy for women's status in two different environments—their natal homes and their marital homes; that is, in their roles as daughters/sisters and as wives/daughters-in-law (although, and this is important, there is the very different mother and mother-in-law role that the woman also plays out in the affinal home).

To begin with the natal home, there are three aspects of hypergamy that can plausibly influence women's status, one potentially positive and two potentially negative. The potentially positive effect derives from the value attached to having a daughter to give to a family of superior status in the first place. The divine and earthly merits of *kanyadaan* have already been touched upon; at least one daughter therefore should be and is generally described by anthropologists of all persuasions as being a much wanted and loved member of the household.

On the other hand, the joys of *kanyadaan* often go with some awesome responsibilities for performing this duty well. First, *kanyadaan* requires the gift of a virgin daughter. An important implication of this is that tight control must be exercised on the sexuality of the unmarried daughter, as well as, for the diehard father, on her emotional virginity. Such control is typically exercised in two important ways in the Northern Indian culture (which comes closest to bridging the gap between precept and practice as far as hypergamy is concerned). These are by restricting the movement of young girls as soon as they reach a potentially corruptible age, and by marrying them off as soon as is decently possible given the constraints of custom, law, and resources. The restraint on movement means a more frequent withdrawal from school (if indeed there was an entry to begin with), as well as from economically productive activities outside the home, in addition to a kind of mental isolation from the world at large, all of which, as every demographer believes, are believed to encourage high fertility for a variety of intentional as well as involuntary reasons. Early marriage too has important demographic implications, being associated everywhere with higher fertility (see Coale 1991), although it may not necessarily imply an earlier start of childbearing (Basu 1993). All three factors—less female education, lower female economic activity, and an early age at marriage—as well as their concomitants, relatively high fertility and mortality, have been well documented for North India as compared with South India and will not be reiterated here.

The second problem with a system of hypergamy is that bridegrooms of superior status are not exactly waiting to be foisted with brides of inferior status. They have a wide field to play, and the best father of the girls concerned wins. More and more, the 'best' father is the one most able to buy his daughter's way into a ritually or otherwise superior household, through what the traditional literature calls a handsome 'dowry' but what is perhaps more appropriately described as 'groomwealth'. Naturally, the higher the status of the groom—that is, the more intense the hypergamy— the higher the price he can command, leading to my second negative implication of hypergamy for the woman in her natal home: daughters are now an expensive proposition, made more expensive by the simultaneous curbs placed on their own economic productivity as mentioned above.

The custom of dowry in India in general and in North India in particular has been extensively discussed in the sociological literature of the country, and the consensus now does seem to be that, not only is dowry a kind of economic drain on household resources which makes a mockery of attempts such as Tambiah's (1973) to equate it with a daughter's pre-mortem inheritance, but also, the system of dowry currently practised in North India in particular is far from the *stridhan* that the traditional scriptures eulogize. The latter kind of gift is meant to be for the daughter, and is supposedly under her control upon her marriage, while dowry instead is much more an affinal gift rather than a gift from a father/brother to his daughter/sister. Indeed, some anthropologists would go as far as to say that the daughter and the dowry are both different gifts to the affinal household, to do with as it pleases. For embodied in the concept of *kanyadaan* is the complete giving away of the parental rights on the daughter to her new home (Trautman 1979). The gifts that go with the married daughter (as well as those that follow at all life-cycle events) are similarly under the control of her marital home for the most part. Sharma (1984) testifies that the convention is for the mother-in-law to gain control over gifts in kind and the father-in-law over those in cash, both often being used to subsidize a daughter's wedding in turn, in a kind of chain birthday-present game.

There is a lively literature on the nature of affinal presentations in hypergamous societies in North India, which stresses (*a*) the frequency and value of such presents, (*b*) the minimal control that the bride has over these gifts, and (*c*) the unidirectional flow of these gifts, given the theoretically non-reciprocal nature of a hypergamous marriage. Indeed, this obligation to maintain a unidirectional flow of gifts and deference even when the marriage is hypergamous only by the fact of having taken place means that an escape through isogamous marriage is not an escape in any real sense. Such an escape is possible only in a hypogamous marriage, in which case the situation may be reversed and involve a 'brideprice' rather than a dowry. But such marriages are only the refuge (an increasingly unwelcome refuge at that) of the lower castes, where the marriage squeeze works in the direction of a shortage of eligible brides. For the upper castes, the ignominy of a hypogamous marriage is more painful than the burden of an extravagant dowry and is to be strictly avoided.

All these factors naturally lead to dowry being a severe economic liability, especially where there is more than one daughter; and the secondary data, which document greater sex differentials in mortality in societies that anthropologists tell us are primarily hypergamous, do plausibly seem to be at least partly connected to such hypergamy norms. Almost all recorded instances of female infanticide relate to caste groups concerned with the problem of marrying daughters in a system of conventional or more modern-day hypergamy.

For example, Clarke (1989) has recorded the acuteness of the problem of female infanticide among the Kanbis of central Gujarat in the mid-nineteenth century. This could be attributed almost entirely to the high costs of getting daughters married into families of the Patidars of Charotar, who occupied the highest position in the Kanbi caste hierarchy. The colonial administration of that time pragmatically decided that, instead of ineffectively banning infanticide, it would be preferable to help the Kanbis to form smaller isogamous endogamous groups, thereby lessening the burden of dowry and also preventing the economic ruination of the Kanbis, which reduced government revenues from land. (See also Pocock 1954 for a discussion of more recent systems of hypergamy among the Patidars.)

Hypergamy also partially explains why the worst sex ratios are found among the highest caste or class groups, where a cultural rather than demographic shortage of grooms is created by the competition for them between girls from their own groups and those from economically or politically important lower groups. Conversely, at the lower end of the scale an artificial shortage of brides is created, associated with the common practice of brideprice at this level together with much greater egalitarianism in survival.

Then there are the implications of hypergamy for women in their marital homes. The explicit and implicit inequality between the households of the wife-givers and the wife-takers has already been mentioned. The first question then is which household the married woman is presumed to belong to. Much anthropological research suggests that the complete integration of the woman into her affinal home takes time and may sometimes never occur. Madan (1975) has documented how, from the terminology of the Kashmiri Pandits, it appears that the woman's status as an incoming wife is so significant that even her sons may classify her as *Amati* (recruited to the descent group through marriage as opposed to a consanguine). In addition, the young wife is believed to herself be insufficiently detached from her natal kin in any case, thus strengthening the resolve of her affinal family not to accept her completely to begin with.

Such a characterization of the wife's place, together with the inferior position accorded to her natal family, is consistent with the bride being accorded an inferior position in her marital home. Intra-household relationships as a whole are very clearly defined and hierarchical, with the young wife generally occupying the lowest rung until she proves herself in some way. This devaluation has important implications for both fertility and mortality. The fertility implication is that one major way for the wife to improve her status in her new home is through her reproductive success, and especially through the bearing of sons to continue the lineage: 'Only when a girl becomes the mother of a boy does she feel completely at home in her husband's house [in North India]' (Karve 1965). She also has another vested interest in childbearing in that her children are her sole consanguines in her marital home, and often her sole effective consanguines, her links with her natal home having been reduced to a formality for everyday purposes. The anthropological literature is replete with descriptions of the rise in status and in confidence associated with the woman's transition from bride to mother, rivalled only by the much later transition to mother-in-lawhood for the woman fortunate enough not to have borne only daughters: 'Generally the woman is so dominated by the affinal kin or the husband that she rarely makes a positive impression except as a mother. It is not rare to see women who were nothing but meek nonentities, blossom out into positive personalities in their middle-aged widowhood, or boss over the weak old husband in the latter part of the married life' (Karve 1965).

All these considerations make a strong case for high-fertility preferences in general and an even stronger case for high fertility as a result of strong son preference; as pointed out in several studies, the two ideals are for a man to have a son to perform his mortuary rites and for a woman to have a son to establish her as a member of her husband's lineage (see e.g. Hershman 1981; Mandelbaum 1970). At the same time, the daughterless woman is not really particularly blessed in this regard. Most studies (even Miller 1980) are agreed that the mother–daughter bond is a particularly strong one in such gender-differentiated cultures and even the father–daughter relation is very close, neither being very exaggerated in the scores of highly charged emotional songs bemoaning the snapping of this parental link upon marriage. Indeed, there is very little evidence of overt emotionally harsh treatment of daughters even in areas that otherwise record severe gender discrimination in the allocation of material resources.

To this high-fertility motivation one can add the indirect, positive effect on fertility associated with the normative domestic and extra-domestic seclusion imposed on married women in hypergamous societies. This has two main roots. First, her junior position as an outsider from an inferior household requires her to behave with relatively greater restraint and invisibility *vis-à-vis* other members (especially older males) in her affinal home; and second, from the groom's family perspective, the main underlying aim of a hypergamous marriage is the bringing in of a woman to continue the family line. Paternity thus has to be guaranteed, and one way to do this is to place severe restraints on the woman's access to sexual freedom through, among other things, limiting her extra-domestic activities. This stronger control on her sexuality in North India has been commented on by several authors (see e.g. Mandelbaum 1970; Sharma 1984) and is also believed to be the reason for the low participation of women in public or community life. Both kinds of restraint, domestic and extra-domestic, stand in the way of fertility as well as mortality decline for pragmatic reasons of the kind that demographers are familiar with; survey after survey has recorded the relatively worse knowledge of and attitudes towards birth control as well as a poorer ability to handle health problems, among women in real or notional *purdah* (although this is one area where an aggressive family planning programme, especially through the mass media, appears to be making some dent). Nor is all this helped by the more restricted and formal husband–wife relationship in such a system of marriage to begin with. Interspousal communication is very limited when, to quote Pettigrew (1981), often 'the only place of contact between men and women is the bed'. Madan (1965) too describes how, among the Kashmiri Brahmins, the wife is called the 'parrot of the pillow', because she is free to talk to her husband only at night. Decisions about fertility control can hardly be taken either jointly or by the woman on her own in such a situation.

North–South Differences

Much of the anthropological literature on hypergamy and some of its consequences, especially those to do with dowry practices, relates to the northern part of India. While a part of the relative neglect of the South may be accidental, I think at least a part is due to the fact that these are (or at least were until recently) less interesting and alive issues in the South Indian milieu, both from the observer's point of view and in the perceptions of the actors in the drama. In other words, except for communities such as the Nayars of Kerala, South India has offered less 'meat' for feminist anthropologists. Its conventional marriage and kinship systems, while full of the stuff of which general kinship theory is derived (theories based on kin terminology make particularly heavy use of South Indian data), have had less dramatic implications for the life of the woman as ego. Indeed, we have much less by way of ethnographies of South Indian women.

However, most anthropologists and ethnographers do now seem to be agreed that hypergamy, as defined in the North Indian context, is not a crucial component of marriage alliance in the South, even if the Great Tradition is the same in both regions. Attempts such as that by Dumont (1966) to emphasize North–South similarities rather than differences in marriage and kinship systems have been viewed as almost tautologous hair-splitting by many researchers (see e.g. Goody 1990) and the debate is in any case somewhat irrelevant to the question of North–South differences in the roles and status of women. This is not to say that women's status is not an important issue in the South; indeed, any advantages are only relative, and furthermore all evidence suggests some regression of this advantage in recent times. However, in the context of the role of practices such as hypergamy, these have conventionally been less important influences on marriage and women's status in the South.

One important custom in much of the South mitigates against the stark inequality between wife-givers and wife-takers implicit in the hypergamy of the North. This is the custom of marriage between close kin, which is completely forbidden in the Brahmanical code that governs marriage in the North. Indeed, by the rules of kinship, Dravidians are *expected* to marry their cross-cousins, the other common category of close kin marriage being between uncle and maternal niece. In North India, on the other hand, the ideal is to proscribe marriage with anyone who shares a common ancestor within seven generations on the father's side and five on the mother's. However, since this kind of genealogical knowledge is often lacking in practice, the prohibition is usually phrased in terms of known consanguinity (Hershman 1981; Mayer 1960; Dumont 1966).

How the Brahmanical code, which is in many ways pan-Indian, has been adapted to allow within kin marriage even among many of the upper castes in Southern India is not very clear and is debated in the literature (see e.g.

Trautman 1981; Goody 1990). But the relevant point here is that such bilateral cross-cousin marriages are less likely to embody a real or expected hierarchy between wife-givers and wife-takers for three reasons: first, the partners are more likely to belong to closely related families of equal rank rather than ritually or socially unequal rank to begin with; second, it is difficult to feel oneself to belong or to be treated as belonging to an inferior natal home when one's mother-in-law is also perhaps one's aunt or one's grandmother; finally, it is difficult to maintain a distinction between wife-givers and wife-takers when exchange marriages continue to occur, whatever the ideal (see e.g. Gough 1956; Dube 1967), which place two families in both positions relative to each other.

It is true that in actual practice not all marriages in South India are consanguineous;[7] if nothing else, one needs a cousin or niece of the right age (and with a few other attractions) if one is to actually follow the norm. But even where marriages are not within the extended kin, the fact that such unions are not proscribed in principle leads to a very different cultural setup, especially where women's status is concerned.

To take up the influences on women's status of hypergamy discussed earlier, in the southern region there is first less need to control so strictly the movements and possible sexuality of young girls. Indeed, growing up as they do in the company of potential husbands, it is quite common practice to tease boys and girls about their cross-cousins; to quote Srinivas (1976), 'village society did not provide congenial soil for ascetics'. One outcome of this ease of flirtation, as well as the relatively greater freedom in the marital home, does seem to be a shorter first birth interval, possibly at least partly because of the greater exposure to pregnancy in the first years of marriage (Basu 1993).

However, this relatively greater female freedom associated with more isogamous marriages also means a less strong compulsion to withdraw girls from school or from economic activity or to get them married as soon as they are sexually mature (see also Caldwell et al. 1982), all of which are believed to raise eventual family size even if they do restrict access to intercourse within the first few years of marriage.

Then there is the question of dowry as traditionally practised in South India. Dowry is a demographically very important issue, since institutionalized high dowry (not so much to the observer as to the observed) is believed to justify both the highest son preference and, even more, the greatest gender discrimination. The often crippling costs of marrying daughters in hypergamous societies has already been discussed; if, as is concluded here, such hypergamy is weaker in the South, do we have any evidence of a corresponding reduction in a daughter's marriage costs and a correspondingly smaller sex differential in welfare, especially survival?

This last, i.e. a smaller sex differential in survival in South India, has been well documented. As for the evidence on lower marriage costs, Miller's extensive search of the ethnographic literature does suggest that this too is not improbable. This review reaches two conclusions. First, marrying daughters is in general a less expensive business in the South, with the system of dowry being relatively less extensive and the amount of dowry being closer to the pre-mortem inheritance implied by the concept of *stridhan*, and with the greater sharing of marriage expenses between the families of the bride and the groom. Second, dowries seem to be smaller in consanguineous marriages than in marriages between unrelated persons. Other writers support the general contours of this conclusion (see e.g. Goody 1990).

This comparison of the incidence of hypergamy in North and South India and its consequent implications for women's status and demographic behaviour cannot be complete without a consideration of the recent tendency to a regional convergence in behaviour to the detriment of women's status in the South. Several factors have been recorded in the more recent anthropological literature on South India, all leading to an increased emphasis on dowry as it has been practised in the North and an increased devaluation of women, symbolized at one extreme by a fall in the population sex ratio, especially in Tamil Nadu (Basu 1994).[8]

Territorial Exogamy

Besides favouring hypergamy, the North Indian marriage system is characterized by two distinct kinds of exogamy—proscribing marriage between close kin, and proscribing marriage between partners living in the same village/geographical area. That is, in much of the North a village is an exogamous unit, so that in effect all persons belonging to the same caste (and indeed often all members of a village community, regardless of caste) in the same village behave as if they had a common ancestor. One of the characteristics of such common ancestry is a taboo on marriages within a group thus bound. As pointed out by Dube (1974), such territorial exogamy is also legitimized by the tendency for lineages to be concentrated in a geographical area, ruling out marriages within the same locality. Gould (1961) has another practical explanation for the persistence of territorial exogamy in the North. Because of the North Indian distinction between affines and agnates, keeping affines physically removed from the village means that the agnatic kinship group avoids interference by affines, and daughters-in-law can more easily be absorbed into their husbands' households. At the same time, such exogamy is also believed to be in the interests of girls' natal families because it reduces the threat they represent to the income and property of the natal group (Sharma 1980). In particular, excluding immovable property (especially land) from the dowry and marrying one's daughter away from one's village are believed to be two ways of controlling the fragmentation of scarce property. Village exogamy may also be seen as one way of controlling the sexuality of a girl. Since every male in her village is a brother to her, given norms about intra-kin relationships, he cannot also be a potential sexual partner.

Territorial exogamy is realized in many ways. On the whole, the further apart the affinal and natal villages are, the better, though only up to a point. Marriage distance is constrained by the need to also keep in mind linguistic, caste, and communal endogamy. In addition, too great a distance makes it difficult to ensure pedigree and feel confident about past behaviour. (The standard practice, for example, is to get girls who have had 'wrong' relationships married far away where their misdemeanours are not common knowledge.)

In addition, many groups in North India will not marry into any village whose lands touch the boundaries of their own village (Mayer 1960). Relations between men in such villages are called *sim-simna bhaichar*, i.e. like brothers because the village boundaries meet (Hershman 1981). Other groups, primarily the Rajputs, will marry their daughters only into villages that lie to the west of their own (L. Dube 1974). This is supposedly to conform to norms about hypergamy, the clans in the east being considered inferior to those westwards. For the same reason that a village that provides a daughter to another is considered inferior to the village of the wife-taker, there is a prejudice against exchanging daughters between villages (Karve 1965). Finally, if a daughter is given into a certain family of a certain village, a second daughter is generally not given into the same family or village in that generation, and usually not in the next two generations at least (Karve 1965). These practices are all more than mere prescriptions. All anthropological accounts of North India record the influence of exogamy norms in deciding marriage partners for one's offspring.

The Southern Indian situation is not marked by any such emphasis on the relative locations of the bride and groom's natal homes. Indeed, the preference given to cross-cousin and uncle–niece marriage often means that the families of both partners belong to the same village, perhaps even the same street. This is in keeping with the probable objective historically of such intra-kin marriages to consolidate rather than expand existing kin and property networks.

Implications of Exogamy for Women's Status and Demographic Behaviour

Thanks to territorial exogamy, the North Indian woman can be one of only two things in the village she lives in: the daughter or the daughter-in-law— never both. Correspondingly, her relatives can be either her cognates or her affines, never both. Such exclusivity makes it much more difficult for the woman to break out of her ascribed (especially daughter-in-law) roles and much easier for her affines in particular to enforce appropriate behavioural norms. The very visible distinction between the daughter and daughter-in-law of the North Indian village has been noted by several commentators (see e.g. Karve 1965; Mandelbaum 1970; Sharma 1980). 'The entire social world of many village women consists of these contrasting venues, the place where she is the constrained daughter-in-law and the wonderfully freer home where she is the beloved daughter' (Mandelbaum 1988). This distinction applies to the freedoms given to women in the home as well as those outside. The latter distinction operates on the principle that, in a system of village exogamy, the daughter of a household is a daughter of the village itself—that is, she is like a sister to the other men of the village and they are thus duty-bound to protect, not assault, her.

In her marital home, on the other hand, norms about veiling and seclusion and avoidance of male affines in general 'constantly remind a woman of her position as a daughter-in-law who must quietly submit her individual wishes to those of the group' (Jacobson 1977). This same pattern of invisibility is carried forward outside the home because other members of the village are also classificatory affines.

The demographic implications of all this are of two kinds. In the first place, 'a woman isolated among affines clearly lives in a more restricted social milieu' (Goody 1990). In turn, this restricts what Dyson and Moore (1983) call the extent of her 'autonomy' to manipulate the conditions and events of her life, including those related to childbearing and childrearing. Apart from the effects of KAP-type variables on fertility as well as health-related behaviour, she is also under greater pressure to conform to existing norms about the need for children in general and sons in particular; indeed, she has a strong vested interest in conforming to these norms as one way of raising her own position in her affinal home. In addition, in the system of territorial exogamy, her children are her only consanguines in her marital village. To quote Karve's (1965) only slightly exaggerated fears, 'early marriage out of the native village to a complete stranger is a terrible crisis in a girl's life', attenuated somewhat only when she becomes the mother of a boy.

In much of the South, on the other hand, 'a man does not bring a stranger as a bride to his home, a woman is not thrown among complete strangers upon her marriage' (Karve 1965). Nor is this solely a result of intra-kin marriages, which are in any case rarely more frequent than the proportion of non-kin marriages. The more important factor reducing the constraints on a married woman's behaviour is probably the fact that she often continues to live among people she has known since childhood, who have other kinds of interaction with her and her parental family besides those arising out of her marriage. As a consequence, not only is she freer to be herself in her new home, she is also better able to retain the contact with and support of her natal kin.

This brings us to the second factor through which territorial exogamy influences demographic behaviour. Marriage does not so effectively cut a daughter off from her parents in the South, if for no other reason than because geographic proximity between the two homes is more common. As for the value of such regular and sustained contact between a woman and her natal kin, it may be argued that such contact increases the sense of security with which the woman can risk taking some control of her own life. In addition, the potential for such continued post-marital contact increases the value of daughters to parents; even when they cease to be economically useful to the natal home, there is much to be said for the emotional and psychological benefits of a daughter living nearby, and parents in the South seem to be well aware of this additional advantage of daughters.

Finally, there is the very real physical support that influences demographic outcomes in areas where territorial exogamy is associated with a sharper snapping of informal ties between a girl and her parents after some years of marriage. The overall tendency is for visits to the parental home to become more and more infrequent and shorter once the first pregnancy sets in. Various reasons have been adduced for this, to do with an emphasis on children growing up in their own lineage and with the gradual resentment felt by a woman's brother (and more often his wife) at her frequent unproductive and expensive visits.

In much of the South, on the other hand, the custom is for the first child and sometimes even subsequent children to be born in the girl's parental home, a practice made considerably easier by the custom of intra-kin and intra-village marriage. It does seem that the attention and care a pregnant wife can demand and receive in her natal home are qualitatively and quantitatively different, as several fictional and real accounts testify. It is certainly not inconsistent that the use of and demand for professional services for delivery is the lowest in those areas where the woman remains in her husband's home throughout her pregnancy and for her delivery. However exaggerated our notions about the friction between a young wife and her husband's family, there is certainly less personal interest in making things easier for the daughter-in-law than there is for the daughter. The data sets that have probed the question do find lower levels of maternal and infant mortality when the woman goes to her parents for a delivery.

Conclusion

This paper has tried to illustrate the value of seemingly non-demographic discussions in mainstream anthropology for the interpretation of quantitative findings in demography. It has used two examples from the anthropological literature on South Asia in general and on North India in particular. These examples relate to the customs of hypergamy and territorial exogamy which are prevalent in much of North India even today and seem to influence greatly the status of women in this region. In turn, it is hypothesized, these effects of women's status get translated into worse demographic outcomes—that is higher fertility, higher mortality, and greater sex differentials in mortality—in this part of India.

The paper has also described the development of anthropological interest in women's issues in an attempt to relate some of the phases of this development to demographic research on the question of women's status and demographic behaviour.

Both parts of the paper highlight the potentially valuable contribution of anthropological demography. Instead of becoming anthropologists themselves, demographers can often benefit greatly by studying the findings, be they field descriptions or theories, of mainstream anthropology and using them in a comparative perspective to better understand demographic differentials across cultures.

Notes

1. Throughout the paper, I use the words 'women's status' mainly for convenience and as a recognizable shorthand for all the complexities that go to make up gender relations in a culture. The term itself has received much criticism in the gender-sensitive anthropological literature of recent years. The strongest criticisms have been expressed of the tendency to equate the status of women with simple indicators such as education and employment (on this see, in particular, Watkins 1993) and of the assumption that more of these imply better status; both these criticisms are especially valid for demographic research on this subject (see Greenhalgh 1994).
2. For greater accuracy, read 'white' for 'foreign'.
3. That is, one can carry destructively far the argument that one can be meaningfully studied only by one's like. Indeed, there is probably a strong case to be made for at least some experience in studying an alien society so that one's ethnocentric biases are exposed to oneself.
4. To cite Mandelbaum's (1988) reference to an Englishwoman writing of the life of upper-class women in North India, she repeatedly urged 'her English readers not to judge Indian Muslim customs by the standards of their own society, or to gauge a Muslim woman's unhappiness by how an Englishwoman might feel if she were placed in purdah'.
5. In an even less obvious way, I would categorize as ethnocentric the clucking attitude of a recent BBC documentary on discrimination against the female child in India, which blatantly implied a harshness rather than a helpless concern in the woman interviewee who justified female infanticide saying that she would rather give her daughter to the goddess of death than to a total stranger.
6. For everything is relative, after all. The anthropologist bemoaning the high marriage costs of daughters in Karnataka is greatly helped to see things in perspective by other studies on dowry demands in Punjab. And, perhaps more ambitiously, a smug attitude about low gender differences in mortality in, say, Kerala will appreciate how much of that state's female mortality is still preventable by looking at the greatly excess *male* mortality in Japan.
7. What is surprising is how large a number still are consanguineous. For example, the National Family Health Survey in Tamil Nadu found almost half the married women in its sample being married to a relative (International Institute for Population Studies 1994).
8. In particular, there is some evidence to suggest that there has been an increase in the state in female infanticide, which was earlier confined to one or two local communities but now seems more widespread.

References

Amadiume, A. (1987), *Male Daughters, Female Husbands: Gender and Sex in an African Society*. London: Zed Books.

Ardener, E. (1975), 'Belief and the problem of women', in S. Ardener (ed.), *Perceiving Women*. London: Dent.

Barnes, J. A. (1973), 'Genetrix: genitor: nature: culture?' in J. Goody (ed.), *The Character of Kinship*. Cambridge: Cambridge University Press

Basu, A. M. (1992), *Culture, the Status of Women and Demographic Behaviour: Illustrated with the case of India*. Oxford: Clarendon Press

—— (1993), 'Cultural influences on the timing of first births in India: large differences that add up to little difference', *Population Studies*, 47: 85–95.

—— (1994), 'On the many routes to a demographic transition: fertility decline and increasing gender inequalities in Tamil Nadu, India'. Mimeo, Cornell University.

Boon, J. (1974), 'Anthropology and nannies', *Man*, 9: 137–40.

Caldwell, J., Reddy, P. H., and Caldwell, P. (1982), 'The causes of demographic change in rural South India: a micro approach'. *Population and Development Review*, 8: 689–727.

Clarke, A. (1989), 'Limitations on female life chances in rural central Gujarat', in J. Krishnamurty (ed.), *Women in Colonial India: Essays on Survival, Work and the State*, Delhi, Oxford University Press.

Cleland, J. and Wilson, C. (1987), 'Demand theories of the fertility transition: an iconoclastic view', *Population Studies*, 41: 5–30.

Coale, A. J. (1991), 'Some relations among cultural traditions, nuptiality and fertility'. Mimeo, Office of Population Research, Princeton University.

Dube, L. (1974), *Sociology of Kinship*. Bombay: Popular Prakasan.

Dube, S. C. (1967), *Indian Village*. New York: Harper & Row.

Dumont, L. (1964), 'Marriage in India: the present state of the question, II. Marriage and status'. *Contributions to Indian Sociology*, 7: 77–98.

—— (1966), 'Marriage in India: the present state of the question, III. North India in relation to South India'. *Contributions to Indian Sociology*, 9: 90–114.

Dyson, T. and Moore, M. (1983). 'On kinship structure, female autonomy and demographic behaviour in India', *Population and Development Review*, 9: 35–60.

Geertz, C. (1973), *The Interpretation of Cultures*. New York: Basic Books.

Goody, J. (1990), *The Oriental, the Ancient and the Primitive: Systems of Marriage and the Family in the Pre-industrial Societies of Eurasia*. Cambridge: Cambridge University Press.

Gough, E. K. (1956), 'Brahman kinship in a Tamil Village', *American Anthropologist*, 58: 826–53.

Gould, H. A. (1961), 'A further note on village exogamy in North India'. *Southwestern Journal of Anthropology*, 17: 297–300.

Greenhalgh, S. (1994), *Anthropological Contributions to Fertility Theory*. Working Paper no. 64, Population Council, New York.

Greer, G. (1984), *Sex and Destiny: The Politics of Human Fertility*. New York: Harper & Row.

Hershman, P. (1981), *Punjabi Kinship and Marriage*. Delhi: Hindustan Publishing House.

Hooks, B. (1982), *Ain't I a Woman? Black Women and Feminism*. London: Pluto Press.

International Institute for Population Studies (1994), *National Family Health Survey: Tamil Nadu, 1993*. Bombay: IIPS.

Jacobson, J. (1977), 'The women of North and Central India: goddesses and wives', in D. Jacobson and S. Wadley (eds.), *Women in India: Two Perspectives*. New Delhi, Manohar.

Jong, E. (1985), *Parachutes and Kisses*. New York: Signet Books.

Karve, I. (1965), *Kinship Organization In India*. Bombay: Asia Publishing House.

Madan, T. N. (1965), *Family and Kinship: A Study of the Pandits of Rural Kashmir*. Bombay: Asia Publishing House.

——(1975), 'Structural implications of marriage in North India: wife-givers and wife-takers among the Pandits of Kashmir'. *Contributions to Indian Sociology*, 9: 217–43.

Mandelbaum, D. G. (1970), *Society in India: Change and Continuity*. Berkeley: University of California Press

Mayer, A. C. (1960), *Caste and Kinship in Central India: A Village and its Region*. London: Routledge & Kegan Paul.

Mayo, K. (1927), *Mother India*, New York: Harcourt Brace.

Miller, B. D. (1980), *The Endangered Sex: Neglect of Female Children in Rural North India*. Ithaca, NY: Cornell University Press.

Moore, H. L. (1992), *Feminism and Anthropology*. Cambridge: Polity Press.

Mukhopadhyay, C. (1988), 'Anthropological studies of women's status revisited', *Annual Review of Anthropology*, 17: 461–95.

Ortner, S. (1974), 'Is female to male as nature is to culture?' in M. Rosaldo and L. Lamphere (eds.), *Woman, Culture and Society*. Stanford, Calif.: Stanford University Press.

Pettigrew, J. (1981), 'Reminiscences of fieldwork among the Sikhs', in H. Roberts (ed.), *Doing Feminist Research*. London: Routledge & Kegan Paul.

Pocock, D. F. (1954), 'The hypergamy of the Patidars', in K. M. Kapadia (ed.), *Professor Ghurye Felicitation Volume*. Bombay: Popular Press.

Rosaldo, M. Z. (1974), 'Woman, culture and society: a theoretical overview', in M. Rosaldo and L. Lamphere (eds.), *Women, Culture and Society*. Stanford, Calif.: Stanford University Press.

Satia, J. K. and S. Jejeebhoy (eds.) (1991), *The Demographic Challenge*. Delhi: Oxford University Press.

Sharma, U. (1980), *Women, Work and Property in North-West India*. London: Tavistock Publications.

——(1984), 'Dowry in North India: its consequences for women', in R. Hirschon (ed.), *Women and Property, Women as Property*. London: Croom Helm.

Srinivas, M. N. (1976), *Remembered Village*. Berkeley: University of California Press.

Tambiah, S. J. (1973), 'Dowry and bridewealth and the property rights of women in South Asia', in J. Goody and S. J. Tambiah (eds.), *Bridewealth and Dowry*. New York: Cambridge University Press.

Trautmann, T. R. (1979), 'The study of Dravidian kinship', in M. M. Deshpande and P. E. Hook (eds.), *Aryan and non-Aryan in India*. Ann Arbor: University of Michigan Press.

——(1981), *Dravidian Kinship*. Cambridge: Cambridge University Press.

Uberoi, P. (ed.) (1993), *Family, Kinship and Marriage in India*. Delhi: Oxford University Press.

Vatuk, S. (1975), 'Gifts and affines in North India'. *Contributions to Indian Sociology*, 9: 155–96.

Watkins, S. C. (1993), 'If all we knew about women was what we read in *Demography*, what would we know?' *Demography*, 30: 551–606.

5 Kinship Structures, Marriage Systems, and Reproductive Behaviour: The use of Anthropology and Demography in a Brazilian Case Study

GEORGIA KAUFMANN

In families the greatest tension and disagreement often centre on similarities. In the family of social sciences, anthropology and demography have much in common, much to contribute to each other, and plenty to disagree over. Their respective approaches to the analysis of the social processes of reproduction are an example of this. Over the last twenty years many anthropologists have increasingly turned their backs on the study of kinship, even disavowing the existence of such a concept (Needham 1971; Schneider 1984). Demographers, on the other hand, have over the same period discovered the importance of the family in determining demographic behaviour both historically and in contemporary societies.

In this paper, I set out to explore some of the commonalities and divergences that the two disciplines share in a brief overview of family demography. More particularly, I will use material from my own fieldwork in Brazil to illustrate the richness to be found in using the disciplines jointly to study the social organization of reproduction.

Demography, the Family, and Reproduction

Looking back over research in social demography, there seem to be two distinct branches, historical and Third World demography, that evolved an interest in anthropological concepts such as kinship, marriage, and family, but for quite different purposes. In the case of historical demography the driving force was the paucity of information; the very nature of the reconstituted data necessitates a holistic view of demographic events happening within a social framework; for example, reconstitution of birth data through parish records is dependent on the social and cultural event—the baptism—not the demographic event—the birth. In the demography of the developing countries, interest in social and cultural factors began emerging in the work of Caldwell (1982), and subsequently among microdemographers, as attempts were made to unpack the factors that maintained the proximate determinants of fertility. On quite another scale, the work of Goody and Boserup set Lesthaeghe on a trail of macroanthropology, harnessing Murdock's Human Relations Area Files to the demographic data of sub-Saharan Africa (Lesthaeghe *et al.* 1989). Both the microdemography and the macro-anthropology were attempts at using the variation in social and cultural organization to throw light on demographic patterns of behaviour. Both historical demography and the demography of the contemporary South have increasingly turned to cultural factors to explain patterns of fertility and, to a lesser extent, mortality. But in both cases the use of concepts such as family, household, and marriage evolved out of the structuralist–functionalist practices of anthropology and has been bypassed by recent developments in the discipline (Lockwood 1995).

Nevertheless, in mainstream demography the desire to model and test continues to drag the quantitative elements of the discipline well away from the muddy waters of social and cultural reality. The need to abstract in order to model means that the units of observation are arbitrarily chosen: the choice of unit for demographic analysis depends on the problem to be solved (Keyfitz 1987: 3). From an anthropologist's point of view, this is bad practice. What Keyfitz is referring to is the tendency to swing between the family, the household, and individuals as the unit of analysis. Not only is this messy, but it is inappropriate to assume that these are interchangeable categories.[1]

This lack of discipline also underlines a significant difference between the two fields. Anthropologists have tended to be passionate about distinguishing between the many different kinds of family. Demographers' interest in families, kinship, and other social constructs lies in their influence on demographic outcomes. The result is that demographers have tended in the past to be loose with their use of kinship and family, or overly simplistic in assuming that marriages and families are all stable, long-term, cyclical, and nuclear (de Oliveira 1992). As Höhn (1987) argues, there is a real need to take demography beyond the confines of the stable conjugal unit to embrace divorce, remarriage, and lone parenthood. While demographers have, to some extent, changed their approach to dealing with social change, household and family are still used interchangeably, and the difference not always well understood (see *Demography* 1995).

Anthropology, the Family, and Reproduction

At one level, the approaches of anthropology and demography to social reproduction are conflicting. Contemporary anthropological ideas focusing on process, succession, and meaning may seem counterintuitive to a demographic audience. While demographers were discovering kinship, anthropologists were radically reworking the concept. The study of kinship forms one of the basic building blocks of the discipline of social anthropology; yet family, the central institution of kinship, has been virtually deconstructed out of existence. The functionalists separated the social world into the politico-juridical and domestic spheres, and the existence of the family was taken for granted. The domestic world was seen to arise out of the functional necessity imposed by blood ties and reproduction (Yanagisako 1979: 189). The home and the family shared the same domestic locus.

More recently kinship itself has been taken to task. Rather than assuming it to be some sort of platonic ideal that exists ontologically, it is thought of as both a social and an analytic category. Families exist, as real and social phenomena, but The Family and Kinship do not. This is a significant change in tack for anthropologists, but it is not one that has been appreciated by the demographers using anthropology (Lockwood 1995).

I am taking on board some of the notions that have emerged from the theoretical deconstruction of family and kinship. 'Domestic', 'family', and 'household' are words that are in many senses overlapping; 'domestic' encapsulates the latter two. Goody pointed out the different functions of the domestic group as production, reproduction, consumption, and shelter (Goody 1972: 4). The concepts that constitute 'the family' are to do with consanguinity and reproduction. The concepts that are packed into 'household' are more specifically to do with shelter—residence, the *domus* being the home, the place where you sleep.[2] It may be that often these categories collapse into one social unit. As Robertson points out, there is 'a mounting uneasiness with conventional notions of "family" and "household": a sense that these are weak analytic categories, social epiphenomena with a great diversity of empirically observable forms' (1991: 3).

The household and the family should not be conflated. Members of one family often live in one household, but equally, family members can be scattered over several households and households can consist of no familial members. The tendency to conflate these notions is arguably to do with the cultural ideal-type family of European culture, with the notion of the nuclear family as the seat of both production and reproduction. For the purpose of this paper, the household and family shall be treated as different categories. Although in our own culture we have come to see many activities as domestic, it would be erroneous to infer the same distribution of consumption, production, and reproduction in other social environments.

Another effect of treating the family as something in and of itself was the manner of conceptualizing it as belonging to its own sphere of influence. In considering the family to be merely another social category or institution, it is necessary to treat it as part of the social world and as subject to influences and constraints arising from the social order rather than from just the biological imperatives of reproduction. A variety of economic, demographic, and social factors, such as property relations, labour, age at marriage, and social stratification, influence the specific forms of families that emerge, rather than the family manifesting itself in different social settings.

It may seem irrelevant to a demographer whether or not there is an ontological family, because clearly there are families out there in the real world reproducing, but these ruminations do bear on demographic concerns. What demographers want to know is whether different families or kinship systems influence demographic behaviour, especially fertility. It is not kinship, nor family *per se*, that attracts the interest of demographers, but the processes of reproduction that they are organized around. Marriage, the lynchpin of any familial or kinship system, is the cultural manifestation of the control of reproduction and fertility. Marriage, in this sense, means the socially sanctioned, regularized sexual union for the purposes of reproduction. But, like kinship and families, there are many kinds of marriages, and many sexual unions that are not marriages. Anthropologists are concerned not just with the control of procreation, but also with the social relations that are formed through reproduction and marriage: namely, affinity and descent. This social setting, kinship, does not have to be seen in a functional way, but can be viewed constructively. Kinship and affinal relations, cultural constructs themselves, in their turn influence the reproductive functions.

Demographers, however, take a functionalist view of marriage and have often treated all 'regular sexual unions' as marriages (Merrick and Berquó 1983, pp. 30–9). Much formal demographic theory is premissed on the assumption that in general procreation is restricted to marriage. Henry's model of natural fertility, for example, times the onset of sexual behaviour with marriage. Bongaart's indices assume that most fertility occurs within marriage. This might well have been plausible among the Hutterites, but it would be inappropriate in many other societies.

Families and Fertility

One of the products of anthropological research is the understanding that there is little that is natural about human reproductive behaviour. The choice of partner, and the age, timing, and place of mating are all highly circumscribed by cultural norms. It is not that we lack biological imperatives: it is that the biological drives are funnelled into prescribed channels of behaviour. Yet the idea of a 'natural' fertility regime is, as mentioned above, a cornerstone of formal demographic theory. If we are to question what influence family forms may have on fertility, than we can use natural fertility regimes as comparative measuring sticks.

Over the last few decades, the painstaking work of historical demographers has provided us with a rich perspective on the demographic regimes of Europe (see e.g. Flinn 1981; Laslett 1972; R. M. Smith 1981; Wrigley 1981; Wrigley and Schofield 1983). England, in particular, exemplifies the

North-west European marriage pattern identified by Hajnal (1965). Typically, a large portion of the rural population spent some of their young
adulthood in service, and waited until their mid to late twenties before
marrying. Residence was neolocal rather than on family land, except for
the first born, and this resulted in the relatively late mean ages at marriage:
individuals had to accumulate sufficient wealth before embarking on their
own families. The high portions remaining permanently celibate testify to
the difficulty of securing a marriage in such circumstances. It seems that the
late age at marriage and high proportions remaining single were closely
related to the inheritance patterns (primogeniture), the residence patterns
(neolocal), and the looseness of non-corporate, bilateral kinship. Translated
into Caldwell's (1982) terms, North West Europe could be characterized as
having a net downward generational wealth flow, which meant that children
were a net cost on parents. They were consequently ill-provided for (Why
invest in children if they will not in turn secure your old age?) and left to their
own resources to provide for their own marriages. The net outcome of this
familial arrangement is that, despite having a natural fertility regime, the
total fertility rates (TFRs) in pre-industrial England, and in Europe in
general, were well below the Hutterite levels.

The European pattern of late and not universal marriage contrasts markedly with the early and universal marriage of sub-Saharan Africa (van de
Walle 1968). Up until recently, fertility in sub-Saharan Africa has been
maintained at high levels through early and universal marriage. The level
of natural fertility was lower than the theoretical maximum because of
traditional practices of prolonged lactation leading to extended child spacing
(Lesthaeghe and Page, 1981). But it is all too easy for Northern social
scientists to assume uniformity in distant cultures, and it is tempting to
assume that there is a single African fertility or nuptiality regime. In fact,
there are regional variations in family formation, nuptiality, and fertility
(Lesthaeghe *et al.* 1989). Far from being homogeneous, African family forms
vary between unilineal descent groups, both patrilineal and matrilineal, and
bilateral descent. At the most simplistic level, those peoples that organize
themselves in corporate lineage groups are more likely to favour higher
fertility, inasmuch as the intergenerational wealth flows are more likely to
be upwards. Several centuries of trade and colonization have had their
impact, however, as have the imported religions of Christianity and Islam.
Even within the context of indigenous African culture, the different value
and status accorded women in matrilineal and patrilineal societies, as well as
in agricultural and pastoral regimes, results in different nuptiality regimes
(Kaufmann and Meekers 1992). West Africa is marked by a higher incidence
of polygyny, larger differences in the mean age at first marriage between the
sexes, more divorce, and more remarriage than Eastern or Southern Africa.
Southern Africa felt the British colonial presence most keenly, and has had
the fabric of social life ruptured most dramatically, especially through male

labour migration. The result is changes in familial organization with a marked increase in the number of female-headed households and consensual unions. This can have serious implications for individuals in cultures where kin, and therefore social status, is fixed by marriage, e.g. bridewealth payments (Izzard 1985; Kuper 1987). More recently, there is evidence of declines in fertility occurring in some countries, noticeably Kenya. It is not clear why, after decades of family planning campaigns, that a fertility transition should occur finally in the midst of economic decline and structural adjustment (Lesthaeghe and Jolly 1992). In so many countries, like Brazil, fertility declines closely accompany rapid economic development.

Brazilian Kinship, Marriage, and Reproduction

In the following section I will be examining more closely the interrelationship between fertility and family forms. Moving away from the past and Africa, I shall be focusing on Brazil, more specifically a *favela* (shanty town) in Belo Horizonte, the third city of Brazil, where I conducted fieldwork. Throughout 1988 I lived in the *favela* Alto Vera Cruz (AVC), conducting participant observation and a microdemographic survey. The data presented here are the result of this fieldwork.

In all, 76 women who had given birth in the year prior to the survey were interviewed using the survey questionnaire. The sample was drawn from the records of a local residents' association and represents a fair cross-section of the *favela* population. It was not, however, randomly drawn. Despite the small sample size, the use of non-parametric tests in the analysis ensures that statistical significance can be calculated. The demographic data are complemented by ethnographic information collected throughout the entire year, and this ensures the high quality of the data set.

Brazilian Fertility

In many respects, Brazil appears to be a perfect example of a country undergoing demographic transition alongside economic development. The economic 'miracle' of the 1970s was accompanied by an equally spectacular decline in fertility rates throughout the country (Merrick and Berquó 1983; Fernandez and Carvalho 1986; Martine 1996), as shown in Table 5.1.

At the most general level, it is clear that the fertility decline had begun in the urban areas prior to 1950. In the large metropolitan, heavily urbanized states of Rio de Janeiro and São Paulo, fertility levels were already low by 1950; the period up until 1970 was fairly stable, and thereafter the dramatic fall occurred. Throughout the 1970s the crude birth rate (CBR) and, total fertility rate (TFR) both fell some 25%–30%. In 1960 the CBR was 40 per 1,000 and by 1980 it had fallen to 30 per 1,000.

Table 5.1. Total Fertility Rates (TFRs) and Percentage of Population Urbanized, Brazil, 1950–1986

	1950	1960	1970	1976	1980	1983–6
Brazil	6.32	6.18	5.83	4.44	4.10	3.5
Urban	4.68	—	4.61	3.48	3.47	3.0
Rural	7.70	—	7.71	6.36	5.83	5.0
% urban	36.2	45.1	55.9	61.2	67.6	70.9

Sources: 1950–80: Merrick and Berquó (1983: 21); 1983–86: Arruda *et al.* (1987: 26).

The purely demographic explanations of the Brazilian fertility decline, emphasizing proximate determinants, suggest that the decline can be attributed more or less in total to a decline in marital fertility; in other words, once women are married or cohabiting they have lower fertility (Merrick and Berquó 1983: 1, 29). The consensus view is that contraception in marriage is the key (Wood and de Carvalho 1988: 154; Merrick and Berquó 1983: 6). Merrick and Berquó think that is related to increasing consumption expectations and endemic inflation. In their view, as people confront increasing economic difficulties, and concurrently contraception becomes more available, heightened consumer expectations inevitably lead to a decline in fertility (Merrick and Berquó 1983: 6). Martine (1996) argues that it is the unintended result of other economic and social development policies and changes.

The Brazilian Family

In the preceding sections I briefly examined the relationship between family form and fertility. In sub-Saharan Africa a higher natural fertility regime had been supported and this was related to the flow of wealth between generations. Equally, the lower fertility found in historical North-western Europe was also related to inheritance patterns and family structure. In Brazil there is a clearly defined notion of what the family should be like (extended, patriarchal), and some considerable variety in what it is actually like (Brühl 1989: 38–43; Durham 1991: 55–7).

A characterization of the Latin American household can illustrate the diversity of families. Using World Fertility Survey data, de Vos argues that Latin American households share the following characteristics: idealization of patriarchal and extended families, idealization of gender-specific roles, patterns of high marital instability and common consensual unions, and a large flow of female rural–urban migration (de Vos 1987: 503). Although Brazilian data were not used in the formation of this typology, it could be usefully extended to Brazil. What is significant is that, by drawing up the schema from empirical survey data, rather than testing out the existence of

an ideal and measuring reality against it, de Vos demonstrates the importance of both traditional ideology and the praxis of consensual unions. By
emphasizing the discrepancy between the praxis and the ideals, she shows
that neither ideal—the traditional nor the alternative—can necessarily
account for the families found in practice.

The idea of the traditional, extended patriarchal family is still prevalent,
although as a viable form in urban areas it is not common. It is this
patriarchal ideal that has been enshrined as the 'Brazilian Family'.

In practice, however, there are only vestiges of this system left. If kinship
and family were platonic ideals, it would be correct to see many of the actual
family formations as deviant from the ideal. But since kinship is an ideological category, it is necessary to look at the interplay between the ideology
and practice of kinship. Kinship and family practices are: the result of an
interaction, and frequently of a conscious manipulation, of the two levels of
the ideological system: an 'ideal' model corresponding approximately to the
dominant culture, and an adaptive model, emerging from the daily praxis of
the poor (Woortman 1987: 12; my translation).

The patriarchal Brazilian Family is an ideal type. The alternative, but
perhaps more common, family type is what is perceived as the dysfunctional,
matrifocal, urban, poor, Black Family. This latter is viewed as the outcome
of slavery and deculturization of the poor blacks. This alternative is also an
ideal type. The widespread existence of the Black Family has been documented (Hannerz 1969; Martinez-Alier 1974; R. T. Smith 1956). A variety of
arguments have been put forward to explain this phenomenon, and can be
summed up as follows. In view of a common African ancestry (most slaves
came from what is now Nigeria and Ghana), one line of argument is that the
powerful position of West African women and the tendency to polygamy
with children living with their mother has been retained in the shape of
matrifocal families. For this to explain the incidence of black matrifocality it
would be necessary to demonstrate a continuity in both the institutions and
values. A second popular explanation directly contradicts the notion of
continuity. Slavery, it is argued, was so disruptive that the family disinteg-
rated under the pressures of low status and because of the control of the
slave owners, who broke up families at whim. In other words, matrifocality
was a result of the lack of continuity and the social trauma of slavery. The
third argument is that these former causes are negligible, and that contemporary matrifocality is an expression of contemporary socioeconomic pressures in conditions of urban poverty (Patterson 1982: 137; R. T. Smith 1956).
These arguments are premissed on the existence of female-headed households or families, in which men occupy a marginal *de jure* or *de facto* role.
Rather than discuss which of these causal arguments is the most explicative,
I contend that the Black Family has taken on an ideological status as the
alternative form to the traditional family. It is taken for granted, as an
empirical fact.

Families in the *Favela*

Having read about both of the ideal family types in the anthropological literature, their lack of ubiquity in the field was surprising. The most striking feature of the families in Alto Vera Cruz (AVC) was their diversity (Kaufmann 1991: 85–103). Using two simple criteria, a typology of families was constructed. Levi-Strauss designated the elementary relationship of families as the mother–child relationship. This is the fundamental reproductive bond. Since reproduction is usually effected through sexual union, the presence or absence of a conjugal couple is a second salient characteristic of families. Another feature of the family is the number of generations found living together. I have termed three generations or more as 'complex', and two generations as 'simple'. In Table 5.2, the locus of the families' residence is also shown. Land is scarce among the urban poor, so that a third of the families live on land that belongs to their parents. In Portuguese they are said to be living *de favor* (by favour).

In the introductory passages of this paper I made a distinction between household and family. Family ties extend beyond immediate co-residence and it can be useful to think in terms of households and housefuls. A *household* is a domestic group that lives in one dwelling and shares various activities and kinship, whereas a *houseful* means all persons inhabiting the same set of premises (Laslett 1972: 36), which could consist of several households in the same building or compound.[3]

Convergence theory used to be popular, postulating that, as societies industrialized and urbanized, reproduction would take place increasingly in nuclear families, and kinship systems would converge on this particular family form. Although for many social change does not necessitate Westernization, others still favour this idea. It has been argued that this is one of the few consistent demographic trends (Prado 1985: 72). But there is a distinct difference between the West and many Third World countries. In Northwest Europe the nuclear family was prevalent long before industrialization and was not a result of it (de Vos 1987: 501). One of the salient features of the Western nuclear family is neolocal residence and economic independence

Table 5.2. The Relationship between Family Types, Residence, Households, and Housefuls in Urban Brazil

Family type	Residence	Household or houseful	%
Conjugal/simple	Virilocal	Virilocal houseful	19
	Uxorilocal	Uxorilocal houseful	16
	Neolocal	Simple conjugal household	23
Conjugal/complex	Neolocal	Complex conjugal household	15
Matrifocal/simple	Neolocal	Simple matrifocal household	8
Matrifocal/complex	Uxorilocal	Complex matrifocal household	18

(Hajnal 1965). Although many of the families in AVC appear to be simple, nuclear families, they are rarely neolocal and often live on the same plot of land as their parents.

None of the family types used above fit exactly into the ideal types of the Brazilian or Black Family. The virilocal housefuls approximate most closely to the norm of the extended, patriarchal Brazilian family. These families tend to be more conservative, practising Catholics. Just over half of the simple conjugal couples are living *de favor* of the man's family. But the form of the locality does not guarantee that the content of the family fulfils the ideal type. For example, Edna was living with her husband in a tiny three-room house, with two of her children. The land belonged to her mother-in-law. Living in other houses on the plot were her two married brothers-in-law and their six children. Although she was only 21, she had been married for five years, and in that time had separated and gone to live with another man, had had a child by him, and had then come back. Her mother-in-law was disapproving. Like 57% of the women living virilocally, Edna came from a rural area. Another example was Maurisa, who was cohabiting with a man seven years her junior. She had four children by three different men, and the oldest was being brought up by her mother. They lived in a house at the top of her mother-in-law's plot of land, and although they wanted to buy it from her, she would not sell.

The women living conjugally but uxorilocally were by contrast much more likely to have come from the city, rather than rural areas. A quarter of the conjugal couples lived *de favor* of the woman's family. All of these women come from Belo Horizonte, and 75% of them were born in AVC. Access to land may play a significant part in the kind of family that emerges. On average, these women are better educated; 67% had got as far as fifth to eighth grade.

The real nuclear families—the neolocal, simple conjugal families; just under a quarter of all families studied—were in a disadvantaged position. They tended to have rural origins and had had to either buy or rent their land. It is not so much choice as necessity that drives people to adopt this modern family form. I am not convinced that there is a trend towards the nuclearization of the family. It might just be a question of access to land. Those arriving from the countryside without kin have no choice but to become nuclear households in rented or bought accommodation. For those whose families live in AVC, it makes economic sense to use the resources that the family already possesses. Nuclearization could be said to be happening if those who could afford to do so moved away. Geni and her sister Dalila were among the least poor families in the survey. Both were married, educated and skilled. They each owned a house, on or adjoining their mother's property. In other words, despite relative economic comfort, they had both chosen to stay close to the parental plot.

A quarter of the women in the sample were living without the presence of either a male partner or male family head (e.g. a father). The matrifocal households fell into two categories; complex, nearly 80% of the cases, and simple. The women living with their mothers in multi-generational female-headed households approximated most closely to the ideal type Black Family. Interestingly, these families were disproportionately black compared with the overall sample. The women were all urban-born, a high proportion having been born in AVC itself. If modernization is said to be having any effect, it is arguably not nuclearization so much as feminization of the family.[4]

Marital Status in the *Favela*

Thus far I have made mention only of the structure of the families. Of the women interviewed in Alto Vera Cruz, 33% were single mothers, 27% were living in consensual union with a man, and 40% were married. The point here is that there are, at the most superficial level, at least three types of family. The marital status of the women in these different families is not without significance. There is a clear pattern in the distribution of family types by marital status: 79% of married couples lived alone, citing either the man or both as head. An even greater portion of cohabiting women, 85% live in nuclear families. Conversely, only 25% of the single women live in simple families, 50% live in female-headed complex families, and 25% in conjugal/complex families.

At this point, I have to make some comments about some of the weaknesses of the AVC data. The survey had not been drawn from a random sample, but from a sample of women selected by a shared event (a birth the previous year and membership of a local residents' association). This means that the data are probably not perfectly representative and probably a bit skewed. Other comparable surveys show a higher proportion of women in unions, and it is reasonable to expect that this survey might be weighted in favour of the women in unions (although this does not initially seem to be the case). Second, interviews were easier to secure with women who were not working. This in fact favoured the women in unions, since a far higher proportion of the single women had to work.[5] I would therefore imagine that, if anything, I have an under-representation of fertile single women.

Fertility in the *Favela*

In this section the relationship between the family types, marital status, and fertility will be discussed. One of the interesting characteristics that has emerged is that the family type is a far less useful predictor of fertility behaviour than marital status. In Brazilian society considerable meaning is still attached to marriage (Martine 1975). The following data demonstrate that the meaningful social category in organizing reproduction is still marriage. Unlike the demographic habit of collapsing cohabitation and marriage into a unitary package of 'in sexual union', the data indicate the need to disaggregate these groups of women.

As shown in Table 5.3, there are no statistical differences in family type when it is ranged against the age of the various fertility events, the number of births, and the gaps between the various demographic events.[6] The fertility events shown in the table are first sexual intercourse, first cohabitation, and first birth. Apart from the single women living on their own, who form a small and variable group, the women living in simple, nuclear families (who tend to be married) display the longest gap between first sexual intercourse, and first cohabitation and first birth.

Only the gap between first sex and first birth is statistically meaningful. The Mann–Whitney U-tests (MWUTs) reveal that most of this significance emerges between the simple-matrifocal and the virilocal, uxorilocal, and complex households. The majority of women living virilocally come from rural areas. These women are also the most likely to have had sex before marriage and tend on average to start living with their partner just after they have given birth. The conjugal units and uxorilocally based couples are more likely to be urban in origin and this is reflected in longer gaps.

This sparse pattern of significance contrasts starkly with the analysis of fertility and marital status. It was noted above that it is generally axiomatic in studies of fertility that the factors affecting cohabiting and married women are the same in terms of fertility. Furthermore, in some instances fertility data have been 'improved' by assuming that single women reported

Table 5.3.   The Mean Number of Years Between Two Events for Women by Family Type*

	(1)		(2)		(3)	
women	sx–chbt	N	sx–bth	N	chbt–bth	N
Total	2.09	58	2.91	73	0.95	58
Simple-matrifocal	6.00	3	6.07	6	2.24	3
Complex-matrifocal	2.67	6	2.97	13	0.83	6
Simple-conjugal	2.59	17	3.92	17	1.39	17
Uxorilocal	0.75	12	2.21	12	1.35	12
Virilocal	2.14	14	2.01	14	−0.04	14
Complex	0.67	6	1.47	11	−0.73	6
Significant			0.004			
F			3.809			

* sx–chbt (gap 1): first sex to first cohabitation/marriage
 sx–bth (gap 2): first sex to first birth
 chbt–bth (gap 3): first cohabitation/marriage to first birth

as fertile are in fact cohabiting and are therefore, to all intents and purposes, like married women: 'In order to reduce the impact of underreporting of consensual unions, single women reporting a birth were considered married' (Merrick and Berquó 1983: 34). From an anthropological perspective, this seems to be a rather wild claim to make, unsubstantiated as it is.

The present research began from the opposite position. I assumed that single and married mothers were fertile at different stages of their lives, perhaps for different reasons. By looking at the fertility data that we have for the women in AVC and analysing it by marital status, this second hypothesis is confirmed and expanded. In Table 5.4, the ages of women at key events in their lives are presented for each type of marital status.

At first glance, it is apparent that, on average, married women pass through all these events later than both the single and cohabiting women. But what is remarkable about the data is that, on average, the single women also first experience sex, and bear their first child, later than the cohabiting women. This implies that, not only are single women different from married women, but cohabiting women are also.

Further analysis of these data by way of the MWUT confirms this discovery that married and cohabiting women are significantly different. First, the MWUTs reveal that no significance need be attributed to the fact that the married women are on average older. This finding is of great significance. It is tempting to hypothesize that women living in such marginal circumstances share a life-cycle that takes them from being single, through cohabitation, into marriage. The results presented in Table 5.4, and the underlying statistical analyses, suggest that there is not one such single life-cycle. Instead, marriage and cohabitation are mutually exclusive alternative life courses.

The differences in the age at first sex was seen in Table 5.4 to be statistically significant. The MWUTs reveal that, indeed, the married women experience sex significantly later than the single and cohabiting women,

Table 5.4. Average Current Age and Age at First Sex, Cohabitation and Birth, and Average Number of Births by Marital Status*

	Age	Sex	Cohabitation	Birth	N births
Total	26.09	18.21	20.07	21.07	2.48
Married	27.50	20.18	20.87	22.38	2.76
Cohabiting	25.06	16.29	19.36	19.34	2.45
Single	25.25	17.43	19.07	20.94	2.17
Significant		0.004		0.05	
F		6.09		3.13	

* The significance levels in this and the following table are shown only if the value is significant, i.e. less than 0.05, and the means and significance are the result of analysis of variance tests.

who are not significantly different from each other. For the differences in the age at first birth, again it is the married and cohabiting women that demonstrate the most significant variance. There are, however, no significant differences between the ages at first cohabitation and the number of births for women in any of the groups.

At this point, then, we can state that the cohabiting and single women have more in common as groups than either have with the married women. Although the actual fertility itself does not vary significantly between the groups, the table indicates that married women have marginally more children than the cohabiting women and the single women in turn.

The analysis thus far points to the necessity for a discussion of the difference, if any, between cohabitation and marriage. The assumption that cohabiting and married women have the same reproductive behaviour seems to be wrong. Fertile single women and cohabiting women have more in common with each other than either have with married women. What is important is to determine whether or not there is a linear development (a 'life-cycle') through which all the women pass, or whether there are alternative life courses (de Oliveira 1992). Can marriage be viewed as the end result of a process that begins with single-parenthood and cohabitation, or does marriage belong to an independent process? If the latter, it would still be possible to argue that cohabitation and single-parent status themselves may constitute a distinct cycle—that is, that there is fluctuation between the two statuses, rather than a linear sequence from being alone through to living together permanently. In Table 5.5, the average amount of time that passes between two events is shown for the women in different marital statuses. It is clear that there are definite and discrete patterns in the timing of these events that differ for women in different categories.

The interest of demographers in nuptiality is based on the assumption that in most instances exposure to sex is dependent on nuptial union; hence the treatment of fertile women as effectively the same, regardless of marital status. If, however, the advent of sexual activity is seen as something that is culturally determined, but most usually—though not necessarily—falling within nuptial union, i.e. marriage, then we can explore the relationship between sexual activity and nuptiality and the implications for fertility. Looking at the first column in Table 5.5, we see that on average women have sex just over two years before their first cohabitation. Although 29% of the married women had had sex before they married, all the cohabiting women had lost their virginity first. Prenuptial sex for the married women happened on average eight months before marriage, while the cohabiting women first had sex on average three years before they first cohabited, and the nine single women who had previously cohabited first had sex four years before that.

The significance of this result is confirmed by the MWUT, which shows that single and cohabiting women do not behave significantly differently

Table 5.5. The Mean Number of Years between Selected Pairs of Events by Marital Status*

	sx–chbt	sx–bth	chbt–btn	N	chbt–btn (excl. single)	N
Total	2.09	2.91	0.95	58	0.89	49
Married	0.69	2.23	1.51	29	1.51	29
Cohabiting	3.25	3.13	−0.02	20	−0.02	20
Single	4.00	3.56	1.32	9		
Significant	0.011		0.023		0.011	
F	7.784		4.053		7.083	

* sx–chbt (gap 1): first sex to first cohabitation/marriage
  sx–bth (gap 2): first sex to first birth
  chbt–bth (gap 3): first cohabitation/marriage to first birth
  chbt–bth–single (gap 3a): first cohabitation/marriage to first birth (excl. single mothers).
The figures represent the mean number of years between a pair of events; for example, '1.5' represents one and half years. A negative figure, e.g. '−0.02', means that in fact the 'first' event occurred after the 'second', e.g. cohabitation followed a birth.

from each other. Nevertheless, the long period of sexual activity before cohabitation is significantly different from the relatively short span of pre-nuptial sex engaged in by the married women. This finding is crucial, in that it shows that sexual behaviour and morality are still determining influences on the women's life chances. For instance, 32% of the women who had ever lived with or been married to a man had had sex before they cohabited, but only 24% of the women who had had prenuptial sex ended up marrying.

In the second column of Table 5.5, the gap between first sex and first birth is shown. The married women have the smallest gap between the two events. Curiously, the differences between the three groups are not significant in an analysis of variance. The MWUTs revealed that there is, however, a significant difference between the two years that married women wait to have the first child and the three-and-a-half years on average that single women wait. As the next column shows, the relationships between conception and marriage and conception and cohabitation are quite distinct.

In the third column, it can be seen that for married women the first baby is born, on average, a year and a half into matrimony, thereby being conceived well after the wedding. Cohabiting women, on the other hand, begin to cohabit on average about a week *after* the birth of their first child. The MWUTs not only support this, but also show that for this variable the single and cohabiting women are also different. The single women who have cohabited were usually cohabiting first. Since only nine of the single women had cohabited, they were dropped from the analysis of variance to see if the difference between the cohabiting and single women would be strengthened in an analysis of variance test, in the fourth column of Table 5.5. This proved to be the case.

To summarize Table 5.5, it can be argued that the cohabiting and married women have distinct life courses. The married women wait until shortly before their wedding to start having sex. Engagement is taken seriously, and being a *noiva* (financée) is an accepted social status. It means that marriage is intended. *Noivas* are given more freedom to be with their *noivo*, because parents feel less protective, more sure of the future. It was not infrequent to hear a woman explaining that she had had premarital sex with her *noivo*. In other words, once the couple have earnest intentions, which have been made public, and the wedding date has been fixed, then an engaged woman might cede to her *noivo's* (and her own) desires. They will then marry and, after an interval, she will have her first child.

Assuming that marriage is the desirable life course, the cohabiting and single women make a strategic mistake. They have sex before they are engaged, or take engagement to mean legitimation of sex, but too early on, so that the man does not feel beholden to, or forced to, marry them. In general, women are greatly pressurized by their boyfriends to have intercourse. Exceptionally, a man may decide that he wants to marry the woman, and then may choose to 'respect' her. More usually, sexual behaviour involves negotiation, coercion, and/or frustration. The women's dilemma is not facilitated by the common prevalence of naivety and changing social mores.

Some men, after the birth of their child, set up a home with the woman and child. Others desert the woman the moment she is pregnant. (This was the most common complaint of the single women.) The situations of the married and cohabiting women are, therefore, dissimilar. The married woman has planned her marriage, has sex with a man she trusts, and plans the baby for after the wedding. The cohabiting woman has sex with a man before there are any such concrete plans and, through a probably unplanned pregnancy, ends up cohabiting. The single women have less chance and often slide into a series of relationships. In other words, these are discrete life courses that result from early decisions. Although most women aspire to marriage, few actually succeed in their goal.

A woman's chances of marriage, therefore, are affected by whether she has premarital sex and, if so, with whom and when. In fact, we find that, whereas a third of ever-cohabiting women had had sex before they cohabited, only a quarter of the married women had.

An initial observation of these differences suggests that single and cohabiting women may have more in common than do married and cohabiting women, apparently contradicting the other findings. It is my contention, however, that each set of women has characteristics that importantly distinguish it—or at least the associated choice of men—from the other two. The married women were clearly more careful than the other two groups about what they did and with whom. The cohabiting women tend to end up in fairly stable unions, but not to marry. There is some fluctuation between cohabitation and being alone for the single women, since a quarter had previously been living with the fathers of their children, but I think that the timing of the cohabitation is crucial. The partners of the cohabiting women on average moved in with them after the birth of their first child. In other words, the partners were assuming their responsibilities as fathers and 'husbands' by moving in. In such circumstances, it is presumably a thought-out decision. Paternity, when acknowledged, is generally taken seriously. The rest of the babies are then born into the cohabiting union.

The single women, however, had often already been living with the man before the birth of the child. It seems plausible to suggest that, if a woman offers a man uxorial services, including sexual ones, without the man having many responsibilities, then the risk that he will run off at the onset of duty are high. Living together for sex is quite another matter from living together for childrearing.

Those women who lose their virginity young have a much higher chance of having more than one mate. This is reflected in the fact that those who are very young when they first enter a union have a much higher chance of going on to have a child with another man. This observation serves to strengthen my view that marriage is the outcome of planning and fortitude: if a woman's objective is marriage, she must choose to withhold herself, and keep her virginity, until such time as her future with her husband-to-be is secure. Those women who slip early find it much harder to achieve the stability of the married women who waited first.

Conclusion

This paper began by arguing that, while demographers have been keen to take on board anthropological concepts of kinship, marriage, and reproduction, there is a danger of the discipline borrowing outmoded notions. Anthropologists have moved away from using fixed, hold-all categories of social organization to looser, processual accounts of social life. For example, the manner in which demographers have sometimes treated interchangeably single, cohabiting, and married women has been seen to be misplaced, in Brazil at least. More detailed analysis reveals that poor, urban Brazilian culture attaches great significance to the marital status, unlike some demographers, and that, accordingly, married, cohabiting, and single women have significantly different patterns around reproductive behaviour (Kaufmann 1991).

The studies of historical and contemporary Third World demography increasingly indicate the need to take a variety of cultural, social, and economic variables into account. Systems of inheritance and land division, and the care and provision of the elderly, have been shown to have impact on the demographic regimes that are shaped by and shape the social setting.

The more contextualized data become, the harder it is to make generalizations. Changes in the social arrangements surrounding reproduction in the West have led to conceptual shifts in the approach to social demography (Lesthaeghe 1992). However, despite the recognition of the importance of cohabitation, there is still a tendency to rely on marital status as a conceptual backbone (Prinz 1995:3).

At an aggregate level, I would have to argue that there is no such thing as a *favela* family or reproductive regime. Yet by decomposing, even in my small sample, it is evident that small, subtle differences in livelihood security (access to land, or the need to rent accommodation) affect in real terms the form of families. The form and locale of families in turn impacts on demographic behaviour. The advice, support, and information flows open to a woman living in a houseful, with other households, is distinct from the relative isolation of a woman in a neolocal, nuclear family.

It is at this micro level that the veins of anthropology and demography can be most richly mined. Aggregate data can never be used to extract meaning from the social fabric. There is evidence world-wide, for instance, of increasing levels of female-headed households, or matrifocality. Statistically, inferences can be made that associate this with increasing female autonomy. (Single mothers are more likely to work, and do not have male household heads to subordinate them.) It is only by placing such data in a cultural context that it becomes possible to gauge the meaning of such changes in social practice. In Alto Vera Cruz, the least well-off and the most disadvantaged women were the single mothers who suffered the additional burden of low status. The married women were in every way more 'successful'—better educated, better off, and better contraceptors. But it is only by putting together the two sets of data, the qualitative and the quantitative, that I have been able to build up a picture of both the form and content of *favela* families.

Notes

1. It is interesting to note that economists also tend to collapse the family and the household into interchangeable categories (Evans 1989: 8; Kabeer 1991: 7–8).
2. Yanagisako (1979) gives a thorough and useful account of the evolution of anthropological thought on the family and household. In particular, she cites (p. 162) Bender (1971) as arguing that family and household are logically distinct categories.
3. Although Laslett (1972: 29) is careful to decompose the various households into their constituent parts, his analysis has one major failing. He takes the conjugal couple as the fundamental building block of the family, thus placing the 'conjugal family unit' (CFU) as the core of every family. Although he allows for widowhood as the remains of a CFU, his definition implicitly deprives matrifocal families of their status as families.
4. I am omitting the complex conjugal families from this discussion, in part because they were few in number, and in part because they display little in the way of significant patterns.
5. Of the women interviewed, 70% of the single women worked, compared with 41% of the married, and 15% of the cohabiting women. (Married women are more likely to work than cohabiting women.)

6. The techniques for analysis employed were analysis of variance in conjunction with the Mann–Whitney U-tests (MWUTs).

References

Arruda, J. M., Rutenberg, N., Morris, L., and Ferraz, E. A. (1987), *Pesquisa Nacional Sobre Saúde Materno-Infantil e Planejamento Familiar: PNSMIPF— Brasil, 1986*. Rio de Janeiro: BEMFAM.

Bender, D. R. (1971), 'De facto families and de jure households in Ondo'. *American Anthropology*, 7: 223–41.

Bongaarts, J. (1978), 'A framework for analyzing the proximate determinants of fertility'. *Population and Development Review*, 4(1): 105–32.

Brühl, D. (1989), *A terra era nossa vida: Armut und Familie in Nordost Brasilien*. Frankfurt: Verlag für Interkulturelle Kommunikatioin.

Caldwell, J. C. (1982), *Theory of Fertility Decline*. London: Academic Press.

Demography (1995), 'Special issue on The Family and Household Demography', *Demography*, 32(3).

de Oliviera, M. C. F. A. (1992), 'Family change and family process: implications for research in developing countries', in E. Berquó and P. Xenos (eds.), *Family Systems and Cultural Change*. Oxford: Clarendon, pp. 201–14.

de Vos, S. (1987), 'Latin American households in comparative perspective'. *Population Studies*, 42: 501–17.

Durham, E. R. (1991), 'Family and human reproduction', in E. Jelin (ed.), *Family, Household and Gender Relations in Latin America*. London: Kegan Paul International/UNESCO, pp. 40–63.

Evans, A. (1989), 'Gender issues in rural household economics', IDS Discussion Paper 254.

Fernandez, R. E. and Carvalho, J. A. M. (1986), 'A evolução da fecundidade no Brasil, período 1957–1979: aplicação da técnica dos filhos próprios para se estimar a fecundidade ano e ano.' *Revista brasileira do estudos de população*, 3(2): 67–86.

Flinn, M. W. (1981), *The European Demographic System, 1500–1820*. Brighton: Harvester.

Fonseca, C. (1991), 'Spouses, siblings and sex-linked bonding: a look at kinship organisation in a Brazilian slum', in E. Jelin (ed.), *Family, Household and Gender Relations in Latin America*. London: Kegan Paul International/UNESCO, pp. 133–60.

Goody, J. (1972), *Domestic Groups*. Reading, Mass.: Addison-Wesley.

Hajnal, J. (1965), 'European marriage patterns in perspective', in D. V. Glass and D. E. C. Eversley (eds.), *Population in History: Essays in Historical Demography*. London: Edward Arnold, pp. 101–43.

Hannerz, U. (1969), *Soulside: Inquiries into Ghetto Culture and Community*. New York: Columbia University Press.

Höhn, C. (1987), 'The family life cycle: needed extensions of the concept', in J. Bongarts, T. Burch, and K. Wachter (eds.), *Family Demography: Methods and their Applications*. Oxford: Clarendon, pp. 65–80.

Izzard, W. (1985), 'Migrants and mothers: case-studies from Botswana'. *Journal of Southern African Studies*, 11: 258–80.

Kabeer, N. (1991), 'Gender, production and well-being: rethinking the household economy'. IDS Discussion Paper 288.

Kaufmann, G. (1991), 'Family formation and fertility in a *favela* in Belo Horizonte, Brazil: an analysis of cultural and demographic influences'. D.Phil. thesis, Oxford University.

—— and Meekers, D. (1992), 'A reappraisal of the state of women and nuptiality in sub-Saharan Africa'. Working Paper 1992-23, Population Research Institute, Pennsylvania State University.

Keyfitz, N. (1987), 'Form and substance in family demography', in J. Bongaarts, T. Burch, and K. Wachter (eds.), *Family Demography: Methods and their Applications*. Oxford: Clarendon, pp. 1–16.

Kuper, A. (1987), 'The transformation of African marriage in South Africa', in *South Africa and the Anthropologist*. London: Routledge & Kegan Paul, pp. 134–48.

Laslett, P. (1972), 'Introduction: The history of the family', in P. Laslett and R. Wall (eds.), *Household and Family in Past Time: Comparative Studies in the Size and Structure of the Domestic Group over the Last Three Centuries in England, France, Serbia, Japan and Colonial North America, with Further Materials from Western Europe*. Cambridge: Cambridge University Press, pp. 1–89.

Lesthaeghe, R. (1992), 'The second demographic transition in Western countries: an interpretation'. IPD Working Paper, Brussels.

—— and Jolly, C. (1992), 'The start of the sub-Saharan African fertility transition: some answers and many questions'. IPD Working Paper 1992-4.

—— and Page, H. (1981), *Child Spacing in Tropical Africa: Traditions and Change*. London: Academic Press.

—— Kaufmann, G. L. and Meekers, D. (1989), 'The nuptiality regimes in sub-Saharan Africa', in R. Lesthaeghe (ed.), *Reproduction and Social Organization in Sub-Saharan Africa*. Berkeley: University of California Press, pp. 238–337.

Lockwood, M. (1995), 'Structure and function in the social demography of Africa', *Population and Development Review*, 21(1): 1–32.

Martine, G. (1975), *Formación de la Familia y Marginalid Urbana en Río de Janeiro*. Santiago: CELADE.

—— (1996), 'Brazil's recent fertility decline, 1965–95: a fresh look at key factors'. *Population and Development Review*, 22(1): 49–75.

Martinez-Alier, V. (1974), *Marriage, Class and Colour in Nineteenth Century Cuba: A Study of Racial Attitudes and Sexual Values in A Slave Society*. Cambridge: Cambridge University Press.

Merrick, T. W. and Berquó, E. (1983), *The Determinants of Brazil's Recent Rapid Decline in Fertility*, Committee on Population and Demography Report CM 22. Washington: National Academy Press.

Needham, R. (1971), 'Remarks on the analysis of kinship and marriage', in R. Needham (ed.), *Rethinking Kinship and Marriage*. London: Tavistock, pp. 1–34.

Patterson, O. (1982), 'Persistence, continuity, and change in the Jamaican working-class family'. *Journal of Family History*, 7(2): 135–61.

Prado, D. (1985), *O que é família*. São Paulo: Abril Cultural/Brasiliense.

Prinz, C. (1995), *Cohabiting, Married or Single: Portraying, Analysing and Modelling New Living Arrangements in the Changing Societies of Europe*. Aldershot: Avebury.

Robertson, A. F. (1991), *Beyond the Family: The Social Organization of Human Reproduction*. Cambridge: Polity.

Schneider, D. M. (1984), *A Critique of the Study of Kinship*. Ann Arbor: University of Michigan Press.

Smith, R. M. (1981), 'Fertility, economy and household structure in England over three centuries'. *Population and Development Review*, 7(4): 595–622.

Smith, R. T. (1956), *The Negro Family in British Guiana: Family Structure and Social Status in the Villages*. London: Routledge & Kegan Paul.

van de Walle, E. (1968), 'Marriage in African censuses and inquiries', in W. Brass *et al.* (eds.), *The Demography of Tropical Africa*. Princeton: Princeton University Press.

Wood, C. H. and de Carvalho, J. A. M. (1988), *The Demography of Inequality in Brazil*. Cambridge: Cambridge University Press.

Woortmann, K. (1987), *A família das mulheres*. Rio de Janeiro: Tempo Brasileiro.

Wrigley, E. A. (1981), 'Marriage, fertility and population growth in eighteenth century England', in R. B. Outhwaite (ed.), *Marriage and Society: Studies in the Social History of Marriage*. London: Europa, pp. 137–85.

——and Schofield, R. (1983), 'English population history from family reconstitution: summary results 1600–1799'. *Population Studies*, 37: 157–84.

Yanagisako, Silvia J. (1979) 'Family and household: the analysis of domestic groups', *Annual Review of Anthropology*, 8, 161–205.

6 Education, Fertility, and Child Survival: Unravelling the Links

JOHN CLELAND AND GEORGIA KAUFMANN

Introduction: The Achievements and Limits of Traditional Demographic Inquiries

It is widely accepted that education affects fertility and mortality. The education–mortality link has been enshrined in the UNDP's Human Development Index, which takes indices of both as key components of an overall level of development (UNDP 1990). Despite the statistical strength of these associations, however, the nature of the relationships is still far from perfectly understood.

The major purpose of this paper is to discuss the contributions that intensive methods of investigation, and particularly those of an anthropological nature, have made and can make to illuminate the effects of education on demographic outcomes. Nevertheless, it is prudent to precede this discussion by reviewing the knowledge that demographers have already assembled. More focused, smaller-scale investigations are best used in conjunction with a thorough understanding of the nature of the statistical evidence. As we shall see, the latter provides many clues to identify the more fruitful avenues to pursue.

There have been numerous reviews of the evidence concerning the relationship between parental education and child mortality, and an almost equal number on the topic of education and fertility. It is less common to compare and contrast the nature of the links between education and these two types of demographic outcome simultaneously. This is the approach adopted here.

Linear Relationship or Threshold Effects

One of the more astonishing features of the link between maternal schooling and child survival is its essentially linear relationship. There appears to be no threshold; for instance, the difference in mortality between the offspring of mothers with no schooling and those with lower primary schooling is often as great as the difference observed between offspring of mothers with lower- and upper primary school education. Typically, the risks of under-5

Table 6.1. Total Marital Fertility Rates in Four Countries, mid-1970s (%)

| Survey | Year | None | Wife's schooling | | |
			Incomplete primary	Complete primary	Secondary or higher
Colombia	1976	7.2	6.2	4.2	3.4
Jordan	1976	9.7	7.9	6.5	4.8
Kenya	1977	7.9	8.8	7.9	7.0
Pakistan	1975	7.2	6.8	6.9	5.5

Source: taken from Cleland and Rodriguez (1988).

mortality fall by some 2%–5% with each single year's increment in the length of mother's schooling (Cochrane *et al.* 1982). Thus, the link takes the form of a straightforward dose–response type of relationship.

In the case of fertility, however, there is a much wider diversity of relationships. While the fertility of women with secondary schooling is invariably lower than that of less educated women, few other simple generalizations can be made. In Latin America and the Arab states the relationship is typically monotonic, mimicking the mortality results. However, in Africa and many Asian countries, the highest levels of fertility may be found among the group with incomplete primary schooling. The results presented in Table 6.1 above taken from Cleland and Rodriguez (1988) illustrate this diversity.

There have been many attempts to account for this diversity of relationship in terms of proximate determinants. In those African and Asian countries where highest fertility is found in the intermediate educational categories, a relaxation of the traditional restraints of prolonged breastfeeding and postpartum sexual abstinence offers a partial explanation, but not a complete one (Singh *et al.* 1985); there must be other fertility-enhancing forces associated with modest exposure to schooling that remain uncaptured by standard demographic surveys. However, we can be fairly confident that these forces are non-volitional, because there is no evidence that wives in Africa or Asia with primary schooling *want* larger families or are less likely to use birth control than wives with no schooling.

Sensitivity to Context

The fact that the education–fertility relationship takes a variety of forms shows that it is sensitive to economic, cultural, or programme contexts. There is certainly corroborative evidence that programmatic factors must be taken into account in the interpretation of educational differentials in fertility. For instance, Entwistle and Mason (1985) demonstrated that, in economically poor countries, the dominant effect of education on cohort fertility is positive in the absence of a family planning programme but becomes negative in the presence of one. The general point can be elaborated with specific examples, albeit ones that run counter to Entwistle and Mason's results. In rural Java, in the mid-1970s the lowest fertility was found among the least educated (Freedman *et al.* 1981). The reason for this atypical pattern almost certainly concerns the nature of family planning services. Strong community pressure was placed on couples to adopt birth control, and it appears that this policy impinged with greatest force on the poor and uneducated.

Family planning programmes that offer generous compensation payments to couples willing to undergo sterilization or IUD insertion achieve a similar dilution, or even a reversal, of the expected education–fertility relationship. In Bangladesh, for instance, sterilization is much more prevalent among the least educated than among those couples with some schooling. The reason is well established. The cash payment is disproportionately attractive to the very poor, though there are no grounds for believing that couples sacrifice reproductive aspirations for financial benefit. The not-so-poor, and better educated, are more likely to use reversible methods, and hence the differences in fertility according to educational status are very modest (Cleland and Mauldin, 1991).

At this juncture, it is relevant to point out that high levels of adult literacy do not inevitably lead to low fertility. Consider the Philippines for instance. This is a country with exceptionally high levels of adult education, particularly for women (and an unusually high level of labour force participation by women); yet fertility in the late 1980s remained well above 4 births per woman, considerably higher than neighbouring Indonesia, where the educational attainment of the adult population is lower. Jordan provides another example. According to the most recent survey in 1990, 54% of ever-married women in the reproductive age span had received secondary or higher schooling, an impressive achievement compared with many other developing countries (Jordan Ministry of Health 1992). At the national level, however, the total fertility rate remained high at 5.6 births per woman and was only slightly lower—at 5.4 births—among couples where the wife had received secondary schooling. In both Jordan and the Philippines, there must be strong countervailing forces, presumably of a political or religious nature, that offset the normal, expected influence of schooling on reproductive performance.

Education should not be regarded as a context-free variable. The provision of education is usually associated with and determined by a host of other social, economic, and political factors. The various transformations of social development that are associated with the mass provision of education seem to result in a variety of predictable demographic outcomes. It is overly simplistic to assume that in each case the various processes and transformations interact in the same way and produce similar outcomes. As we can see in the Philippines and Jordan, cultural and political processes can re-direct demographic outcomes. Conversely, similar demographic outcomes may arise from different internal processes.

Does the education–mortality association exhibit a similar sensitivity to context and vulnerability to offsetting factors? More specifically, is the association conditioned by the quality and coverage of health services? The dominant theoretical stance on this issue is that the influence of personal characteristics, such as maternal education, on child welfare will attenuate in settings where good services are widely available (e.g. Palloni 1985; Rosenzweig and Schultz 1982). There is certainly some supporting evidence, but also many contrary examples where access to services appears to make little difference to educational differentials. (For a more detailed discussion, see Cleland and Van Ginneken 1989.) Perhaps the most telling analysis is that by Bicego and Boerma (1991), who find a stronger effect of maternal education on child survival in urban areas (where presumably health services are more widely accessible) than in rural areas.

We may conclude that the education–mortality relationship tends to be much more ubiquitous, invariate, and robust than does the education–fertility link. These characteristics are all the more surprising in view of the great diversity of school curricula and styles. In some countries, primary school teaching is performed in the national language and emphasis is placed on traditional values; in other settings, ex-colonial languages are used and the ethos of education is radical. Yet these huge variations in schooling styles appear to make little difference to the association between length of schooling and child survival.

Relationship to Stage of Demographic Transition

The relationship of educational differences in fertility to stage of demographic transition can be summarized succinctly. In pre-transitional societies these differences are very modest. Typically, only the tiny élite of couples with secondary or higher schooling record distinctively lower fertility. Among the great mass of the population with no schooling or a modest exposure to primary schooling, variations in reproductive levels are both small and, as we have already seen, erratic in nature. During the process of transition, there is typically, though not always, a divergence between educational strata; huge differences of up to three or four births per woman may emerge between upper and lower strata. However, as transition proceeds these gaps narrow again and eventually disappear.

This process has been documented most adequately in Latin America. In Colombia, for instance, marital fertility decline commenced in the early 1960s for women with completed primary schooling, in the late 1960s for those who failed to complete this level of schooling, and in the 1970s for women with no schooling (Rodriguez and Hobcraft 1980). More recently, Rodriguez and Aravena (1991), using survey data from both the World Fertility Survey (WFS) and the Demographic and Health Surveys (DHS), have further confirmed this process of diffusion from more to less educated strata. The largest declines in fertility during the late 1970s and 1980s were observed among the least educated strata, with the net result of a convergence in reproductive behaviour. The ephemeral nature of educational differentials in fertility carries major implications for the type of determinant that may be operative. A diffusion-of-innovation perspective appears much more plausible than a search for deep-seated and enduring institutional or economic factors that might account for the educational effect. It also opens up the question of whether education is itself merely a marker of other social processes that are also in operation.

Once again, examination of the education–mortality relationship over the course of demographic transition leads us to rather different conclusions. In Western Europe and North America, educational and social class differences in child mortality were modest at the end of the nineteenth century; they subsequently widened and then narrowed. Preston (1985) has attributed this sequence to the advent of a scientific basis for preventive and curative medicine in the early part of this century, which permitted better educated mothers to translate their skills into a health advantage for their children. The widespread declines in infant and child mortality actually preceded mass education.

In the Western experience, then, the education–mortality relationship varies over the course of transition in a similar way to that described above for fertility. However, the situation with regard to developing countries is different. Even at the very early stages of transition, large effects of parental education are observed. As overall mortality declines, the absolute size of educational differentials obviously diminishes but proportional or relative differences tend to remain more or less constant. For instance, the comparison by Cleland *et al.* (1992) of WFS and DHS data found no evidence of appreciable changes between the mid-1970s and mid-1980s in the relative risks of under-five mortality by the educational status of mothers. It is also true that, even in very low-mortality industrialized countries, social class and educational effects on health and mortality persist (e.g. Townsend and Davidson 1982).

The key conclusion is clear-cut. Whatever advantages education confers with regard to the health of children, they are persistent and continue to operate to some extent in highly literate, low-mortality settings. Conversely, the effect of education on fertility is much more transient.

Unadjusted and Adjusted Effects

Many demographic analysts have reassessed the effect of parental, and particularly maternal, education on child mortality and fertility after controlling for other socioeconomic factors that are themselves correlated with education. The aim is to isolate and quantify a 'pure' effect of education, purged of its obvious economic component. The results have been fairly consistent. With regard both to fertility and mortality, between one-third and one-half of the maternal educational effect can be attributed to the economic advantages enjoyed by more educated mothers. This is in line with the argument that education is an aspect of a series of social and economic processes. We need to examine more closely the flow of causality between income and education, and how the dynamics of this relationship in turn influence demographic behaviour.

Two specific results are of special theoretical importance. First, the link between the wife's education and fertility and contraceptive use cannot be attributed to employment. Indeed, employment outside the home appears to have surprisingly little bearing on reproductive patterns, once education is controlled (United Nations 1987). Thus, the commonly held thesis that education reduces fertility by raising the opportunity costs of childbearing can muster little empirical support. But again, this is a context-bound finding. Better-off, better-educated working women may be able to buy the child care that poorer, less well-educated working women cannot afford. The opportunity cost of children depends on factors other than work itself.

The second result concerns the relative effect of husband's and wife's educational status on demographic outcomes. Is our obsession with the education of women rather than men justified? There is of course a correlation between the educational attainment of spouses. The United Nations (1987) found a coefficient of 0.57 between years of schooling of husband and wife, as recorded in WFS surveys. When education was grouped in five categories, approximately half of all spouses belonged in the same category. However, this degree of collinearity is not so severe that it disallows attempts to isolate effects. The most powerful relevant analysis concerning mortality is that by Hobcraft *et al.* (1984). The general finding, averaged across many surveys, is that mother's schooling emerges as the more decisive influence. Even after controls for husband's education and other socioeconomic factors, one to three years of maternal schooling is associated with a 20% fall in childhood risks of dying, (the risks of dying between age one and five) while father's education (net of similar controls) has no effect. At higher educational levels, the influence of maternal schooling is about twice as large as that of father's schooling. The emphasis on the education of women is indeed vindicated.

In the case of fertility, similar but less emphatic results have been obtained. In the Arab states and the Caribbean, there appears to be little difference between the net effect of husbands' and wives' education. In Africa, Asia, and Latin America, however, maternal education emerges as the more decisive influence (Cleland and Rodriguez 1988).

Fertility-Specific Pathways

Through innumerable analyses of the proximate determinants of fertility, the behavioural pathways linking education to reproduction are well established. Educated women marry later and are more likely to use contraception within marriage than the less educated. More surprisingly, however, the educated do not appear to be more effective users of specific contraceptive methods (Moreno 1991); nor is their choice of methods strikingly different in most countries from that of the uneducated. In terms of family formation patterns, educated couples tend to start later and finish earlier, but birth-spacing patterns do not diverge much.

It is often assumed that the lower fertility of the more educated must reflect a lower desire or demand for children, suggesting the need for anthropological and other intensive studies into the utilities and costs of children. Although the fertility preference data collected in large demographic surveys have attracted much criticism, they should not be lightly dismissed. Over the last thirty years, survey information on desired family sizes and percentages wanting no more children have been broadly predictive of subsequent fertility trends. For instance, the earliest surveys in Asia and Latin America indicated that desired fertility was much lower than actual reproductive performance. As we now know, fertility has declined throughout both continents. Conversely, desired family sizes have always been much higher in Africa, and it is in this region that fertility still remains high. Indeed, demographers have a better record of predicting demographic change than anthropologists, few of whom anticipated the huge changes in family formation patterns that would engulf much of the developing world.[1]

The analysis of educational differentials in fertility preferences is fraught with difficulties. Age compositions differ and so do actual numbers of surviving children. Because fertility preferences are partly, and by no means wholly, rationalizations, straightforward comparisons may be misleading. It is thus advisable to control age and existing family size in analyses of desired fertility. When this precaution is taken, the general finding is that educational differentials, though often in the expected direction, are modest, and certainly much smaller than differences in fertility itself (Lightbourne 1987; Martin and Juarez 1993). This verdict is consistent with abundant evidence that the 'unmet need' for contraception and 'unwanted' childbearing is invariably greater among the less than the more educated sectors (Westoff and Ochoa 1991).

This finding has profound implications for anthropological and other more intensive studies. The question of overriding importance appears to be 'Why are the educated more likely to implement reproductive preferences?' rather than 'Why do educated couples want smaller numbers of children?' This perspective implies a focus on the determinants of effective reproductive decision-making, including such aspects as the domestic autonomy of women, interspousal communication, feelings of self-efficacy or instrumentality, attitudes towards birth control, and ability to access and utilize family planning services.

Mortality-Specific Pathways

While motivation for small family sizes has played a prominent role in discussions of the education–fertility relationship, this is not the case in discussions of mortality. Rather, it is implicitly or explicitly assumed that mothers of different educational backgrounds are equally committed to the health and survival of their children. The huge differences in mortality thus must spring from variations in the resources or skills that mothers are able to bring to the task of child welfare. Although some (e.g. Scrimshaw 1978; Das Gupta 1987; Simons 1993; Scheper-Hughes, 1992) have challenged the view that the strength of parental motivations to maximize child survival is always and necessarily high, there is little evidence to suggest that a modest exposure to schooling has an influence on maternal commitment to child survival. Education clearly does not affect discrimination in favour of sons over daughters (Weinberger and Heligman 1987). By extension, it is there-fore unlikely to influence maternal valuation of children in general.

WFS inquiries offered little scope for investigation of possible bio-medical or behavioural pathways linking education to the survival of children. The mediating effects of birth order, birth spacing, maternal age, and breastfeed-ing could be assessed but were found to be of little importance. Use of antenatal care, medical supervision of delivery, and immunization could also be examined; large educational differentials were usually found, parti-cularly with regard to antenatal and obstetric care, though it remains unclear how these divergences in behaviour could account for differences in child survival.

The advent of the Demographic and Health Survey (DHS), with its greater emphasis on morbidity and health care, allowed more proximate determinants to be assessed. Sufficient data have now been published to permit rather confident generalizations (e.g. Boerma *et al.* 1991). Childhood morbidity appears not to vary greatly according to the educational status of mothers. With airborne pathogens, this is perhaps not surprising because of the difficulties of prevention. With pathogens transmitted in a liquid or solid medium, however, the results are of more profound significance. The fact that diarrhoeal morbidity is equally common among children of more and less educated mothers suggests that domestic hygiene is not an important mechanism, though the possibility remains that differential reporting may mask genuine variations.

DHS results, in fact, reveal the existence of an educational effect on the treatment of childhood illnesses in most, though not all, surveys, Thus, the children of educated mothers with fever or respiratory infections are more likely to have been taken to a medical facility than the children of the less educated. In conclusion, the demographic evidence suggests that response to, and treatment of, infection may be a more important pathway than prevention of infection.

Implications

The most important implication of this brief resumé of the demographic evidence concerns child mortality. Despite huge variations in cultural and economic setting and in the nature and quality of educational systems, the strong link between a mother's schooling and the survival of her children persists. Given the very different types of schooling that abound, two major research agendas are opened up. We should be trying to uncover whether this effect is a universal consequence of the schooling experience, or of some near-universal process of selectivity that determines school enrolment and retention and thus leads to the apparently universal mortality outcomes. Additionally, we should continue to examine the contexts and natures of specific schooling experiences so as to try to extract the array of significant processes involved in schooling that determine mortality outcomes.

The implication with regard to fertility is different. Clearly, its relationship to education is more variable and context-specific and thus more obviously amenable to the traditional strengths of social anthropology. Moreover, as discussed earlier, reproductive goals, unlike child-survival goals, vary among cultures; their elucidation will require a more holistic understanding than can be obtained in standardized surveys. Anthropological approaches have much to offer in this area.

A further strong clue offered by the demographic evidence is that the interface between women and the outside world, in particular the world of modern health and family planning services, may be of critical importance. We need to know precisely what factors inhibit the less educated from seeking services and to what extent they receive a lower-quality service when they do attempt to access facilities. Does the experience of schooling inculcate an inner sense of confidence in dealing with the outside world, and superior knowledge and skills to manipulate these resources? To what extent does the social esteem accorded to the more educated facilitate effective health seeking?

Anthropology on the Effect of Education

One of the problems with demographic analysis, especially with large-scale surveys, is the difficulty in reading meaning into the statistical associations. In the preceding section the strong relationships between maternal education and infant mortality and fertility have been discussed. Demographic evidence shows that the more educated a woman is, the less likely her children will die, but 'we do not know why this should be so' (Ware 1984: 210). More specifically, Das Gupta (1990: 490) has shown that, despite the importance of maternal education, the clustering of deaths in some families results from the 'basic abilities and personality characteristics of the mother'. Caldwell (1979: 408) has also argued that the explanation for child mortality has to be sought in the reactions of women to infant illness, the decision-making process, and how this is affected by a variety of social and cultural conventions. The dilemma is that, although demography has demonstrated that there is a strong relationship between certain demographic outcomes and education, it cannot provide the contextual and cultural data that may be used to explain these relationships. Increasingly, demographers have looked to anthropology for the contextual explanation of these demographic patterns.

When anthropology and demography are employed to elucidate the patterns of reproductive behaviour, they work in a complementary fashion. The object of analysis is fairly straightforward, be it called fertility, offspring, or procreation. With respect to education, the complementarity of the two disciplines is less evident. For demographers, the fact of having completed x years of schooling, of being literate, is of significance. Yet anthropologists, inconveniently, have been addressing not what it is that education *does*, but rather what education *is*. The anthropology of education focuses on issues such as modes of thought of literate and non-literate people, educational institutions, and pupil–teacher relations (Goody 1977, 1986; Pelissier 1991; Willis 1977).

Both disciplines have similar assumptions about the transformatory power of education and/or literacy which have much in common with evolutionary social theories. The acquisition of learning is likened to an evolutionary development capable of transforming demographic regimes and society (Akinnaso 1981: 164; Goody 1977: 2–3; Street 1990: 6). Education is a factor associated with the processes of socioeconomic development. The mechanisms of this relationship are not well understood, but the fact of the relationship is not questioned. For demographers, used to notions such as the Demographic Transition, it is not alien to view social change as evolutionary. The alignment of the illiterate, uneducated, and un(der)developed against the literate, educated, and developed seems logical, given the strong statistical associations found within these categories.

For anthropologists, the evolutionary theme runs through the discussion on whether or not the acquisition of literacy transforms the mode of thinking of individuals or cultures (Pelissier 1991: 76–7). Lévy-Bruhl initiated the debate with *Les Fonctions mentales dans les sociétés inférieures* in 1910. He argued that 'primitive mentality' was qualitatively different from modern mentality. It was not logical but 'pre-logical'. Primitive thinkers were not capable of abstract thought, only concrete thought. This set the stage for the

Great Divide debate. The supporters of Lévy-Bruhl argued that there is a marked difference between 'us' and 'them'. Others, e.g. Evans-Pritchard and Levi-Strauss, argued that there is a continuum, that modes of thinking do not vary. For Levi-Strauss, culture, the outcome of thinking, arises out of the process that all societies are occupied in, namely thinking a social order into being. Culture is the thought classification of the natural world. In other words, culture is social knowledge shared between people. Communication is an essential aspect of culture, and one that is transformed by literacy. But the absence of literacy does not mean impaired mental activity (Street 1993: 11). Whether there is a continuum or divide between oral and literate cultures, the difference is, in either view, critical (Goody 1977: 10).

The demographic dilemma is to ascertain whether it is the knowledge or the thought mode—or a mixture of both—of 'educated' people that determines shifts in social behaviour that then alter demographic behaviour. For demographers, like anthropologists, it is therefore necessary to understand what is entailed by the educative process that affects behaviour. Recent changes in anthropological approaches to the study of literacy and education have moved the emphasis away from the Great Divide debate, which distinguished between oral and literate cultures, to focus on knowledge and power (Street 1990: 5; 1993: 7). Education is recognized to be the 'social processes involved in instructing, acquiring and transforming knowledge' (Pelissier 1991: 75). If culture is constituted of the way we think about the world, i.e. knowledge, then access to, and control of, that knowledge is central. This is not the place to delve into discourse theory, but the concentration on issues of power and knowledge that has followed from Foucault bears on the question of what is it about education that changes people's behaviour.

The moment power enters into the equation, the potential for a simple resolution to the problem evaporates. In the past it was easier: 'educationalists, linguists and psychologists conceptualised literacy as a universal constant whose acquisition... will lead to higher cognitive skills, to improved logical thinking, to critical inquiry, and to self-conscious reflection' (Street 1993: 11).

The recognition that education may be a process that unfolds in the web of social relationships disallows the possibility of such a simplistic causal outcome. It is not enough to know that an individual has been to school, but becomes a question of what school, what knowledge, and for what purpose (Willis 1977; Freire 1970, 1992). Schooling opens doors to new discourses, new ways of viewing the world. The new vista is not necessarily less constricted. For instance, we know that Koranic schooling in sub-Saharan Africa does not have the same effect on demographic outcomes as 'Western' schooling. The learning process involved in schooling is about participating in a community of practice (Lavé and Wenger 1991). In this sense, schooling opens doors to other cultural communities.

If anthropologists have the key to understanding what it is about education that is significant to the demographic process, then there is a slight dilemma for the interested demographer. Is it really necessary to dive into the recesses of post-modern, post-structuralist discourse theory, or is there another way to seek an answer? As Giles Pison once wrote, it is a matter of asking the right question. What demographers need to learn from anthropologists is some more of the right questions about education. For example, when Caldwell (1979: 412) observed that better educated, younger women had a greater chance of making decisions independently of their affinal kin, he was touching on the same issues, involving the nexus between knowledge, power, and self-determination. Demographers know that education changes behaviour; anthropologists know that schooling changes the cognitive and social world of individuals. Demographers need therefore to harness the meaning-orientated investigative techniques of anthropologists in order to resolve their own set of questions. Anthropologists, alone, will not ask the demographers' questions.[2]

Investigating Education Anthropologically

A recent study that attempted to unravel the effect of education on economic development in Kenya and Tanzania posited three hypotheses for why people have higher incomes if they have been educated (Knight and Sabot 1990: 5). First, the human capital theory argues that education changes people, improves their cognitive skills, and makes them more able. Second, the screening theory advocates that people who succeed in getting educated are more able to begin with, and therefore do better in life in general. Third, the credentialist theory posits that it is the fact of having been to school, the credential, that wins people better jobs. The economists conducting the study 'measured' all these factors, and analysed and modelled the results to show that it was the acquisition of cognitive skills that was most significant (Knight and Sabot 1990: 19). Whilst the statistical evidence in favour of cognitive skills might be conclusive, this study does not explain in a satisfactory manner what is meant by cognitive skills. Unpacking the meaning of such concepts requires a systematic, ethnographic approach.

If the task of the anthropologist is to comprehend the knowledge that demographic actors learn, and the way in which they use it, a contextualized understanding of that knowledge is necessary. This search for meaning is best conducted using anthropological techniques. In its classic form, participant observation, the anthropological method par excellence, is conducted over a period of a year or more of low-key, constant observation and interviewing. Such a methodology, like a survey, is a snapshot, however detailed, of one period of ethnographic time. Anthropology produces static pictures, and it can not easily accommodate change and process (Woods 1985: 54).

In pursuit of the meaning of education, it is not sufficient to conduct participant observation without selecting aspects of social behaviour and attitudes to form the focus of study. It seems that the central question to be asked is whether or not educated people have different knowledge or beliefs, think in different ways, or act differently (or some combination of all three). What is it that education teaches? The issues are, therefore, of attitude and behaviour.

Anthropological research is well suited to the task of comprehending the attitudes and beliefs that may guide behaviour. While surveys can elicit palatable, computer-digestible material, the answers to attitudinal questions are often normative and formalized (Kaufmann 1991: 52). The manner of anthropological inquiry, although producing less measurable results, facilitates the extraction of meaningful responses.

A number of explicitly anthropological or similar small intensive studies have compared the health knowledge of educated and uneducated mothers. The expectation is not that the school curriculum directly imparts relevant knowledge that is then retained for a decade or more. It is instead that those who have had the experience of schooling may be more exposed to health messages in adulthood and more able to comprehend them. However plausible this connection may appear, the balance of evidence is negative, at least in South Asia (Lindenbaum *et al.* 1985; Zeitlyn and Islam 1993; Caldwell *et al.* 1983; Basu 1993). Mothers with primary schooling hold views about disease aetiology and prevention similar to those of uneducated mothers. Thus, the behavioural changes that presumably underlie the education–child survival link do not appear to have a cognitive origin. McClain (1977) has discussed this relationship between cognitive and behavioural change. Health beliefs, it is argued, may be core items of cultures that are resistant to change. Further, the theory behind allopathic medicine is not readily accessible, even to educated persons. Yet allopathic services and treatments are demonstrably superior in at least some regards. Hence educated persons, perhaps because of a greater social identification with modern institutions, may be particularly likely to use modern services, without necessarily understanding their aetiological principles.

One of the traumas of fieldwork is being offered potentially harmful food or drink. In 1992 there was a cholera scare in Brazil. People responded to the threat of contaminated water by renewed hygiene measures. Hygiene, however, is culturally conceived. It is a custom among low-income but cleanliness-conscious people always to rinse a glass or plate in running water before filling it, still wet. In terms of avoiding cholera, this is a disastrous practice. It seems that the more educated the woman, the more likely she is to adopt such a practice, and the more effort she will make to be 'clean', when there is an imminent threat of cholera. Similarly, women will argue that, as boiling water kills germs, so does freezing it; the same logic is applied incorrectly to different processes. The women have learnt that water needs to be made harmless for consumption (by altered status, hence freezing is equated with boiling), and that water cleans. The jump they have not made or been taught is that 'cleaning' with water can kill. Both these examples illustrate how knowledge, once acquired, is used, misused, and reinterpreted.

There is increasing interest in the question of female autonomy. It is argued that female education increases levels of female autonomy, which may affect behaviour. In 1988, one of the authors of this paper conducted a microdemographic survey in Brazil interviewing women who had given birth the previous year (Kaufmann 1991). It was found that half of the married women had studied beyond fourth grade, while less than a third of the single and cohabiting women had. The married women were not only better educated, but also more likely to be working, to share higher household incomes, and in most measures to be more successful than the unmarried women. It is not obvious how the measurable variables relate to female empowerment. Is a more educated, married woman more or less empowered than a single woman? Is a less educated, single woman more or less autonomous than a married woman? The author also conducted participant observation in the same community, alongside the survey. Rather than collecting data in one-off interviews, she repeatedly visited specific respondents and transformed them into informants. Questions about aspirations and beliefs are more likely to be answered truthfully in the context of an informal visit, over a cup of coffee, than in a formal interview situation. The data thus become contextualized and richer; from the information gathered this way, it becomes possible to interpret the quantitative associations. In this instance, contrary to the findings of Knight and Sabot, the screening hypothesis seems most plausible. The characteristics of individual women push them along specific life trajectories of varying degrees of success. The women who have the ability to apply themselves to schooling are also the ones most likely to find employment, to marry, and to contracept more effectively. By contextualizing the data, education ceases to be a determining influence but becomes a manifestation of other processes of self-betterment in the women's lives. Those women who seek or seize empowerment or autonomy are those who get educated.

The problem for anthropologists is the need to unravel the contextual tangle, while still looking for further links. The variable that determine the level of educational attainment probably impinge directly on demographic behaviour as well.

This issue of domestic empowerment forms the central hypothesis of one of the few anthropological studies that has been devoted to an elucidation of the education–child survival link (Zeitlyn and Islam 1993). A total of 50 rural and 50 urban Bangladeshi families—equally divided between those with an educated or uneducated mother—were studied by extended participant observation and by questionnaire methods. Contrary to expectations, the results suggested that educated mothers were generally less autonomous than their uneducated counterparts. For instance, they claimed less control over the management of vegetable plots and over decisions regarding the care of sick children or the purchase of medicines. They were also more likely to observe purdah, or seclusion.

The explanation given by Zeitlyn and Islam is that, in societies with a long tradition of religious literacy, the experience of schooling may reinforce, rather than challenge, religious values. These values support women's sub-ordination within the family and seclusion from public life. In other words, one of the main and more lasting effects of schooling in Bangladesh, and perhaps in other Islamic societies, is greater familiarity with and internaliza-tion of mainstream values and institutions. This is not an isolated finding. In Pakistan, for instance, Shah and Bulatao (1981) found that conformity to Islamic standards of dress was strongest among women with primary school-ing. Clearly, the notion that there is a linear relationship between length of schooling and degree of modernity or Westernization is a gross over-sim-plification. Furthermore, extreme poverty, associated with a total lack of schooling, may represent a forced form of emancipation from the dictates of female deference and respectability. In Bangladesh, poverty may put pres-sure on women to disregard the system of purdah and to seek paid employ-ment outside the homestead. It is only the more wealthy households, where women are more likely to be educated, that can afford to maintain purdah.

While the Zeitlyn–Islam study provides little support for the conventional assumption that education enhances autonomy and power, it is clear from their analysis that educated persons are accorded considerable respect. Exactly the same impression emerges from another anthropological study in North India (Jeffery and Jeffery 1996). Particularly among the Jats, education was ascribed a considerable value in its own right. Uneducated persons were defensive about their inability to read and write and frequently commented that their lack of schooling represented a lasting damage. Despite the obvious esteem attached to education in this North Indian community, Jeffery and Jeffery, like Zeitlyn and Islam, found little evidence that women's education resulted in empowerment. In matters of reproduct-ive decision-making, control of household resources, or choice of a marriage partner, there appeared to be little divergence between uneducated and educated women. The main reason advanced in the analysis is that women, educated or not, neither own productive property nor control significant sources of income. The potentially empowering effects of education wither in the face of this structural powerlessness. A further reason may be much more context-specific. The very concept of autonomy carried connotations of immodesty or shamelessness when applied to women. Far from finding autonomy an attractive proposition, even educated women regarded it as frightening.

These two examples illustrate the point that the process of schooling has varying effects and meaning in different contexts. In these instances education seems to operate as a desirable asset that increases a woman's wifely value within the context of marriage. In other words it reinforces a tradition rather than changes it.

Classic long-term participant observation also provides a wealth of data on social networks and information flows. With regard to educational achievement, this might not at first sight seem significant. If the argument is that educated mothers make better decisions, then close observation will enable their decision-making processes to be tracked. It is only through such observation that it will be possible to deduce the effect of education on daily tasks and practices that constitute the determinants of some demographic outcomes. In the cases of fertility and contraceptive practice, the correlation with education is strong. But the content of that correlation is unclear unless directly observed. The fact that a woman says she takes the pill in a certain way does not necessarily mean that she does. Repeated informal interviews might lead to better understanding of possible discrepancies between self-reports and actual behaviour.

What is difficult to ascertain is the manner in which education may affect such vital practices as information networking, the use of public services, and the ability in general to manipulate the social system. As we noted above, the education differential in mortality outcomes persists even when services are widely available (Bicego and Boerma 1991). We also argued above that education permitted an entry into other discourses. What is unclear is whether or not this is empowering. Targeted monitoring of the behaviour of people around medical services might yield fascinating results. Health services are often protected by complex bureaucracies and inconvenient queuing systems that only the most desperate and most capable succeed in negotiating. It is all too easy for the illiterate to be put off by such threatening systems. Additionally, using medical systems well, and knowing which clinics open when and which provide free treatment or prescriptions and so on, requires networking and cognitive abilities which may be enhanced by education. The skills and determination required in many Third World settings to access adequate services are not inconsiderable (Kaufmann 1993: 11; Nations and Rebhun 1988: 153–7).

There is abundant evidence from large-scale demographic surveys that the education of the mother is a powerful predictor of the use of both preventive and curative services. Moreover, the educated may receive higher-quality treatment because they can command more respect from providers and because they can communicate more fluently and more cogently than the uneducated. Maclean (1974) demonstrated that literate patients received better treatment at government hospitals and health centres, particularly in the form of more specific diagnoses. Using the technique of the 'bogus' client, the study by Schuler *et al.* (1985) vividly demonstrates the arrogance and abuse that poor, illiterate visitors to family planning clinics may experience. Clinic staff had a low opinion of the intelligence of uneducated clients and made little attempt to understand their needs. The rapidly growing literature on the quality of client–provider transactions indicates that these exchanges typically fall well short of expected standards of interpersonal care (Simmons and Phillips 1992). Most such studies have not disaggregated the results by the social distance between provider and client in terms of education or socioeconomic status, but it is reasonable to expect that the greater the distance, the lower will be the quality of interchanges.

In a recent study, which is in many ways a pioneering one, Joshi (1994) tested the ability of mothers of different educational levels to report to doctors about the health of their children. The fluency of these reports was assessed by counting the number of idea units presented in the first 90 seconds of the interchange with the doctor and dividing this number by the number of prompts that the doctor had to use. A second more subjective test was used, whereby the doctor, who was unaware of the educational status of mothers, rated the conversation in terms of confidence and communicative adequacy. The results showed that education in this semi-urban Nepalese community led to enhanced linguistic abilities, which in turn resulted in a greater ability to communicate fluently and convincingly with a doctor.

Anthropologists have developed other techniques which can be applied more specifically to behaviour, namely time allocation studies, spot sampling, minute-by-minute observation, and continuous monitoring. These methods offer no utility in uncovering beliefs and attitudes but can expose contradictions and concordances between ideas and practice.

The assumption that maternal education improves child-care practices and the use of medical services can be tested by direct observation (Das Gupta 1990: 503). To ascertain whether child-care practices really are different, a researcher might choose to adopt continuous monitoring. This approach generates masses of data, and can be structured in minute-by-minute observation styles or by activities and chronologies (Bernard 1988: 271–6). Although this method is activity-based, there are problems of recording when more than one activity is taking place. This may be crucial in terms of child care. The data yielded from such intense observation, especially if the observed are accustomed to the observers and behave naturally, can be used to illustrate the dynamics of the relationship between education and child care, and education and mortality.

A less intensive approach is spot sampling with time allocation. With this method the researcher turns up at randomly selected times and places and records what people are doing at the moment of meeting. By making enough visits, the researcher can calculate the percentage of times that people are observed to be engaged in specific activities, and deduce from that the percentage of time that they spend on those activities altogether (Bernard 1988: 280–2). For women engaged in child care, which can be a fairly constant activity, this might well produce little useful data. What such methods do provide, however, is good overview of what it is that people do differently.

Joshi (1994) used the spot observation method in the Nepal study on a sub-sample of households. These observations, carried out over a 12-month period, revealed a significant difference in time allocation for child care between educated and uneducated mothers, despite the fact that the total number of household members were closely similar for the two groups. Unschooled mothers contributed 49% of total child-care time, compared with 62% among schooled mothers.

Perhaps more important than the quantity of mother's time devoted to child care is its quality. Levine has advanced the thesis that the demographic transition is accompanied by, and perhaps partly powered by, profound changes in the nature of the mother–child relationship (Levine *et al.* 1991, Levine 1993). In traditional agrarian societies, the dominant pattern of mothering may be characterized by lengthy physical contact but by low intensity, which permits the mother to continue with other tasks. This style tends to produce undemanding and compliant children. By contrast, the more modern style of mothering involves less physical contact but a much higher level of verbal and visual contact, which produces more active and assertive children. The possible implications for health and survival are that a 'modern' mother may be more likely to notice distress in her child and that the child itself is more socialized to make its needs known. Speed of reaction to childhood illnesses may be critical in determining length of illness and case fatality.

Scheper-Hughes's (1992) devastating account of the selective neglect practised by impoverished women in the North-east of Brazil underlines the applicability of Levine's thesis. The poor women in the Scheper-Hughes study enable their children's deaths through lack of intervention and a re-interpretation of their malnourished listlessness as inevitable lifelessness.

The main empirical evidence that maternal education may be an important determinant of the shift from passive to more active styles of mothering comes from a study in Mexico (Levine *et al.* 1991). Detailed observation revealed that educated mothers were much more likely to interact visually and verbally with children between the age of 5 and 15 months. Having internalized in early life the roles of teacher and pupil, educated mothers were acting as teachers to their children, and thus forming a new type of relationship based on reciprocal verbal interactions.

Future Directions

As we have seen, both demographers and anthropologists have made major contributions towards a better understanding of the relationships between parental schooling and demographic outcomes in the last fifteen years. In this final section, we will attempt to identify the most promising avenues for future research, recognizing that both quantitative and less structured approaches will play valuable roles.

One obvious priority, in which demographers and anthropologists can contribute equally, is to achieve a better understanding of the determinants of school enrolment and retention, a topic that has been neglected by demographers though not by anthropologists. If indeed length of exposure to formal schooling is a major predictor of demographic behaviour in adulthood, then we need to know why this exposure varies so much between individuals, communities, and societies. Large data sets, such as the DHS inquiries, permit certain types of analysis. The influence of income, number of siblings, birth order, sex, household characteristics, and proximity to the nearest school can be assessed (e.g. Lloyd and Gage-Brandon 1992). The contribution of anthropologists is the classic one of promoting better understanding of the social meaning of education in different cultures, in a way that will illuminate the statistical results (e.g. Lindenbaum 1991).

With regard to more specific links, we need to recognize at the outset that research on mortality and fertility is circumscribed in different ways. The main behavioural determinants of fertility—coitus and contraception—cannot be directly observed. The bedroom door is closed, even to anthropologists. Conversely, many of the behavioural pathways that may link parental schooling to child survival are amenable to observation, for instance time and food allocation within households, styles of mother–child interaction, and domestic hygienic practices. Thus, the skills of the anthropologist as an observer—either using highly structured techniques or in a more informal participant mode—can be more readily harnessed for mortality-related than for fertility-related research.

Of necessity, then, the intensive study of fertility will have to concentrate largely on values, attitudes, and beliefs. There is, however, one key exception that brings together fertility and mortality concerns and is open to observation. This exception concerns the study of interactions between health or family planning providers and clients. There are good *a priori* reasons, and some empirical evidence, to suggest that the better educated are able to extract and implement a higher quality of service than the less educated. Such differentials in treatment may go some way to explaining why there are such wide divergences in service utilization between educational strata. In the family planning literature there is much rhetoric about quality of care, but so far there have been few attempts to document in detail what happens to different types of women when they enter a family planning (or health) clinic. This is surely a priority area for future research, one that lies well beyond the traditional domain of the demographer but well within the scope of the anthropologist.

A tentative conclusion drawn earlier in this paper is that anthropological investigation of values and attitudes towards family size and fertility regulation may prove to be more fruitful than parallel research on child survival. The main reason for this conclusion is that fertility behaviour appears to be more sensitive to context, and connections to education more variable, than is the case with mortality. We already know (with the obvious exception of education that is purely religious in purpose) that the effect of schooling on child survival is broadly constant. The work of Levine offers one clue in the search for some subtle, yet near-universal, consequence of exposure to schooling. He has adduced evidence that educated mothers think in different ways than the uneducated. Specifically, they are more able to use decontextualized language. Some studies have shown that education opens people to other discourses and, with that, to new cognitive skills (Pelissier 1991:80). However, it remains to be demonstrated how this difference could lead to such a wide divergence in demographic outcomes. What anthropologists can offer demographers in the understanding of mortality is clarification about how thinking and decision-making is altered by education. Decision-making in particular is affected by the social status of individuals, and, as we have seen in India, education can affect women's status in surprising ways.

Further clues may come from social psychology rather than anthropology. It is possible that a modest exposure to formal education, in addition to influencing powers of conceptualization, may indicate a greater sense of instrumentality or self-efficacy. In societies where women have little structural power and where strong traditions of female subordination exist, any such change might not be readily apparent in observable behaviour but yet might underlie both fertility regulation and child survival behaviours. Social psychologists have articulated both the concepts and the measures that are relevant for further investigation of this topic (see Simons 1993 for a review).

Finally, we should consider whether the content of large-scale standardized survey research in the demographic tradition can be expanded in ways that will permit further exploration of education–fertility–mortality linkages. The possibilities are rather limited. Clearly, observations of behaviour are impossible to accommodate and it is doubtful whether modes of thought or the concept of instrumentality could or should be measured in such surveys. On the measurement of women's autonomy and values that may intervene between schooling and demographic outcomes (such as religiosity or individualism), there are conflicting views between disciplines. Anthropologists tend to scorn attempts to quantify such complex concepts through standardized instruments, particularly if they are applied cross-culturally; demographers may be less sceptical but have shown little inclination to incorporate these types of measure into their studies.

When demographers do stray from the relatively straightforward and descriptive variables to which they are so wedded, it is by no means certain that they will reach the same conclusions as anthropologists. This point is well illustrated by recent work on the relationships among maternal education, autonomy, and fertility behaviour in Bangladesh. As already discussed, several anthropological studies in that country have concluded that education has little impact on autonomy. Analyses based on the 1989 Bangladesh Fertility Survey, however, give very different indications (Cleland *et al.* 1993). In that survey, two dimensions of autonomy were measured in an admittedly simple-minded manner. Geographical mobility was measured by asking women whether or not they could do certain things alone (i.e. unaccompanied), such as visit a health centre or go outside the village. Domestic autonomy was measured by asking whether specified decisions (such as type of food to be purchased or education of children) were taken by her alone, by the husband alone, or by both jointly. Maternal education proved to be a strong predictor of both dimensions in the expected direction. Furthermore, mobility and domestic decision-making autonomy were themselves powerful predictors of contraceptive use and fertility. Whom should we then believe?

Notes

1. Some anthropologists predicted a convergence of familial forms on the nuclear family (Goode 1963), but few anthropologists or demographers (if any) envisaged the increased nuclearization to single parenthood that is now rapidly spreading.
2. The lack of interest among anthropologists in the effect of education on social behaviour is quite stark. Almost nothing pertinent to this paper could be gleaned from over a decade of the *Anthropological and Education Quarterly*. A history of educational anthropology demonstrates the lack of shared interest (Eddy 1985).

References

Akinnaso, F. N. (1981), 'The consequences of literacy in pragmatic and theoretical perspectives'. *Anthropological and Education Quarterly*, 12(3): 163–200.

Basu, A. (1993), 'Maternal education and childhood mortality: the status of women as a "proximate" proximate determinant', in L. Visaria, J. Simons, and P. Berman (eds.), *Maternal Education and Child Survival: Pathways and Evidence*. Ahmedabad: Gujerat Institute of Development Research.

Bernard, H. R. (1988), *Research Methods in Cultural Anthropology*. Newbury Park, Calif.: Sage.

Bicego, G. and Boerma, T. (1991), 'Maternal education and child survival: a comparative analysis of DHS data', in *Proceedings of the Demographic and Health Surveys World Conference*, i. Columbia, md: IRD/Macro Int. Inc., pp. 177–204.

Boerma, T., Summerfelt, A., and Rutstein, S. (1991), 'Childhood morbidity and treatment patterns'. *DHS Comparative Studies*, no. 4.

Caldwell, J. C. (1979), 'Education as a factor in mortality decline: an examination of Nigerian data'. *Population Studies*, 33(3): 395–413.

——Reddy, P. H., and Caldwell, P. (1983), 'The social component of mortality decline: an investigation in India employing alternative methodologies'. *Population Studies*, 37: 185–205.

Cleland, J. and Mauldin, W. P. (1991), 'The promotion of family planning by financial payments: the case of Bangladesh'. *Studies in Family Planning*, 22: 1–18.

—— and Rodriguez, G. (1988), 'The effects of parental education on marital fertility in developing countries'. *Population Studies*, 42: 419–42.

—— and Van Ginneken, J. (1989), 'Maternal education and child survival in developing countries: the search for pathways of influences'. *Social Science and Medicine*, 27: 1357–60.

—— Bicego, G., and Fegan, G. (1992), 'Socioeconomic inequalities in childhood mortality: the 1970s to the 1980s'. *Health Transition Review*, 2: 1–18.

—— Kamal, N., and Sloggett, A. (1993), 'Links between fertility regulation and the education and autonomy of women in Bangladesh'. Unpublished paper, Centre for Population Studies, London School of Hygiene and Tropical Medicine.

Cochrane S., O'Hara, D., and Leslie, J. (1982), 'The effects of education on health', World Bank State Working Paper no. 405. Washington: World Bank.

Das Gupta, M. (1987), 'Selective discrimination against female children in rural Punjab'. *Population and Development Review*, 13: 77–100.

—— (1990), 'Death clustering, mother's education and the determinants of child mortality in rural Punjab, India'. *Population Studies*, 44(3): 489–505.

Eddy, E. M. (1985), 'Theory, research and application in educational anthropology'. *Anthropological and Education Quarterly*, 16(2): 83–104.

Entwistle, B. and Mason, W. M. (1985), 'Multilevel effects of socioeconomic development and family planning programs on children everborn'. *American Journal of Sociology*, 91: 616–49.

Freedman, R., Khoo, S-E., and Supraptilah, B. (1981), 'Use of modern contraceptives in Indonesia: a challenge to conventional wisdom'. *International Family Planning Perspectives*, 7: 3–15.

Freire, P. (1970), *Pedagogia do Oprimido*. São Paulo: Paz e Terra.

—— (1992), *Pedagogia da Esperança: Um reencontro com a Pedagogia do oprimido*. São Paulo: Paz e Terra.

Goode, W. J. (1963), *World Revolution and Family Patterns*. New York: Free Press.

Goody, J. (1977), *The Domestication of the Savage Mind*. Cambridge: Cambridge University Press.

—— (1986), *The Logic of Writing and the Organisation of Society*. Cambridge: Cambridge University Press.

Hobcraft, J., McDonald, J., and Rutstein, S. (1984), 'Socioeconomic factors in infant and child mortality: a cross national comparison'. *Population Studies*, 38: 193–223.

Jeffery, R. and Jeffery, P. (1996), 'Jats and sheikhs in Bijnor: education, women's autonomy and fertility outcomes', in R. Jeffery and A. M. Basu (ed.) *Girls' Education, Women's Autonomy and Fertility Change in South Asia*. New Delhi: Sage.

Jordan Ministry of Health (1992), *Jordan Population and Family Health Survey*. Amman: Department of Statistics.

Joshi, A. R. (1994), 'Maternal schooling and child health; preliminary analysis of the interviewing mechanisms in Nepal'. *Health Transition Review*, 4: 1–28.

Kaufmann, G. (1991), 'Family formation and fertility in a favela in Belo Horizonte, Brazil: an analysis of cultural and demographic influences'. Unpublished D.Phil. thesis, Oxford University.

—— (1993), 'Family planning in urban Brazil: gaps between policy and practice'. IDS Discussion Paper no. 329, Brighton.

Knight, J. B. and Sabot, R. H. (1990), *Education, Productivity and Inequality: The East African Natural Experiment.* Oxford: Oxford University Press.

Lavé, J. and Wenger, E. (1991), *Situated Learning: Legitimate Peripheral Participation.* Cambridge: Cambridge University Press.

Levine, R. (1993), 'Effects of schooling on mother–infant interactions: the implications for child survival and development', in L. Visaria, J. Simons, and P. Berman (eds.), *Maternal Education and Child Survival: Pathways and Evidence.* Ahmedabad: Gujerat Institute of Development Research.

— — Levine, S., Richman, A., Uribe, F., Correa, C., and Miller, P. (1991), 'Women's schooling and child care in the demographic transition: a Mexican case study'. *Population and Development Review,* 17: 459–96.

Levy-Brohl, L. (1910), *Fonctions mentales dans les sociétés inférieures.* English translation by L. A. Clare (1971), *How Natives Think,* New York: Arno Press.

Lightbourne, R. (1987), 'Reproductive preferences and behaviour', in J. Cleland and C. Scott (eds.), *The World Fertility Survey: An Assessment.* Oxford: Oxford University Press.

Lindenbaum, S. (1991), 'Maternal education and health care processes in Bangladesh: the health and hygiene of the middle classes', in J. Caldwell *et al.* (eds.), *What We Know about Health Transition,* i. Canberra: Australian National University, pp. 425–40.

— — Chakraborty, M., and Elias, M. (1985), 'The influence of maternal education on infant and child mortality in Bangladesh', Special Publication no. 23. Dhaka: International Centre for Diarrhoeal Disease Research, Bangladesh.

Lloyd, C. and Gage-Brandon, A. (1992), 'Does sibsize matter? The implications of family size for children's education in Ghana', in C. Lloyd (ed.), *Fertility, Family Size and Structure; Implications for Families and Children.* New York: Population Council.

Maclean, U. (1974), *Magical Medicine: A Nigerian Case Study.* London: Penguin.

McClain, C. (1977), 'Adaptation in health behaviour: modern and traditional medicine in a West Mexican community'. *Social Science and Medicine,* 11: 341–7.

Martin, T. C. and Juarez, F. (1993), 'Women's education and fertility in Latin America: exploring the significance of education for women's lives'. Paper presented at General Population Conference, Montreal.

Moreno, L. (1991), 'Differentials in contraceptive failure rates in developing countries: results from demographic and health surveys', in *Proceedings of Demographic and Health Surveys World Conference,* i. Columbia, Md: IRD/MACRO Int. Inc., pp. 695–786.

Nations, M. and Rebhun, L. A. (1988), 'Angels with wet wings won't fly: maternal sentiment in Brazil and the image of neglect'. *Culture, Medicine and Psychiatry,* 12: 141–200.

Palloni, A. (1985), 'Health conditions in Latin America and policies for mortality change', in J. Vallin and A. Lopez (eds.), *Health Policy, Social Policy and Mortality Prospects.* Liege: Ordina.

Pelissier, C. (1991), 'The anthropology of teaching and learning'. *Annual Review of Anthropology,* 20: 75–95.

Preston, S. (1985), 'Resources, knowledge and child mortality: a comparison of the US in the late nineteenth century and developing countries today', in *Proceedings of the International Population Conference, Florence 1985*, iv. Liège: IUSSP, pp. 373–88.

Rodriguez, G. and Aravena, R. (1991), 'Socio-economic factors and the transition to low fertility in less developed countries', in *Proceedings of the Demographic and Health Surveys World Conference* i. Columbia, Md: IRD/Macro Int. Inc. pp. 39–72.

—— and Hobcraft, J. (1980), 'Illustrative analysis: life table analysis of birth intervals in Colombia', WFS Scientific Report no. 16. Voorburg, Netherlands: International Statistical Institute.

Rosenzweig M. and Shultz, T. P. (1982), 'Child mortality and fertility in Colombia: individual and community effects'. *Health Policy and Education*, 2: 305.

Scheper-Hughes, N. (1992), *Death without Weeping: The Violence of Everyday Life in Brazil*. Berkeley: University of California Press.

Schuler, S. R., McIntosh, E. N., Goldstein, M. C., and Pande, B. R. (1985), 'Barriers to effective family planning in Nepal'. *Studies in Family Planning*, 16: 260–70.

Scrimshaw, S. (1978), 'Cultural values and behaviours related to population change'. *Population and Development Review*, 3: 336.

Shah, N. and Bulatao, R. (1981), 'Purdah and family planning in Pakistan'. *International Family Planning Perspectives*, 7: 32–6.

Simmons, R. and Phillips, J. (1992), 'The proximate operational determinants of fertility regulation behaviour', in J. Phillips and J. Ross (eds.), *Family Planning Programmes and Fertility*. Oxford: Oxford University Press.

Simons, J. (1993), 'Components of cultural variation in the mother's contribution to child survival', in L. Visaria, J. Simons, and P. Berman (eds.), *Maternal Education and Child Survival: Pathways and Evidence*. Ahmedabad: Gujerat Institute of Development Research.

Singh, S., Casterline, J. B. and Cleland, J. G. (1985), 'The proximate determinants of fertility: sub-national variations'. *Population Studies*, 39: 113–35.

Street, B. V. (1990), *Cultural Meanings of Literacy*. Paris: UNESCO/IBE.

——(1993), 'Introduction: the new literacy studies', in B. V. Street, (ed.), *Cross-Cultural Approaches to Literacy*. Cambridge: Cambridge University Press, pp. 1–21.

Townsend, P. and Davidson, N. (1982). *Inequalities in Health: The Black Report*. Harmonsworth: Penguin.

UNDP (1990), *Human Development Report*. Oxford: Oxford University Press.

United Nations (1987), *Fertility Behaviour in the Context of Development: Evidence from the World Fertility Survey*. New York: ST/ESA/SER.A/IUD.

Ware, H. (1984), 'Effects of maternal education, women's roles, and child care on mortality', In W. H. Mosley and L. C. Chen (eds.), *Child Survival: Strategies for Research*, Supplement to *Population and Development Review*, 10: 191–214.

Weinberger, M-B. and Heligman, L. (1987), 'Do social and economic variables differentially affect male and female mortality?' Paper presented to the 1987 Annual Meeting of the Population Association of America, Chicago.

Westoff, C. and Ochoa, L. H. (1991), 'Unmet need and the demand for family planning'. *Demographic and Health Surveys Comparative Studies*, no. 5. Columbia, Md: Macro International Inc.

Willis, P. (1977), *Learning to Labour: How Working Class Kids Get Working Class Jobs*. Aldershot: Gower.

Woods, P. (1985), 'Ethnography and theory construction in educational research', in R. G. Burgess (ed.), *Field Methods in the Study of Education*. Lewes, Sx: Falmer Press.

Zeitlyn, S. and Islam, F. (1993), 'Mother's education, autonomy and innovation', in L. Visaria, J. Simons, and P. Berman (eds.), *Maternal Education and Child Survival: Pathways and Evidence*. Ahmedabad: Gujerat Institute of Development Research.

7 A Rereading of Historical Material: An Alternative Account of the Position of Women in Ancient India

SUKUMARI BHATTACHARJI

Introduction

Not only do events in our demographic history influence the present, but our understanding of the past also informs our understanding of the present. This latter premiss is the basis of much historical demography, and the European demographic transition in particular has attracted a lot of research attention which is motivated by its potential for understanding and predicting demographic transitions in contemporary populations. However, not only is the past not always a good guide to the present, but understanding and interpreting the past can be fraught with difficulties. This is especially the case when one looks at the relatively ancient past, for which records are likely to be selective, incomplete, and, for the large part, descriptive or even merely prescriptive. Such records call for careful critical scrutiny before being used to advance a thesis, and this paper illustrates this problem by providing an alternative interpretation of the ancient Indian texts. The plausibility of such an alternative interpretation and a critique of existing interpretations highlight the political processes that influence not just the writing of a text, but also the reading of it. This awareness brings one closer to acknowledging the biases possible in one's attempts to apply politically loaded and value loaded ideas from other disciplines to a supposedly 'objective' discipline such as demography. Such caution is particularly warranted by the increasing politicization of demography and of the policy prescriptions that it generates.

Until quite recently, the ancient Indian texts, especially the Vedic, epic, and Puranic literature, were explained in a subjective and tendentious manner. Tendentious because, as Indians chafed under foreign domination, this national subordination led them to a sense of humiliation and inferiority. This they sought to mitigate by reading into these texts a history of unprecedented glory, power, honour, and the predominance of all human values. Among these values came the subject of the treatment of women: ancient India, it was claimed, treated her women with a measure of respect never accorded elsewhere or at any other time. Passages were often culled out of context, myths interpreted as reality, and unpalatable passages suppressed.

Scholars now look upon the ancient texts not as descriptively realistic, but as sociologically real documents which the mentors or socio-religious law-givers composed to solve the ideological problems of a particular age to suit the interests of the group in power without provoking widespread revolt among the people. The assumptions now are that (1) the texts were produced as solutions to real socio-political, religio-philosophical, and economic problems thrust up by the exigencies of a real society at a real point of time; (2) society had accepted the superior wisdom of a section of people and would abide by the solutions offered by them; (3) this section of law-givers was a power group which had assumed power through (a) superior lineage, (b) economic affluence, (c) political power, and (d) mendicity or asceticism which was believed to generate clairvoyance and/or greater wisdom; (4) this power group was not homogeneous but often comprised sections with mutually conflicting and contrary interests; (5) of these conflicting, power-wielding groups, whichever enjoyed the benefit of patronage of the royalty or chieftaincy of the region came into the limelight and laid down dogmas which people followed abjectly, at least until that group fell from favour; and (6) this knowledge–power group varied from region to region and from period to period; hence the existence of contradictory scriptural dogmas. But since, until the fourth century BC (at the earliest), these dogmas were formulated for a society in a particular region and at a particular point of time, there was no obvious contradiction for that society at that time.

At the same time, the power group succeeded in serving its own group interests, through struggles to remain in a favoured position so that it could continue to pontificate and lay down normative injunctions and compose supportive mythical anecdotes. We now believe that any regulative or hermeneutic text is prompted by the needs of society as a whole as well as by the interests of the controlling group. There were situations when this knowledge–power group had no axe of its own to grind; at such times the dicta were evoked by society's needs alone.

Modern scholarship in the field of decoding ancient texts assumes that each particular normative text-injunction, explication, or anecdote was necessitated by real and specific socioeconomic, religio-philosophical, and/or political predicaments. Social cohesion, the avoidance of mass disaffection, and the fulfilment of the self-interests of the controlling élite were decisive factors in the generation of the regulative or hermeneutic discourses in the texts. Those who were at the helm of social affairs sought to achieve a balance between their own group interests and the interests of society. But only real crisis situations called forth new directives. Pre-literate, proto-literate, or even neo-literate texts observe strict economy of words, hence all texts should be analysed as specific responses to specific problems. These problems arose from conflicting interests among classes, castes, occupation or handicaps, family precedences, and assumptions of male superiority on the one hand; and the equally real common humane urges of kindness, grace, generosity, pity, integrity, and such like on the other. The texts are the end-results or resolutions of the tension between these mutually contradictory pressures. To arrive at a consensus of opinion, we have to add and weigh mutually contradictory injunctions and decide which dicta were repeated for longer periods over wider areas. It will, then, be safe to assume that these directives served the interests of the major knowledge–power groups without provoking an open rebellion for a considerable period of time.

However, as the records are those of the ruling groups themselves, we can never preclude the possibility of the existence of smouldering discontent in the masses of the downtrodden—the *sūdras*, the untouchables, and the women—whose voices are never audible except as background whispers. Some episodes clearly record the rivalry between the brahmins and ksatriyas, or between men and women; when a Brahmana myth describing a ritual detail of beating clarified butter with a stick concludes with 'hence should the wife be thrashed so that she has no power over her body or property', we clearly perceive how the ritual not only endorses a current social practice but advocates its continuance. Wife-beating obviously provoked enough controversy for the law-givers to invent a myth to lend it a myth-ritual justification and a longer life. Most normative texts are solutions to real problems between conflicting interest groups, and were resolved according to the existential needs of the major power groups in society.

The modern methodology for decoding ancient texts is based on a belief not in the descriptive nature of the texts, but in the reality of the social exigencies leading to dilemmatic situations in precise historical times and places which the normative texts solved, however temporarily or regionally, involving the satisfactory preservation of social cohesion. Prescriptions that could contain social conflicts and which provoked the least resistance within a paradigm of viable norms had a longer life-span.

Our sole source for the study of the Vedic woman is the Vedic literature itself, because archaeological material of the period is hopelessly meagre and much of it is without any firm historical sequence. Vedic literature, from the earliest Samhitās (songs and poems) to the latest ancillary vedāṅgas, was composed roughly between the twelfth country BC and the fifth century AD. This whole literature does not concern itself with women directly, and so we glean the material from scattered references, imagery, and some directives and injunctions of considerable significance.

This literature was composed over seventeen to eighteen centuries by several generations of authors, distant from each other in time and place. Hence there is no conceptual homogeneity in the bulk of the texts; we have to depend on an attitude pervasive in the texts. Some corroborative passages from the later epic-Puranic literature have occasionally been used. While most of the normative discourses emphatically point to the very low position of women, a few legends and stanzas dispersed over the texts declare that occasionally women were held in high respect. Yet women's subjugation is conspicuously discernible as a fact and a norm throughout this literature. The discrepancy between some descriptive and most prescriptive passages is continued by later creative literature: Smrtis and Nibandhas, late didactic, and exegetical scriptures repeat the paradox between the model and the actual position of women.

There is no recorded history in India as such until the Moghul period; but soon after the advent of the British we have the rulers' accounts of the state of affairs in the country. With William Jones's discovery of the wealth of Sanskrit literature, there began a period of extravagant and uncritical praise of everything in ancient India, including the status of women. Some Indophiles, both foreigners and patriotic Indians, began to assert that the Indian woman had always been an object of veneration. Growing nationalistic fervour and the mortification of colonial subjection lead to a distortion of the facts, a selection of only the favourable and a suppression of those that were derogatory or unsavoury. Authors created a fanciful portrait of the ancient Indian woman. Poets, novelists, and even dramatists of the nineteenth century sang paeans to the ancient Indian woman's character and conduct; to her noble and stoic self-effacement, her unflinching loyalty to her husband, her lofty sense of duty to her in-laws and children, and so on. Foreign scholars also felt some genuine admiration for the ancient Indian woman based on laudatory texts supplied by Indian Sanskritists.

In the last quarter of this century, with the women's liberation movement gaining momentum and seeking to unravel the roots of woman's present predicament in her past history, there began an attempt to face history squarely, to sift fact from fiction, to present facts not flattering to her mythical self-image, and thus to unearth a truer picture through heuristic attempts. My study of the ancient Indian literature over the last forty years has impressed me with a picture of the ancient Indian woman vastly different from the one we have absorbed from earlier reading. In consequence, I have felt compelled to debunk this mythical presentation by bringing into the light texts that have been ignored and banished into oblivion so far. There is much in the ancient Indian culture that is truly positive, but in uncovering history the truth cannot be avoided. The present paper is an attempt to move in that direction.

The nineteenth-century glorification of the ancient Indian woman, notably in Bankim Chandra Chatterji's essays, in scattered remarks in his novels, and also in the literatures of some other provinces, has fed this mythical ego of the ancient Indian woman. This trend continued and culminated in some of the early writings of Tagore himself and has proceeded in an unbroken chain until the twentieth century.

Cultural historian's like A. Barth (translated 1882), Monier-Williams (1883) and, much later, Majumdar (1953), or Apte's chapter in Majumdar

(1951) share the view that Vedic women enjoyed much greater freedom than those in the epic-Puranic age. It is true that the early Vedic women coming straight from the nomadic pastoral tradition did enjoy a modicum of social liberty, but it was only marginal at best—at least as far as the records testify—and was withheld quite soon. Besides, these authors magnify every bit of favourable evidence and explain away the unpalatable parts as myths. Kane's (1930) masterly work on the history of the *Dharmashastras* is the product of stupendous scholarship, yet it betrays some accepted prejudices regarding women's high status in the very ancient past. Even a later work like Hopkins (1972) idealizes the image of women in the *Mahabharata*. Still later Leslie (1989) upholds this view, although in a much more critical vein regarding a medieval text on the perfect wife. These are but a few instances, picked at random in the vast literature on ancient Indian women, but they have cast a spell over the vast majority of uncritical Indian and foreign readers, and steered them into accepting a well-fashioned myth in place of reality.

It must, however, be stated that all these discussions are based on literature and this literature is a record of the upper echelons of society; those lower down were beneath the notice of such authors, and the chances are that they enjoyed a greater measure of freedom. But we cannot come to any firm conclusions, for that would be *deductio ab silentio*, and hence logically untenable.

The present paper is the result of a critical appraisal of India's past; its data are culled chiefly from literature but have been checked against whatever evidence for material life is available. The study brings to light much data hitherto suppressed, neglected, underplayed, or distorted tendentiously. I seek to correlate literary data with archaeological, numismatic, and epigraphical evidence unearthed in the last fifty years, although most of such evidence is relevant to a later period. Yet this material evidence throws much light on trends or consistent attitudes to women over the past millennia.

Life did not remain static during this period, but changed and evolved considerably. The texts themselves are not uniform; there was very little social homogeneity in this vast geographical area over such a long period. The texts differ because there were regional variations, differences in the authors' personalities and in the social milieu in which they were composed. But because social norms and values are heavily conditioned by the means and modes of production and the production relationships, and by the surplus value and the management of the surplus, women's fate revolved round this axis throughout the three millennia of known Indian history. This paper is an attempt to make connections, wherever possible, between the existing material and the descriptive and prescriptive accounts. In particular, it presents an unorthodox picture, especially through the use of texts, many of which have remained unearthed to date.

The Earliest Period

Between the earliest Samhitas and the latest auxiliary Vedic manuals,[1] there elapsed some seventeen to eighteen centuries. Evidently social relationships and codes of conduct evolved, changed, and grew to a considerable extent, and by the end of this period the Vedic age had advanced well into the early classical age. But the social freedom of women throughout this period is largely a myth. What is true is that in the earliest Vedic age women enjoyed a few rights and were looked upon as normal and comparatively uninhibited human beings who did not need to repress their feminine desires and passions. 'Usha' (dawn) is a beautiful well-dressed woman, clad in a red garment, looking like a maid freshly washed and decked out by her mother with loving care.[2] She is also called 'a shameless hussy'[3] because she bares her breasts to the public eye. Love between man and woman was regarded as normal and was depicted without any prurience: 'The fire-god enjoys the devotee's praise just as a loving husband takes delight in his wife';[4] 'As a beloved wife finds joy in a loving husband, O Bhaga, may you find the same joy in me.'[5] In one instance, the devotee and his god are likened to a loving couple; 'the stream of clarified butter flows towards Soma as a well-dressed, pretty young woman goes to her husband'.[6] An unusual insight into the woman's status in the earliest period is provided in an image of the sun following dawn (mythologically, his wife) from behind.[7] The wife was also honoured by her husband: 'the fire-god is as pure as a wife honoured by her husband'.[8] A very common image is 'as a man follows the woman from behind'.[9] While in later literature and life it is always the woman who walks behind her husband, these images are rather striking and evidently belong to that very early period when women did enjoy a modicum of respect and independence. Then, 'she could even choose her own partner'.[10]

The Maid, the Old Maid, and the Widow

We do not hear about the maiden, except as the old maid who 'grew old in her parents' house';[11] as a social being she is hardly ever mentioned in the texts. Nor is the widow paid much attention except in a late Ṛgvedic passage[12] where she lies beside her husband's corpse and then is ritually raised by the brother-in-law to join him in the land of the living. A Ṛgvedic image points to the widow's marriage with the brother-in-law. Although Vedic and early epic literature does not refer to widow-burning, the *Atharvaveda* has two references to co-cremation: (1) 'a living woman is being taken as a bride to a dead person', and (2) 'this woman is going to the region of her husband, she follows an ancient custom'.[13] We do not know how ancient the custom was, but as other ancient Indo-Europeans—the Greeks, Romans, Celts, or the Germanic people—did not burn their widows except very occasionally, it may be presumed that this was a pre-Aryan, possibly Indus Valley, custom which would explain its appearance in the late part of the *Rgveda* and the *Atharvaveda* which was compiled later. In ancient northern India it never became obligatory, but its prevalence increased with time from the epic and early Puranic age. 'Widow burning dramatically removes the awesome danger of women who are still potentially procreative but without legitimate male partners.'[14] But evidently widowhood was dreaded; a prayer says, 'may I ever remain unwidowed like Indraur'.[15] Possibly the widow was socially ostracized in some ways and led a comparatively abject life.

Widow remarriage was sanctioned in the *Yamasamhita*, a late text, but the literature mentions no instances of this except for one or two marginal references in the Vedic literature; however, a widow could beget sons through her brother-in-law. (Vyasa, for example, had sons through his widowed sister-in-law.)

Education

Five things were desirable in a woman at marriage: wealth, beauty, learning, intelligence, and good lineage. But it must be borne in mind that, since the woman was debarred from the investiture of the sacred thread ceremony,[16] she was not given any formal education. A text says that 'in an earlier age, a woman was initiated with the sacred thread', but this is a very late medieval text.[17] The woman thus had no formal education, and her syllabus presumably was primarily domestic lore, hearsay, legends and tales, rudimentary arithmetic, and possibly, at an early stage, singing and dancing. The *Rgveda* says that the woman fetched water and watched over the fields.[18] A later text says that she carded wool and possibly knitted it.[19] Women sometimes actively participated in warfare; the *Rgveda* mentions Mudgalini winning a battle,[20] and Vadhrimatī and Śaśiyasī were noted for their heroism on the battlefield. At the daily rite of offering water to the ancestors, three women's names figured in the list of those to whom water was to be offered: Gārgī Vācaknavī, Vaḍavā Ātreyī, and Sulabhā Maitreyī. We should remember that all three were learned and had participated in philosophical discourses. Also, when the Vedic student completed his studies, on the final 'utsarga' day, a seat of honour had to be accorded to Vasistha's wife Arundhatī, and she belonged among the venerables to whom ritual honour was paid.

Only in exceptional cases do we hear of women learned in other subjects like cosmogony, metaphysics, etc. Some girls who had physical blemishes which made marriage difficult, some young widows, and possibly some women suffering from long-term diseases, or, in exceptional cases, an intelligent girl with some promise—these were taught by a kind father, brother, husband, or teacher. True, Panini has grammatical rules for forming words with two sets of feminine suffixes, one that means a teacher's wife and the other referring to a woman teacher.[21] But the literature gives us only a few instances of learned women.[22] One example, the Ṛgvedic rsikas, were female seers named Viśvāvāra, Ghoṣā, Apālā, and Godhā.[23] These were known as 'brahmavadinis' in the *Yamasamhitā* (a late Dharmasūtra) and to all evidence constituted a minuscule minority in society at all times.

How the learned woman was looked upon is clear from Yājña-valkya's censure to Gārgī when she cornered him in an argument: 'Do not ask overmuch, Gārgī, your head will fall.'[24] And Sulabhā, who came for a metaphysical discourse, was accused of attempting to seduce Janakā. Vāc, sage Ambhṛha's daughter, was the first to utter the 'so ham' theory, the bottom board of all Upanisadic metaphysics. And here in India, as in Greece and Rome, the deity of learning was a goddess—Vāc, Bhāratī, or Sarasvatī, like Athene or Minerva—yet the living woman was generally debarred from formal education. Yet, among the five things coveted in a bride, learning was included. Yājñavalkya even lays down a rite for obtaining a learned daughter.[25] The educated woman however was despised (feared?)—'although women, they are really men'.[26]

The Wife

The average woman was trained in those household chores, such as minding children, cooking, etc., which she would be called upon to perform after marriage. Hence she did not acquire any special skills and was not given any equipment that she could use lucratively, so that she was wholly dependent on men for her livelihood. But this is particularly true of the upper echelons of society as a whole; poorer women acquired practical skills and worked alongside their men. For her food needs, however, the average woman was dependent on her husband. The Sanskrit synonym for wife is *bhāryā*, derived from *bhṛ* from which *bhṛtya*, servant, is also derived. One remembers that even in Elizabethan England the wife addressed her husband as 'lord' (as did the servant); the word is derived from Old English *hlaf* (loaf) + *ward*. This dependence on the husband for food increased with time and the wife's movements were increasingly circumscribed. With the territorial expansion of the Aryans through their conquest of the indigenous population, the conquered people became slaves who took over many of the heavier chores which women had been performing earlier; this reduced women's contribution to productive labour and enhanced their dependence on men even more.

Virginity has a premium. Many episodes record girls regaining their virginity through a boon granted by the ascetics to whom they had yielded sexually. Marriage was obligatory for all women except the professional prostitute. Penance is normally prohibited for women, but is permitted if practised for gaining a husband.[27] What was the marriageable age of the prospective bride? Vedic evidence seems to be in favour of adult marriage, but from the epic period child marriage came into vogue, although post-puberty marriage also continued. However, from the early medieval period adolescent and child brides grew in number, until the scriptures also came to endow the child bride's father with religious merit. 'Child marriage ensures that when the girl begins to menstruate she has a husband capable of transforming her destructing capability into generative power.'[28] Rites at a girl's birth were minimal; no more notice was taken of her childhood and girlhood, either. Only at marriage did the ritual texts take any notice of her; and even then, all the prayers at a wedding were directed towards the well-being and long life of her husband and the in-laws, presumably because at her wedding 'a girl is given to a family' (*Kula*).[29] This gives the whole family a proprietory right over the bride. The marriage vow for the woman is uttered by the husband, 'may your heart be settled in my vow...may you follow my mind...'; she is thus required to submerge her whole personality into her husband's. One notices that there is no corresponding vow for the husband. The wife's duty was clearly stipulated: she was to serve abjectly the interests of husband, in-laws, and children. Although a Ṛgvedic text blesses the bride with 'be an empress to all your in-laws';[30] yet we read in the *Atharvaveda* that 'at sunrise ghosts flee just as a daughter-in-law flees from her father-in-law';[31] this turns the Ṛgvedic blessing into a mere pious wish.

We hear that a woman's place was at home: 'She should remain in the seclusion of the inner chambers or she loses her energy.'[32] One wonders what kind of energy it was that thrives only in seclusion. 'A good woman is one who pleases her husband, delivers male children and never talks back to her husband.'[33] Her major function was to bring forth male children, and 'she who fails to do so may be discarded'.[34] In ritual, her presence was necessary but she could not utter mantras; 'she may not offer oblation',[35] although we hear also that 'the wife is the posterior half of the sacrifice'.[36]

Social prohibitions for married women were many and various. 'The husband should not dine in front of the wife', or the reverse, 'she should eat his left-overs'.[37] She could not drink honey (possibly honey-mead) because 'she says, "I fulfill this vow for the sake of my sons"'.[38] 'She could not attend assemblies.'[39] 'A wife should remain behind her husband.'[40] This emphatically demonstrates society's firm belief that the woman was inferior *per se*. We are, however, given a ritual justification; at a Soma rite, some vessels are put on the ground while others are held up high; 'therefore, the newborn girl child is put down on the ground while a boy is held up high'.[41] Such discrimination persists all through her life. 'Women should follow in the paths of their husbands.'[42] The scriptures look upon the wife as 'bringing enjoyment'; hence 'cattle, land, and the wife should not be enjoyed excessively'.[43] 'The wife is a necessity'; 'he who is without a wife is without sacrifice'.[44]

One passage says, 'a wife is a comrade, a daughter misery, a son a light in the highest heaven'. Another text says, 'the wife is one half of one's self', which is comforting until we read the next part: 'therefore, as long as one does not obtain a wife one has no progeny'.[45] There is no rite for the woman herself until she is pregnant; even after pregnancy, the rite is directed not towards her well-being or health, but for the family's desire for a male issue.

Within marriage, sex was comparatively free. The bar imposed during the wife's menstrual period, on certain inauspicious days, and before and after certain ritual days was observed by the couple; otherwise sex depended mainly on the husband's desire. There was no ban on sexuality as such, and certainly the much later Islamic influence did not permeate brahmanical ideas and practices about sex.

In her conjugal life the woman's sexuality was controlled absolutely by her husband, and indirectly by her in-laws, and even by the society at large, because there was pressure from them all for her to conceive and bring forth male children. Her personal inclination or disinclination was not relevant 'When a wife is reluctant to oblige her husband's sexual desire, he should first cajole her with sweet words, then try to purchase [here the verb used is *avakrinīyāt*, or should buy] with gifts, and if she still refuses then he should thrash her with his fist or with a stick and force her into subjugation.'[46] In the sacrificial rite, *agni patnīvat*, clarified butter, is beaten with a stick; 'so should a woman be thrashed so that she has no right on her person or property'.[47] Again, in the Varuṇapraghāsa rite the priest asked the sacrificer's wife: 'with whom have you committed adultery?'[48]—the sacrificer himself was never required to confess his own lapses in a public assembly. The punishment for married woman's adultery was horrendous, cruel, and sadistic.[49] We notice society's double standards: for women chastity was obligatory and unchastity, punishable; but if a man transgressed against conjugal fidelity, one or two scriptural passages prescribed half-a-day's fasting—although the literature does not record even one instance of such expiation. 'The sacrificer was required to abstain from a prostitute's company only on the day of his initiation [for the sacrifice], the day before he was to avoid enjoying another's wife, and his own wife on the day of the sacrifice.'[50] We see how lenient society was to aberrations in the man's sexual life, whereas a woman in a similar situation paid heavily for her remissness. The prescribed punishment may not have been carried out every time, but, if and when a 'wronged' husband wished to inflict it, society and its law were on his side.[51]

However, premarital or extramarital sex was not unrecorded. The scriptures mention the '*sahodha*' son—a pregnant bride's son born after her marriage to a man other than the begetter. A maiden's son was known as *kānīna*. The *Mahabharata* has an episode where princess Kuntī received a boon from an ascetic she had pleased with her service. With this boon she invoked the sun-god who gave her a son. This is a mythic version of a maiden's conception. The *gūdhotpanna* was the married woman's son begotten by someone other than the husband. Satyavati's son in the *Mahābhārata* was *kānīna*; so was Gaṅgā's son Bhīṣma. There are other instances strewn across the later literature.

Scriptural laws vary in their moods and tones both regionally and temporally. Some texts enjoin lenience to women—'even if a wife is quarrelsome, unclean, has left home, is raped, or abducted by thieves, she may not be abandoned'.[52] 'Even a seduced wife is purified by atonement.'[53] 'The husband who forsakes his wife is liable to be punished heavily, whereas a wife who leaves her husband is purified by expiation. The husband who speaks harshly to his wife has to fast and expiate for it.'[54] That these were merely pious dicta is amply borne out by Rama humiliating and abandoning Sītā on mere suspicion, by Ahalyā whose husband Gautama cursed and abandoned her, and by Reṇukā who was murdered at her husband's behest. Numerous other instances bear testimony to the social reality: the humanitarian rules were seldom followed.

Prostitution

Prostitution, the world's oldest profession, is known even in the Ṛgvedic times under many names.[55] Possibly these names signified their social and economic status. Later, the names multiplied and the prostitutes' social position and obligations also became diverse and increasingly stratified. The *ganikā* was the most accomplished and affluent of prostitutes and enjoyed the highest social status. She was served by a number of attendants, both male and female, had a professional procurer, and was controlled by a supervisor appointed by the state who collected taxes from her. She was educated at the state's expense. The *avaruddhā* was a woman kept in seclusion and paid by a man. In principle, the laws regarding prostitution did not confine the prostitute permanently to prostitution. In a kind of general amnesty, the king could set her free. Her lover too could buy her out with a rich ransom. Such women could then marry and lead an honourable housewife's life.

Apart from courtesans, there were temple dancers, 'devadāsis', who drew their subsistence from the state and were at the disposal of the priests, the king, and the nobility, with the priests' connivance. We know from the later scriptures that buying girls and donating them to the temple was deemed a pious act; and at times of famines, battle, or epidemics, parents sometimes sold their daughters to the rich. Young women in their hundreds formed an essential item in the catalogue of sacrificial fees and donations to brahmins and their guests; they also formed part of a bride's dowry entourage to her husband's home. In most cases of such lump gifts of girls, some of them were enjoyed by the recipient, some sold as slaves, and some, after serving for a time at their owners' houses, slowly but surely found their way to the brothel. Distress sales, war captives, exodus from foreign countries, and donations swelled the number of prostitutes and temple girls.

Abduction of women was known even in the Ṛgvedic times. A man about to abduct a girl—presumably with her consent—prays that the entire household be lulled into deep sleep, that her brothers, relatives, and even the dogs do not wake up so that he can elope safely.[56]

Polyandry and Polygamy

Polyandry in ancient India must have been regionally and exceptionally practised, judging by the infrequency of references to it in the literature. The *Atharvaveda* says that 'if a woman marries a second time she has to offer a food offering';[57] another passage says that, 'even if a woman has ten husbands, the brahmin alone is her true husband and not the 'rājanya' [baron] or the 'vaiśya' [merchant or farmer]'.[58] Women, therefore, occasionally (and possibly, regionally) could and did marry more than once.

On the other hand, polygamy was extremely common. Men's bigamy was sanctioned with pseudo-logic: 'because two pieces of cloth are twined around one stake, and not *vice versa*, therefore, a woman may not take two husbands, but the man can take two wives.'[59] Another text says, quite unambiguously, 'with the sense organs one enjoys a second wife... therefore men can enjoy two wives each'.[60] The king married four wives[61] and could retain any number of women in his vast seraglio. Polygamy had ritual sanction, whereas polyandry was almost universally prohibited. 'Even though one husband has many wives, one husband is enough for one woman.'[62] Clearly, there was a double standard for male and female sexuality, as was the case in most ancient civilizations.

An extremely revealing passage throws a flood of light on polygamy: 'that is prosperity, when a man's wives are fewer than his cattle.'[63] We cannot fail to notice that cattle and wives are uttered in the same breath in the context of prosperity or status symbols. When in a pastoral-agricultural milieu a comparison is made between a prosperous man's cattle and his wives, the number of his wives is simply anybody's guess. Ṛgvedic and Atharvavedic prayers for destruction of co-wives presuppose polygamy as a common social practice. The *Maitrayani* Samhita mentions the ten wives of Manu and the *Tattirīya* Saṃhitā the moon-god's twenty-seven wives. Needless to say, these are the mythological reflection of social reality.

That wives could be pawned is also clear from a Ṛgvedic passage and the infamous game of dice in the *Mahābhārata* when Yudhiṣṭhira staked his wife and lost. Also in the same epic, when Kṛṣṇa went on a peace mission to the Kuru court, he sought to appease them with the gift of large tracts of land as well as of Draupadī, the Pandavas' wife.

At one stage of the wedding rite, the husband says to the newly wedded wife, 'come, let us unite so that we can produce male children who will continue the line, so that we may gain sons, grandsons, servants, pupils, garments, blankets, metals, *many wives*, a king, food, and security.'[64] The crudity of praying for 'many wives' right in front of the new bride, and involving her in the prayer, did not disturb men in ancient times. I shall probe this later. Even with a society permissive about male sexuality and its concomitant licentiousness, men kept a large number of concubines and visited brothels; for the woman, however, no such avenue existed. Very occasionally does a text condemn the husband's deception and promiscuity. 'He was to cover himself in ass-hide and wander about begging alms and proclaiming his sin.'[65] But in literature there is not a single instance of such expiation by an unfaithful husband; he follows his inclinations with complete impunity.

The woman is inherently 'evil' (inauspicious) in herself; 'one should not look upon the untrue [*sic*], the woman, the dog, and the black bird.'[66] 'A woman entices her husband at night and gains her objectives.'[67] As early as the eighth or ninth century BC, in the *Yajurveda*, we hear, 'woman is false, she is a misfortune, she is nothing but a passion like wine or dice';[68] and 'the woman endowed with every virtue is inferior to the most worthless man'.[69] This is one of the most categorical appraisals of the ancient Indian woman's social standing. The expiation for killing the following is the same (one day's penance): a 'black bird, a hawk, a mongoose, a rat, a dog, *a woman*, and a sūdra'.[70]

In the 'Sārasvatānāmayana' sacrifice, the fee was a mare and a maid-servant with her son.[71] The mare would produce colts, the maid servant had already proved her fertility; she would serve the master as a concubine, a housemaid, and a prospective mother of servants; her son would grow into a servant and would eventually beget other servants. Fertility thus has a premium on it already, and was a special virtue in gifts. In other sacrifices we hear of women in their hundreds being included in the list of sacrificial fees, gifts, and articles for entertainment of guests.

The Economic Position of Women

'Economic theories as well as legislature treat the family as a private economic unit ... Fundamentally the housewife's legal position is a reflection of the husbands.'[72] Furthermore, this economic subjugation of the woman was bound with her sex, in that 'sexual inequalities are bound to the control of property'.[73]

In the early period we hear of the groom paying bride-price; the custom later changed into dowry whereby the girl's father paid the bridegroom. Behind this was a process of the steady devaluation of the woman's social position. 'Dowry is characterized by asymmetry, uncertainty and unpredict-ability.'[74] Even under Roman law, 'brides could be purchased.'[75] So this was not unique to India, in that the ancient world as a whole during the first period of urbanization instituted dowry, or bridegroom-price, switching over from the earlier practice of bride-price. At marriage the bride received *strīdhana*, *yautaka*, and *saudāyika*, which were hers to enjoy freely, especially the *strīdhana*, which was exclusively her property; even so, the later literature bears ample evidence that quite frequently her in-laws helped themselves to these. Manu says 'friends or relations of a woman, who out of folly or avarice *live upon the property belonging to her*, or the wicked people who deprive her of the enjoyment of *her own belongings* such as cloth, etc., go to hell.'[76] 'Relations of a woman who lives by selling carts, clothes, and gold ornaments which are her *strīdhana* commit a sin and suffer worse fate in the next world.'[77] This is quite an early text from about the eighth century BC. So misappropriation of the bride's personal property started quite early, and one wonders about the extent to which the prospect of going to hell actually deterred the in-laws from this act.

When a husband married a second time, he paid a consolatory gift to the first wife; and 'what has been given to her on her husband's next marriage, what was given to her by kindred [as *saudāyika* or *yautaka*, i.e. gifts to the couple] and her bride-price, or what was given to her after marriage, was the woman's property, her *stridhana*.'[78] In these circumstances, one-third of the husband's property had to be given to the first wife, says Narada, and this was entirely hers to enjoy, sell, pawn, or give away.[79] Manu says: 'to a woman whose husband marries a second wife, let him give an equal sum as compensation for the suppression, provided no *strīdhana* has been bestowed on her, but if she has been allotted, let him allot half'.[80]

This money paid to the first wife was clearly a kind of alimony, but it is doubtful whether it was sufficient to meet her needs, since she now receded to the background and was neglected for the rest of her life. 'What wealth a woman earns through crafts or what was given by others in love, the husband is the proprietor of all that; what remains is *stridhana*.'[81] Obviously, precious little would qualify as *strīdhana* if she could not call her own gifts and her own earnings her own. Between the husband's proprietory rights and the in-laws' avarice, little, if any, of her possessions would remain to her. At least one law-giver says that 'a husband is not liable to make good the property of his wife taken by him during a famine, or for the performance of a duty, or during illness or under restraint'.[82] Yājñavalkya also says that 'the husband has no right to touch the *strīdhana* except during a famine, a necessary religious purpose, at times of disease, or during his imprison-ment'.[83] Thus, the extenuating circumstances multiply and one can imagine the bride frequently being deprived of her possessions, so that her property was in an extremely precarious condition. Society saw to it, in fact, that the woman was debarred from possessing property.

Some law-givers lay down that 'on the death of a sonless woman, the husband shall unhesitatingly take the entire estate left by her'.[84] Clearly, when a woman with affluent parents, who has received rich *strīdhana*, *yautaka*, and *saudāyika*, died, the husband gained substantially at her death. But then, in life also, 'she did not have an incontrovertible right over her property and none over her own body'.[85] Husbands appropriating the dead wives' property deprived the daughters.

In the house, the couple jointly administered the family finance. We should remember that the Sanskrit word for couple, *dampatī*, was formed from the Indo-European *domos* and *pati*, i.e., 'lords of the house'; hence the word denotes duality and means that together the couple controlled the house. This is a far cry from the later situation, when the husband managed the *nomos* of the *oikos* single-handed. 'When a husband leaves home on a business trip he must make provisions for the wife's maintenance.'[86] 'If during his absence she drinks or attends public dances, she should be fined five *krsnalas*.' One wonders how she paid the fine.

Woman as Property

In India women could be staked as a pawn in dice and be lost; the *akṣa* (dice) hymn in the *Ṛgveda*[87] and the *Mahābhārata* episode[88] bring this out clearly. When Duhsasana came to drag Draupadi to the court because her husband Yudhisthira had staked and lost her in a game of dice, she asked whether Yudhiṣthira had lost her *before* or *after* losing himself. The insinuation is quite clear: if the husband had been a free agent, he had the legal right of staking and losing her. In another anecdote of the *Mahābhārata*, Galava, a student, begged King Yayati for his teacher's fees. Yayāti pleaded a depleted treasury and instead, offered his pretty young daughter Mādhavī, whom Gālava should rent out to three kings for a year each. When she delivered a son, then the King concerned would pay Gālava a sum so that at the end of three years he would be able to pay his teacher. The girl was thus used as a machine for producing sons to serve the interests of six men—her father, Gālava's teacher, Gālava, and the three kings.

In both the above instances, the woman is some man's property who could be invested, staked, and lost. Hence, at least theoretically, she could not own property herself, nor did she have control over her body or her sexuality. The *Taittirīya* Saṃhitā deprives her of control over those.[89] One remembers that under the Gortyn law even a married woman slave had the right over the movable property and small livestock.[90] In India only exceptionally could a woman own property, since she herself was the property of her father until adolescence, her husband's in youth, and her sons' in old age; a common dictum emphatically states that 'she is not worthy of freedom.'

Motherhood

With a few exceptions, a woman is praised in literature only on two counts: for her pretty, youthful body, and her ability to bring forth male children. 'The apotheosis of motherhood has reached a greater height in India than anywhere else.'[91] But social reality was not reflected in that apotheosis, which was but compensatory; her actual position in society was vastly different. A glance at the ritual aspects of conception, gestation, parturition, and post-parturition stages brings this out unambiguously. A wedding prayer says, 'Come let us join so that we may generate a *male child, a son* for the increase of wealth.'[92] Even at the expected moment of conception, the husband prays for a male child.[93] A gestation rite, *pumsavana* (literally, the birth of a male child), and another, *sīmantonnayana*, have the same objective: a male child. At the latter, a mess of cooked rice is placed before the pregnant woman; the husband asks her, 'what do you see?' to which she replies 'offspring', followed by his response, 'be a mother of valiant sons'.[94] In another text she replies, 'sons and cattle',[95] and in yet another, 'children, good fortune for me, and long life for my husband'.[96] And all this when she is about to go through a life-and-death crisis. No one prays for her safe delivery, health, or long life. Apparently, the child's life is much more important than the mother's, who can be replaced at any time.

Fertility in Ancient India

Simone de Beauvoir says that, unlike the case of being a man, there is a contradiction between being a woman and being a human being, and, 'since woman has been subjected as mother, she will be cherished first of all as a mother'.[97] Motherhood was actually two different things to woman in a patriarchal society. As a mother, she had an experience with her child through her body, an experience unique to her; but she also experienced motherhood as an institution imposed upon her, often against her will, which she had to endure because of social pressure, fear of social stigma, and in apprehension of social ostracism, and so it was not an unmixed blessing. Barrenness was a curse and had a stigma attached to it. A woman was recognized as a useful cog in the social wheel only when she bore a child, and more specifically a son, and this was often an oppressive burden to her. Adrienne Rich distinguishes between these two aspects of motherhood.[98] But, whether voluntarily or through pressure from the patriarchal value system, the wife submitted and sought to redeem her womanhood through maternity. Motherhood had a special premium attached to it in all agricultural and feudal societies. 'Motherhood was the only function society came to recognize for "ladies" until they themselves forced a change.'[99] Until quite recently, women were conditioned to subscribe to these widespread views regarding motherhood. 'Women's capacities for mothering and abilities to get gratification from it are strongly internalized and are built developmentally into the feminine psychic structure.'[100]

Society was aware that the pregnant woman needed more food. A scriptural passage says, 'the newly wedded bride, the unmarried daughter, a sick person, and *a pregnant woman* must be fed even before the guest.'[101] After the initial birth rites, however, the mother receded into the background; except for looking after the child's physical needs, she had no part in its bringing-up.

If a woman strayed from the path of virtue, her son was nevertheless obliged to feed her. 'The mother is never an outcaste for the son.'[102] 'The son should serve food to such a mother without speaking to her.'[103] For a mother guilty of moral transgression, the son prays at the obsequial (*śrāddha*) ceremony 'wherein my mother has done anything amiss...may my father take that sperm as his own'.[104] The social attitude was possibly generated by the need not to let such a child go to waste, since society needed children. Hence 'a barren woman could be cast away after fifteen years' because she was possessed by Nirṛti' (an evil spirit).[105] 'The barren woman could be discarded after ten years, a mother of girl-children only after twelve, and the mother of still-born children after fifteen years.'[106]

Like many ancient civilizations, ancient Indians also believed that the upper air and the nether world were infested with evil spirits which sought to prevent conception, kill foetuses, and devour them in the womb. This was because the scientific explanation of miscarriages was yet unknown, and male infertility was inconceivable. Such beliefs in forces destructive to foetuses is an inverse evidence of society's craving for children. 'A good woman is one who pleases her husband, *gives birth to male children*, and never talks back to the husband.'[107] Later literature invented the goddess Sasthi, who presided over conception, gestation, parturition, and the well-being of infants.[108] Vows and rites like Saṣṭhī-Kalpa and Vināyaka-Kalpa were invented to placate this goddess, as also was the god Kartikeya who protected infants.[109]

One indirect result of the social appreciation of the value of motherhood was that the female body in its youthful beauty was glorified in literature and women themselves took greater interest in becoming and remaining physically attractive. But they paid a price for this. Women's reproductive function required that more energy be directed toward pregnancy and maternity, hence less was available for the higher functions associated with learning and reasoning. Barren women were made to feel guilty because they had failed to discharge their social obligation. Women without sons poignantly felt the social slur and ritual ostracism that went with it.

Values pertaining to the social superstructure tend to be transmitted over centuries, even millennia. We can easily imagine the early tribal society's desire for sons, for sons fought in tribal warfare and often died; hence a steady replenishment was urgently needed. One proof of this hankering for sons is society's recognition of various categories of sons: (1) begotten by the father (*aurasa*), (2) born of a premarital conception (*kanina*), (3) born of a foetus in the bride's womb (*sahoḍha*), (4) a daughter's son whom the sonless father adopted as his own (*putrīkāputra*), (5) a child secretly born to a man other than the husband (*gudhotpanna*), and (6) a child born of a levirate (*niyoga*). Of these, society looked askance at the *kānīna*, *sahoḍha* and *gūḍhotpanna*; the other three were organized openly by society itself. Besides these, sons could be (7) bought (presumably from a distress sale or from one with too many) and (8) adopted. The society's anxiety for sons is thus very obvious. Populations often were depleted through natural calamities or warfare. Hence, for a society to thrive and prosper, it was obligatory to maintain a reserve force of manpower. The number of children was thus more than a status symbol: it was a source of security. Thus too, the 'apotheosis of motherhood had reached a greater height in India than anywhere else.'[110]

Earlier as a pastoral people and later as an agricultural people, the Aryans and the miscegenated Aryan–pre-non-Aryan population followed and analysed the process of reproduction, especially the relative roles of seed/semen and land/womb. They also framed a paradigm of the social value system, which postulated: 'of the seed and the womb, the seed is superior';[112] 'The qualities of the womb are never shared by the seed.'[112] The question arises: 'to whom does the offspring belong?'

Manu is quite explicit, and he declares unequivocally: 'as in cattle, horses, camels, and maidservants, in buffaloes, goats, and sheep, the male [partners of these] do not possess the calves, etc.; so it is for women'.[113] But this is relevant only when a man other than the husband begets the child; in such cases, the 'field' becomes more significant than the seed. As is to be expected, there is controversy regarding who owns the child—the begetter or the husband.[114] After the painful experiences of gestation and parturition, it was the mother who tended the children from infancy to adolescence. 'Given the social monopoly over children by women, the father became a significant and known quantity much later.'[115] Yet in India, a common formula which the father often muttered over the child is 'born limb by limb from me, born from my heart, son, you are my other self.' So the mother is notionally relegated to a completely insignificant position.

Yet motherhood established the wife's role as the cultivable field, and the husband became the owner and sower-cum-tiller of the seed. As the field receives the seed passively, while the sowing is a volitional act of a sentient agent, so the wife has always been regarded as a field at the sower's disposal. Hence Yājñavalkya's directive to thrash an unwilling wife. The crop belongs not to the field, although the field yields it, but to the sower and owner of the field; so were the children the father's property. As a big harvest depends primarily on the field and the seed, but is modified and influenced by other factors such as moisture, rainfall, manure, freedom from natural calamities, etc., so has a pregnancy to be tended. But fertility was the woman's avenue for gaining honour in the family and prestige in society.

Yet 'woman was dethroned by the advent of private property and her lot through the centuries was bound up with private property'.[116] Dethroned, she became a machine for conceiving and delivering children, preferably sons. Hence Gāndhārī has a hundred sons, King Sāgara's wives gave him sixty thousand sons, and Savitri prayed for a hundred sons for herself and a hundred for her mother. Gods had one, two, or no children, but man's strength was in numbers. There are prayers and vows for chain conceptions. Pāṇḍu, who could not beget children, prodded his wives to conceive from others. Society's hankering for male children partially explains the wide prevalence of polygamy; prayers for many sons had a better chance of fulfilment if there were many wives to conceive them.

As long as a woman was potentially fertile and capable of childbearing, she was put under various restrictions in order to ensure the parentage of the issue; but the social shackles slackened after due period of time. 'It is only when the wife has first become a mother, especially of sons, and then advanced to the relatively safe waters of post-menstrual infertility, that the restrictions began to be lifted.'[117]

Fertility was a value in itself; sexuality was notionally potential fertility. This explains the chief queen ritually cohabiting with the carcass of the virile sacrificial horse; it also explains the inclusion of apparently bawdy, even obscene, hymns like 'Etasa's delirium' of the 'Āhanasyā' in the supplementary (*Khila*) hymns of the *Rgveda*. This also explains why soil from a prostitute's courtyard was an essential ingredient in the clay component of the image of the goddess Durgā. The prostitute is a sexually powerful agent, and Durga, the primary harvest goddess, blesses fecundity (hence implicitly sexual potency) in plants, animals, and women. Motherhood was female fertility, sanctioned and endorsed by the scriptures, hence it was hallowed. Repeated pregnancies enhanced a woman's social prestige; it brought the security that society needed against various perils threatening its survival through numerical depletion and hence against eventual extinction.

The shift from a nomadic pastoral life to a settled agricultural life magnified the importance of the land and seed to the mixed population of northern India about the middle of the first millennium BC: it was then that woman came to be looked upon as the field. A little before this time the maritime trade with Europe via the Middle East, discontinued after the Aryans' advent, had been resumed; also, the iron ploughshare made it easier to cultivate vast tracts with comparative ease, surplus was produced in agriculture, and craft and trade brought extra affluence. All this plenty was controlled by a privileged section at the apex of society. Now arose the problem of the legitimate heir of these fortunate few. This put increasingly severe restraints on the liberty of a woman, who had moved indoors after the captive pre-Aryans replaced her in productive labour. Her sole occupation became reproduction and looking after the husband and his people. In an agricultural context the field now belonged to the sower, a concept not known to their pastoral ancestors. Hence the mother's, even the prospective mother's, maids', and young widows' movements were controlled to ensure the parentage of the heir. Class division, prosperity, and exemption from outdoor productive labour confined the woman indoors, and reproduction (especially of male children) became her sole *raison d'être*.

Conclusion

A critical rereading of historical and, for that matter, anthropological accounts greatly increases their validity for informing the correlates of demographic behaviour today. No descriptive or prescriptive text can be isolated from the circumstances in which it was written, nor can it be isolated from the circumstances in which it is read. This paper has tried to illustrate both these propositions through an alternative, politically less palatable, analysis of the ancient Indian texts to question the widespread belief that women in the past had a special status in Indian society. In the process, the paper has also tried to illustrate the problems that the careful demographer must acknowledge in his attempt to apply the material from other disciplines to his own subject of inquiry.

Abbreviations

AR   Āraṇyaka
AV   Atharva Veda
Br   Brāhmaṇa (texts on sacrifice)
DS   Dharma Sūtra (texts on social and caste conduct)
GS   Grhya Sūtra (texts on domestic rites)
RV   *Rgveda*
S   Samhita (Hymns)
T   Taittirīya
Up   Upaniṣad (philosophical texts)

Notes

1. Linguistic, sacrificial and social directives.
2. *RV* I: 124: 7.
3. *RV* I· 46. 4.
4. *RV* III: 62: 8.
5. *T* Br II: 4: 6: 56.
6. *RV* IV: 58: 9.

7. *RV* III: 61: 4.
8. *RV* I: 73: 3.
9. e.g. *RV* III: 80: 2, of *jāro na maryam abhyeti pascāt*.
10. *RV* X: 27: 12.
11. *Amāju, amājurā, kulapā kanyā, jaratkumārī* or *vṛddhakumārī*.
12. *RV* X: 18: 8.
13. *AV* XVIII: 3: 3.
14. Allen and Mukherji (1982: 4).
15. *T* Br III: 7: 5: 51.
16. Presumably, because after the Aryans began taking non-Aryan wives; they were reluctant to admit aliens to their sacred lore.
17. *Smṛticandrikā*, Mysore GOIS edn.: 62.
18. *RV* IV: 5: 5.
19. *Śatapatha* Br XII: 7: 2: 17.
20. *RV* X· 102: 2.
21. *Acāryānī, upādhyāyānī* and *ācaryā, upādhyāyā*.
22. Gārgī, Ātreyī, Sulabhā, Panditakaurśikī, and Sāṃkṛtyāyanī.
23. *Śāṅkhāyana* GS IV: 10: 3; *Āpastamba* GS III· 4: 4; *Kausītaki* GS I. 28: 22.
24. *Bṛhadāraṇyaka* Up III: 6· 1.
25. *Bṛhadāraṇyaka* UP VI: 4: 13.
26. *Taittirīya Āraṇyaka* I: II· 4.
27. *Atharvaveda* XI: 5: 18.
28. Allen and Mukherji (1982: 3).
29. *Āpastamba* DS II: 10: 27: 3.
30. *RV* X: 85: 46.
31. *RV* VIII: 6: 24.
32. *Aitareya* Br III: 24: 27; *Śatapatha* Br XIV: 1: 1: 31; *Āpastamba* DS II: 10: 27· 3.
33. *Śatapatha* Br X: 5: 2: 9.
34. *Vaśiṣṭha* DS XXVIII: 2, 3.
35. *Maitrāyanī* S IV: 7: 4.
36. *Gautama* DS XVIII: 1.
37. *Khādira* GS I: 4: 11.
38. *Āpastamba* DS I: 10· 51–3.
39. *Jaiminīya* Up Br XVII: 3: 1.
40. *Baudhāyana* DS II: 2: 3, 44–5.
41. *Taittirīya* S VI: 5: 10: 3.
42. *Śatapatha* Br IV: 4: 2: 13.
43. *Gautama* DS XII: 39.
44. I Br II: 2: 13.
45. e.g. *Maitrāyanī* S I: 10. 11: IV: 6: 4; *Taittiriya* S VI. 5: 8.
46. *Bṛhadāraṇyaka* Up V: 4: 7.
47. *Taittiriya* S, II: 5: 8: 2.
48. Ibid. II: 5: 2: 20.
49. *Āpastamba* DS XXIII: 4, *Hiranyakeśin* GS I; 4. 14: 2.
50. *T* S VI: 6: 8: 5.
51. cf e.g. *T* Br II· 2: 2: 13.
52. *Vaśiṣṭha* DS XXI: 8–10.
53. *Āpastamba* DS I: 10: 19, 28.
54. *Baudhāyana* GS II: 2: 63, 64.
55. e.g. *hasrā, agrū, sādhāranī, sāmānyā, puṃścaī, apaskadvarī, atiskadvarī*.
56. *RV* I: 112: 7; also I: 116: 1.
57. *AV* IX, 5: 27.
58. *AV* V: 17: 8, 9.
59. *T* S, VI: 6: 43, *T* Br I: 3: 10: 58.
60. *T* Ar: I: 3: 10: 50.
61. Mahiṣī, Vāvātā, Parivṛkti, and Pālāgalī.
62. *Aitareya* Br III: 5: 3: 47.
63. *Śatapatha* Br II: 3: 2: 18.

64. *Hiraṇyakeśin* GS I: 6: 12: 18.
65. *Kāthaka* S I: 10: 11: III.
66. *Maitrāyaṇī* S III: 8: 3; *T* S, VI: 5: 8: 2.
67. *Āpastamba* DS I: 9: 23: 45.
68. Ibid.
69. Ibid. VI: 5: 8: 2.
70. Ibid.
71. *Satapatha.*
72. *Śāṅkhāyana* SS XII: 29: 2; italics mine.
73. Smart and Smart (1978: 18).
74. Kelly (1984: 11).
75. Srinivas (1989: 16).
76. Grant and Kitzinger (1988).
77. *Manu* S III: 52.
78. *Maitrāyaṇī* S I: 11.
79. *Vaśiṣṭha* DS XII: 11: 18.
80. *Manu* S, V: 953.
81. *Manu* S, III: 52.
82. *Kātyāyana* DS V: 904.
83. *Yājñavalkya* DS II: 151.
84. Ibid. V: 95
85. *Vyāsa* DS IV: 30.
86. *Maitrāyaṇī* S III: 6: 3; IV: 6: 7; IV: 7.4; X: 10: 11; *T* S IV: 5: 8: 2.
87. *RV* X: 34: 4.
88. Mahābhārata II: 58: 32–7.
89. I VI: 5: 8: 2.
90. Gortyn law preserved in a fifth century inscription in Crete.
91. Pomeroy (1975: 41).
92. *Hiraṇyakeśin* GS I: 6: 22: 14; italics mine.
93. *Atharvaveda* III: 23; V: 25; VI: 11.
94. *Gobhila* GS II: 7: 1–2; *Khādira* GS II: 2: 214–28.
95. *Bharadvāja* GS I: 2.
96. *Jaiminīya* GS I: 17.
97. de Beauvoir (1986: 204).
98. Rich (1976: 21).
99. Kelly (1984: 129–30).
100. Chodorov (1978: 39).
101. *Viṣṇu* DS LXVIII: 46; italics mine.
102. *Vāsiṣṭha* DS XXI: 10; XIII: 47; *Viṣṇu* DS LVII: 1–5.
103. *Baudhāyana* DS II: 2: 48.
104. *Hiraṇyakeśin* GS II: 4: 10: 7; *Manusaṃhitā.*
105. *Śatapatha* Br II: 5: 2–20.
106. *Baudhāyana* DS II 4: 6; *Āpastamba* DS II: 5: 11–14; *Yājñavalkya* S I: 73: 81; *Manusaṃhitā*
     IX: 4.
107. *Aitareya* Br III: 24: 27; *Āpastamba* DS I: 10: 51–3; italics mine.
108. She is the Indian counterpart of Greek Eileithiya.
109. *Mānava* GS III: 13: 6; 11: 4.
110. el Saadawi (1980: 63).
111. *Manu* S IX: 35.
112. Ibid. IX, 37.
113. Ibid. IX: 48.
114. Ibid. IX: 52; X: 32.
115. Eisenstein (1988: 81).
116. de Beauvoir (1986: 113).
117. Allen and Mukherji (1987: 7).

References

Abbott, J. (1932), *The Keys of Power: A Study of Indian Ritual and Belief*. London: Methuen.

Allen, M. and Mukherji, S. N. (1982), *Women in India and Nepal*. Canberra: Australian National University.

Altekar, A. S. (1956), *The Position of Women in Hindu Civilization*. Delhi: Motilal Banarsidass.

Ardner E. (1980), *Perceiving Women*. London: Malaby Press.

Auerbach, N. (1982), *Women and the Demon*. Cambridge, Mass.: Harvard University Press.

Bachofen, J. J. (1981), *Myth, Religion and Mother Right*. London: Routledge & Kegan Paul (first published in 1967).

Barker, D. L. and Allen, S. (eds.) (1976), *Dependence and Exploitation in Work and Marriage*. London: Longman.

Baroda, Maharani of and Mitra, S. M. (1911), *The Position of Women in Indian Life*. Delhi: Longmans, Green and Co.

Bennett, L. (1983), 'Sex and motherhood among the Brahmins and Chhetris of east central Nepal'. *Contributions to Nepalese Studies*, 3: 1–52.

Bhattacharya, A. (1948), 'The cult of Shasthi in Bengal'. *Man in India*, 28: 152–62.

Bhattacharya, N. N. (1977), *The Indian Mother Goddess*. Columbia: South Asian Books.

Boserup, E. (1970), *Women's Role in Economic Development*. London: George Allen & Unwin.

Briffault, R. (1959), *The Mothers* (abridged edn.). London: Macmillan.

Chodorov, N. (1978), *The Reproduction of Mothering Psycho-analysis and the Sociology of Gender*. Berkeley: University of California Press.

Daly, M. (1978), *Gun/Ecology: The Metaethics of Radical Feminism*. Boston: Beacon Press.

Davies, M. (ed.) (1978), *Maternity: Letters from Working Women*. Montreal: Eden Press Women's Publications.

de Beauvoir, S. (1949), *The Second Sex*. Bombay: Penguin, 1986 edn.

Durkheim, E and Mauss, M. (1963), *Primitive Classifications*. Chicago: University of Chicago Press.

el Sadaawi, N. (1980), *The Hidden Face of Eve*. London: Zed Press.

Evans-Pritchard, E. E. (1962), *Essays in Social Anthropology*. London: Faber & Faber.

Gimbuttas, M. (1982), *The Goddesses and Gods of Old Europe*. London: Thames & Hudson.

Ghosh, S. K. (1989), *Indian Women through the Ages*. Chicago: University of Chicago Press.

Grant, M. and Kitzinger, R. (eds.) (1988), *Civilization of the Ancient Mediterranean* Vol. 1: *Greece and Rome*. New York: Scribner's.

Hall, E. T. (1966), *The Hidden Dimension*. New York: Doubleday.

Harris, M. (1983), *Cultural Anthropology*. London: Harper & Row.

Jacobson, D. and Wadley, S. (1986), *Women in India*. Delhi: Manohar.

Kelly, J. (1984), *Women, History and Theory*. Chicago: University of Chicago Press.

Krishnaswamy, S. (1983), *Glimpses of Women in India*. New Delhi: Ashis Publishing House.

Lazarre, J. (1976), *The Mother Knot*. New York: McGraw Hill.

Madan, T. N. (1976), *Family and Kinship*. Bombay: Asia Publishing House.

Mandelbaum, D. (1970), *Society in India*, 2 vols. Berkeley: University of California Press.

Mannheim, R. (1963), *The Great Mother: An Analysis of the Archetype*. Princeton: Princeton University Press.

Morgan, L. H. (1877), *Ancient Society*. Calcutta: K. P. Bagchi (1982 edn.).

Neumann, E. (1955), *The Great Mother*. New York: Bollingen Foundation.

Pomeroy, S. B. (1975), *Goddesses, Whores, Wives and Slaves: Women in Classical Antiquity*. New York: Scholar Books.

Preston, J. (ed.) (1983), *Mother Worship: Themes and Variations*, 2nd edn. Chapel Hill, NC: University of North Carolina Press (first published in 1982).

Raphael, D. (ed.) (1989), *Being Female: Reproduction, Power and Change*. The Hague: Mouton.

Rich, A. (1976), *Of Women Born: Motherhood as Experience and Institution*. New York: W. W. Norton.

Richter, D. (1971), 'The position of women in classical Athens'. *Classical Journal*, 67: 1–6.

Rossi, A. (1977), 'A biological perspective on parenting', *Daedalus*, 106: 1–31.

Ruddick, S. (1980), 'The maternal thinking', *Feminist Studies*, 6: 342–67.

Seltman, C. (1956), *Women in Antiquity*. London: Thames and Hudson.

Smart, C. and Smart, B. (eds.) (1978) *Women, Sexuality and Social Control*. London: Routledge & Kegan Paul.

Srinivas, M. N. (1989), *The Cohesive Role of Sanskritization*. Oxford: Oxford University Press.

Srinivas, M. N. (1977), 'The changing position of women in India', *Man*, 12: 221–38.

8 Political Economy and Cultural Processes in the Fertility Decline of Sicilian Artisans

JANE SCHNEIDER AND PETER SCHNEIDER

This paper analyses the transition from high to low fertility of the artisan class in a rural town of the Sicilian interior. The transition occurred between the First and Second World Wars, a time of severe dislocation and economic downturn. We argue that the resulting hardships motivated artisans to want smaller families; yet we do not treat their impressive new commitment to family limitation as a mere economizing gesture, but regard it as reflecting, as well, pan-European cultural processes that contributed to the diffusion of a particular technique of family limitation: coitus interruptus. We ask specifically how the inter-war crisis affected local artisans. In addition, we examine their life ways in relation to both the gender dynamics of this technique and the communications networks carrying news of its contraceptive efficacy. Overall, we hope to present a culturally sensitive, political economy approach to population change.

The rural town in question is referred to as Villamaura. Located at around 9,000 feet in altitude in what was once a grain-producing zone, its history has been shaped by the vast *latifundia* that dominated interior Sicily from Roman colonization until the Second World War. Villamaura's inhabitants were, as a result, divided into highly unequal social groups. Fieldwork experience in the mid-1960s, reinforced by extensive reading of Sicilian history, led us to define four categories for comparison: a class of quasi-aristocratic gentry landowners, the *civili* (singular, or as an adjective, *civile*); a class of artisans (*artigiani* or *mastri*); a class of relatively well-off peasants (*burgisi*, singular *burgise*); and, by far the largest group, a class of landless and landpoor peasants called *braccianti* (singular *bracciante*) because their only means of production was their arms (*braccie*).

By the mid-1960s, Villamaura's population had contracted from its early twentieth-century peak of 11,000 to around 7,500, reflecting both out-migration and fertility decline. Members of the gentry class began to have fewer children around 1900 with artisans following, as noted above, between the two world wars. The movement of the peasantry in this direction also began in the inter-war years but did not engage a majority of either prosperous or poor peasants until the 1950s and 1960s.

Our initial residence in Villamaura occurred between 1965 and 1967. Later field trips of direct relevance to the study of population change occurred over eight months in 1977–8, and for three summers thereafter. In the course of these sojourns, we used vital records to reconstitute the families formed by marriages at ten-year intervals from 1850 to 1920. Household registers, dating to the late nineteenth century and continuing into the present, facilitated tracking families from the 1920s on.

Both household registers and the vital records consistently indicate men's occupations and sometimes women's, but not necessarily in ways that corresponded to the four social groups we wanted to compare. For example, only around the turn of the century did record-keepers begin to use the term *bracciante*. Until then other words—*contadino, villano, mezzadro*—indicated a paucity of land. At the other end of the scale, a descendant of one of the best known *civile* families appeared in the records as a 'gold merchant'. There were also numerous craft specializations with which we were unfamiliar. Older interviewees, many of them good, informal historians, helped us interpret these labels and make coding decisions, explaining, for example, that the gold merchant was indeed a '*civile*', that a *villano* was likely impoverished, and that the crafts of weaving baskets and making sieves were better considered extensions of peasant than of artisan life. Our understanding of class was further enhanced through retrospective interviewing, and through a material culture survey. In conducting the latter, we asked elderly informants to explain the social and cultural contexts of their families' past houses, furnishings and wardrobes—items that, in many instances, we could see, handle, and compare for ourselves. Overall, we have sought to interpret Villamaura's social hierarchy less as a 'structure' than as a reflection of on-going processes of class formation, set off by the commercialization of agriculture after 1860 (see Schneider and Schneider 1996).

Political Economy and Population Change

As is well known, the earliest theory of demographic transition, popular in the 1950s, attributed instances of rapid population expansion to falling mortality, then defined each subsequent drop in fertility as a homeostatic 'adjustment'. A cluster of interacting changes associated with modernization was held to account for this adjustment: mortality decline, urbanizing and industrializing trends, new patterns of work and leisure for women, and an expanded presence of secular beliefs and institutions. Declining child labour, a widening availability of contraceptives and contraceptive information, and the emergence of social security systems for the aged have also been on the list. Interpreting fertility behaviour in relation to so wide a range of 'factors'—social, economic, medical, intellectual, technological, and cultural— the theory had a relatively holistic cast. Only politics was absent as a domain of change, no doubt because so many political regimes appeared to be either uninvolved in, or an outright obstacle to, the spread of birth control.

We are intrigued that, by around 1970, this holism was diverging into two, seemingly opposite, orientations towards population change. Researchers associated with the Princeton Project for the study of historical demography in Europe exemplify one orientation; researchers influenced by neo-classical economics exemplify the other. Both schools have confronted the task of comprehending what in technical language are called 'differentials'—the tendency for processes of fertility decline, as they unfold in any particular, localized setting, to engage some groups but not others—indeed, to side-step some groups whose rates of growth not only remain high, but may actually be increasing. Because it is so often the least advantaged social groups that 'lag' behind in the transition to smaller family size, both historical and economic demographers confront the task of 'explaining' the coincidence of high fertility and immiseration. Does one cause the other? In what ways do they interact? Are both but manifestations of wider problems?

Two contrasting answers have dominated much of the literature. For the Princeton-affiliated historical demographers, the decisive element is people's ideas and values, their world view or *mentalité*, as shaped above all by religion. In their reconstructions of the European fertility decline, groups that 'failed' to adjust to falling mortality and other modernizing processes by limiting the size of their families did so because of a 'traditional' or fatalistic mind-set which discouraged subjecting the realm of reproduction to 'rational control'. Conversely, for most economic demographers, fertility rates are always an aggregate of the conscious, rational decisions that couples make upon weighing the relative costs and benefits to them of the *n*th child. According to this approach, if the transition to small family size comes later in some groups than in others, it is because, for those groups, children continue to add more to their parents' short-term or long-term well-being than they take away.

Both of these alternatives—the culturalist and the rational choice models—are considerably one-sided in imagining human behaviour to be motivated either by culture or practical reason (see Sahlins 1976), by emotion or interest, by values or by advantage. In contrast to both, we treat as a positive, rather than negative, feature of early transition theory its emphasis on a cluster of changes that simultaneously influence all, or most, domains of human activity, however uneven the effects. Such a model, messy as it might be, resonates with the lived experience of fertility decline more fully than the polarized caricatures that result from searching for one, pre-eminent cause. The point is to grasp the historical context for the changes, to see their variable effect within as well as across local settings, and to trace how people in these settings generate collective as well as individual responses, drawing upon the full range of indigenous and external cultural materials at their disposal.

First, the historical context. Because the fertility decline in Europe was coterminous with the emergence and spread of capitalism, shifts in investment trends—the so-called boom and bust cycles—are among the most important shaping forces to consider. Each punctuation or 'conjuncture', we propose, can be consequential for all the domains of life of any given social group. In other words, the concept of the conjuncture or phase as a marked moment in the erratic, discontinuous, and chaotic expansion of capitalism is our solution to the problem of handling a wide range of variables at the same time.

Put somewhat differently, the concerted actions of political and economic power-holders, operating as they do in a highly competitive field, affect people's lives by exposing them to bouts of expansion and contraction, optimism and anxiety about the future. Not only our bread and butter, but our outlook or mood, can be influenced by these shifts, with implications for reproductive behaviour. Whereas the first theory of demographic transition envisioned a long list of variables interacting to induce fertility decline through the generalized evolutionary trajectory of 'modernization', we fasten on capitalism's historic, always politically conditioned, moments of exuberant entry into new arenas of commodification, and its moments of disinvestment and depression. Such times, we think, accelerate demographic changes already underway, above all by encouraging a redefinition of family ideals—the adoption of new standards for evaluating one's own and other people's families.

It must be emphasized that such redefinition is not the work of isolated couples, acting as individuals who want, or feel compelled, to adjust to change. Rather, as cultural work, it occurs in groups—face-to-face reference groups whose members share a similar relation to the conjuncture in question. Nor do we think of this cultural work as a matter of one-dimensional diffusion. Among the members of any face-to-face community, some will be innovators in the creation of new standards, inspired, perhaps, by the behaviour of outsiders, and others will follow. But this does not require our adopting the hegemonic assumption that the only cultural process worth considering is the historic spread of 'Western values' from the first centres of capitalism into a backward or 'traditional' geographical and social periphery. After laying out the political–economic motivation for fertility decline among Villamaura's artisans, we consider, below, the pitfalls of so narrow an understanding of culture.

Artisans and the Inter-War Conjuncture

Making up about 15%–25% of the local population around the turn of the century (Gabaccia 1988: 40–1), Villamaura's artisans were a diverse group. Some made agricultural implements and had a largely peasant clientele.

Others, for example shoemakers, catered to a mix of customers that included members of the gentry class as well. Stone-cutters, especially if they worked in marble, and cabinet-makers, if they worked in luxury woods like ebony, oriented their activity to the upper end of the social scale. Because in Villamaura the gentry occupants of this upper end had set themselves up to 'live in style', their grand *palazzi* and graceful villas transforming what was once a rural backwater into a bustling, cosmopolitan town, craftsmen and women of considerable skill were a noteworthy local presence.

Back in the 1880s, Europe's first great depression had brought about a collapse of grain prices—the background, in Sicily, for a decade of political turmoil (the 1890s) and the related exodus of artisans and especially peasants to North America. It was in the context of this conjuncture that the gentry class of Villamaura, feeling undermined, first began to limit family size. There was nothing, however, in the political–economic dynamics of the decades leading up to the First World War that confronted craftsmen with a similar imperative. On the contrary, if gentry orders for artisanal production atrophied, returned migrants, and recipients of emigrants' remittances, more than filled the gap. Eager to enlarge and embellish their homes, these new consumers commissioned furniture and fittings and clothes that expressed their aspirations for a better life. Artisan couples of the early twentieth century continued to produce large birth cohorts, notwithstanding that members of the gentry were setting out another course.

To say this is to dramatize the speed and thoroughness with which small families appeared among Villamaura's artisans in the following, inter-war period. Our analysis of this period benefits from a new data source: local household registers instituted by the Mussolini government in 1931. Called *foglie di famiglia* (family files), the registers are a useful supplement to the vital records of marriage, birth, and death, revealing both household composition and information on emigration. We were able to find 206 such records for artisan families in Villamaura's archive, describing households formed by marriages between 1860 and 1950. They display a strong and consistent pattern: until the 1920s, the great majority of artisan couples had between five and thirteen living children; from the 1920s on, and particularly after 1930, most had two or three and none had more than four.

Our first task in comprehending this change in family composition is to look at the political economy of the inter-war years. Not surprisingly, given its class structure and vulnerability to crises, Villamaura participated in the surge of labour and peasant unrest that swept through Italy at the end of the First World War. The years 1919 and 1920 were 'hot years' for this country as for much of Europe. Workers occupied factories in Turin and Milan; the fledgling Socialist Party, like Russia's Mensheviks and Bolsheviks, split into minimalist and maximalist wings; and in 1921 a breakaway group formed the Italian Communist Party. In Sicily worker organizations asserted themselves in strategic domains, for example the Palermo shipyards. Miners struck in the sulphur zone, while restive peasants, hungry for land and improved agricultural contracts, staged demonstrations and strikes in several of the large rural towns (Ganci 1980: 94–7; Marino 1976: 85–8).

Along with severe inflation, the claims of war veterans to be rewarded with land stoked the militancy. In 1919, the more or less 'liberal' national government promulgated decrees providing for the orderly occupation of uncultivated holdings by certified leagues and cooperatives formed by veterans. At the same time, leagues of both socialist and Catholic–populist orientation mobilized to claim land too (Ganci 1980: 94–7). In the words of one historian, the First World War was 'the yeast of the class struggle', setting in motion an assault on the entire parasitic and exploitative structure of productive relations (Marino 1976: 90).

In Villamaura, artisans were in the vanguard of a local socialist movement, which in 1913, aided by a further expansion of the suffrage, elected a handful of representatives to the town council. According to Gabaccia, in 1916, 150 socialist-led locals 'organized one of the earliest Sicilian protests against the war' (1988: 161). In 1919 there were local echoes of larger strikes, especially nearby Ribera's 'four days of Bolshevism' (Ganci 1980: 154–8). Three peasant leagues—one socialist, one Catholic, and one of veterans—occupied *latifondi* in order to gain land and improve tenancy and sharecropping arrangements. Finally, in 1921 Villamaura's 'maximal' socialists spawned a circle (*circolo*) of the Communist Party. (Sicily supported 37 party sections with 776 members in this, the first, Communist year.) (Ganci 1980: 102–9; Gabaccia 1988: 161; Schneider and Schneider 1976: 128).

The crushing defeat of these revolutionary initiatives took different forms in Italy's varied regions. In the case of Sicily, only the economically most developed province of Ragusa in the south-eastern quadrant of the island generated indigenous fascists. Nevertheless, titled elements of the landed class, resident in Catania and Palermo, felt sufficiently terrified by the 'poisonous' spectre of peasant power to create an 'anti-Bolshevik' agrarian party. When, after Mussolini's March on Rome in 1922, the national fascist regime set about consolidating a presence in the South, its leaders sought out an alliance with this group (Ganci 1980: 98–109; Marino 1976: 207).

While in the previous era the national government had nourished free trade and open borders, fascism took Italy in an autarchic direction. The changed global context of the post-war years encouraged this step. For one thing, the United States Immigration Acts of the early 1920s heavily restricted—indeed, virtually dammed up—the migration stream from Italy. The fascist regime in Italy quickly developed a negative discourse on emigration, thereafter defined as a shameful, 'proletarian' way of spreading one's influence in the world. In contrast to colonizers, emigrants drained off national resources and lowered a nation's prestige—the opposite of what Britain and France had achieved.

Once the transatlantic connection was broken, Italy faced a new and serious balance of payments problem, in part the motivation for a reversal in tariff and agricultural policies. In 1925 Mussolini launched a 'Battle for Grain', designed to put pastures back into wheat, to reclaim unused land, and thereby to break the country's reliance on imported cereals. Historian Salvatore Lupo offers a comprehensive account of what this meant for Sicily. The protectionist bent, intensified by revaluations of the *lira* between 1926 and 1929 and by the global depression of 1929–33, was especially damaging to the coastal and urban sectors of the island economy where a strong commerce in fish, wine-grapes, irrigated fruits, and fruit products had flourished. A modern, dynamic, entrepreneurial sector tied to this commercial activity was subjected to the restored predominance of the *latifundia* (Lupo 1981).

Thanks to the unrest and migration remittances of the previous era, some *latifondi* had been divided, others rented out to peasant cooperatives, in both cases with encouragement to a varied polyculture as against the old tyranny of grain. Now, the Battle for Grain established a context for reconsolidating that tyranny, and with it the largest properties. Argued to favour the mechanization of reaping and threshing, in fact the reconsolidation satisfied the *civile* desire for class vengeance. In Lupo's words, there occurred a veritable inversion of the tendencies of 1900–14 as landowners sought to recoup complete control over productive activity and the social fabric (Lupo 1981: 70; Mack Smith 1968: 516).

During the inter-war years, the neo-mercantilist fascist government adopted a series of populationist measures in support of its bellicose posture in the world community of nations. As early as 1924, Mussolini had reversed his earlier support for a neo-Malthusian movement that had begun to disseminate birth control propaganda in Italy. In 1926 he promoted a national commission to protect 'the family' from such propaganda and instituted a tax on bachelors. The tax was increased in 1928, with benefits added for fathers of seven or more children if they worked for the state, ten or more children if they worked in the private sector. Meanwhile women were exhorted that their pre-eminent duty was to bear the nation's children (de Grazia 1992: 44; Glass 1967; Saraceno 1992: 258–61; Triolo 1989). Yet, although the population of Sicily continued to grow after 1914, there is scant evidence that these measures were the reason. Conducting fieldwork in Villamaura in the mid-1960s, we learned of one local family that had become a target of ridicule for having twelve children 'just because of Mussolini'— eight of the twelve were daughters, leaving the poor father with a ludicrous number of dowries to provide. It is more likely, rather, that a continued decline of mortality, plus return migration, accounted for most of the inter-war population growth.

Within this overall expansion, artisans had clearly embarked on something new. Before we turn to the cultural processes that supported their innovation, let us summarize why the political and economic conjuncture of the inter-war years motivated them to want fewer children. First of all, even in the absence of competition from imported manufactures—a threat that would ruin local craftsmen after the Second World War—the curtailment of emigration and currency revaluations, capped by the depression, affected them deeply. Accustomed to marrying within their class ('everyone with their own *ceto*' was a characteristic slogan), they expected their male offspring to succeed them. Shoemakers gave rise to shoemakers, carpenters to carpenters, and so on. Sometimes boys acquired the necessary skills from their fathers, for example by straightening nails for them after school. More often they were apprenticed to another craftsman. Apparently, each artisan shop had seven or eight such learners during the period in question. Apprentices earned neither room and board nor income—only a token gift on festival days or a pair of shoes each year if this were their trade. Should the apprenticeship require a sojourn in Palermo, there were fees to pay. In addition, artisans aimed for their children to obtain some schooling. Once migration to America ceased to be an option, outlays for apprenticeships became an increasing burden, the more so as the promise of eventual adult employment began to dim. Villamaura had some thirty shoemaking shops between the wars, an over-saturation of the market even without a dip in the business cycle.

The depression, coming on the heels of the revaluations, was devastating. Much artisan activity focused on the annual festival when everyone needed new attire, and on weddings and the creation of new households. But these were not the moments when clients paid. Typically, a craftsman advanced his services to entire families, whether peasant or gentry, on an annual basis and worked out a system of reckoning credit based on the agricultural calendar. Every 31 August, following the grain harvest, all debts were called in, whether in money or in kind. Unfortunately, artisans procured their raw materials from suppliers in Palermo who, except in unusual cases of 'good faith', advanced credit for three to four months at best. And, whereas local craftsmen were reluctant to charge interest, preferring to include the service of the loan in the cost of the product, Palermo suppliers charged 5% or 6%. The revaluations had a pincer effect: suppliers' terms became ever less generous just as local clients began to default. An old shoemaker, reminiscing about the 1930s, recalled having to make shoes from donkey skins because he could no longer acquire leather, then showed us his ledgers of the time in which a vast number of debts were simply cancelled. According to the ledgers, even his better-off clients let him down, although generally speaking, work for the *civili* was more likely to be remunerated than work for the other classes.

Like smallholders, artisans risked bankruptcy during the inter-war years. We were told that those with mainly peasant clients sometimes became agricultural labourers, forced to make ends meet by seeking a daily wage harvesting crops. Family limitation seemed a way to avoid this fate. By all accounts, artisans embraced the idea of the small, early stopping family both to be able to provide for each child under deteriorating economic circumstances, and to shore up a resource—in this case skills rather than land—that the ever growing class of 'beggars' did not have. The alternative was to lose both a livelihood and a respected social position.

In addition to this motivation, at once economic and cultural, the way of life of artisans positioned them to learn about, and develop a positive orientation towards, the 'French method' of coitus interruptus. As we will see, this practice was simultaneously 'rational' and 'moral'—a means of birth control and, as a symbol of sexual continence, an anchor for family respectability or honour. It is to this aspect of the artisans' fertility decline that we now turn.

Cultural Aspects of Western Europe's Demographic Transition

In the forefront of an unprecedented population explosion, Western Europeans had to pioneer new and uncharted territory in bringing about their fertility decline. They did not get much help from Church or State. The first opposed the idea of birth control on moral and religious grounds; the second remained overtly pro-natalist until the twentieth century (and in some cases, beyond). Moreover, until this century, there was no effective 'family planning' establishment to counsel women and distribute mechanical or chemical contraceptives, improved through the linked efforts of scientific research and the medical and pharmaceutical professions. Such a network and such efforts were, in fact, consequences of the transition to a low birth rate in Europe. The transition depended, instead, on some combination of the following strategies: celibacy and abstinence within marriage, coitus interruptus, and abortion. Of the three, coitus interruptus, also known as withdrawal, is considered to have been pre-eminent (Santow 1993; Schneider and Schneider 1991, 1996; Wrigley 1969: 188–200).

Like abortion, coitus interruptus meant very different things to different people. Condemned by religious and moral authorities as an enhancement to irresponsible sexuality, as a method of birth control it appears to have demanded considerable sexual restraint: the 'rational' modulation or redeployment of gratification (Foucault 1980: 120–2, 154; Gay 1984: 262–77; Schneider and Schneider 1991, 1996). Moreover, for most Europeans fertility decline meant not only fewer live births—the average number per married woman fell from seven or eight in 1870 to two or three by 1960—but what is called 'early stopping': the compression of childbearing into the first few years of a mothering career. Completing a birth cohort some ten to fifteen years before the menopause of the wife, married couples who relied on withdrawal to reduce the risk of unwanted pregnancies did so for heroic stretches of time.

Most of the literature on Europe's declining fertility overlooks this fact. Coitus interruptus is mentioned only in passing, as if it obviously belonged to a wider, more inclusive account of 'birth control' or 'family limitation'. Often it is taken for granted as a 'male method'. Yet, notwithstanding these lapses, it can be argued that the central role of withdrawal in the European transition to a low birth rate exerted a subtle influence over theory. Both the culturalist and the economistic approaches put great store in men's and women's 'rational control' of sexual desire as the core means to smaller family size. Culturalist theory, in particular, posits such defiance of nature as part of the package of (hopefully diffusing) 'Western values' whose presence constituted a necessary, if not a sufficient, condition for modern demographic practice.

According to Ansley Coale, the first to articulate the culturalist position as a theory, the Western values package hinges on a secular, rational, or calculating world view that enables people to consider the otherwise 'unthinkable' idea of controlling fertility (Coale 1973; Alter 1992: 20–3). Additional features include a nuclear family system that pivots around the gender-balanced, companionate form of marriage and encourages its members to pursue paths of individual achievement. In retrospect, as Susan Watkins has commented, the standard seems derived from the aspirations of sexually continent middle-class families of Victorian Europe and America—families in which coitus interruptus served as both mechanism and symbol of empowerment and respectability (Watkins 1993; Gay 1984).

An important application of the culturalist approach is found in Massimo Livi-Bacci's monograph on Italy, written for the Princeton Project in 1977. Having determined that the Italian South 'lagged' behind the North in the decline of fertility, Livi-Bacci went on to demonstrate, using measures developed by Coale, a greater homogeneity for southern than for northern fertility patterns. The reason, he argued, was that in the South, culture 'explained' more of the variance, binding not only peasants, but urban and artisan classes as well, into a seamless whole:

What seems to be at work is the force of residual factors, which we cannot measure statistically. Attachment to traditions; a more extended and tightly knit family system; the stronger weight of social control; the lack of women's emancipation; the weight of the often very conservative teaching of the Church—these are some of the manifold factors of Southern culture [which] affect, in a degree not appreciably different, all sectors of the population without regard to income, profession, or residence. (Livi-Bacci 1977: 244)

Did Villamaura in the early twentieth century harbour the cultural obstacles to fertility decline that Livi-Bacci identified for the Italian south as a whole? On two points—family and religion—the picture is less than clear. For example, even if Sicilians were not consciously socialized to strike off on their own, pursuing opportunities that would cut them off from a close and continual relationship with their kin, can we assume that families were always extended and 'closely knit'? Emigration, certainly, had led to dramatic estrangements even though many migrants established lifelines of remittance payments, letters, and gifts; even though many eventually returned home. Locally, the Catholic Church, represented by several priests, two monasteries, and several lay organizations, reinforced a proverbially conservative idea—that 'every child is the child of God' (*ogni bimbo, figlio di dio*) and should be accepted as such. But God's providential role in reproduction was not necessarily presented as the negation of contraception. In retrospective interviews, two elderly priests, one doctor, and several non-specialists emphasized that birth control was not an issue that was aggressively pursued in the pulpit or in confession. Besides, they pointed out, Villamaura fairly bubbled with both intellectual and popular forms of anticlericalism, among them the free masonry of the *civile* class and the free-thinking of artisans.

Easier to defend is Livi-Bacci's claim regarding the emancipation of women, for Villamaura participated in a Mediterranean culture long associated with the patriarchal complex of 'honour and shame'. Recent analyses, however, question the uniformity, distribution, and consistency of the honour–shame complex over geographical and social space, and over time. Michael Herzfeld, whose ethnography of Crete pioneered this more nuanced view, in particular asked if the very word 'honour' did not mean different things in the different contexts to which English-speaking anthropologists had applied it (Herzfeld 1980, 1984). In the following account, we attempt to assimilate the lessons of the last few years.

According to George Saunders's useful review, there is considerable evidence that, in southern European societies, the conjugal bond was not traditionally a source of pronounced affection or intimacy. Although it involved cooperation, marriage competed with the affective ties that united a wife with her children (especially sons), a wife with her family of origin, and a husband with his family of origin. In order to attract husbands, women had to be endowed by their families; but the land or house they received as dowry, plus the valuable hand-embroidered bed linens that constituted their trousseaux, did not become spousal property. Destined for transmission to their children, these resources could be drawn upon by a husband only if he sought legal authorization. And, should a wife die childless, the trousseau and dowry reverted to her family, rather than her spouse (Saunders 1981: 442–4; Brettell 1991).

More than one Villamaura resident whom we queried on the subject of dowry in the 1960s held up as diagnostic the apocryphal case of the woman who died along with her first issue, in childbirth. If she were the first of the two to expire, the child would inherit her property (if only for a matter of seconds); then upon his or her death the property would revert to the child's heir—the father. But if, on the other hand, the child died first, the dowried property would be restored to the wife's kin, her family of origin. So clear were these rules that both husband and in-laws were expected to mobilize witnesses on behalf of their respective claims. Nor is Villamaura the only Sicilian community to substantiate Saunders's conclusion regarding a weak marriage bond. Charlotte Gower Chapman, conducting fieldwork in a Sicilian rural town she called 'Milocca' during the 1920s, also thought that the marital relationship was undermined by ties of lineality. In the absence of children, the wife's dowry belonged to her and her kin, the husband's inheritance to him and his (Chapman 1971: 97–8).

Nancy Triolo, author of a (1989) dissertation on Sicilian maternity in the 1930s, draws upon Chapman to make the same point, adding other revealing details. For example, children in Sicily were customarily named for a grandparent of their same sex—the first born for those on the paternal side, the second born for those on the maternal side. Triolo suggests that the naming practice kept alive the significance of consanguineal, as distinct from marital, relationships, especially when these relationships were celebrated on the name day, or *onomastico*, of the saint whose name they shared (Triolo, n.d.). According to Triolo, we should also ask whether, upon marriage, women kept their family names. In the 1960s, when we were first in Villamaura, people would identify a married woman by the often humorous, unflattering, or legendary nickname (*sopranome*) of her natal extended family, even though they used her married name to her face.

If the marriage bond was traditionally weak in Sicily, did this mean that wives were subordinated to husbands, or women to men? One clue might be a discrepancy in spousal age. It is therefore noteworthy that in Milocca a proverb declared the ideal bride to be 18 (never over 30), whereas 28 was the ideal age declared for a groom (Chapman 1971: 98–101). Villamaura residents of the 1960s also considered a discrepancy of ten years to be ideal, so much so that young men of 20, imagining their future wives, looked over girls who were 10. Yet the ideal gap is at odds with overall statistics showing youthful marriage on the part of men as well as women. 'Late marriages make early orphans' was another proverb that Charlotte Chapman recorded in Milocca. Moreover, as both her study and ours on Villamaura show, different social classes exhibited different orientations towards marriage age. The most likely to realize the ideal of a groom ten years older than his bride were members of the landed peasant or *burgise* class, whose men were obliged to amass a respectable amount of property before taking the plunge. In Villamaura, during the decades of the 1920s and 1930s, which are the focus of this paper, a destabilized economy resulted in postponed marriages by *burgise* women as well as men, cancelling out much of the difference in spousal age.

Rather than rely on marriage-age data to arrive at the quality of gender relations, Saunders follows the lead of Ann Parsons, whose social–psychological study of Neapolitan families in the late 1960s raised the issue of the male peer group. To a surprising degree, the women depicted by Parsons tolerated in their husbands, as they appreciated in their sons, a modicum of irresponsible and carefree roving outside the home. Peer groups of adult men gave space to obscene and sacrilegious joking—a welcome escape from the constraining, madonna-like image of the wife and mother at home. The converse of men's freedom to flaunt domestic and religious authority was women's subjugation. As Saunders shows, numerous ethnographies report that father and brothers chaperoned a girl before she married, guarding her reputation for chastity; mothers and mothers-in-law inspected the bridal sheets for blood stains after the wedding night; husbands gave their brides a black dress in anticipation of their widowhood and remained jealous of their chastity throughout their married years; men flaunted a jealous control of 'their' women.

In marriage negotiations, the value of a woman's dowry was pivotal, but her purity mattered as well. Except in poor families, where it was difficult to isolate daughters from public view, parents enhanced the value of their female offspring by keeping them home, or chaperoning them when they did leave the house. Between the demand for dowry and the need for constant vigilance, people sometimes referred to their daughters as 'burdens'. 'Blessed is the door out of which a dead daughter goes', eerily joked a proverb quoted by Chapman (1971: 30). By the same token, an unchaste or unfaithful wife might be returned, dowry in hand, to her kin (p. 110). Conversely, although most Milocca husbands were faithful, male infidelity 'was not a sin'. Nor were men constrained by law in this regard. Had Sicilian women of the 1920s been able to seek adjudication in the national courts, they would have found the double standard legally enshrined. In the 1970s, partly in response to political campaigns on the part of Italian feminists, a series of enactments changed family law dramatically. Until then, legislation had favoured patriarchy. Indeed, the telltale principle of *patria potestà* was not erased until 1975. According to this concept, husbands ruled over their wives, who were the legal equivalent of children. Under the penal code, moreover, women could be punished for appearing disreputable, and for assuming careers that detracted from family life (Rodotà and Rodotà 1982; Saraceno 1992: 253–4).

To the extent that 'the male version of culture is publicly dominant', Saunders argues, women are 'socialized from childhood to accept the male view of reality'. Although women of the past may have harboured cynical doubts, 'their public acceptance of a role that devalued their intelligence probably also eroded their respect for each other and aspirations for themselves' (Saunders 1981: 448–9). Nancy Triolo is convinced otherwise. Women's activities were separated from men's in Sicily's rural communities of the early twentieth century. Except in very poor families, wives and daughters rarely accompanied men to the fields. Their dress emphasized modesty. But none of these conditions defined women as dominated, passive, or shy. Attached to the home, they also ran it (Triolo, n.d.). As the Sicilian folklorist Salamone-Marino (1968) insisted, married women over-saw the preparation of their daughters' trousseaux and the negotiation of their children's marriages—a pivotal role.

Several sources suggest that, although 'prudish' or, better, 'modest', Sicilian women of the past were not puritanical. Chapman records hearing licentious conversations, rich with metaphors for sexual intercourse—for example the lever on a kneading board pressing on a piece of dough, or an embroiderer's needle moving in and out of a piece cloth (1971: 91). Nor were young girls so protected as to preclude their falling in love. Although a proverb said that marriages based on love or pre-marital acquaintance were doomed, such unions did occur, in part because determined girls and their suitors could elope, forcing the hands of their parents and prospective in-laws (Chapman 1971: 91–5).

A girl who became pregnant out of wedlock also had an 'out'. Guided, perhaps, by her mother, she could anonymously place her baby in an institution for foundlings. According to a recent study by David Kertzer, in 1750 the Bourbon monarchy then ruling Sicily obliged all local govern-ments to provide for the reception, wet-nursing, and family placement of illegitimate offspring at public expense. By the mid-nineteenth century, 69 % of the island's communities had done so, if not without some resistance, creating the most extensive network of homes for abandoned infants in Italy (Kertzer 1993: 95–8). After national unification in 1860, a movement emerged in northern Italy to transform such homes into a modern child-support system that would enable unwed mothers to keep their offspring. But the changeover faltered in the South. While most northern homes were closed by 1867–75 (Kertzer 1993: 160–1), the Sicilian town of Villamaura, and many other Sicilian communities, continued to pay for the reception and feeding of foundlings until the Second World War.

Thanks to Kertzer's (1993) reconstruction of infant abandonment in Italy, it is possible to appreciate the state's role in mitigating what is known as the 'crime of honour'. This concept, which exonerates a father who kills his daughter and her lover, or a husband who kills his adulterous wife and her lover, was upheld in legal thought for twenty centuries. Eva Cantarella, tracing its development from Roman jurists who systematized earlier ideas about killing to erase a sexual transgression, reminds us that 'homicide for honour's sake was removed from the Italian penal code only . . . in 1981' (1991: 244). Even the fascist regime, which otherwise brooked no competi-tion in the use of force, compromised in this area: crimes of honour might be punished by the state, but only with sentences so mild as to be a joke.

Sicily figures significantly among the regions of Italy where, according to Cantarella, 'the concept of family honor still makes an occasional appear-ance, and vestiges of a code of honor exist in the vulgar use of the term *cornuto* (cuckold) as an insult' (p. 244). Northern Italians often identify southerners, Sardinians, and Sicilians with the associated implication of violence, above all towards women. In fact, however, actual crimes of honour were unusual in Sicily, in part because few men commanded the wherewithal to commit them. Notwithstanding a favourable legal climate, there could be retaliation, so that most cuckolds, or imagined cuckolds, remained *bastonati*, beaten down. Meanwhile, because the foundling homes masked illegitimate relationships, families had a way of avoiding the shedding of blood in order to purify their name. Abortion could also cancel an illegitimate conception (see Chapman 1971: 80), but this seems not to have been the usual remedy. As Kertzer shows, in creating the foundling system, both State and Church enacted their strong, ideological opposition to abortion. Among its regulations was one that prohibited engaging the foundlings' mothers as wet nurses. To do so would have contradicted the very condition that made infant abandonment a credible competitor to the abortionist: anonymity.

Abortion, though, did occur in Sicily, as documented by Triolo (1989; n.d.), by the Palermo physician Vincenzo Borruso (1966), and by a scattering of other surveys. Of 50 women interviewed by Borruso in the 1960s, 30 had undergone abortions, averaging three apiece. Triolo's sample was of 22 married women of poor, rural backgrounds, born between 1892 and 1931 and living in Palermo at the time of her fieldwork in the 1980s. Twelve of the 22 spoke about having had abortions, with about three per person; 39 of the 82 pregnancies she recorded had been terminated in this way. A mix of self-inflicted methods, from ingesting herbal concoctions based on parsley and maidenhair fern to inserting parsley into the vagina, were reported to both researchers. Both also describe non-physician specialists who used surgical instruments to puncture the amniotic sac. According to Triolo, it was usually married women who sought abortions in Sicily, and they did so because, burdened with children, they yearned for a way to lengthen the time between pregnancies, or to bring a long career of childbearing to a close. Interpreting the intervention as 'restoring their menses', they especially appreciated the fact that it did not require their husband's cooperation. 'Things of women' (*cosi di fimini*), abortions were even paid for out of women's petty cash, earned through selling eggs and chickens. Nor was there any need to inform outsiders, unless a medical problem arose. Only then might a husband be informed, and explode in anger, as Triolo learned from a few of her inform-ants (see Triolo n.d.).

It is difficult to evaluate the meaning of abortion for Sicilian women. On the one hand, its existence was proof that women enjoyed a sphere of autonomy *vis-à-vis* men that belied their caricatured lack of independence. On the other hand, though, its very segregation as a 'thing of women' also revealed an ultimate vulnerability because communication with men was so tenuous. According to Triolo (n.d.), for the women in her sample, it was husbands who determined the when and where of sexual intercourse.

Talking with them about sex, pregnancy, or any sort of family planning was awkward and rare. This, indeed, was partly what made abortions necessary. In other words, abortion experiences confirmed, at the same time as they called into question, the subordination of women to men. In this regard, they underscored the absence of a criterion that Livi-Bacci considered crucial to the onset of fertility decline: women's emancipation from structures of patriarchy.

As far as we can tell, although abortion practice was certainly more widespread than has been documented, it did not become the main vehicle for fertility decline in Sicily any more than in Western Europe as a whole. Religious and moral opprobrium, plus a high risk to women's health during the eras of these transitions, rendered coitus interruptus preferable to (we think) most people, most of the time. Unlike abortion, this route to family limitation necessarily implicated men. Moreover, if our interviewees are any guide, its success depended upon the joint motivation and mutuality of husbands and wives. Were it not that mistakes could be repaired through abortion, we might imagine an inverse relationship between aborting unwanted pregnancies and using coitus interruptus for birth control.

Given the imbalance in gender relations that characterized early twentieth-century Sicily, how did this method become so widespread? The question brings us back to artisans, whose way of life was to some extent at odds with the patriarchal system just described.

The Artisan Transition

Villamaura's artisan parents became skilled practitioners of coitus interruptus in the 1920s and 1930s. Telling us about this in retrospective interviews, elderly men and women seemed to favour the euphemism *marcia in dietro*, or reverse gear. Associated with automotive history, it is strongly evocative of male activity. As one old man proudly explained, 'the train can go forward, the train can go backward. I practised reverse gear for 18 years.' Also common, especially among women, is to call the practice 'making sacrifices'—*fare sacrifici*—or simply to refer to withdrawal by the noun *sacrifici*. Although we conducted interviews with men and women of every social stratum on the subject of birth control, we found no variation in these designations, with the exception that a few artisan women also volunteered a culinary metaphor: 'you can't cook anything if you don't put something in the pan!'

According to the elderly veterans of the artisan transition, men perceived coitus interruptus as a learned skill. This is not to confirm, however, the widely held assumption among demographers that withdrawal 'makes the decision to employ contraception and limit family size . . . a male prerogative' (Wrigley 1969: 200). Most artisan men whom we interviewed characterized their birth control effort as requiring a high level of communication and cooperation between spouses, the more so if their wives were to experience orgasm. Most women seemed appreciative, using words like 'honest', 'attentive', and 'careful' to describe a good man. When women spoke of sacrifice, moreover, it was usually with pride rather than regret or resentment.

Several aspects of the artisans' way of life (different from that of peasants and gentry) contributed to this seeming mutuality, not the least of which was an already existing companionate form of marriage. Shoemakers, cabinet-makers, blacksmiths, and tailors pursued their crafts close to home, in a *bottega* or shop on the ground floor of their two-store dwelling. They ate their main meal at midday, seated at table with wife and children; peasant men, in contrast, ate after sundown, following an exhausting day outdoors, and quite possibly in the absence of other family members who had already eaten. Among artisans, the conjugal pair was also likely to cooperate in work. Thus a shoemaker's wife might use a Singer sewing machine to stitch the uppers of shoes being made by her husband, or the seamstress-wife of a cabinet-maker might ask him to critique her designs. Many artisans' wives were themselves artisans, or ran small shops, and most helped out in the training and discipline of apprentices. As such they participated in their husbands' daytime activities to a far greater degree than did the wives of the agricultural classes, including the gentry.

Artisans enjoyed a unique pattern of leisure. Known for arranging evenings of dance and song in each other's houses, they also set aside each Monday—the day that neither blacksmiths nor barbers worked—for convivial gatherings in the countryside. Situated in one of the small rustic houses that some of them owned on the outskirts of the town, such occasions engaged men in political discussions punctuated by music, for artisans were knowledgeable about opera and often played tambourines, whistles, horns, or violins. More or less limited to a single afternoon and evening of the week, these exclusively male gatherings were less a contradiction to the partnership marriage than were the leisure activities of men in the other classes—further support for the gender-balanced quality of the artisans' fertility decline.

In addition to their 'pre-adaptive' marriage arrangements, artisans' acceptance of coitus interruptus as a route to family limitation reflected their long exposure to secular and worldly political ideologies. As already noted, skilled craftsmen, literate since the late nineteenth century, were conduits of international socialism in the Sicilian interior (P. Schneider 1986; Gabaccia 1988: 44–9). In Villamaura, a strong artisan contingent formed the backbone of the fledgling Communist Party that broke away from its socialist forerunner in 1922. Persecuted under fascism, this group nevertheless continued to receive international publications, and to hide them, read them, and debate them in their shops. It is said that, unlike other men in Villamaura, if artisans attended church it was not to pray but to listen and criticize. Although we were told by priests that the local clergy had never considered contraception a priority matter for pastoral counselling, or pursued it as a moral issue in confession, Catholic dogma nevertheless held that reproduction was up to God, not men and women. The artisans challenged this view, even satirizing clerics who preached against the 'incomplete act'. ('The priest told Tizio that it would be a sin to spill his seed on the ground, so he dumped it in a sack.')

Elderly male artisans, interviewed by us in the early 1980s, recalled how they first became used to the idea of small families, and of coitus interruptus as the way to achieve them—goals that matched women's wish for a safe route to fewer births and babies. The main contexts for change were their Monday gatherings, their shops, and the *Circolo degli Operai* or 'Worker's Circle' that had been founded by about 70 craftsmen in 1907. Here, in animated conversations, they raised each other's consciousness about 'the French'—a people they had become familiar with through the Ditta Ducrot, a French cabinet-making firm in Palermo that employed small-town cabinet-makers and carpenters alongside workers from France. Their discourse characterized Frenchmen as *più evoluto* ('more evolved') than Sicilians, in part for having small families through sexual restraint. 'The French', it was said, 'can pick up a glass of water, drink half of it and put it down again, in contrast to we Sicilians who can't stop before the glass is empty.' But among Sicilians, artisans were the 'most advanced'; for, although they had little land, they could read. Literacy, plus the urban origins of their respective crafts, linked them to a wider world.

We were also told, finally, that the workshop conversations included recounting dreams with sexual content—a sort of improvizational psychoanalysis for those who were having trouble reversing gears. What better contradiction could there be to the hypostasized dichotomy of 'cultural' versus 'rational choice' models that appears in so much of the writing on demography? Villamaura's artisans suggest how the adoption of a practice—coitus interruptus—indeed involved a 'rationalizing' change of behaviour, but did so within a familiar social and cultural context. Social interactions among men, and men's (and women's) culturally conditioned concepts of family honour, were critical to the change. Rationality, in the abstract sense of *either* cost-accounting *or* diffusing Western values, is simply not the issue.

Conclusion

Today the Italian birth rate is below replacement, the absolute lowest in Europe, not least because citizens of the southern provinces have severely limited the size of their families. Did southerners, Sicilians, the people of Villamaura, change their behaviour in response to a barrage of 'Western values', traceable to local élites, to role models in northern Italy, or to leaders in northern Europe? In Villamaura there is no evidence for the diffusion of a new family ideal through such intrusive avenues as education, campaigning, propaganda, or advertising. Nevertheless, because the turn of the century was, as we have seen, the point of transition to low fertility of Villamaura's *civili*, could not this class have mediated a process of 'Westernization' whose source point was France or England? Members of the gentry class were certainly enthusiastic about the Continent, elevating their status through travel and connections there. Our material culture survey turned up a large number of landlords who absorbed French culture by commissioning tailors and seamstresses to follow the fashions and use the fabrics of this neighbour to the north. Around 1900, the Liberty Style of English provenence spread through Sicily, leaving its mark on the clothing and the furniture of high status groups in the interior as well as in Palermo.

Yet, Villamaura's *civile* élite were hardly leaders in the local adoption of coitus interruptus, or role models for its transmission to other classes—and this even though their fertility decline anticipated that of the others by three to six decades. Elsewhere we describe, to the contrary, how *civile* men disliked this option, preferring to arrange costly clinical abortions for their wives in Palermo, or to cease sleeping with these women, recruiting peasant mistresses instead (see Schneider and Schneider 1984, 1996). Some *civile* men also ignored the economic pressures that motivated low fertility for their class, 'siring' broods of up to thirteen offspring as if to ridicule the new, truncated family. Perhaps more telling still, members of the *civile* élite believed that peasants were condemned to high fertility as a condition of their servitude—a prejudice they expressed in frequent and jarring ways.

Artisans were different. As this paper suggests, they learned about the French, and about birth control, through independent networks of craft activity and political opposition. Moreover, given their already established preference for the companionate form of marriage, the messages they received through these channels found a ready home. Although we do not discuss this here, artisans ended up having a significant demonstration effect: numerous peasant men heard about the skills of reversing gears from talk in their shops.

Even so, rather than account for Villamaura's eventual membership among demographically fully 'modern' communities in terms of these cultural processes alone, we conclude by revisiting the political–economic context. It has been our argument that the dislocations of Italian fascism and the great depression motivated artisans' commitment to limit family size. Peasants, exposed to the same events, experienced them differently. As we show elsewhere (Schneider and Schneider 1991, 1992, 1996), instead of propelling this class towards a lower birth rate, the conjuncture in question trapped most of them, and certainly the poorest of them, in a high-fertility, low-mortality regime. Only later, in the 1950s and 1960s, would another phase of capitalist development crystallize for peasants Sicily's on-going, at times only gradual, fertility decline.

References

Alter, G. (1992), 'Theories of fertility decline: a non-specialist's guide to the current debate', in J.R. Gillis, L. A. Tilly, and D. Levine (eds.), *The European Experience of Declining Fertility: A Quiet Revolution, 1850–1970*. Cambridge, Mass., and Oxford: Blackwell, pp. 13–31.

Borruso, V. (1966), *Pratiche abortive e controllo delle nascite in Sicilia*. Palermo: Libri Siciliani.

Brettell, C. B. (1991), 'Kinship and contract: property transmission and family relations in northwestern Portugal'. *Comparative Studies in Society and History*, 33: 443–65.

Cantarella, E. (1991), 'Homicides of honor: the development of Italian adultery law over two millennia', in D. I. Kertzer, and R. P. Saller (eds.), *The Family in Italy from Antiquity to the Present*. New Haven: Yale University Press, pp. 229–47.

Chapman, C. G. (1971), *Milocca, A Sicilian Village*. Cambridge, Mass: Schenkman.

Coale, A. (1973), 'The demographic transition', in *International Population Conference, Liege, 1973*, i. Liege: International Union for the Scientific Study of Population, pp. 53–72.

de Grazia, V. (1992), *How Fascism Ruled Women: Italy, 1922–1945*. Berkeley and Los Angeles: University of California Press.

Foucault, M. (1980), *The History of Sexuality*, i, *An Introduction*, trans. R. Hurley. New York: Random House.

Gabaccia, D. (1988), *Militants and Migrants: Rural Sicilians become American Workers*. New Brunswick, NJ: Rutgers University Press.

Ganci, M. (1980), *La Sicilia Contemporanea: Storia di Napoli e della Sicilia*. Palermo, Napoli: Società Editrice.

Gay, P. (1984), *Bourgeois Experience, Victoria to Freud*, i, *Education of the Senses*. New York: Oxford University Press.

Glass, D. V. (1967), *Population Policies and Movements in Europe*. London: Frank Cass.

Herzfeld, M. (1980), 'Honour and shame: problems in the analysis of moral systems', *Man* (n.s.), 15: 339–51.

——(1984), 'The horns of the Mediterraneanist dilemma'. *American Ethnologist*, 11: 439–54.

Kertzer, D. I. (1993), *Sacrificed for Honor: Italian Infant Abandonment and the Politics of Reproductive Control*. Boston: Beacon Press.

Livi-Bacci, M. (1977), *A History of Italian Fertility During the Last Two Centuries*. Princeton: Princeton University Press.

Lupo, S. (1981), *Blocco Agrario e Crisi in Sicilia tra le Due Guerre*. Napoli: Guida.

Mack Smith, D. (1968), *A History of Sicily: Modern Sicily after 1713*. London: Chatto & Windus.

Marino, G. C. (1976), *Partiti e Lotta di Classe in Sicilia; da Orlando a Mussolini*. Bari: De Donato.

Rodotà, S. and Rodotà, C. (1982), 'Il Diritto di famiglia', in AAVV (eds.), *Retratto di Famiglia degli Anni '80*. Bari: Laterza, pp. 161–201.

Sahlins, M. (1976), *Culture and Practical Reason*. Chicago: University of Chicago Press.

Salamone-Marino, S. (1968), *Costumi e Usanze dei Contadini di Sicilia*. Palermo: Il Vespro.

Santow, G. (1993), 'Coitus interruptus in the twentieth century'. *Population and Development Review*, 19: 767–93.

Saraceno, C. (1992), 'Constructing families, shaping women's lives: the making of Italian families between market economy and state interventions, in J. R. Gillis, L. A. Tilly, and D. Levine (eds.), *The European Experience of Declining Fertility: A Quiet Revolution, 1850–1970*. Cambridge, Mass., and Oxford: Blackwell, pp. 251–70.

Saunders, G. R. (1981), 'Men and women in southern Europe: a review of some aspects of cultural complexity'. *Journal of Psychoanalytic Anthropology*, 4: 435–66.

Schneider, J., and Schneider, P. (1976), *Culture and Political Economy in Western Sicily*. New York: Academic Press.

————(1984), 'Demographic transitions in a Sicilian rural town'. *Journal of Family History*, 9: 245–73.

————(1991), 'Sex and respectability in an age of fertility decline: a Sicilian case study'. *Social Science and Medicine*, 33: 885–95.

————(1992), 'Going forward in reverse gear: culture, economy, and political economy in the demographic transitions of a rural Sicilian town', in J. R. Gillis, L. A. Tilly, and D. Levine (eds.), *The European Experience of Declining Fertility: A Quiet Revolution, 1850–1970*. Cambridge, Mass., and Oxford: Blackwell, pp. 146–75.

————(1996), *Festival of the Poor: Fertility Decline and the Ideology of Class in Sicily, 1860–1980*. Tucson: University of Arizona Press.

Schneider, P. (1986), 'Rural artisans and peasant mobilisation in the Socialist International: the Fasci Siciliani. *Journal of Peasant Studies*, 13: 63–81.

Triolo, N. (1989), 'The angel-makers: Fascist pro-natalism and the normalization of midwives in Sicily'. Ph.D. dissertation, University of California, Berkeley.

——(n.d.), *Cosi di Fimmini: Fertility Decision-making and Abortion in Sicily, 1900–1940*. Unpublished paper.

Watkins, S. C. (1993), 'If all we knew about women was what we read in *Demography*, what would we know?' *Demography*, 30: 593–603.

Wrigley, E. A. (1969), *Population and History*. New York: McGraw-Hill.

9 Anthropological Perspectives on Migration in Africa

JOHN KWASI ANARFI

Introduction

For reasons that are not easy to explain, demographers seem to have a greater understanding for the fertility and mortality aspects of population than they have for migration, the third of the components of population change. While social scientists in other disciplines also work in the area of fertility and mortality, they seem to have accepted the lead of demographers, and there is very little or no controversy over concepts and definitions. This is not so with migration. Geographers as well as economists regard migration with special interest and have, in fact, contributed much to the study of its development at both the theoretical and empirical levels.

Finding a general theory of migration with universal validity and acceptability is the perpetual dream of those working in migration research. Some writers have claimed to have established 'theories' or 'laws of migration' (Ravenstein 1889; Lee 1966; Zelinsky 1979). It is not my intention to review these theories, because that has been done competently elsewhere. Suffice it to say that, while many such studies on migration are useful and informative, all the theories propounded 'suffer from one or several fundamental shortcomings in accounting for even the traditional, "normal" phenomena of migration. They are even more deficient in coping with the turnaround in the Western countries or the peculiarities of present day migration in the Third World' (Zelinsky 1983: 33). It is on the latter that attention will be focused in this paper, with greater emphasis on Africa.

An emphasis on Africa is predicated upon the fact that much of what falls beyond the 'normal' migration phenomenon occurs in the Third World including Africa. This abnormality stems from the fact that 'most theoretical efforts drew almost solely on Western experience, and more particularly, the British and European variety' (Zelinsky 1983; see also Kearney 1986). Mabogunje's (1970) systems approach to migration studies, which is one of the few deeply rooted in African situations, has been hailed as one of the most comprehensive theories of the social and environmental context of migration (Findley 1987; De Jong and Fawcett 1981). Yet even here, little seems to have been actually done beyond the statement of the model.

In demography, migration researchers have used several techniques to understand the process involved. One of demography's major concerns is to understand the nature of population change. Migration being one of the components of change, emphasis has been placed on identifying its patterns and trends, the distinguishing characteristics of migrants, and the analysis of socioeconomic or ecological factors associated with systems of population movement. Such goals have necessitated the adoption of an aggregate approach to the study of migration. In this respect, migration studies suffer the same fate as the other aspects of demography in their reliance on censuses and large-scale survey data.

Most migration studies are 'restricted by narrow conceptual and analytical frameworks which have focused on the act of migration rather than the underlying circumstances of which migration is merely a secondary symptom' (Izzard 1985: 259). This is where anthropology is appropriate. As the study of humankind, it seeks to produce useful generalizations about people and their behaviour and to arrive at the fullest possible understanding of human diversity. This approach gives anthropologists a uniquely broad perspective that equips them to deal with that elusive thing called human nature. Migration is not just numbers and distances, and the migration phenomenon is in fact very complex. Attention in this paper will be focused only on aspects of migration that are salient and of particular relevance to African and Third World situations.

Towards a Better Understanding of Some Migration Implications

Migration Decision-Making

The most deficient areas of migration knowledge concern individual-level and family-level explanations of migration decision-making behaviour (De Jong and Fawcett 1981). Here the concept of decision-making is used in its most general form to refer to the formation of an intention or disposition that results in a migration behaviour. The decision itself is sometimes conceptualized as actually composed of two parts: the decision to move or stay, and the choice of one destination among various alternatives. In its wider implications, the migration decision-making process involves the determinants of migration and the reasons or motives for migrating.

The basic elements of migration decision-making at the micro level start with a consideration of the motivations for migration. According to De Jong and Fawcett (1981), motives can be briefly characterized as one of the proximate causes of intentions to move. They explain that motives can be conceptualized at both the subjective and the objective level. Subjectively, when the individual is said to be considering cost–benefit ratios, levels of stress and satisfaction, and values and expectancies, the underlying concept

is that of motivation. Objectively, discussions of place utility and of opportunity structures often incorporate inferred motivations. For adequate
understanding of migration decision-making and subsequent behaviour,
Taylor (1969) and Pryor (1975), among others, have pointed out the need
to integrate societal-level motives. Taylor emphasizes that area and community opportunities form a context for psycho-social determinants such as
motives. Pryor, for his part, questions whether the answers that people give
to the question 'Why did you move?' constitute analytically valid micro-level
motives, and he argues that the analysis of reasons for migration is a 'meso
analysis' which must be pursued further by a micro analysis of the information context and of decision-making factors that coalesce in motivated
behaviour. De Jong and Fawcett (1981) conclude that, in addition to the
personal characteristics of the actors and the social, economic, and demographic characteristics of the individual and family, the decision-making
process and the ability to actualize decisions are affected by the community
context, social networks, and norms that surround the individual.

In an overview paper in which he draws on a wealth of African experience
to put forward a systems theory of rural–urban migration, Mabogunje
(1970) spells out explicitly the need to take into account the migration
decision-making context. Findley (1987) builds up a convincing argument
for a contextual model for studying family migration by analysing migration
decision-making in a very wide context. Her analysis concludes that the
migration decision-making phenomenon makes it possible for consideration
to be given to a wide range of factors that have a bearing on the migration
process including the actors, the scope, and context of migration decision-
making; the causes/motives or determinants of migration; and factors
influencing and specific events triggering migration decision-making. Pryor
too, in his review of the literature with respect to the motivation for migration, sees 'the social and cultural context of migration as having a crucial
role in either facilitating or inhibiting the interplay of economic and other
motivations and demographic differentials which result in an individual's
spatial relocation' (Pryor 1975: 2).

It is important to look at the different approaches to the study of migration decision-making chosen because 'the way in which information relating
to the decision to move or stay is collected, in what context it is collected,
and from whom, exerts a frequently overlooked but critical influence on the
picture of the decision-making process that emerges' (Hugo 1981: 188).
Findley (1987) employs a contextual analysis in her study of rural development and migration in the Philippines, explaining it as the study of individual behaviour which takes into consideration the group or environmental
setting of individual behaviour. This context includes societal or group
phenomena including norms, social institutions such as families, clubs, and
communities, and physical factors of the individual's environment (Blalock
and Wilken 1979; Lazarsfeld and Menzel 1961). Findley concludes that

economic consideration is the main driving force behind a family's migration decision-making.

Hugo (1981) for his part explains that three interrelated socio-cultural phenomena appear to exert a strong influence on the move/stay decision-making process in Third World situations: these are village/community ties, village norms, and village and other ethnic social networks. He concentrates on the village or community of origin of migrants in which the actual decision to move or stay is made.

Units and Dimensions of Analysis

One of the unending problems in migration research in Third World countries relates to the units and dimensions of analysis and the locus of fieldwork. It is accepted that structural economic forces have an overriding influence in determining the distribution of economic opportunities in developing countries and hence in shaping macro patterns of migration in those contexts (see e.g. Amin's 1974 work in Africa and Titus's 1978 in Indonesia). Village-level research conducted in Third World contexts has confirmed that structural factors, together with such demographic factors as life-cycle stage, are of considerable importance in causing individuals and groups to migrate. It also indicates, however, that, 'if one is to approach an understanding of the migration process, it is important to have an appreciation of the social and cultural context in which those forces operate and are perceived by the people involved' (Hugo 1981: 187). The approach to this has been micro-level research at the community, the family, and the individual level.

It has been observed that macro-level studies are superior in describing broad patterns of migration whereas micro-level studies are superior in explaining migration behaviour. There is the tendency for macro models to be deterministic and to place heavy stress on the fundamental economic causes of movement, with social and cultural influences being regarded as epiphenomenal. One unfortunate reason for this state of affairs is that very little attention has been given to research into the socio-cultural factors influencing migration decisions. There is a general failure to identify and specify the precise nature of these influences in terms other than those so vague that any attempt to include them in a model would be extremely difficult. Another reason often given for excluding socio-cultural factors in models is that it is very difficult to quantify many such variables (Hugo 1981). Migration researchers, however, working at the community and/or individual levels as distinct from those dealing with aggregate (usually secondary) data, are acutely aware of how poor a predictor of population mobility economic variables are when considered in isolation from social and cultural influences. One advantage of the macro approach is that under survey situations it is possible to employ variables that do give quantitative expression to such influences as kinship and family linkages or community norms (see Speare 1971; Hugo 1978; Du Toit 1975; Germani 1965).

In his study in Indonesia, Hugo (1978) found that villages located in ecologically similar situations with almost identical economies, as well as approximately the same levels of pressure on agricultural resources, differed widely with respect to the level and/or type of population mobility that was dominant. Following a similar experience, Cardona and Simmons (1975: 45) remarked, 'Many men have relatively poor job opportunities in rural areas but only some individuals go to the city.'

Hugo concludes from his study that:

the weight of evidence from microlevel studies of the process of migration decision making is that the social and cultural context in which such decisions are made exerts an important influence upon economic and other motives of potential migrants and thus shapes (1) whether or not migration occurs; (2) if it does, what form this migration takes (permanent, circular or other); (3) the destination of the migrant; and (4) the nature of the migrant's experience at that destination. (Hugo 1981: 188)

He adds:

such influences are not to be viewed as distinct and separate elements explaining a small proportion of movement but as having a more fundamental role where they are frequently tied up inextricably with the economic motivation that so many movers articulate as their reasons for moving when they are asked directly. (Hugo 1981: 190)

Germani stresses that:

the so-called economic objective influences do not operate in a vacuum but in a normative context so that people will evaluate and perceive the attractions or repulsions of particular locations against the framework of institutionalized roles, expectations and behaviour patterns that in a particular society regulate migration. Such norms can operate to facilitate or retard mobility. (Germani 1965; quoted in Hugo 1981: 186–224)

The Frafra of northern Ghana present a very good illustration of the conclusions of Hugo and Germani. The Frafra are highly mobile, and their practice of moving to the south of Ghana dates back to the early part of the century (see Fortes 1945). Explanation for their high mobility lies, in part, in the patrilineal and patrilocal inheritance. In this system, inheritance passes through the male line of the family by age and successive generations. The inheritance in the extended family will not pass to a father's sons' generation until all the male members of the father's generation die. This arrangement has implications for migration when young men feel cheated, particularly if the family head is wicked or not tactful (Nabila 1974).

Fortes found this to be the situation in the 1930s:

when young men who have been abroad working in Ashanti or the colony for a period of years are questioned about their motives for leaving home, the commonest reason they give is the death of a parent. 'My father died, and my junior father took over the house and so I went away', is the usual formula. One soon discovers that there was always some tension and often friction between the youth and his father's brother. (Fortes 1945: 140)

Who Makes the Decision?

Many migration researchers have concentrated on the individual as the sole decision maker (see Stone 1975; Sjaastad 1962; Bowles 1970; Da Vanzo 1981). Sell and De Jong (1978: 315–16) note that 'the use of aggregate data confounds important aspects of migration decision making, such as the impact of wife's employment and job dissatisfaction, and the ways in which so-called "chronic movers" differ from other migrants'.

There is an increasing interest in the household or family as the unit of analysis bridging the gap between social and individual levels (Graves and Linneman 1979; Harbison 1981; Mincer 1978; Sandell 1977; Stark 1982; Urzua 1981; Wood 1981; Findley 1987). According to this view, individuals do not act alone in choosing the locations of their residence and work. Migration is undertaken as part of a family's strategy to maximize its welfare, in either the short or long run (Nelson 1976a; Findley 1987). The decision is made collectively by adult members of the family or by the family head alone, who is usually a male.

Often family and household are used interchangeably. Findley (1987), however, argued in favour of the family as the unit of migration analysis in a contextual model. Whereas households are defined as a group of co-residential individuals, families must be related by blood, adoption, or marriage, and may or may not be co-residential (Yanagisako 1979: 161–5). Also, migration of any member can affect the welfare of other family members, whether or not they also move, even though migration does not alter family membership while altering household membership. Furthermore, families are preferred to households because family units are considered the appropriate unit for analysis of collective micro-level welfare decisions (Becker 1981; Da Vanzo 1976, 1981). Elsewhere Caldwell *et al.* (1988) observed that the survey household was to a large extent an artefact of the survey interviewer or supervisor (because of problems of applying definitions or obtaining agreement from respondents to use that definition). Zelinsky (1983) has cautioned about the uncritical reliance on official decisions and information. Migration researchers tend to use the 'household' instead of the 'family' as a unit of analysis in migration studies to conform to the conventional practice in censuses all over the world. 'The hazards in accepting convenient data are greater in migration work than for the student of fertility or most other demographic items' (Zelinsky 1983).

The adoption of the family as the basic unit for migration decision-making may look simple in developed countries where the nuclear family is the norm. In Africa, however, the situation is different and one has to grapple with the question of what constitutes a family. In many places the idea of a family implies the extended family, which has even more conceptual problems than the household. There is also the issue of the continuing membership of children as they go through the life-cycle. Whatever the age and/or marital status of a person, there seems never to be a complete break from the family. The problem is made even more complicated when these extended families are organized by lineage systems— matrilineal or patrilineal. Anthropology, with its historical interest in kinship and family structures, certainly has much to offer in the study of these issues.

At whatever level of analysis we look at it, females generally received less attention than males in migration studies until the late 1970s (Pessar 1985; Brydon 1987; Izzard 1985; Chaney 1980). Pessar relates the virtual non-existence of the female migrant to two central premisses of the modernization theory that was the epistemiological framework for most research on population movement. One was that migration was viewed as a matter of individual choice whereby people relocated from backward rural areas to modern urban locales. It was hypothesized that those individuals with the ability to take risks made it to the modern cities. Modernization theorists often assumed that a dichotomy existed between men and women, and since the former were allegedly more apt to be risk-takers and achievers, they were generally the focus of migration studies. Females were explained away as wives and mothers who were the passive followers of male pioneers.

The second factor that contributed to the disregard of female migrants was 'the common conflation of "migrant" with "waged labour" and the misapprehension that women migrants do not work' (Pessar 1985: 274; see also Morokvasic 1979; Ware 1981). This idea underlies gender roles in capitalist societies wherein women are *a priori* assumed, along with children, to be dependants of men. Recent findings, however, indicate that, either as women left behind (Meillassoux 1981; Chaney and Lewis 1980; Smale 1980; Izzard 1985) or as accompanied migrants (Pessar 1982), women have been very productive and have, in fact, contributed to the household income in or out of migration. Other researchers have documented the large supply of, and demand for, female immigrant labour in the secondary sector of advanced capitalist societies (Guhleman and Tienda 1981; Sassen-Koob 1981). Independent women migrating alone have also been captured by studies in some developing country areas of late (Anarfi 1982, 1990a; Brydon 1987; Recchini de Lattes 1989; Pittin 1984).

When the woman was perceived as a dependant of a male primary migrant, she was not considered as playing any role in the migration decision-making of the household, or at most was considered as playing just a passive role. Boserup (1970) has analysed the relative strengths of women in decision-making in general under different socioeconomic conditions, and

Ware (1981) has reviewed women's role in relation to migration decision-making. The truth is that no serious attention has been given to the role of women in migration decision-making in Africa, which is seen mainly as consisting of male-dominant societies.

Recent researches on independent women migrating in Africa have recognized that women migrate for the same reason as men, which is to better their economic conditions (Anarfi 1982, 1990a; Brydon 1987; Eades 1975; Pittin 1984). A study of Ghanaian women immigrants in Abidjan, Côte d'Ivoire, revealed that almost all the unmarried women in the study took the decision to migrate alone. Moreover, these women were more likely to inform their mothers than any other member of the family about their intention to migrate. This was found to be part of their arrangements to get care-takers for children left behind, as over 60% of the sample women (both married and unmarried) had children (Anarfi 1990a). The situation is different in Taiwan, where even when women migrate on their own they are not autonomous movers, since the decision is rarely independent of parental supervision (Huang 1984). These observations confirm findings from elsewhere that women's migration decision is influenced by their age, conjugal status, and other family-cycle characteristics (Garcia-Castro 1986).

It is in the area of women left behind that the passiveness of women in migration decision-making is best portrayed. The woman is left behind, it is assumed, to take care of the family property (Izzard 1985; Obbo 1980). Some studies have observed that both the family and the community suffer when young men leave to work as wage labourers in agriculture or in distant cities or countries (Chaney and Lewis 1980). In contrast, Izzard (1985) examines the contribution of mobility to the development cycle of the household and, in turn, to the observed differences in wealth and income within Tswana society (in Botswana) and concludes that a lack of resident adult men does not automatically disadvantage female-headed households. She emphasizes that the success or failure of the migrant household depends very much on the income-earning activities the household is engaged in and the propensity of absent members to contribute to the household in terms of remittances or transfers, in cash or in kind. In this respect it is very simplistic to see the woman left behind as a mere simpleton who plays no part in an arrangement, the success of which depends so much on her. Perhaps this explains in part why more and more writers are seeing migration decision-making as a collective responsibility of the family (Findley 1987).

This also brings up the issue of the place of women left behind in the persistence of circulation migration in Third World societies. Is the presence of the woman in the area of origin just part of the migration strategy, or is it the cause of such circulation, which is still pervasive in many Third World areas?

The Persistence of Circulation in Third World Areas

Circulation, which includes 'a great deal of movements, usually short-term repetitive or cyclical in character, but all having in common the lack of any declared intention of a permanent or long-standing change of residence' (Zelinsky 1971), is one of what are termed the peculiarities of present-day migration in the Third World (see Gould and Prothero 1975; Nelson 1976a; Goldstein 1978; Conaway 1977; Hugo 1978). Gould and Prothero (1975) emphasize that permanent migration in the conventional sense of the term, that is definitive movements with no propensity to return to the home area, is relatively uncommon in tropical Africa, though this is less so now than in the past. Zelinsky (1983) for his part speculates that 'circular migration may be a modern phenomenon, as in much of Central and Southern Africa, or an extension of traditional patterns'. This apparent state of confusion is explained by the fact that much of what is known about circulation is based largely upon unsystematic observation, and no major examination has attempted to specify the actual elements involved in the phenomenon, particularly at the non-migrant level (Hugo 1981).

Hugo (1981: 194) explains that circulation may result when there is only a marginal difference in the evaluation of conditions in the place of origin and the potential destination, so that the individual decides to attempt to 'get the best of both worlds' by taking advantage of positive attributes at both locations, while at the same time alleviating somewhat the impact of negative factors at both places. This explanation certainly has an economic outlook and points to the deduction that, if the difference in evaluation of the places of origin and potential destination were substantial and in favour of the destination, movers would choose permanent migration. However, other studies have observed strong socio-cultural influences on migrants' continuous ties with their home areas. A third of respondents in a West Java study indicated that the most pleasant thing about living in their village was that it allowed for closeness to their family (Hugo 1978).

If economic considerations were the only forces behind circular migration in Third World areas, it could be deduced that migrants would lose ties with their places of origin when they became successful at their destinations. But the evidence shows that many movers to Third World cities appear to maintain, or even enhance, their location-specific capital in their village of origin by buying land, building houses, contributing to village projects, and participating in important family and village ceremonies while living in the city.

Another dimension of the strong ties between migrants and their home areas is the desire to be buried in their home village. Caldwell observes that 'to most West Africans the ancestral village always remains "home". This is true not only of the recent migrant to the town but also of the long-standing migrant and, even in rural areas, of families who have migrated for some generations to new farming areas' (1969: 185). This observation is confirmed by Gugler (1969), and Hugo (1978) has made a similar observation about the Javanese.

The intensive attachment of people to their place of birth in many Third World areas is strongly demonstrated by the resistance that many resettlement programmes have encountered. The difficulties that successive governments have experienced in persuading large numbers of inhabitants of densely populated Java to resettle in the less densely settled islands of the archipelago have been attributed to this attachment (Hugo 1981). It cost the government of Ghana a number of heads of cattle and sheep in sacrifices to persuade the inhabitants of a particular settlement to move to a new settlement with their fetish as part of a rehabilitation programme associated with the Volta hydroelectric project.

What are the elements operating to bind people to their home areas in parts of the Third World? While the presence of strong community and kinship ties is one of the most ubiquitous characteristics of traditional and semi-traditional societies, the influence of such ties on migration is by no means clear (Hugo 1981). This is partly because the literature is concerned mainly with the role of such ties in encouraging the migrant to maintain contact with the place of origin and/or to return eventually to live there permanently. Hugo adds, 'Unfortunately we know little of the extent to which the relative strength of such ties influence the decision to move or stay. Moreover, research into migration in the Third World has concentrated upon studies of migrants and been little concerned with people who have not migrated' (Hugo 1981: 196). The few studies on stayers (e.g. Hugo 1978; Anarfi 1990*a*) have tended to concentrate on those living in communities from which there is heavy out-migration. The answer to the problem may lie with non-migrating communities.

Migrants' Settlement in the Receiving Society

At the opposite end to migration decision-making on the migration continuum is the settlement of the migrant in the host society. Mangalam has posited that migration takes place as a society undergoes a social change, which is the 'difference between the social organization of a given society at two different points in time, comprising changes in any or all the three component systems, namely the culture, social and personality systems' (1968: 13). He further observes that migration affects and is affected by the social organization of the society of origin and destination, and in the process the cultural values, norms, and goals of migrants also change.

The sociological aspects of migration have been given more expression in the study of migrants' assimilation into the host society (see Eisenstadt 1954). The term 'assimilation' retains a substantial trace of its physiological analogy. Like it, it implies that every suggestion of separate origin disappears. Assimilation may, in some senses and to a certain degree, be described as a function of visibility. As soon as the migrant no longer exhibits the marks which identify him or her as a member of an alien group, the actual if not the legal status of a native is acquired.

The successful assimilation of a migrant can be said to represent the final stage of the migration process (Mabogunje 1970). But can there be complete assimilation? The controversy over this question has led to a longstanding argument over the precise meaning of assimilation and of such words as 'integration' and 'absorption'. Whatever the difference, all are concerned with a process of economic, social, and cultural adjustment.

There has been a growing awareness of the persistence of the cultural traits that immigrants bring with them, and of the significance of the retention by immigrants of many of these traits as a stabilizing link between their old life and their new (Reid 1955). Assimilation (or the merging of immigrant and native cultures), if it happens at all, is a very long process taking generations rather than years; so the important and more immediate problem is the degree of adaptation that can reasonably be expected from the first generation and at what levels it should occur. To meet this middle-way approach, the term 'integration' is often used. It is a happier and more exact term than others to describe the successful inclusion of a new group into an existing society (Borrie 1956).

Again, assimilation, besides its misleading biological connotation, implies a one-way street in group relations. It suggests that the newcomer is divested of the old culture completely and is virtually remoulded in everything from clothes to ideology (see Eisenstadt 1954). It denies or ignores the many gifts brought by the migrant to the new home, and the impact of the migrant's ideas, talents, and hopes upon the host community. Integration, on the other hand, is a dual process which carries more clearly the notion of adjustment by both migrant and non-migrant groups.

The theory of rural–urban continuum opines that rural migrants in the city become more urbanized the longer they stayed in the city (McGee 1975). An element of this theory is the claim that rural migrants suffer grave problems of social adjustment to the city. An increasing body of research in the Third World since the 1950s has challenged this assertion. About Mexico, Lewis writes:

the preliminary findings of the present study of urbanization in Mexico City indicate quite different trends, and suggest the possibility of urbanization without breakdown. They also show that some of the hitherto unquestioned sociological generalizations about urbanization may be culture-bound and in need of re-examination in the light of comparative studies of urbanization in other areas. (Lewis 1952: 31)

Similar observations have been made by Bruner (1961: 518) on South-east Asia, Mayer (1961) about the Bantu in East London, South Africa, Abu-Lughod (1961) on migrants in Cairo city, and elsewhere by Mangin (1970),

Turner (1967), and Nelson (1970). In challenging earlier models of urban transformation, McGee (1975: 110) observes two main weaknesses:

1. they portrayed cities as places inducing social maladjustment, and
2. they ignored the fact that at, the level of individual adaptation, the majority of rural migrants exhibit attitudes that may be regarded as both rural and urban at the same time. He explained that such attitudes might change with time, but felt it was dangerous to argue that they would necessarily change because of the influence of the city.

Very pertinent to the observations is Gluckman's (1958) assertion that 'all culture tends to survive'. So when people from one cultural group migrate to the town, they retain a great deal of their culture even without forming a corporate political group. They thus constitute a cultural category initially, and, with increasing interaction and communication between its members, transform into cultural groups with well-defined political identities. This process is an important element of the migration process in many Third World societies. It has been mentioned earlier that movements generally occur through well-defined contact networks (Germani 1965). Interpersonal friendship and kinship connections, while facilitating the move, also have a cushioning effect on the adjustment of migrants after arrival. This informal segment of what Mabogunje (1970) calls the urban control sub-system plays a strongly positive and supportive role in the absorption of migrants. It also provides them with social and emotional support. This assistance may be extended through formal or semi-formal urban associations about which there is considerable literature (e.g. Skeldon 1977; Little 1965, 1973).

In his study on Hausa migrants in Yoruba towns, Cohen (1969) mentions two closely related social relationships among migrants. One is 'detribalization', in which an ethnic group adjusts to the new social realities by adopting customs from other groups or by developing new customs which are shared with other groups. The other is 'retribalization', in which an ethnic group adjusts to new realities by reorganizing its own traditional customs, or by developing new customs under traditional symbols, often using traditional norms and ideologies to enhance its distinctiveness within the contemporary situation. Cohen (1969: 2) emphasizes that 'nowhere are these two processes so dramatically evident as in African towns today, where social interaction is particularly intense and change very rapid'. The former is more likely to be found in 'industrial' type towns than in the 'traditional' type and is synonymous with what some sociologists call 'modernization', a process by which various types of local, traditional, and status groups are drawn together into a common institutional organizational framework. McGee (1975: 127) notes that 'social scientists doing research in the non-western world make much of the concept of westernization, often using it synonymously with "modernization" to mean an individual or group of individuals that has adopted the mores and value judgements of supposedly advanced individuals of capitalist societies'. He adds that ultimately the individual is the product of the society and not of the city.

Gender Differences in the Settlement of Migrants

Not unexpectedly, most of the models that have been developed to explain migrants' settlement in the host society have been steeped in the modernization theory which has dominated most research on population movement. According to one popular variant of the modernization approach championed by Piore (1979), the migrant arrives as a pure economic maximizer. As such, he or she is willing to accept any job, no matter how demeaning, because the self-defined status of temporary worker promotes a sharp dichotomy between work and social identity. Piore notes: 'work performed in the receiving society is purely instrumental: a means to gather income, income that can be taken back to his or her home community and used to fulfil or enhance his/her role within that social structure. From the perspective of the immigrant, work is essentially asocial' (1979: 514).

A major criticism of Piore's (1979) model centres on its failure to address the contrasting orientations of men and women to migration. In Pessar's (1985) observation, its shortcoming lies, in large part, in Piore's failure to develop a purely phenomenological framework in which the gender-determined aspects of social identity and volition are included. Writing on Latin American and Caribbean women and migration, Garcia-Castro *et al.* (1984) remarked that most studies fail to consider simultaneously migrants as individuals—who resist or acquiesce to their cooptation—and as participants in a structurally determined process beyond the individual's control. Similar observations have been made by other writers (see e.g. Bertaux-Wiame 1979; Connell 1984; Fawcett *et al.* 1984; and Sudarkasa 1977), leading to the call for women migrants to be studied as a separate category from male migrants and from non-migrant women (Youssef *et al.* 1979; Morokvasic 1984).

Along with the upsurge of studies on autonomous women migrating alone, the literature shows growing interest in the dominant images of migrant women, and a more general focus on the relationship between female migration and prostitution (Nadel 1942; Little 1973). Migration by young women on their own is often viewed as tantamount to prostitution, and prostitution in turn can be assumed through migration (Pittin 1984). Caldwell (1969: 103) writes of the objections of rural families to their daughters and sisters moving to the towns because they fear that they will be 'led astray' easily and will end up as prostitutes. Sudarkasa (1973, 1977), reacting to Nadel's (1942) and later Little's (1973) work, argues against 'the creation of [the] stereotypic image of female migrants as actual or potential prostitutes' (1973: 183), pointing out that in the Nigerian and Ghanaian area in which she worked only a small minority of female migrants relied on the sale of their sexual services as sources of income. Brydon (1987), writing about the Avatime of Ghana, makes a similar observation. However, Pittin's (1984) work on Hausa women in Nigeria found that most young and unattached migrant women were in *karuwanci* (courtesanship), and Anarfi's (1990b) sample of Ghanaian women immigrants in Abidjan worked predominantly as prostitutes. Such varying findings underscore the need for better data on the socio-cultural background of these women and for new ideas about appropriate work and behaviour.

In the search for such data, Pittin (1984) advises that reasons for migrant women's occupational choices must be sought within the context of specific socio-cultural provisions and constraints, as well as within the wider socio-economic framework. She notes that, without socially sanctioned access to opportunities even in the informal sector, and subjected to seclusion and social control, Hausa women play the roles traditionally accorded to and expected of them. To the question of why she left the village and became a prostitute, one of the few women in the profession encountered by Brydon said 'to get work to get money. Anyway, it was not my intention, but circumstances beyond my control forced me to come here' (Brydon 1987: 171). Another explanation of why migrant women became prostitutes was offered by one of the respondents in Anarfi's (1990b) Abidjan study. On why she went into prostitution she said, 'in Ghana men were using me for free, so what is wrong if I come here to do it for money' (author's field notes).

The above responses become more meaningful if we look at them in relation to gender roles in the establishment of sexual relations in the African context. In the first place, the woman's sexual role tends to be more or less marginal and passive. She does not take the initiative in sexual activity, and she is normally not expected to give any indication that she is enjoying the sexual act (Amoah 1990). Second, much sexual exchange in Africa has a monetary component, even if it would be quite inappropriate culturally to define it as prostitution. This is because the reward comes voluntarily from the man and may not be given immediately after the sexual act. Interestingly, most prostitutes in Africa manipulate these two cultural ideologies about sexual relations to their advantage.

Pittin (1984) reports that Hausa women live together in 'houses of women' and expect to be 'courted' by a prospective client. Similarly, commercial sex workers in Ghana towns and Abidjan generally sit in their rooms and wait for their clients to come (Anarfi 1990b). In a sense, the women seem to adhere to one facet of the appropriate behaviour demanded of them, that of being passive. But in this case the man is 'lured' into the woman's residence, which constitutes an open manifestation that he needs her. That gives the prostitute a certain control over the male client and compels the latter to pay for his needs, an action that is not compulsory under normal circumstances. In this way, the myth of women seeing sex as a favour to men (Janeway 1974) is broken.

From the foregoing, it becomes clear that cultural ideology has a pro-found influence on the individual's behaviour, and upon others' perceptions of the individual. One effect of this is that under survey conditions female migrants' responses tend to be justifications for entering into prostitution. Such responses are influenced by the narrowness of their perceived roles. For example, in the case of the Hausa women in Nigeria, Pittin (1984) observes that, by projecting their self-image as victims of circumstances and male whims, their pursuit of the *karuwanci* profession is used as an excuse to remain, even to thrive, in the profession they may have willingly chosen. Similarly, Ghanaian women in prostitution in Abidjan justified their entry into the profession by highlighting contemporary male partners' non-giving of rewards, which is one of the traditionally accepted rules of the game, and their partners' failure to take up the responsibility of bringing up the children that often result in the sexual relationship. The upkeep of their own children and other members of the family was cited as the main reason for sending remittances by female immigrants in Abidjan (Anarfi 1990*a*). Thus, there may be considerable inconsistency between women's stated and actual reasons for migration, and between men's and women's perceptions of migrant women's roles, activities, and associates. To understand female migration and its implications fully, therefore a thorough understanding of the culture of the society out of which they migrated is required, which means using anthropological techniques.

There is a high degree of perceptual accentuation on the part of female migrants themselves and non-migrants alike which relates to the moral association with prostitution. Brydon (1987) traces the current concept of prostitution in West Africa to the increasing influence of Europeans, more especially with colonization, which also introduced Christian moralistic attitudes to it. Hence there is a general stigma attached to the profession in the whole of West Africa which has a profound influence on the attitudes of those who practise it themselves. To a very large extent, it is the stigma attached to the profession that compels women to practise it far away from home. In the Hausa case, Pittin remarks that 'there is no question of a woman admitting to an outsider, or to men, for example, that she had actively chosen her life-style, although this is of course exactly what many women do' (1984: 1307).

In the Abidjan example several women shed tears openly in course of the interview, by which they seemed to say that 'you know we don't like what we are doing but we are compelled by circumstances to do it'. To find out how the women reconcile their Christianity with their behaviour, there was a question about how often they went to church. Interestingly, several of them responded 'how can you go to church when you are in this kind of job' (Anarfi 1990). Only a few of them were active church-goers and their churches were mainly syncretic. There was evidence that such sects were set up to take a psychological advantage of immigrant woman prostitutes by exploiting their guilt feelings. One such sect established by some Ghanaian male immigrants was called Fa woho ma Awurade (Give yourself to the Lord). A popular hymn at their service was:

> Bra na obegye wo
> Ogye abonefo, ogye ayarefo
> Yesu de, ompa mu o.

(Come and He will receive you; He receives sinners, he receives the sick; Jesus does not discriminate.)

A non-migrant component of the Abidjan study brought another dimension to the moral approbation associated with migrant women and prostitution. The study sought the views, attitudes, and expectations of non-migrant women from a high-emigration area about the emigration of Ghanaian women to Abidjan (Anarfi 1990*a*, 1990*b*). There was general resentment of the emigration of Ghanaian women to Abidjan because of dislike of the work they do there. While there was evidence that incomes and living conditions were better in Abidjan than in Ghana, almost all the non-migrants insisted that not even an offer of a lucrative job at the destination would make them migrate to Abidjan. This stand adopted by the majority of non-migrants brings into focus the issue of the mover–stayer dichotomy, which has remained a mystery in migration studies to date. Why do a few people move out of a place because of supposedly unsatisfactory conditions (mainly economic) while the majority stay on?

The non-migrants' refusal to migrate to Abidjan may be related to a Ghanaian saying, 'Fere ne owu, afanyinam owu' (Between disgrace and death, the latter is preferable.) Certainly, the level of stigma attached to the emigration of Ghanaian women cannot be underestimated. That is why, although non-migrant incomes were much lower than those of migrants and living conditions in Abidjan far better than those in Ghana, many women still stayed on. The few who emigrate perhaps take solace from another Ghanaian saying, 'W'ani anhu adebi a, enye wo tan' (If it is out of sight, who cares if it is unpleasant.) That may explain why they do what they do not in Ghana, but in far-away Abidjan.

Recently, however, these women emigrants have begun to bring not only wealth from Abidjan, but also diseases (see Anarfi 1990*b*). That brings us to our final consideration: the implications of migration for the health of migrants.

The Health of Migrants

Relationships between population movements and health have long been recognized in the literature. The range of issues covered include the effects of movements on the transmission of disease and their impacts on programmes for disease control (Ford 1971; Molineaux and Guammiccia 1980), the effects of movements on the physical and mental conditions of those who move (Wessen 1974; Prothero 1977), and the effects of movements on the need for, the nature of, and the provision of health services in both rural and urban areas (Prothero 1989). Others have looked at the effect of health conditions on mobility patterns (Hunter 1966, 1981). To put the complexity of the variety of migration and health relationships into better perspective, Prothero (1977) advanced the now long-established typology of population movements in a variety of spatial/temporal forms and a number of major categories of health hazards. The typology was intended as a summary indication of what needs to be considered in a more penetrating social/ medical interdisciplinary concern than exists at the present time. A modified form of the typology has been successfully applied to movements and specific diseases (e.g. on malaria in Thailand, and on guineaworms in Nigeria: see Prothero 1989: 3).

One disease that has strong implications for population movements and which requires a penetrating interdisciplinary approach to its study is AIDS. The need to understand the relationship between migration and AIDS stems from the fact that, with a few exceptions, the disease appears currently to be concentrated in urban populations. African populations are very mobile and, given the circulatory nature of population mobility in the continent, the interrelatedness of urban and rural populations is a fact of existence. The current view is that heterosexual transmission through vaginal penetrative sex is the major conduit for HIV/AIDS infection in Africa. Unfortunately, there are cultural and political constraints on the open discussion of sexuality. As a result, not enough is known about sexuality in Africa to enable the interrelationship between it, migration, and HIV/AIDS to be properly constructed. While much effort has been expended to understand the disease and sexuality in the African context, not much has been done on the migration component of the interrelationship (see Anarfi 1993).

Most of Africa is still rural and traditional, which means that in many parts of Africa traditional restrictions and regulations still prevail, particularly pertaining to sexuality. It would appear that migration offers an opportunity for people to shake off such restrictions just by physically moving away from the agents and custodians of tradition and/or into the anonymity provided by the urban area.

The town is a place of qualitatively different forms of social relationship from those found in rural areas and a place which lends itself to the exploitation of new opportunities. Prostitution tends to be seen as part of this opening up of new opportunities. It is generally agreed that promiscuity increases in cities because of both the destitution of women and the 'rootlessness of male migrants'. The transformation of African rural economies in the colonial period did bring about far-reaching changes in marriage, kinship, and gender relations. As sexual behaviour is constructed within these relations, it cannot have remained unaffected. The result is the development of sexual sub-cultures in the cities and urban centres. There is the need, therefore, to link the domains of sexual relations to the wider socio-cultural, economic, and political contexts within which they are embedded. Anthropological techniques can certainly be useful in placing sexual behaviour in context and by shifting emphasis from risk behaviour in general to which partner and under what circumstances, the latter of which will include migration.

Conclusion

Of the major components of population change, migration is the one to which least attention has been given. It remains the most difficult component to conceptualize, measure, and analyse. None the less, the literature on migration is so diverse and voluminous that it is impossible, within limited space, to more than touch upon some of its major aspects. This paper has mentioned just a few of the basic concepts, methodological problems, and implications of migration that are of particular relevance to Africa and Third World situations.

It has been emphasized that the basic explanation for the general unsatisfactory status of migration studies lies in the realm of the conceptual and the social-psychological (Zelinsky 1983). The continuing reliance on questions and answers about migration that were developed years ago for a particular setting at a particular time has been questioned by some scholars (e.g. Goldstein 1978). To break the inertia, certain issues require careful consideration. First, there is a need to broaden the geographical and historical bounds of the migration enterprise. Second, there is the need for an interdisciplinary approach to attack questions of mutual interest. Third, there is a need for grounding migration work in basic, comprehensive social theory.

It is apparent that migration decision-making holds the key to the understanding of some of the behaviours of migrants and non-migrants alike and to the gender differences in these. To make any headway, much research needs to be done in connection with socio-cultural influences on migration decision-making. Hugo (1981) has suggested the adoption of more innovative approaches, including the study of the entire process of migration by interviewing migrants at various stages of the process via longitudinal studies and resurveys of specific populations examined in previous migration studies. He stresses the need to take a fuller account of the rural decision-making context in rural–urban migration studies and a closer investigation of the decision to stay through studies devoted specifically to non-migrants. Given that the cost of longitudinal studies is often prohibitive both in temporal and financial terms, the life history approach has been suggested as a useful alternative (see Hugo 1981; Pryor 1975; and Bertaux-Wiame 1979).

Economic versus non-economic causes of migration continues to generate a lot of argument. It has been pointed out that most of the generalizations in migration based on economic models are still begging for social and psychological explanations. But the fact remains that it is impossible to get a purely non-economic explanation of migration behaviour. Whatever the cause, the essential issue is that the migrant must survive. That requires rational economic decisions and entrance into an economic venture or relationship which alone can ensure the satisfaction of the basic necessities of food, shelter, and clothing. However, in order to generate an all-pervading theory of migration, and for policy purposes, we need to go beyond narrow and obvious economic thinking and take a holistic view of the migration process.

The need for a combination of qualitative ethnographic fieldwork with quantitative methods of censusing and surveying in the study of population problems, including migration, has been articulated by many researchers with varied backgrounds (e.g. Kearney 1986; Hugo 1981; Caldwell *et al.* 1988; Du Toit 1975). The consensus is that the greater use of participant observation techniques and the case study approach of intensive examination of particular individuals, families, groups, and communities will be rewarding and should reveal new hypotheses that can be tested in conventional questionnaire surveys. A major advantage of the micro approach is the identification and isolation of the domestic community, which is the usual place and object of anthropological fieldwork; this also allows gender differences to be observed and examined in detail.

References

Abu-Lughod, J. (1961), 'Migrant adjustment to city life'. *American Journal of Sociology*, 67: 22–32.

Amin, S. (1974), 'Modern migration in western Africa', in S. Amin (ed.), *Modern Migrations in Western Africa*. London: Oxford University Press, pp. 65–124.

Amoah, E. (1990), 'Femaleness: Akan concepts and practices', in J. Bercher (ed.), *Women, Religion and Sexuality*. Geneva: World Council of Churches, pp. 129–53.

Anarfi, J. K. (1982), 'International labour migration in West Africa: the emigration of Ghanaians to Lagos, Nigeria'. MA thesis, Regional Institute for Population Studies at the University of Ghana, Legon.

——(1990a), 'International migration of Ghanaian women to Abidjan, Cote d'Ivoire: a demographic and socio-economic study'. Ph.D. dissertation, Regional Institute for Population Studies at the University of Ghana, Legon.

——(1990b), 'Female migration, occupation and diseases linkages: the Abidjan case study'. Paper presented at an informal workshop on Researching Sexual Networking in West Africa, Ibadan, 22–3 March.

——(1993), 'Sexuality, migration and AIDS in Ghana: a socio-behavioural study'. *Health Transition Review: Sexual Networking and HIV/AIDS in West Africa*, 3 (supplement): 45–67.

Anderson, J. (1971), 'Space–time budget and activity studies in urban geography and planning'. *Environment and Planning*, 3: 353–68.

Becker, G. S. (1981), *A Treatise on the Family*. Cambridge, Mass.: Harvard University Press.

Bertaux-Wiame, I. (1979), 'The life history approach to the study of internal migration'. *Oral History*, 1: 249–65.

Blalock, H. and Wilken, P. H. (1979), *Intergroup Processes*. New York: Free Press.

Borrie, W. D. (1956), *The Cultural Integration of Immigrants*. Paris: UNESCO.

Boserup, E. (1970), *Woman's Role in Economic Development*. London: George Allen & Unwin.

Bowles, S. (1970), 'Migration as investment: empirical tests of the human investment approach to geographical mobility'. *Review of Economics and Statistics*, 52(4): 356–62.

Bruner, E. M. (1961), 'Urbanization and ethnic identity in North Sumatra'. *American Anthropologist*, 63: 508–21.

Brydon, L. (1987), 'Who moves? Women and migration in West Africa in the 1980s', in J. S. Eades (ed.), *Migrants, Workers and the Social Order*. London: Association of Social Anthropologists, pp. 165–80.

Burch, T. K. (1978), 'The decision to migrate: a synthesis and theoretical application'. Unpublished paper, Population Studies Center, University of Western Ontario.

Caldwell, J. C. (1969), *African Rural–Urban Migration: The Movement to Ghana's Towns*. New York: Columbia University Press.

——(1976), 'Towards a restatement of demographic transition theory'. *Population and Development Review*, 2: 321–66.

——(1982), *Theory of Fertility Decline*. New York: Academic Press.

——Reddy, P. H., and Caldwell, P. (1988), *The Case of Demographic Change: Experimental Research in South India*. Madison, Wis.: University of Wisconsin Press.

Cardona, R. and Simmons, A. (1975), 'Toward a model of migration in Latin America', in B. M. Du Toit and H. I. Safa (eds.), *Migration and Urbanization*. The Hague: Mouton, pp. 19–48.

Chambers, R. (1983), *Rural Development: Putting the Last First*. New York: Longman.

Chan, T. H. P. (1981), 'A review of micro migration research in the Third World context', in G. F. De Jong and R. Gardner (eds.), *Migration Decision Making: Multi-disciplinary Approaches to Microlevel Studies in Developed and Developing Countries*. New York: Pergamon Press.

Chaney, E. M. (1980), 'Women in international migration: issues in development planning'. Washington, DC: USAID.

——and Lewis, M. W. (1980), 'Women, migration and the decline of smallholder agriculture'. Report prepared for the Office of Women in Development, US Agency for International Development, Washington, DC.

Cohen, A. (1969), *Custom and Politics in Urban Africa*. London: Routledge & Kegan Paul/University of California Press.

——(1974), *Two-Dimensional Man*. Berkley and Los Angeles: University of California Press.

Conaway, M. E. (1977), 'Circular migration: a summary and bibliography'. *Council of Planning Libraries Exchange Bibliography*. Monticello, Ill.: Council of Planning Libraries.

Connell, J. (1984), 'Status or subjugation? Women, migration and development in the South Pacific'. *International Migration Review*, Special Issue, 18: 964–83.

Da Vanzo, J. (1976), 'Family migration decisions: an econometric model'. Paper presented at the annual meeting of the Population Association of America, Montreal.

——(1981), 'Microeconomic approaches to studying migration decisions', in G. F. De Jong and R. W. Gardner (eds.), *Migration Decision Making: Multidisciplinary Approaches to Microlevel Studies in Developed and Developing Countries*. New York: Pergamon Press, pp. 90–129.

De Jong, G. F. and Fawcett, J. T. (1981), 'Motivations for migration: an assessment and value-expectancy research model', in G. F. De Jong and R. Gardner (eds.), *Migration Decision Making: Multidisciplinary Approaches to Microlevel Studies in Developed and Developing Countries*. New York: Pergamon Press.

Du Toit, B. M. (1975), 'A decision-making model for the study of migration', in B. M. Du Toit and H. Safa (eds.), *Migration and Urbanization*. The Hague: Mouton, pp. 49–76.

Eades, J. S. (1975), 'The growth of a migrant community: the Yoruba in northern Ghana', in J. R. Goody (ed.), *Changing Social Structure in Ghana*. London: International African Institute.

Eisenstadt, S. N. (1954), *The Absorption of Immigrants*. London: Routledge & Kegan Paul.

Fawcett, J. T., Khoo, S. E., and Smith, P. C. (1984), 'Urbanization, migration and the status of women', in J. T. Fawcett, S-E. Khoo and P. C. Smith (eds.), *Women in the Cities of Asia: Migration and Urban Adaptation*. Boulder, Color.: Westview Press, pp. 3–11.

Findley, S. (1987), *Rural Development and Migration: A Study of Family Choices in the Philippines*. Boulder, Colo., and London: Westview Press.

Ford, J. (1971), *The Role of the Trypanosomiases in African Ecology*. Oxford: Clarendon Press.

Fortes, M. (1945), *The Dynamics of Clanship among the Tallensi*. London: Anthropological Publications/Oxford University Press.

Fox, R. (1968), *Encounter with Anthropology*. New York: Dell.

Garcia-Castro, M. (1986), 'Work versus life: Colombian women in New York', in J. Nash and H. Safa (eds.), *Women and Change in Latin America*. Boston, Mass.: Bergin & Garvey.

——Gearing, J., and Gill, M. (1984), *Women and Migration: Latin America and the Caribbean: A Selective Annotated Bibliography*, Occasional Paper 2, Centre for Latin American Studies. Gainesville: University of Florida.

Germani, G. (1965), 'Migration and acculturation', in P. Hauser (ed.), *Handbook for Social Research in Urban Areas*. Paris: UNESCO, pp. 159–78.

Gluckman, M. (1958), *Analysis of a Social Situation in Modern Zululand*. Manchester: Rhodes Livingstone Institute.

Goldstein, S. (1978), 'Circulation in the context of total mobility in Southeast Asia', *Papers of the East–West Population Institute*, No. 53. Honolulu: East–West Population Institute.

Gould, W. T. S. and Prothero, R. M. (1975), 'Space and time in African population mobility', in L. A. Kozinski and R. M. Prothero (eds.), *People on the Move*. London: Methuen.

Graves, P. E. and Linneman, P. D. (1979), 'Household migration: theoretical and empirical results'. *Journal of Urban Economics*, 6(3): 383–404.

Gugler, J. (1969), 'On the theory of rural–urban migration: the case of sub-Saharan Africa', in J. A. Jackson (ed.), *Migration*. Cambridge: Cambridge University Press.

Guhleman, P. and Tienda, M. (1981), 'A socioeconomic profile of Hispanic American female workers: perspectives on labour force participation and earnings'. *Centre for Demography and Ecology Working Papers* 81–87. Madison: University of Wisconsin.

Harbison, S. F. (1981), 'Family structure and family strategy in migration decision making', in G. F. De Jong and R. W. Gardner (eds.), *Migration Decision Making: Multidisciplinary Approaches to Microlevel Studies in Developed and Developing Countries*. New York: Pergamon Press, pp. 225–51.

Huang, N. C. (1984), 'The migration of rural women to Taipei', in J. T. Fawcett, S. E. Khoo, and P. C. Smith, (eds.). *Women in the Cities of Asia: Migration and Urban Adaptation*. Boulder, Colo: Westview Press, pp. 247–68.

Hugo, G. J. (1978), *Population Mobility in West Java*. Yogyakarta: Gadjah Mada University Press.

——(1981), 'Village–community ties, village norms, and ethnic and social networks: a review of evidence from the Third World', in G. F. De Jong and R. W. Gardner (eds.), *Migration Decision Making*. New York: Pergamon Press.

Hunter, J. M. (1966), 'River blindness in Nangodi, Northern Ghana: a hypothesis of cyclical advance and retreat'. *Geographical Review*, 56: 398.

——(1981), 'Progress and concerns in the World Health Organization Onchocerciasis Control Programme in West Africa'. *Social Science and Medicine*, 15D: 261–75.

Izzard, W. (1985), 'Migrants and mothers: case-studies from Botswana'. *Journal of Southern African Studies*, 11(2): 258–80.

Janeway, E. (1974), *Man's World, Woman's Place: a Study in Social Mythology*. New York: W. Morrow.

Kearney, M. (1986), 'From the Invisible Hand to visible feet: anthropological studies of migration and development'. *Annual Review of Anthropology*, 15: 331–61.

Lazarsfeld, P. F. and Menzel, H. (1961), 'On the relation between individual and collective properties', in A. Etzioni (ed.), *Complex Organizations*. New York: Holt, Rinehart & Winston.

Lee, E. S. (1966), 'A theory of migration'. *Demography*, 3: 47–57.

Lewis, O. (1952), 'Urbanization without breakdown: a case study'. *Science Monthly*, 75: 31–41.

Little, K. (1965), *West African Urbanization: A Study of Voluntary Associations in Social Change*. Cambridge: Cambridge University Press.

——(1973), *African Women in Towns*. Cambridge: Cambridge University Press.

Mabogunje, A. L. (1970), 'Systems approach to a theory of rural–urban migration'. *Geographical Analysis*, 2: 1–17.

Mangalam, J. J. (1968), *Human Migration: A Guide to Migration Literature in English*. Lexington, Ky: University of Kentucky Press.

Mangin, W. (ed.) (1970), *Peasants in Cities: Readings in the Anthropology of Urbanization*. Boston: Houghton-Mifflin.

Mayer, P. (1961), *Townsmen or Tribesmen*. Cape Town: Oxford University Press.

McGee, T. G. (1975), 'Malay migration to Kuala Lumpur City', in B. Du Toit and H. Safa (eds.), *Migration Models and Adaptative Strategies*. The Hague: Mouton. pp. 143–78.

Meillassoux, C. (1981), *Maidens, Meal and Money*. London: Cambridge University Press.

Mincer, J. (1978), 'Family migration decisions'. *Journal of Political Economy*, 86(5): 749–73.

Molineaux, L. and Guammiccia, G. (1980), *The Garki Project: Research on the Epidemiology and Control of Malaria in the Sudan Savanna of West Africa*. Geneva: WHO.

Morokvasic, M. (1979), 'The migration of women in Europe'. Paper presented at a conference on the Continuing Subordination of Women in the Development Process, Institute for Development Studies, Brighton, Sussex.

——(1984), 'Birds of passage are also women', *International Migration Review*, 4: 886–907.

Nabila, J. S. (1974), 'Migration of the Frafra in northern Ghana: a case study of cyclical labour migration in West Africa'. Ph.D. dissertation, Michigan State University.

Nadel, S. F. (1942), *A Black Byzantium: The Kingdom of Nupe in Nigeria*. London: Oxford University Press.

Nelson, J., (1970), 'The urban poor: disruption or political integration in Third World cities'. *World Politics*, 22: 393–413.

——(1976*a*), 'Sojourners versus new urbanites: causes and consequences of temporary versus permanent migration'. *Economic Development and Cultural Change*, 24: 721–57.

——(1976*b*), 'Temporary versus permanent cityward migration: causes and consequences'. Mimeo, Massachusetts Institute of Technology Migration and Development Study Group, Cambridge, Mass.

Obbo, C. (1980), *African Women: Their Struggle for Economic Independence*. London: Zed Press.

Pessar, P. (1982), 'Kinship relations of production in the migration process: the case of Dominican emigration to the United States', *Occasional Papers* 32. New York: Center for Latin American and Caribbean Studies, New York University.

——(1985), 'The role of gender in Dominican settlement in the United States', in J. Nash and H. I. Safa (eds.), *Women and Change in Latin America*. Boston, Mass.: Bergin & Garvey.

Piore, M. (1979), *Birds of Passage: Migrant Labour and Industrial Societies*. Cambridge: Cambridge University Press.

Pittin, R. (1984), 'Migration of women in Nigeria: the Hausa case'. *International Migration Review*, (Special Issue): 1293–1314.

Prothero, M. R. (1977), 'Disease and mobility: a neglected factor in epidemiology'. *International Journal of Epidemiology*, 6: 259–67.

——(1989), 'Migration and health'. Paper presented for discussion at the conference on the Union for African Population Studies on Migration in African Development: Issues and Policies for the 1990s, Nairobi, 4–9 December.

Pryor, R. J. (1975), *The Motivation of Migration*. Canberra: Australian National University.

Ravenstein, E. G. (1889), 'The laws of migration'. *Journal of the Statistical Society*, 52: 241–301.

Recchini de Lattes, Z. (1989), 'Women in internal migration, with special reference to Latin America'. *Population Bulletin of the United Nations*, 27: 95–107.

Reid, I. A. (1955), 'Immigration and assimilation'. *Current History*, 29: 305–10.

Sandell, S. H. (1977), 'Women and the economics of family migration'. *Review of Economics and Statistics*, 59(4): 406–14.

Sassen-Koob, S. (1981), 'Exporting capital and importing labour: the role of women', in D. M. Mortimer and R. Bryce-La Porte (eds.), *Female Immigrants to the United States: Caribbean, Latin American, and African Experiences*. Washington, DC: Smithsonian Institute Press, pp. 203–34.

Sell, R. and De Jong, G. F. (1978), 'Toward a motivational theory of migration decision making'. *Journal of Population*, 1(4): 313–35.

Sjaasstad, L. A. (1962), 'The costs and returns of human migration'. *Journal of Political Economy*, 70: 80–93.

Skeldon, R. (1977), 'The evolution of migration patterns during urbanization in Peru'. *Geographical Review*, 67: 394–411.

Smale, M. (1980), *Women in Mauritania: The Effects of Drought and Implications for Development Programmes*. Washington, DC: US Agency for International Development, Office of Women in Development.

Speare, A., Jr. (1971), 'A cost–benefit model of rural to urban migration in Taiwan'. *Population Studies*, 25(1): 117–30.

Stark, O. (1982), 'Rural-to-urban migration and intrafamilial risk-taking agreements in LDCs'. Paper presented at the annual meeting of the Population Association of America.

Stone, L. O. (1975), 'On the interaction of mobility dimensions in theory of decision making'. *Canadian Review of Sociology and Anthropology*, 12(1): 95–100.

Sudarkasa, N. (1973), 'Where women work: a study of Yoruba women in the market place and in the home'. *Anthropological Papers* no. 53. Ann Arbor: Museum of Anthropology, University of Michigan.

——(1977), 'Women and migration in contemporary West Africa', in Wellesley College Centre for Research on Women in Higher Education and the Professions, *Women and National Development: The Complexities of Change*. Chicago: University of Chicago Press, pp. 178–89.

Taylor, R. (1969), 'Migration and motivation: a study of determinants and types', in J. A. Jackson (ed.), *Migration*. Cambridge: Cambridge University Press, pp. 99–133.

Titus, M. J. (1978), 'Inter-regional migration in Indonesia as a reflection of social and regional inequalities'. *Tijdschrift voor Economische en Sociale Geografie*, 69(4): 194–204.

Turner, J. F. C. (1967), 'Barriers and channels for housing development in modernizing countries'. *Journal of the American Institute of Planners*, 33: 167–81.

Urzua, R. (1981), 'Population redistribution mechanisms as related to various forms of development'. *Population Distribution Policies in Development Planning*, Population Studies no. 75. New York: UN Department of International Economics and Social Affairs, pp. 53–69.

Ware, H. (1981), *Women, Demography and Development*. Canberra: Australian National University Press.

Wessen, A. (1974), 'The role of migrant studies in epidemiological research'. *Israel Journal of Medical Science*, 1: 584.

Wood, C. H. (1981), 'Structural changes and household strategies: a conceptual framework for the study of rural migration'. *Human Organization*, 40: 338–44.

Yanagisako, S. J. (1979), 'Family and household: the analysis of domestic groups'. *Annual Review of Anthropology*, 8: 161–205.

Youssej, N. *et al.* (1979), *Women in Migration: A Third World Focus*, Washington, DC: International Centre for Research on Women.

Zelinsky, W. (1971), 'The hypothesis of the mobility transition'. *Geographical Review*, 61: 219–49.

—— (1979), 'The demographic transition: changing patterns of migration.' Mimeo, Pennsylvania State University.

—— (1983), 'The impasse in migration theory: a sketch map for practical escapees', in P. A. Morrison (ed.), *Population Movements: Their Forms and Functions in Urbanization*, Liège: Ordina.

10 Are Men Weaker or Do their Sisters Talk Too Much?
Sex Differences in Childhood Mortality and the Construction of 'Biological' Differences

PETER AABY

> 'Men are more often colour-blind than women', said Joanna, 'It's one of those sex-linked things', she added with an air of erudition, 'You know, it passes through the women to come out in the men.'
> 'You make it sound as though it was measles', said Emelyn Price.
>
> Agatha Christie, *Nemesis* (1974: 128)

Popular beliefs in Euro-American culture are characterized by a complementary definition of the sexes. While males have greater physical strength, Nature has gifted females with greater biological resistance. More men than women are born, but survival is better among women (Mims 1976: 205).

Medical research has supported such beliefs by showing higher mortality for men from many infectious diseases (Denny *et al.* 1977; Karzon *et al.* 1961; McGlashan 1969). For example, the measles mortality rate is higher among males than females (Lancaster 1952; T. S. Wilson 1971). One of the few exceptions has been whooping cough, where girls apparently have higher mortality, possibly because of the easier obstruction of their smaller airways. The difference in severity or mortality is generally explained in terms of 'sex-linked immune capacity' or 'hormonal differences having consequences for immunity' (Mims 1976: 205). To most people, these sex differences are perceived to be fully documented by science; greater biological strength has become the natural biological state of women.

However, mortality is not always higher for boys than for girls. In some developing countries, girls have higher childhood mortality or higher mortality from certain diseases (Fargues and Nassour 1988; McGregor 1964; Monastiri 1961). Given the belief that men are weaker, this higher female mortality is explained in terms of differential treatment in cultures with a preference for boys. Much of the literature has therefore discussed whether this differential treatment by sex is more important in relation to infant

This chapter is a development of a paper originally published in French (Aaby *et al.* 1983).

feeding, home care, or utilization of health services (Chen *et al.* 1981). To quote a recent report, the UN Population Division

is undertaking a study of child mortality by sex that will document the determinants of sex differentials in mortality in various socio-cultural settings. This study will include comparisons of mortality rates in childhood among males and females.... A review of the mechanisms that lead to excess female child mortality will be undertaken. Mechanisms of interest include: prevalence of son preference, the differential utilization of health facilities and differential feeding practices by sex of child, and differences in the nutritional status between male and female children.

The question of female excess mortality has received particular attention in Bangladesh (Bhuiya and Streatfield 1991; Chen *et al.* 1981; D'Souza and Chen 1980; Fauveau *et al.* 1991; Koenig and D'Souza 1986) and on the Indian subcontinent (Basu 1989; Das Gupta 1987; Sathar 1987). Sex differences in both nutrition and utilization of health services have been found (Chen *et al.* 1981). In an economically inspired interpretation, it has been emphasized that the tendency towards higher female mortality is not so much a result of a cultural disrespect for girls as it is a consequence of the need to allocate limited resources. Given the strong preference for boys, they may receive more treatment when resources are scarce (Koenig and D'Souza 1986).

The present essay is a result of an attempt made during the last fifteen years to understand sex differences in relation to measles-related mortality (Aaby *et al.* 1983). Since measles is the most severe of the childhood infections and the single largest killer of children in developing countries (Aaby 1991), it is likely that this lesson is important for studying other infections and childhood mortality in general. Common beliefs have assumed males to be weaker and higher female mortality to be an unnatural product of culturally sanctioned preferential treatment of boys in relation to feeding or care. However, this mode of thinking may have been accepted too uncritically. The cultural belief that one sex is stronger than the other because of as yet undocumented genetic mechanisms may be unfounded, and there may well be other and less conscious mechanisms than preferential treatment which generate sex differences in mortality. In this paper it is argued that the question has been wrongly posed by emphasizing one sex as the stronger one. Both female and male mortality need to be explained. There is too much variation in mortality patterns by sex and age for different diseases and in different periods to make it likely that a genetic difference explains very much. It is my hypothesis that much of the variation in mortality may be related to the disease transmission process affecting the sexes differently, producing more intensive exposure and more severe impact of that disease for one sex than the other. The disease transmission process is shaped by both conscious and unconscious behaviour patterns. Cultural beliefs and institutions can have major effects on mortality differentials through the way they construct gender differences in behaviour which in turn affect disease transmission, for example by confining girls to the home and sending boys to school. Since the emphasis is on variations in disease transmission, age differences will also have to be considered. Just as sex differences have been 'explained' by genetic differences, age differences in mortality have also been ascribed to genetic differences. In contrast to these common beliefs, it may be argued that both sex and age differences in mortality can be a product of the disease transmission process. In the process of pursuing this hypothesis, several unexpected tendencies appear which lead to a different understanding of sex differences in childhood mortality (Aaby *et al.* 1986, 1992, 1993*b*).

The present paper, therefore, is not an attempt to assess whether preferential treatment in feeding, home care, or utilization of preventive or curative health services is the more important factor in producing mortality differences between the sexes; nor is it an attempt to understand the cultural or socioeconomic processes that lead to preferential treatment of one sex. Instead, the paper analyses how disease transmission patterns may produce severe infection and mortality differences by sex or age. The focus is the interaction between behaviour patterns and disease transmission, a reality that may interact in important ways with patterns of differential or preferential treatment of the sexes.

Patterns of Severity by Age and Sex

Tables 10.1–10.5 shows some typical tendencies with respect to changes in severity in measles according to age and sex. Infections are most severe for the very young children, but a higher risk reappears in older age groups, as illustrated by the higher measles case fatality ratio (CFR) for individuals over 10 years (Table 10.1) or over 15 years (Table 10.2). A similar pattern also exists for other infections, such as chickenpox, with higher case fatality for individuals over 20 years (Table 10.4), and polio infection, with a higher frequency of paralysis among those over 15 years (Table 10.5). Hence the severity curve has a U- or V-shape indicating greatest severity among younger and older individuals. This tendency is contrary to experimental studies with the measles virus in animals, where the reaction is inversely proportional to the age at infection (Griffin *et al.* 1974). It is also contrary to the experience with live measles vaccine virus, which demonstrates less reaction among adults (Gudnadóttir and Black 1964).

With respect to measles and polio, it appears that boys are more severely affected than girls at the younger ages (Tables 10.2 and 10.5). However, at the later ages where there is a renewed increase in severity, girls or women seem more severely affected than males (Tables 10.2, 10.3, and 10.5). Generally, measles is not a problem among adults in endemic areas as virtually

Table 10.1. Case Fatality Ratio (CFR) from Measles according to Age: Reported Cases, January-June 1961, England and Wales

Age (yrs)	Cases	Deaths	CFR/1,000
0	21,570	24	1.11
1	62,942	34	0.54
2–4	266,984	35	0.13
5–9	294,555	20	0.07
10–14	18,059	8	0.44
15+	6.272	11	1.75

Source: Babbott *et al*. (1963).

Table 10.2. Case Fatality Ratio (CFR) from Measles according to Age, Sex, and Relative Risk (RR) for Women: Reported Cases, 1883–1902, Aberdeen

Age (yrs)	No. of cases	CFR (%) Male	Female	Total CFR	RR for females
0	3,034	14.5	13.56	14.04	0.94
1	5,222	10.9	9.23	10.07	0.85
2	5,195	3,62	3,22	3.43	0.89
3	5,053	1.52	1.72	1.62	1.13
4	4,836	0.92	0.85	0.89	0.92
5	5,352	0.65	0.66	0.65	1.01
6	4,628	0.38	0.54	0.45	1.42
7	2,818	0.30	0.68	0.50	2.27
8–14	3,155	0.33	0.42	0.38	1.27
15+	1,081	0.59	1.04	0.83	1.76

Source: G. Wilson (1905).

Table 10.3. Measles Deaths according to Age and Sex: 1873, Kristiania (Oslo), Norway

Age (yrs)	Male deaths	Female deaths
0	22	23
1–2	56	52
3–4	14	23
5–9	7	22
10–14	2	7
Total	101	121

Source: Irgens (1880).

Table 10.4. Cases and Deaths from Chickenpox (Varicella) according to Age: Reported Cases, USA, 1972–1976

Age (yrs)	Cases	Deaths	CFR (%)
0–4	18,823	140	0.74
5–9	71,321	214	0.30
10–14	16,840	60	0.36
15–19	2,098	8	0.38
20 +	2,103	133	6.32
Total	111,185	555	0.50

Source: Preblud and D'Angelo (1979).

Table 10.5. Polio Occurrences according to Age and Sex, Relative Risk (RR) in Women, and Percentage Paralysed, by age group: USA, 34 states, 1955

Age (yrs)	Polio rate/1,000		RR for women	% paralysed
	Males	Females		
0–4	39.3	27.8	0.71	64.5
5–9	45.9	26.9	0.59	43.9
10–14	33.0	21.7	0.66	43.7
15–19	20.3	16.1	0.79	48.3
20–24	15.3	23.7	1.55	50.2
25–29	17.1	21.4	1.25	53.2
30–34	11.5	12.3	1.07	56.6

Source: Hall *et al.* (1957).

everybody contracts the infection in childhood. However, in virgin-soil areas never touched by the infection, or in isolated areas with a very long interval between epidemics, adults are equally susceptible to the infection. From descriptions of such epidemics, it seems that women are more severely infected than men (Corney 1913; Mancius 1847). For example, when measles was introduced in Greenland in 1951, the mortality rate was clearly higher among women aged 15–54 years (1.9%, 23 out of 1,182) than among the males of the same age group (0.7%, 7 out of 970) ($p = 0.025$); furthermore, measles caused more complications among the women (Christensen *et al.* 1953). Generally, males may have a higher mortality because they are more affected at a young age when the case fatality rate is particularly high, but it does not seem that higher male mortality is an invariate phenomenon.

There is no general explanation of these age- and sex-specific tendencies. It is usually suggested that immunological immaturity is an important factor for the greater severity of infections among the youngest children (Mims 1976). However, there is no explanation as to why infections become more severe among adults (Alter 1976; Mims 1976). There are some indications that people over 40 years of age have less adequate immune reactions (Mims 1976). However, in many societies infections attack young adults more severely (Tables 10.1–10.5), even though they experience fewer reactions to infection with live measles vaccine virus than younger age groups (Gudna-dóttir and Black 1964).

Hormonal factors have been suggested as being important for the higher mortality of adult females. Presumably owing to the associated immunosup-pression, pregnant women experience higher mortality, and this may account for some of the difference in severity of infection among women. In one example, smallpox mortality was clearly shown to be higher among pregnant women compared with non-pregnant women of the same age (Rao *et al.* 1968). However, pregnancy does not explain the whole difference in mortality among adults. For example, in Greenland mortality was 1.7% (19 out of 1,099) among non-pregnant women, which was still considerably higher than for men of the same age group (relative risk = 2.40 (1.01–5.67)). The hypothesis of major hormonal differences between the sexes also seems less likely to explain why the higher severity for females may start as early as 5–6 years of age for some infections (Table 10.2).

Medical science has tended to reconstruct the sex and age patterns observed in Europe and America as a biological reality, and as age- and sex-related factors that are ultimately determined by genetic constitution (Alter 1976; Mims 1976). From this perspective, it is inconsistent that the age of lowest severity varies in different societies and for different infections. For example, in England and Wales in 1961 (Table 10.1) the least severe measles infection was among the age group 2–9 years, in Aberdeen in 1883–1902 (Table 10.2) it was the age group 8–14 years, and in the United States in the 1970s it was the ages 5–19 that suffered the least from chickenpox infection. If this really is a sex-dependent factor, it becomes difficult to understand how females can have higher measles mortality from the age of 6 years in Aberdeen at the turn of the century (Table 10.2), from 3 years in Norway in 1873 (Table 10.3), and only from 20 years of age in polio mortality in the United States in 1955 (Table 10.5). Hence there is a need for explanations that do not assume these age and sex differentials to be determined predo-minantly by nature.

Determinants of Severity of Infection

There are more important determinants of severe disease than age and sex. This is most clearly illustrated by historical and geographical variations in mortality. For example, in the 1960s the measles case fatality ratio (CFR) was 0.07% (10 out of 14,752) for infants in Denmark (Hertz *et al.* 1976), but as high as 14% (426 out of 3,044) at the turn of the century in Aberdeen (Table 10.2). In many West African countries, the CFR for infants has been well over 20% until recently (Aaby 1991). It would seem plausible that the same factors that produce such differences in mortality could be linked to age and sex differences in mortality. Medical research has tended to relate differences in mortality from infectious diseases, including measles, according to the care received, or by detecting differences in host resistance between the individuals who survived or died, emphasizing factors such as state of nutrition, age at infection, genetic differences, or chronic conditions, i.e. the host and care-factor approach (Aaby 1991). For measles, immunological frailty resulting from preceding infections or chronic diseases (Hertz *et al.* 1976; Barkin 1975) and genetic constitution (Black *et al.* 1971) have been assumed to be important determinants of disease fatality. However, malnutrition has undoubtedly been assumed to be a major factor explaining differences in case fatality (Jelliffe 1968; Mata 1978; Morley 1973). While this perspective has been supported by hospital studies showing higher mortality for children admitted with low weight-for-age, there is no published community study showing a significant impact of the pre-infection state of nutrition on the case fatality level (Aaby 1991). In fact, several studies from Guinea-Bissau, Kenya, and Bangladesh (Koster *et al.* 1981) have found no relation between the pre-infection state of nutrition and the subsequent CFR.

Instead, studies from Guinea-Bissau, Senegal, Gambia, Kenya, Bangladesh, England, Germany, and Denmark have found mortality to be related to overcrowding (Aaby 1991). The CFR is much higher in houses with several cases than in houses with only a single case of measles. Mortality is particularly high among the so-called secondary cases, individuals who have contracted measles from someone within their own house, whereas it is lower for the index cases, i.e. the first case(s) in a house infected from someone outside the house. This pattern has been found in all areas with high mortality. In chickenpox infection, where death is rare, differences in severity have been documented by measuring the number of pox; these are considerably higher in secondary than in index cases (Ross 1962). There are also indications from other infections, e.g. polio, that mortality is higher for secondary cases (Aaby et al. 1985). If secondary cases are more severe, this is presumably because secondary cases have been more intensively exposed to the infecting agent within the home and for a longer period than an index case who contracts infection in a brief contact with someone from outside the family. It seems plausible that the underlying mechanism for this pattern of severity is the dose of absorbed virus. In animal models, a high dose of infection leads to a short period of incubation, inability to mount a sufficient immune response, and a high mortality (Aaby 1991). Since secondary cases are most severe, it becomes important to detect which groups become index cases and transmit infection and which groups are infected at home and become secondary cases. Societies differ considerably with respect to what proportion of the children are infected intensively at home. For example, in Bangladesh, where the case fatality is low (less than 3%), only 14%–20% of the children under 3 years of age were secondary cases in the home, whereas more than 60% of the children of the same age group were secondary cases in Guinea-Bissau where the case fatality is as high as 25%. There are also indications that the proportion of secondary cases was more than 50% when mortality was high in Europe at the turn of the century, whereas today it is probably only 5%–10% who become infected at home. If the transmission pattern is so strongly correlated with the severity of infection, it is relevant to examine whether the age and sex patterns of severity can be related to variation in transmission.

Age Patterns

Infectious diseases are transmitted between different families mainly in the age group with a high concentration of susceptible individuals. Earlier on, transmission between families occurred predominantly in the first years of school (Brownlee 1920). Among the older children, there would be too few susceptible individuals to allow for effective transmission in this age group, and among the younger pre-school children there was probably too little contact between children from different homes. Most of the children infected in the age of inter-family transmission would be index cases. However, the children infected before or after this age would have a higher risk of becoming secondary cases, since their most likely source of infection would be a sibling of the age group of inter-family transmission rather than an age mate from outside the family. As seen in Table 10.6 and Figure 10.1, the result of this pattern of transmission is that the proportion of secondary cases by age shows a U-shaped curve. Similar tendencies have been observed for chickenpox infection (Asano *et al.* 1977; Ross 1962). Hence there is a good correspondance between the curve of severity and the frequency of secondary cases by age.

Experiments with infection in animals and studies of reactions to vaccine virus—as a model of natural infection—indicate that the U-shaped curve of severity is 'unnatural'. However, it may be the result of how social institutions affect the risk of becoming a secondary case. Since the secondary cases have been found to be much more severe, it seems plausible that the social pattern of transmission explains a large part of the age pattern of mortality. However, secondary cases among infants and younger children do have a higher CFR than secondary cases among older children. Such differences could be due to age-related maturity of the immune system, though important immunological differences by age have not been found (Aaby *et al.* 1985), or to physical size in relation to a given dose of infection. Since the index cases among the youngest children do not have severe disease, it seems that severity is related to the combination of intensive exposure and insufficient immune capacity.

Table 10.6. Occurrences of measles according to Sex and Age: Hagelloch, 1861[a]

Age (yrs)	Boys	Girls
(a) *Proportion of index cases*[b,c]		
0	0 (0/4)	25 (1/4)
1–2	8 (1/16)	54 (7/13)
3–4	20 (3/15)	44 (7/16)
5–6	30 (3/10)	20 (2/10)
7–9	100 (11/11)	89 (8/9)
10–15	55 (21/38)	55 (17/31)
Total	41 (39/94)	51 (42/83)
(b) *Case fatality ratio*[c,d]		
0	0 (0/4)	0 (0/4)
1–2	13 (2/16)	15 (2/13)
3–4	20 (3/15)	0 (16)
5–6	20 (2/10)	0 (10)
7–9	0 (11)	0 (9)
10–15	8 (3/38)	0 (31)
Total	11 (10/94)	2 (2/83)

[a] Figures in parentheses are the actual numbers of index cases out of the total number.
[b] Percentage of index cases out of all cases.
[c] For 11 children there was no information on sex.
[d] Percentage of deaths out of all cases.

Source: Aaby *et al*. (1992).

Do Sisters Talk Too Much?

If age differences can be related to the pattern of transmission, something similar may apply to the sex pattern. According to popular beliefs, women talk more than men. Some anthropological studies from Norway have supported this notion by showing that even among kindergarten children girls have more verbal contacts, whereas boys compete about the acquisition of objects (Berentzen 1979). Anthropological observations among the Bushmen have also suggested that girls were more likely to have close contact with other persons than boys of the same age (Draper 1973). My own experience from rural Senegal and urban Bissau suggests a similar pattern, in that girls are more likely to be at home and may therefore have closer contact with other persons. Although girls may have closer contacts, boys may have a wider area of operation, and therefore possibly a larger number of contacts. The net impact of such differences in behaviour for disease transmission is difficult to predict and has not been studied systematically. However, there are several indications that girls are in fact the most effective transmitters of infections. According to several studies, more girls than boys

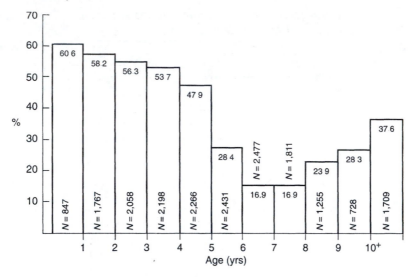

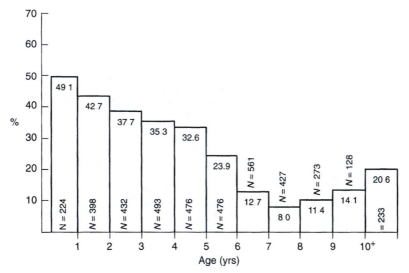

Fig. 10.1. Infectious diseases percentages of secondary cases according to age group

(a) Renfrewshire, Scotland: 19,567 cases

(b) Providence, Rhode Island. 4,121 cases

Sources. Picken (1921) Chapin (1925).

have such infections as measles, chickenpox, mumps, rubella, diphtheria, scarlatina, and whooping cough before reaching school age (Henderson 1916; Hill 1913). According to Danish statistics, a great many more girls than boys have had measles before 7 years of age (Table 10.7), and similar

Table 10.7. Reported Cases of Measles according to Age and Sex: Denmark, 1963–1969

Age (yrs)	Males	Females
0	3,093	6,345
1–6	86,047	95,087
7–14	48,612	39,749
14+	3,574	2,796
Total	141,326	143,977

Source Hertz *et al.* (1976)

patterns have been found for other reported infections. Since equally as many male and female cases are reported, it is unlikely that this tendency represents a sex-specific reporting bias. It is surprising to see that the difference in measles incidence appears even before the age of 1 year.

It is known that girls and boys are equally likely to contract infection when exposed at home (Top 1938). If the girls are contracting infection at a younger age, they must be more effective in contracting infection outside the home. Hence girls should be more likely to be index cases. Conversely, boys should have a higher risk of becoming secondary cases. This possibility has not been studied systematically, though Top (1938) indicated that there were more girls among the index cases. The predicated pattern is clearly visible in an analysis of data from a severe outbreak of measles in Germany in 1861 (Aaby *et al.* 1992). Preschool-aged girls were found to be significantly more likely to be index cases than boys (Table 10.6). In agreement with the European tradition, boys had significantly higher mortality than the girls (Table 10.6). The outbreak occurred in an isolated village which had not experienced measles for fourteen years (Pfeilsticker 1863). All the school-age children contracted measles immediately when the disease was introduced in their class. Hence it was only among the preschool-age children that it was possible to test which sex was more effective in transmitting infection.

In most societies, it is the women and the older girls who take care of small children and the sick. The women and older girls are therefore more exposed to common infections than men of the same age. Hence women and older girls have a higher incidence of common infections than their male age mates (Hillenbrand 1956). Since the secondary cases are more severe, the pattern of exposure may also explain why females of higher ages tend to be more severely affected by common infections like measles (Pison *et al.* 1992).

If girls of a young age are kept at home because of household chores, child-care responsibilities, cultural definitions of appropriate gender behaviour, or simply because of their play patterns, their risk of becoming secondary cases is increased. Such behaviour patterns may explain some of the situations in which girls have been found to have higher mortality from

Table 10.8. Severity of Measles according to Age and Sex: The Gambia and Tunis

(a) *Case fatality rate: Keneba and Jali, the Gambia, 1961*

Age (yrs)	Males		Females	
	Deaths per cases	%	Deaths per cases	%
0–2	23/94	25	18/84	21
3–4	5/43	9	10/36	28
5–9	2/83	2	4/95	4
Total	30/220	14	32/215	15

(b) *Deaths from measles: Tunis, 1952–1960*

Age (yrs)	Deaths (N)	% female deaths
0	569	50.4
1	648	52.2
2–4	320	55.6
5+	53	62.3
Total	1,590	52.6

Sources: (a) McGregor (1964); (b) Monastiri (1961).

measles even at an early age (Table 10.8). Most reports of higher female mortality from measles are from Muslim societies (Bhuiya *et al.* 1984; Fargues and Nassour 1988; Garenne 1982; McGregor 1964; Monastiri 1961; Pison *et al.* 1992), where it seems plausible that cultural rules tend to restrict girls to the home sphere. In Senegal, where the girls are known to have had higher female mortality for the last thirty years (Garenne 1982), girls have been found more likely to be secondary cases than boys, though the difference was not statistically significant (Aaby 1992). Such behaviour differences may explain why there are differences in mortality by sex.

It therefore seems plausible that the severity of infection by age and sex may depend as much on the pattern of disease transmission as on age- and sex-specific factors. In the model suggested here, the age of inter-family transmission may vary considerably as it depends on institutional conditions in the society which facilitate or prevent transmission of infections. For example, at the turn of the century the school often served as the centre of transmission (Brownlee 1920). However, with more public child care at younger ages, the age at transmission has tended to move downwards. In developing countries it is often the youngest children who transmit infections, because they are carried around by their mothers. This process is accelerated where child health programmes and clinics exist which bring together young and sick children. The transmission model suggested here may have many other implications. For example, in families with a large number of children of susceptible age, the risk of becoming a secondary case and therefore of mortality will be higher. In Guinea-Bissau, we found that the case fatality was greater in polygynous families than in monogynous families (Aaby 1991). Hence family and housing patterns may play a major role in affecting mortality trends through their influence on disease transmission.

Cross-Sex Transmission

This simple model of transmission suggests more than a symbolic content to the possibility of 'being talked to death'. However, it becomes even more pronounced with the following observation on the impact of cross-sex transmission of infections (Aaby *et al.* 1986). As an unexpected extension of the transmission perspective, we found in several studies in Guinea-Bissau that secondary cases infected by someone of the opposite sex had a higher CFR than infection from someone of the same sex (Table 10.9). This tendency did not depend on misclassification of transmission, as it could be shown that mortality for children aged 6–59 months was higher in houses where one boy and one girl had measles together (26%) than in houses with two boys or two girls (11%) (RR (relative risk) = 2.65; 95% CI: 1.20–5.84).

Similar situations seem to have existed in several other places. In Copenhagen at the beginning of this century, mortality was significantly higher in families with one boy and one girl having measles during the same outbreak than in families with two boys or two girls (RR = 1.89; 95% CI: 1.06–3.37). In a small outbreak in Keneba, the Gambia, where the children were under close medical observation and there was no mortality, individuals infected by someone of the opposite sex were more likely to get pulmonary complications than a person who contracted infection from someone of their own sex (RR = 2.82, 95% CI: 0.9–9.7) (Aaby and Lamb 1991). Since the severity of the index case could influence the result, it was also examined whether

Table 10.9. Case Fatality Ratio (CFR) among Secondary Cases of Measles according to Age and Sex of Infecting Child: Guinea-Bissau, 1979–1983

Age group (mos)	Same-sex transmission[a]		Opposite-sex transmission[a]	
	M to M	F to F	M to F	F to M
6–35	26 (9/35)	16 (5/31)	49 (22/45)	36 (16/45)
36–59	10 (1/10)	6 (1/16)	20 (3/15)	18 (3/17)
Total	22 (10/45)	13 (6/47)	42 (25/60)	31 (19/62)

[a] The CFR (%) is followed, in parentheses, by the number of deaths out of total cases.
Source: Aaby *et al.* 1986.

sex-opposition or sex-sameness affected the increase in severity from index to secondary case; children infected by someone of the opposite sex were significantly more likely to have an increase in severity relative to the index case than children infected by someone of their own sex ($p = 0.026$). In one area of Senegal, Niokholonko, under demographic surveillance since 1970, 196 deaths have been registered during three outbreaks of measles. In families with only two maternal siblings under 10 years of age, the relative risk of dying of measles during an outbreak was 1.81 times higher (95% CI: 1.17–1.82) in families with one boy and one girl than in families with two boys or two girls when adjustment was made for important background factors including age, age difference between siblings, and size of the village (Pison et al. 1992). Several other studies from Senegal (Aaby 1992), Greenland (author's unpublished observations), Germany (Aaby et al. 1992), and Kenya have suggested similar tendencies. Published case reports of fatal cases of measles with information on the sex of both the secondary case and the index case indicate the same pattern (Aaby et al. 1986). For example, in a children's home in Boston in 1835, a girl introduced measles and infected fourteen girls of whom one died and fifteen boys of whom six died.

This unexpected tendency may not be limited to measles infection. Case reports in the literature of severe and fatal chickenpox infection indicate that cross-sex transmission increases severity (author's unpublished observations). Furthermore, we have found in Guinea-Bissau that male–female twins have a higher risk of post-neonatal mortality than same-sex twins (Aaby and Mølbak 1990). Data from Bangladesh (D'Souza and Chen 1980) support a similar tendency. Since we did not find cross-sex transmission to be important in connection with severe outbreaks of whooping cough in Guinea-Bissau (author's unpublished observations), we may be dealing with a viral phenomenon.

There is obviously a need for an explanation as to why infection contracted from someone of the opposite sex is more severe. The most simple explanation would be that close contact, e.g. kissing, which increases the dose of virus or the risk of complicating infections, is more common between a boy and a girl than between two children of the same sex. Such a difference in contact patterns has not been documented in studies of child behaviour. However, it may be necessary to look more specifically at sex-specific interaction patterns during times of illness. Since the same tendency has been found in very different societies, it seems unlikely that culturally determined behaviour patterns are the cause. Still, biologically based behaviour patterns could mean that transmission of a high dose was more common from someone of the opposite sex.

However, more basic mechanisms at the cellular level may also have to be considered. The simplest hypothesis would be that passage through cells of the opposite sex enhances infectivity and increases the viral load or interferes with the immune system (Aaby et al. 1986).

The increased severity associated with intensive exposure and cross-transmission of infection may help explain differences in mortality by sex. Should one sex be more likely to become index cases, the other sex will have both an increased risk of becoming secondary cases, and also of being infected by the opposite sex. Hence, this sex may suffer a dual disadvantage in terms of survival. In Euro-American societies, the boys seem to have suffered most from this. However, this pattern need not be invariable. In societies where women tend to remain at home while the boys get out or go to school, it would seem plausible that girls are likely to suffer this dual disadvantage. So far, it has been possible to test this model in one society only—Niakhar, Senegal, where girls have been shown to have a higher mortality in measles than boys. In the period 1983–6, girls had a relative risk of dying of measles of 1.30 (0.9–1.9) (Aaby 1992). Cross-sex transmission was associated with a two-fold increase in mortality (RR = 2.44; 1.48–4.02) and girls were significantly more likely to be infected by the opposite sex (RR = 1.26; 1.09–1.47). When adjustment was made for the difference in exposure, there was no longer any difference in CFR for the two sexes (RR = 1.06; 0.66–1.69).

Sex-Specific Vaccines

These observations on the impact of cross-sex transmission suggest that biological factors are more important than originally envisioned. Sex differences in mortality cannot be reduced to a question of differential exposure. Cellular sex differences are likely to be part of the process that produces different mortality for boys and girls. This has not diminished the importance of intensive exposure, but has added new dimensions to the question of sex and mortality. If the severity of infection depends on the sexual origin of a pathogen, the same might very well apply to live vaccines derived from human material. This is obviously a possibility that has not been considered seriously.

Owing to the high incidence of measles in developing countries in babies under nine months of age, the recommended age of immunization with Schwarz standard vaccine, attempts were made in the 1980s to develop a new formula for a measles vaccine which could be used before nine months. These investigations focused on the vaccine developed and used routinely in Yugoslavia, the Edmonston–Zagreb vaccine (EZ). When the vaccine was used in a dose 10 to 100 times greater than the standard dose of Schwarz vaccine, it was capable of immunizing children from the age of four to five months. In 1989, after several studies had found the vaccine to induce a satisfactory antibody response, WHO therefore recommended this vaccine for use in areas with a high incidence of measles for babies under nine months of age. WHO had originally planned no study to test the long-term impact of

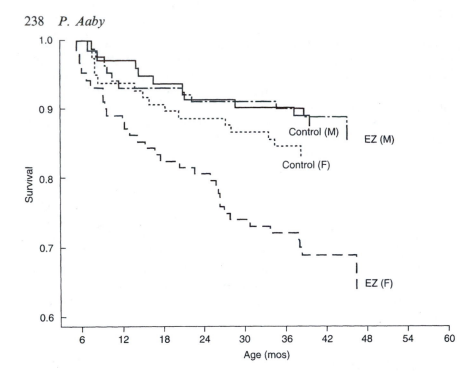

Fig. 10.2. Survival curves according to sex and vaccination group, Guinea-Bissau Bandım cohort 2 (from first vaccination). children born from 1 May 1986 to 30 April 1987; follow-up until May and June 1990.
Source. Aaby et al. (1993a)

this vaccine. However, in Bissau two trials with respectively a medium- and a high-titre dose of EZ were initiated in 1985 and 1987 and follow-up has been on-going. Surprisingly, it turned out that the high-titre vaccine was associated with higher mortality than the standard vaccine received by children in the control group (Aaby *et al.* 1993*a*). However, most surprising was the fact that the difference was found only for girls (Figure 10.2). No one would have believed this observation had other longitudinal studies not used high-titre vaccine as well, which offered a possibility for verifying the observation. Subsequently, very similar tendencies were found in Senegal, where female recipients of both high-titre EZ and high-titre Schwarz vaccine had approximately twice the mortality rate as the female recipients of standard measles vaccine, whereas there was no difference for boys who had received different measles vaccines (Aaby *et al.* 1993*b*). Furthermore, a restudy of children included in a seroconversion study in Haiti also found higher mortality for female recipients of high-titre vaccine, but no difference for the boys (Holt *et al.* 1993). These observations obliged the WHO's Expanded Programme on Immunization (EPI) to withdraw its recommendation of high-titre measles vaccines even though they had no plausible biological mechanism to explain the phenomenon (EPI 1992).

Originally, these results were interpreted as showing that the high-titre vaccine had a damaging effect on girls. However, there are now more data suggesting that an important part of the problem is that standard Schwarz measles vaccine is actually much better than was previously thought possible, particularly for girls (Aaby *et al.* 1993*b*). For example, in Senegal the female–male mortality ratio was 0.94 among unvaccinated children aged nine months to five years of age, whereas it dropped to 0.64 for children who had received standard Schwarz measles vaccine. In the same comparison, the female–male mortality ratio was 1.33 among recipients of high-titre vaccines. Hence a significant part of the explanation for higher mortality among females receiving high-titre vaccine can be found in the inordinately low mortality among girls who received the standard vaccine. Data from other areas of Senegal (Desgrées du Loû *et al.*, unpublished observations) and Bissau have also suggested that the standard vaccine may have particularly beneficial effects on girls. At the moment, the female–male mortality ratio after nine months of age is below 0.60 among children born to a national cohort of 10,000 women of fertile age in Guinea-Bissau. These results suggest that we may have to use sex-specific vaccines in the future. Apparently, a measles vaccine with beneficial effects on boys is needed.

Vaccines for What?

The most important aspect of the measles vaccine story may not be the sex-specific reactions to the vaccine, but the fact that the reduction in mortality following immunization seems much larger than it should have been if the main function of the vaccine was to prevent the acute and long-term consequences of measles infection (Aaby 1995). Several studies from Guinea-Bissau, Senegal, Zaire, Bangladesh, India, and Haiti have documented the fact that the reduction in mortality after measles immunization is of the order of 40–70% from the age of immunization, much larger than the share of deaths attributed to measles in these societies. Furthermore, studies from Guinea-Bissau, Senegal, and Bangladesh have been consistent in showing that the same reduction is found when comparison is made between immunized and unimmunized children not infected with measles (author's unpublished observations).

If the sole function of a measles vaccine was to prevent acute measles and its long-term consequences, there should be no difference in mortality between immunized and unimmunized children who have not had measles. Hence the suggestion is that the vaccine may be beneficial in its own right. The most likely mechanisms seem to be that the vaccine stimulates the immune system or teaches it a lesson. A stimulation is probably most likely, since the effect seems to be temporary, being strongest in the first six to twelve months after immunization (Aaby 1995).

If vaccines can have a beneficial effect apart from protecting against a specific disease, it may be time to consider whether the disease can also have beneficial effects. That does seem to be the case, at least for measles. While there is obviously an important acute mortality connected with measles infection, surprisingly, studies from Bissau, Senegal, and Bangladesh indicate that mortality may be lower in the post-measles period if comparison is made with unimmunized, uninfected children. So for the survivors the infection may have done them some good, possibly through activation of the immune system. Unpublished data from Guinea-Bissau, Senegal, and Bangladesh suggest that the beneficial effect is much stronger for the index cases, who also had low mortality in the acute phase. In the post-measles phase, index cases continue to have significantly lower mortality than the secondary cases.

In Bangladesh, girls have 50%–80% higher mortality than boys in the one to four year age-group (Chen *et al.* 1981). Surprisingly, a reanalysis of Matlab data indicates that, after measles, there may no longer be any difference in mortality between boys and girls. In the period 1983–5, mortality for girls was 60% higher than that for boys; however, from three months after the onset of measles rash, the female–male mortality ratio was 1. Apparently, the stimulation provided by measles infection may be particularly important as a protection against the diseases that otherwise lead to excess female mortality.

Conclusion

Discussions of sex differences in childhood mortality have tended to start from the cultural assumption that medical science has already shown that men are biologically weaker than women (Waldron 1983). From this perspective, the main problem is to find out which form of preferential treatment of boys can reverse this natural tendency, and produce the patterns observed in societies with higher female mortality (Chen *et al.* 1981). It is interesting to consider what would have happened if medical science had been initiated in a society with higher female than male childhood mortality. Then, we would probably all have believed today that men are both physically and biologically stronger than women—after all, women are the weaker sex. To explain higher male mortality in certain societies, this male-being-stronger tradition would presumably have emphasized the preferential care given to girls in these societies. Though it would seem to be a kinder approach, it does not solve the problem of establishing a better understanding of sex differences in childhood mortality. Maybe the major problem is that we have emphasized the *difference in mortality*, thereby giving priority in allocating medical resources to one sex rather than starting from the assumption that both male and female mortality need to be explained.

There are several lessons to be learned from this story. At least for measles, it seems that the sex differences in CFR can be explained by an emphasis on how severe disease is distributed in the society. There are three different ways in which sex skewedness in the distribution of index cases may be important. If one sex is more likely to be index cases transporting infections between families, this sex will be: (*a*) less likely to suffer the high CFR for secondary cases, (*b*) less likely to have increased mortality resulting from infection contracted from the opposite sex, and (*c*) more likely to gain from immuno-stimulation in the post-measles phase.

In the model presented here, the institutional framework facilitating transmission of infection between individuals from different families becomes important. For example, at the turn of the century, schools seem to have been the major transmitters of measles between homes (Figure 10.1 and Table 10.6), and severe cases were likely to occur when older siblings contracted infection at school and then infected their smaller siblings at home (Brownlee, 1920). When public child care became more common, the transmission chain within the family was broken and mortality declined, partly because small children went out more and became infected in the nursery or kindergarten. With data from the infectious disease hospital in Copenhagen, it was possible to show that children infected in kindergarten and crèches had much lower measles mortality than children infected at home by a sibling. Just as social institutions play a major role in shaping mortality patterns through the way they shape disease transmission, society may also affect sex-specific mortality patterns by placing gender-specific restrictions on movements outside the home. The restricted gender would tend to suffer more from infections like measles.

All this is not to say that conscious gender differences in treatment practices regarding feeding, home care, or health service utilization are not important for sex differences in mortality. They may well be. With the enormous impact of immunizations on mortality (Aaby 1991), it is quite clear that a tendency to provide more immunizations to one sex could have significant effects on mortality. However, a transmission model may provide a broader insight. In the studies of higher female mortality, it is often emphasized that this is not so much a result of female maltreatment as an outcome of allocating scarce resources in a culture with a preference for boys (Koenig and D'Souza 1986). If that was the case, one should expect sex differences to diminish with education and socioeconomic status. However, this does not seem to have happened in Bangladesh (Bhuiya and Streatfield 1991). While the higher social groups clearly have lower mortality than other groups, there is no reduction in female excess mortality, and there may even be an increase. It seems likely that with higher socioeconomic status the family would have better possibilities of adhering to traditional female roles which keep the girls at home.

Maybe the most important part of the story of measles and sex differences is the suggestion that the major problem may not be the relative strength of the sexes and differential treatment. Rather, as cross-sex infection increases severity and vaccines can have sex-specific effects, 'sex' itself is part of the process that may generate differences in mortality. Part of the reason for higher male mortality in early life could be that males are the opposite sex of their mother rather than that they are genetically weaker. In some infections, such as respiratory synctial virus (RSV), mothers are believed to be important for disease transmission, and their role may also explain why boys are much more likely to suffer severe RSV infection at an age where the mother is the main contact.

This paper has emphasized my research on measles infection. There are several indications that the important mechanisms—intensity of exposure and dose of infection, cross-sex transmission—may also apply to other virus infection such as chickenpox and polio. It is not known to what extent a transmission perspective is important for infections arising from bacterias and parasites. Though transmission may be less important for such infections, it seems likely that studies of sex differences in mortality can benefit from further studies of transmission. We may find that girls are stronger, not because they have two X-chromosomes (Waldron 1983), but because they have more and closer contacts, and transmit infections more easily than boys. In the end, the problem may be that the boys are not talking enough.

References

Aaby, P. (1991), 'Determinants of measles mortality: host or transmission factors?' in L. M. de la Maza and E. M. Peterson (eds.), *Medical Virology*, x. New York: Plenum Press, pp. 83–116.

—— (1992), 'Influence of cross-sex transmission on measles mortality in rural Senegal'. *Lancet*, 340: 388–91.

—— (1995), 'Assumptions and contradictions in measles and measles immunization research: is measles good for something?' *Social Science and Medicine*, 41: 673–86.

—— and Lamb, W. H. (1991), 'Sex and transmission of measles in a Gambian village'. *Journal of Infection*, 22: 287–92.

—— and Mølbak, K. (1990), 'Siblings of opposite sex as a risk factor for child mortality'. *British Medical Journal*, 301: 143–5.

—— Bukh, J., Lisse, I. M., and Smits, A. J. (1983), 'Les hommes sont-ils plus faibles ou leurs soeurs parlent-elles trop? Essai sur la transmission des maladies infectieuses'. *Anthropologie et Societe*, 7(2): 47–59.

—— Coovadia, H., Bukh, J., Lisse, I. M., Smits, A. J., Wesley, A., and Kiepiela, P. (1985), 'Severe measles: a reappraisal of the role of nutrition, overcrowding and virus dose'. *Medical Hypotheses*, 18: 93–112.

——Bukh, J., Lisse, I. M., and Smits, A. J. (1986), 'Cross-sex transmission of infection and increased mortality due to measles'. *Reviews of Infectious Diseases*, 8: 138–43.

——Oesterle, H., Dietz, K., and Becker, N. (1992), 'Higher male case fatality in severe measles outbreak in rural Germany, 1861'. *Lancet*, no. 340: 1172.

——Knudsen, K., Whittle, H., Thårup, J., Poulsen, A., Sodemann, M., Jakobsen, M., Brink, L., Gansted, U., Permin, A., Jensen, T. G., Lisse, I. M., Andersen, H., and da Silva, M. C. (1993*a*), 'Long-term survival after Edmonston–Zagreb measles vaccination: Increased female mortality'. *Journal of Pediatrics*, 122: 904–8.

——Samb, B., Simondon, F., Knudsen, K., Coll Seck, A. M., Bennett, J., and Whittle, H. (1993*b*), 'Divergent mortality for male and female recipients of low-titre and high-titre measles vaccines in rural Senegal'. *American Journal of Epidemiology*, 138: 746–55.

Alter, M. (1976), 'Is multiple sclerosis an age-dependent host response to measles?' *Lancet*, 307(1): 456–7.

Asano, Y., Nakayama, H., Yazaki, T., Kato, R., Hirose, S., Tsuzuki, K., Ito, S., Isomura, S., and Takahashi, M. (1977), 'Protection against varicella in family contacts by immediate inoculation with live varicella vaccine'. *Pediatrics*, 59: 3–7.

Babbott, F. L., Galbraith, J. C., McDonald, J. C., Shaw, A., and Zuckerman, A. J. (1963), 'Deaths from measles in England and Wales in 1961'. *Monthly Bulletin of the Ministry of Health (England)*, 22: 167.

Barkin, R. M. (1975), 'Measles mortality'. *American Journal of Diseases of Childhood* 129: 307–9.

Basu, A. M. (1989), 'Is discrimination in food really necessary for explaining sex differentials in childhood mortality?' *Population Studies*, 43: 193–210.

Berentzen, S. (1979), 'Ett samhandlingsperspektiv på studiet av barn'. *Tidsskr f samfunndsforskning*, 20: 393.

Bhuiya, A., and Streatfield, K. (1991), 'Mothers' education and survival of female children in a rural area of Bangladesh'. *Population Studies*, 45: 253–64.

——Wojtyniak, B., D'Souza, S., Nahar, L., and Shaikh, K. (1984). 'Measles case fatality among under-fives: a multivariate analysis of risk factors in a rural area of Bangladesh'. *Social Science and Medicine*, 24: 439–43.

Black, F. L., Hierholzer, W., Woodall, J. O., and Pinheiro, F. (1971), 'Intensified reactions to measles vaccine in unexposed populations of American Indians'. *Journal of Infectious Diseases* 124: 306–17.

Brownlee, J. (1920), 'Public health administration in epidemics of measles'. *British Medical Journal*, 1: 534.

Chapin, C. V. (1925), 'Measles in Providence, RI, 1918–1923. *American Journal of Hygiene*, 5: 645.

Chen, L. C., Huq, E., and D'Souza, S. (1981), 'Sex bias in the family allocation of food and health care in rural Bangladesh'. *Population and Development Review*, 7: 55.

Christensen, P. E., Schmidt, H., Bang, H. O., Andersen, V., Jordal, B., and Jensen, O. (1953), 'An epidemic of measles in Southern Greenland, 1951'. *Acta Medica Scandinavica* 144: 430–54.

Christie A. (1974), *Nemesis*. London: Fontana/Collins.

Corney, B. G. (1913), 'A note on an epidemic of measles at Rotuma, 1911'. *Proceedings of the Royal Society of Medicine*, 6: 138.

Das Gupta, M. (1987), 'Selective discrimination against female children in rural Punjab, India'. *Population and Development Review* 13: 77–100.

Denny, F. W., Collier, A. M., Henderson, F. W., and Clyde, W. A. Jr (1977), 'Infectious agents of importance in airways and parenchymal diseases in infants and children with particular emphasis on bronchiolitis'. *Pediatric Research* 11: 234–6.

Draper, P. (1973), 'Crowding among hunter-gatherers: the !Kung bushmen'. *Science*, no. 182: 301–3.

D'Souza, S., and Chen, L. C. (1980), 'Sex differentials in mortality in rural Bangladesh'. *Population and Development Review* 6: 257–70.

EPI (Expanded Programme on Immunization) (1992), 'Safety of high titre measles vaccines'. *Weekly Epidemiological Records* 67: 357–61.

Fargues, P., and Nassour, O. (1988), *Douze ans de mortalité urbaine au Sahel*. Paris: Presses Universitaires de France.

Fauveau, V., Koenig, M. A., and Wojtyniak, B. (1991), 'Excess female deaths among rural Bangladeshi children: an examination of cause specific mortality and morbidity'. *International Journal of Epidemiology* 20: 729–35.

Garenne, M. (1982), 'Variations in the age pattern of infant and child mortality with special reference to a case study in Ngayokheme (rural Senegal)'. Ph.D. dissertation, University of Pennsylvania.

—— and Aaby, P. (1991), 'Pattern of exposure and measles mortality in Senegal'. *Journal of Infectious Diseases* 161: 1088–94.

Griffin, D. E., Mullinix, J., Narayan, O., and Johnson, R. T. (1974), 'Age dependence of viral expression: comparative pathogenesis of two rodent adapted strains of measles virus in mice'. *Infection and Immunity*, 9: 690–5.

Gudnadóttir, M., and Black, F. L. (1964), 'Response of adults in Iceland to live attenuated measles vaccine'. *Bulletin of the WHO*, 30: 753–62.

Hall, W. J., Nathanson, N., and Langmuir, A. D. (1957), 'The age distribution of poliomyelitis in the United States in 1955'. *American Journal of Hygiene*, 66: 214–34.

Henderson, E. C. (1916), 'A census of contagious diseases of 8,786 children'. *American Journal of Public Health*, 6: 971–81.

Hertz, J. B., Sorensen, T. B., and Vejerslev, L. (1976), 'Morbillidødsfald i Danmark 1958–1969'. *Ugeskr Læger*, 138: 589–93.

Hill, H. W. (1913), 'The infectious diseases of 8,900 children'. *American Journal of Public Health*, 3: 1063–72.

Hillenbrand, F. K. M. (1956), 'Rubella in a remote community'. *Lancet*, 268(2): 64–6.

Holt, E. A., Moulton, L. H., Siberry, G. K., and Halsey, N. A. (1993), 'Differential mortality by measles vaccine titer and sex'. *Journal of Infectious Diseases*, 168: 1087–96.

Irgens, A. (1880), 'Spæde børn er mindre udsatte for mæslinger end ældre'. *Norsk Magazin for Lægevidenskab*, 9: 785–8.

Jelliffe, D. B. (1968), *The Assessment of the Nutritional Status of the Community*. Geneva: WHO.

Karzon, D. T., Eckert, G. L., Barron, A. L., Hayner, N. S., and Winkelstein, W. (1961), 'Aseptic meningitis epidemic due to Echo 4 virus'. *American Journal of Diseases of Childhood*, 101: 610–22.

Koenig, M. A., and D'Souza, S. (1986), 'Sex differences in childhood mortality in rural Bangladesh'. *Social Science and Medicine* 22: 15–22.

Koster, F. T., Curlin, G. C., Aiz, K. M. A., and Haque, A. (1981), 'Synergistic impact of measles and diarrhoea on nutrition and mortality in Bangladesh'. *Bulletin of the WHO*, 59: 901–8.

Lancaster, H. O. (1952), 'The mortality in Australia from measles, scarlatina and diphtheria'. *Medical Journal of Australia*, 2: 272–6.

Mancius, A. (1847), 'Mæslinger på Færøerne i sommeren 1846'. *Ugeskrift Læger*, 13–14: 189.

Mata, L. J. (1978), *The Children of Santa Maria Cauqué*. Cambridge, Mass.: MIT Press.

McGlashan, N. D. (1969), 'Measles, malnutrition and blindness in Luapula Province, Zambia'. *Tropical and Geographical Medicine*, 21: 157–62.

McGregor, I. A. (1964), 'Measles and child mortality in the Gambia'. *West African Medical Journal*, 14: 251–6.

Mims, C. A. (1976), *The Pathogenesis of Infectious Diseases*. London: Academic Press.

Monastiri, H. (1961), 'Quelques données statestiques relatives à la mortalité par rougeole dans la Commune de Tunis'. *La Tunisie Medical*, 39: 179–87.

Morley, D. (1973), *Paediatric Priorities in the Developing World*. London: Butterworths.

Pfeilsticker, A. (1863), 'Beiträge zur Pathologie der Masern mit besonderer Berücksichtigung der statistischen Verhältnisse'. Ph.D. thesis, University of Tübingen.

Picken, R. M. F. (1921), 'The epidemiology of measles in a rural and residential area'. *Lancet*, 197(1): 1349–53.

Pison, G., Aaby, P., and Knudsen, K. (1992), 'Increased risk of measles mortality for children with a sibling of the opposite sex among the Fula Bande and Niokholonko, Senegal'. *British Medical Journal*, 304: 284–7.

Preblud, S. R., and D'Angelo, L. J. (1979), 'Chickenpox in the United States, 1972–1977'. *Journal of Infectious Diseases*, 140: 257–60.

Rao, A. R., Sukumar, M. S., Kamalakshi, S., Paramasivam, T. V., Parasuraman, T. A. R., and Shantha, M. (1968), 'Experimental variola in monkeys'. *Indian Journal of Medical Research*, 56: 1855–65.

Ross, A. H. (1962), 'Modification of chickenpox in family contacts by administration of gamma globulin'. *New England Journal of Medicine*, 267: 369–76.

Sathar, Z. A. (1987), 'Sex differentials in mortality: a corollary of son preference?' *Pakistan Development Review*, 26: 555–65.

Top, F. H. (1938), 'Measles in Detroit, 1935'. *American Journal of Public Health*, 28: 935–43.

Waldron, I. (1983), 'The role of genetic and biological factors in sex differences in mortality', in A. D. Lopez and L. T. Ruzicka (eds.), *Sex Differentials in Mortality*. Canberra: Australian National University, pp. 141–64.

Wilson, G. (1905), 'Measles: its prevalence and mortality in Aberdeen'. *Public Health*, 18: 65–82.

Wilson, T. S. (1971), 'A study of the incidence and mortality of measles and whooping cough in Glasgow from 1855, with reference to birth rates, death rates and death rates of children under one year'. *Health Bulletin*, 29: 206–13.

11 Cultural Models and Demographic Behaviour

ANTHONY T. CARTER

Demography is sometimes said to suffer from an absence of theory. Just over a decade ago, for example, Geoffrey McNicoll observed that '[i]t is widely agreed that we do not have an adequate *theory* of fertility, if by theory we mean a coherent body of analysis linking a characterization of society and economy, aggregate or local, to individual fertility decisions and outcomes, able to withstand scrutiny against the empirical record' (1980: 441). More recently, Susan Greenhalgh noted that 'the closer we get to understanding specific fertility declines, the further we move from a general theory of fertility transition' (1990: 85).

In what follows I take a different approach. The problem, I argue, is less one of an absence of theory than of a particular sort of theory. In demographic theory, as in Western social theory generally, agency and cultural are regarded as distinct and separable phenomena.[1] Agency has to do with rational decision-making isolated from context. It is a universal property of autonomous individuals. Culture has to do with norms and social institutions, which stand outside of and constrain agency. In some versions of social theory agency entirely displaces culture. In other versions culture entirely displaces agency. Nowhere is the relation between agency and culture, conceived of in these terms, satisfactory. A better approach, I will argue, lies in theories of practice that focus on flows of conduct or activity-in-setting. These approaches resist the separation of agency and culture. Both terms lose their familiar character as distinct abstractions.

I will not review here theories of culture in anthropology.[2] My intent, rather, is to outline a critique of one pervasive feature of social theory and to point to an alternative. The argument has three parts. In the first two parts, I review and then criticize concepts of agency and culture common to demography and anthropology as well as other social science disciplines. In the third part, I briefly outline and discuss two alternative approaches which may help us overcome the separation of agency and culture, putting fertility in context.

Culture and Agency in Demographic Theory

I take as my text the two-volume report on *The Determinants of Fertility in Developing Countries*, edited by Rodolfo A. Bulatao and Ronald D. Lee (1983) (referred to henceforth as *Determinants*). The material gathered together in *Determinants* comprises the report of a National Research Council Panel on Fertility Determinants. Few, if any, other publications of the period received such elaborate vetting by demographers or were blessed with such an imposing official or quasi-official imprimatur. However, I do not claim that this work represents a demographic consensus—not in the late 1970s and early 1980s and certainly not fifteen to twenty years later. It does provide an unusually full picture of an approach to agency and culture that occurs widely in the social sciences, anthropology as well as demography.

The design of *Determinants* is a classic example of the separation of agency and culture. The volumes consist of forty chapters grouped into six substantive sections—'The Supply of Children', 'The Demand for Children', 'Fertility Regulation and its Costs', 'Fertility Decision-Making Processes', 'Nuptuality and Fertility', and 'Social Institutions and Fertility Change'—plus an introduction and conclusion. The analytical framework sketched in the opening chapter revolves around an economic version of abstract rationality. The position of culture in this framework is marginal and ambiguous. Culture receives sustained treatment only in the last substantive section of the report, 'Social Institutions and Fertility Change'. In that section, chapters reviewing the effects on fertility of modernization, education, 'societal and community institutions', and culture are gathered together with chapters on 'Statistical Studies of Aggregate Fertility Change' and 'Cohort and Period Measures of Changing Fertility'. This heterogeneous collection stands quite outside the analytical framework of the two volumes as a whole with its microeconomic treatment of the supply of and demand for children, the costs of fertility regulation, and decision-making processes. The chapter that focuses on culture—'Effects of Culture on Fertility: Anthropological Contributions' by Robert A. LeVine and Susan C. M. Scrimshaw—is the result of an enterprise separate from, though coordinated with, the work of the Panel on Fertility Determinants. The chapter 'reflects, without attempting to report, the proceedings of a February 1981 Workshop on the Anthropology of Human Fertility at the National Academy of Sciences' (LeVine and Scrimshaw 1983: 666). In an editorial note, Bulatao and Lee observe that '[u]nlike the other papers in this report, this paper does not confine itself to particular fertility determinants but discusses in broad terms the contributions of one discipline, illustrating in its approach the anthropological preference for dealing with specific elements in their social and cultural context' (p. 666).

The analytical framework used in *Determinants* is outlined in the first chapter of the volumes (Bulatao *et al.* 1983) and is graphically summarized

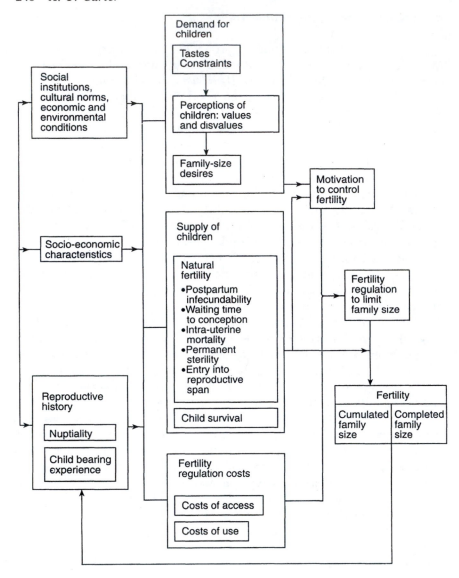

Fig.11.1.   A framework for the study of fertility determinants
Source Bulatao et al. (1983:10)

here in Figure 11.1. Based on Richard Easterlin's (1966; 1978) microeco-nomic model of household production, the framework focuses on fertility decisions made by representative couples or households. Conscious fertility decisions occur in populations in which the supply of children exceeds demand and the costs of fertility regulation are not prohibitively high.

They may be made once, early in a marriage, or repeatedly during the course of a couple's fertility career.

In this approach decisions concerning fertility are abstracted from the milieu in which they are embedded in everyday life. This feature of the economic approach is not emphasized in the introductory statement of the analytical framework, but it appears clearly in a later chapter co-authored by Lee and Bulatao (1983). They specify that '[t]he concept of demand for children refers to a decision maker's views on alternate family-building outcomes, abstracting from attitudes toward the family-building process, including such areas as intercourse, contraception, and breastfeeding'. Thus, survey questions designed to measure demand require that 'the respondent must in answering consider all her particular household circumstances (that is, not answer as if resources were unlimited), and not consider her feelings about the measures necessary (contraception, abortion, abstinence, prolonged breast-feeding) to attain this desired family size' (Lee and Bulatao 1983: 234–5).

The supply of and demand for children and the costs of fertility regulation are each functions of three blocks of fertility determinants (again, see Figure 11.1). Two of these blocks pertain to characteristics of individual couples. One is concerned with the representative couple's reproductive history, including marital history and childbearing experience; the other is concerned with the couple's other socioeconomic characteristics. The third block of determinants pertains to characteristics of social groups containing numbers of couples.

For the anthropologist who has been asked to think about cultural models and fertility behaviour, it is apparent that culture has neither a large nor a clear place in this framework. On the contrary, its role is at once ambiguous, peripheral, and unstable. Culture appears first in the following introductory statement:

Fertility involves both biology and individual choice, the former modified by cultural patterns and the latter strongly influenced by economic and social conditions. The biology, as well as the cultural patterns shaping it, is represented under the rubric of the 'supply of children'. Individual choices about family size, along with the conditions influencing them, are covered under the rubric of the 'demand for children'. (Bulatao *et al.* 1983: 2)

It is subsequently explained that the supply of children is 'the number of surviving children a couple would have if they made no deliberate attempt at limitation' (Bulatao *et al.* 1983: 3). It is thus a function of natural fertility and child mortality. Natural fertility, in turn, is shaped by 'cultural practices relating to such behaviors as intercourse, abstinence, and breastfeeding' and thus 'varies widely among populations' (Bulatao *et al.* 1983: 4).[3]

In Figure 11.1, 'cultural norms' are one element of the block of fertility determinants that includes characteristics of the 'social group, society and culture' to which couples belong. Culture is mentioned twice more when the authors discuss the contents of this block of fertility determinants in greater detail. Here they refer not to 'cultural norms', but to 'social norms understood as shared expectations about how those in particular statuses should behave, usually reinforced by sanctions imposed for deviations' and 'embedded in different social institutions and cultural patterns' (Bulatao et al. 1983: 13). In addition to such social norms and the 'demographic structure of a society' (Bulatao et al. 1983: 12), this block consists of a wide range of 'social institutions' having to do with the economy, polity, family, health care, education, religion, belief system, stratification, ethnic differentiation, demographic structure, and ecological system (Bulatao et al. 1983: 13–15). A brief description of some of the possible effects on fertility of variations in these institutions contains the final reference to culture. Here it is noted that belief systems are equivalent to 'what are often described residually as "cultural factors"' (Bulatao et al. 1983: 15).

In this analytical framework, culture is not treated as a primary object of analysis, defined and analysed in its own terms. Nowhere are 'cultural patterns', 'cultural practices', 'cultural norms', or 'cultural factors' defined. The various appearances of culture may be understood as functions of two related oppositions. One is the distinction between individual choice and group characteristics. It is this that motivates the first references to cultural patterns or practices. Here culture is associated with biology and distinguished from individual agency. Together, biology and culture produce regimes of child supply that are relatively constant across entire populations and change slowly if at all. Individual choice, on the other hand, responds quickly and autonomously to varying economic and social conditions. This opposition also motivates the displacement of cultural norms by social norms and the reappearance of culture as 'cultural patterns'. Social institutions are the sum of individual choices and activities, while cultural patterns presumably have to do with systems of meaning that pre-exist particular individuals and in which the individuals participate. Another conceptual opposition that informs the authors' references to culture is the distinction between belief and knowledge. Where belief is the product of culture and tradition, knowledge is the product of scientific practices that have broken free of culture.[4] It is this opposition that motivates culture's final resting place as an equivalent of belief systems.

Not surprisingly, LeVine and Scrimshaw (1983) take quite a different approach in their contribution to *Determinants*. Their account of anthropological contributions to the explanation of fertility is based on the concept of culture outlined by Clifford Geertz in *The Interpretation of Cultures* (1973). Geertz argues that it is useful to distinguish between culture and social system along the following lines:

to see the former as an ordered system of meaning and of symbols, in terms of which social interaction takes place; and to see the latter as the pattern of social interaction itself. On the one level there is the framework of beliefs, expressive symbols, and values in terms of which individuals define their world, express their feelings, and make their judgments; on the other level there is the ongoing process of interactive behavior, whose persistent form we call social structure. Culture is the fabric of meaning in terms of which human beings interpret their experience and guide their action; social structure is the form that action takes, the actually existing network of social relations. (Geertz 1973: 144–5)[5]

LeVine and Scrimshaw introduce the Geertzian approach to culture into the study of fertility by distinguishing it from approaches that reduce culture to sets of discrete norms. They observe that:

[w]hen demographers and economists write about cultural factors in the determination of fertility in the developing countries, they tend to treat those factors as discrete rules or beliefs: 'irrational' norms, tastes, and taboos on the one hand, and 'rational' perceptions of local cost–benefit contingencies on the other. Anthropologists, however, tend (particularly in recent years) to see culture as an organized system of shared meanings, often more pervasive than explicit, a set of basic assumptions and images that *generates* rules and beliefs, but is not reducible to them. In the influential formulation of Geertz (1973), culture refers to 'models of' and 'models for' reality—organized images and conceptions that reflect environmental contingencies and guide social behavior, respectively. A cultural model thus includes both existential and normative aspects (implications of what is and what ought to be) combined in a single symbolic code that is not merely shared by a community, but taken for granted as a matter of 'common sense'. (LeVine and Scrimshaw 1983: 667)

More specifically, LeVine and Scrimshaw suggest that a cultural approach to fertility would focus on 'cultural models for reproduction'. Such cultural models 'reflect the shared beliefs and expectations of a population about the reproductive process in general and its own fertility–mortality situation in particular, and prescribe and proscribe certain reproductive behaviors' (1983: 669). Anthropological analysis of such models focuses on issues of cultural meaning and cultural rationale. For a particular population, the cultural meanings of the various activities, events, and processes involved in reproduction—'conception, pregnancy, birth, lactation, infant care, infant mortality, and lifetime fertility'—are constituted by their location in that population's cultural model of reproduction. The cultural rationale of a population's fertility pattern—'e.g., its crude birth rate, age-specific fertility rates, and total fertility rate'—is provided by a body of cultural assumptions, 'some "rational" (reflecting the actual environment) and others "irrational" (reflecting normative traditions), but all accepted by the population to be principles of common sense' (1983: 669).

To this, following Alexander Alland (1970), LeVine and Scrimshaw add the idea that culture contributes to humanity's Darwinian adaptive fitness. That is, 'it has helped us to increase our reproductive success and to compete in a wide variety of environments' (LeVine and Scrimshaw 1983: 668). Behaviours involved in rates of birth and death adapt to environmental pressures. Human populations regulate fertility and mortality routinely rather than exceptionally.

LeVine and Scrimshaw also note several ways in which anthropologists can contribute to research on fertility. Two of these are of interest here: a brief critique of the notion of natural fertility, and the concept of context variables.

LeVine and Scrimshaw recognize that the distinction between natural and controlled fertility 'permits operationalization of demographic transition theory'. Nevertheless, they find two major problems with the notion of natural fertility. First, it incorrectly assimilates features of human conduct that have complex cultural rationales to 'something genetically determined, as in "nature vs. nurture"; precultural, as in Levi-Strauss' "nature vs. culture"; or free of technological intervention, as in "natural childbirth"'. Second, it obscures the fact that so-called natural fertility societies constitute a heterogeneous category. If they are alike in lacking parity-dependent contraception, they nevertheless have widely varying total fertility rates caused by variations in the underlying proximate and indirect determinants of fertility.[6] The use of the term 'creates a category which may well prove to be as variable internally as the stages of the demographic transition are from each other'. Levine and Scrimshaw assert that all this is of particular interest to anthropology. 'Anthropologists work largely with societies lacking (or which until recently lacked) parity-dependent birth limitation', and 'the proximate and indirect determinants of fertility are the primary objects of anthropological investigation' (LeVine and Scrimshaw 1983: 670–1).

Another aspect of anthropological research on fertility underlined by LeVine and Scrimshaw concerns what Lucile Newman (1981) has called context variables. Comprised of 'ideological, interpersonal, contraceptive, and reproductive' factors, these influence both the intermediate fertility variables delineated by Davis and Blake (1956) and the proximate variables outlined by Bongaarts (1978). They are of particular interest to anthropologists because they are difficult to derive from survey data, but are accessible to ethnographic investigation (LeVine and Scrimshaw 1983: 673).

A Critique

LeVine and Scrimshaw's contribution to *Determinants* is a sustained, even if collegial, critique of the volumes' analytical framework. If the Geertzian view of culture employed by LeVine and Scrimshaw is correct, then culture must move out of the marginal place it holds in the microeconomic analytical framework outlined by Bulatao *et al.* (1983). If, on the other hand, the universalistic view of individual rationality embedded in the microeconomic framework is accepted, then the strong view of culture urged by Geertz and adopted by LeVine and Scrimshaw must be rejected.

Determinants turns its back on this paradox. With perhaps one exception, the contributors to the report either have nothing to say about culture, or retain, with little or no comment, a vocabulary of 'cultural patterns', 'cultural practices', and especially 'cultural norms' which LeVine and Scrimshaw explicitly reject.[7] At the same time, LeVine and Scrimshaw stop short of explicitly criticizing the analytical framework outlined by Bulatao and Lee and employed throughout the two volumes.

The existence of this fundamental contradiction is disguised by several alternative divisions of intellectual labour. Each of these serves to hold apart the contradictory concepts of agency and culture. None of them can be sustained.

Culture as Context—Culture as Residual Variable

One form of intellectual specialization that obscures the contradiction between the notion of agency employed in *Determinants'* analytical framework and the concept of culture offered by LeVine and Scrimshaw turns on the idea that culture may be treated as the context of agency. In another, closely related, form of intellectual specialization, culture is reduced to a residual variable.

The notion that culture provides the context of agency is briefly introduced by LeVine and Scrimshaw (1983: 673). As I noted above, they argue that culture mediates the effects of proximate and intermediate determinants on fertility outcomes. The use of culture as a residual variable is perhaps clearest in the chapter on 'Perceptions of the Value of Children: Satisfaction and Costs' by James T. Fawcett. Fawcett divides the variables that influence the perception of the value of children into two classes: 'structural features of the society in which the individual lives', and 'more idiosyncratic aspects of the person's life experience'. He divides the structural features into three categories: socioeconomic status, especially class and rural–urban differentials; cultural influences; and sex roles. For Fawcett, culture 'may determine the hierarchy of general values or goals against which children are evaluated, as well as increase or decrease specific satisfactions and costs of children'. However, its effects are revealed only at the end of analysis after other, more rational, effects have been factored out:

culture is a holistic concept, difficult to isolate from other influences, and in some ways elusive. Thus survey research cannot be expected to produce measures adequately representing culture as an independent variable. However, cultural influences can be inferred from survey results, especially in comparative studies. At least two types of survey findings are relevant: (1) a broad response pattern observed in one country but not in others that are comparable on various noncultural dimensions (e.g., level of development); and (2) findings for particular variables that can convincingly be traced, by virtue of their content, to corresponding cultural values or practices. (Fawcett 1983: 435)

Founded on the prior assumption of abstract, universal rationality, both of these ways of carving up the territory of scholarship confine culture to a small and receding corner in the background. The limiting case may be Ronald Lee and Rodolfo Bulatao's (1983) discussion of tastes and demand for children. Here culture is residual almost to the point of invisibility. Lee and Bulatao note that investigations of fertility 'desires' generally 'provide measures not of tastes by themselves but of demand for children, reflecting the interaction of tastes with constraints'. Against this, '[t]he economists term "tastes" permits a more precise reference to one particular component of the demand for children.' It provides, that is, 'a ranking of the satisfactions attached to each possible combination of quantities of different goods, including children and their attributes', without regard to circumstances that may constrain the ability actually to obtain them. The economist's concept of tastes is brought into proximity with the anthropologist's concept of culture as a consequence of the fact that tastes are 'socially patterned'. In this, tastes resemble 'norms' and 'values' even though the latter terms 'have a more diffuse reference'. As Lee and Bulatao observe,

[t]his conception, although analytically convenient, has an important drawback: it makes tastes nearly impossible to measure directly. Some economists therefore disavow variations in tastes, preferring to account for any apparent variations by ingenious extensions of the concepts of prices and incomes (Becker 1960; Stigler and Becker 1977). Most economists, however, rather than treating tastes as invariant, instead treat them as a residual category, consigned to other disciplines for study. (Lee and Bulatao 1983: 257)

Left to its own devices, however, abstract agency routinely proves incapable of producing complete and coherent accounts of fertility. For example, in their chapter on 'Effects of Income and Wealth on the Demand for Children', Eva Mueller and Kathleen Short (1983) note that there are two, contradictory, arguments concerning the effects of increasing income on fertility. The notion that 'development is the best contraceptive' suggests that fertility is negatively related to income. However, if children are 'normal goods' analogous to refrigerators or trips to Barcelona, then fertility should be positively related to income. 'Empirical studies do not show a consistently positive or negative effect of income on fertility, and often the measured relation is not statistically significant' (Mueller and Short 1983: 630). Mueller and Short deal with these complexities in part by suggesting 'that the *pure* income effect on the demand for children is very likely to be positive, while some major *indirect* effects are negative' (1983: 592). In addition, they suggest that the indirect effects of income on fertility are mediated by culture and other intervening factors. 'Because the timing and strength of the indirect effects may be expected to vary among different places and times, depending primarily on the particular culture and economic structure, the *total* income effect may be either positive or negative' (Mueller and Short 1983: 592).

In short, agency can never quite dispense with culture. Regularly driven from the stage with a flourish of theory, culture is just as regularly ushered back into demographic analysis in an *ad hoc* manner.

Culture Is to Agency as Natural Fertility Is to Controlled Fertility

More importantly, it appears to be assumed that the contradiction between the notion of agency employed in *Determinants'* analytical framework and the concept of culture offered by LeVine and Scrimshaw may be mediated by the idea that anthropologists are distinguishable from other scholars interested in demography because they study different kinds of society.

This view may be discerned in the conjunction of the definitions of the supply of and demand for children, on the one hand, with LeVine and Scrimshaw's description of the typical interests of anthropologists, on the other. The supply of children, it will be recalled, is a function of child mortality and natural fertility. The latter, in turn, is a function of biology and cultural norms or patterns. The demand for children is the subject of individual choice. The emphasis in LeVine and Scrimshaw on the concept of culture and their assertion (1983: 670) that anthropologists 'work largely' with natural fertility populations is consistent with the distinction between the supply of and demand for children. Together, these ideas sustain the separation of agency and culture by confining anthropologists and their concept of culture to societies that have not yet begun, or remain in the early phases of, the demographic transition. These are said to be societies in which population processes respond closely to normative and institutional constraints and in which fertility, like child mortality, is 'a group or population characteristic' (Bongaarts and Menkin 1983: 33; see also Knodel 1983: 65). This leaves scholars from other disciplines to devote themselves to societies that have completed the demographic transition or entered its later phases. In these societies individual choice is 'strongly influenced by economic and social conditions' (Bulatao *et al.* 1983: 2). Cultural norms have little impact on fertility.

Separated in this manner and left to their own devices, agency and culture both fall into difficulty. Harvey Leibenstein's (1981) critique of economic decision theory is indicative of the trajectory of approaches that begin with abstract agency. In these approaches, decision-making is assumed to be active and to be based on maximization. As Leibenstein observes, however, maximization is impossibly time-consuming and complex. It is doubtful that such procedures are humanly feasible outside the specialized settings of departments of economics, schools of management, and the public and private bureaucracies with which they are associated. If they are within the reach, in the conduct of our everyday lives, of those of us who are what Jean Lave (1988: 4) calls 'just plain folks', we surely avoid them much of the time.

Leibenstein urges instead an approach built around what he calls 'passive decision-making' or 'non-decision decisions'. Under the impact of sufficiently strong stimuli, the choices involved in fertility may be made actively on the basis of partial or even full calculation. However, in all but the most unusual circumstances, they are made passively or routinely on the basis of an ethnic or cultural convention. Classical transition theory equated modern societies with active decision-making and traditional societies with passive decision-making. Leibenstein sees both forms of decision-making as occurring in both kinds of society but he preserves the distinction between traditional and modern societies:

Those living in a village in a developing country are likely to exhibit a considerable amount of routine behavior, and hence this would appear to be a desirable context within which to study passive decision-making. In other words, the general hypothesis is that so-called traditional behavior is likely to involve a great many passive decisions. (Leibenstein 1981: 397)

Leibenstein's attack on microeconomic maximization, together with his notion of passive decision-making based on convention, carry us from agency to culture. Indeed, convention or culture is now expanded to cover post-transitional as well as pre-transitional societies. But this position, too, is untenable.

At the core of the suggestion that large areas of social life are governed by passive decision-making is the idea that both mortality and fertility in pre-transition populations are group rather than individual characteristics. This idea is supported by two additional assumptions. One is that effective fertility control, the only fertility control worth talking about, requires modern contraceptive devices. The other is that, at least as regards family formation, mortality is a given, an exogenously determined condition which may influence fertility but is not itself the object of deliberate control.

These assumptions are insulated from close empirical study by several routine statistical simplifications and practices. More often than not, demographic analysis focuses on family size without regard to gender. Couples are treated as if they wanted, and got, undifferentiated children rather than sons and daughters.[8] Explanations of the level of fertility in natural fertility populations focus on the incidence of marriage and the length of birth intervals. If completed family size is the sole object of explanation, other concerns involved in family formation can be ignored. Since populations with high, natural fertility also are thought to be characterized by passive decision-making, measures of the population average for all of these aspects of fertility will suffice. Individual variation can be treated as a problem lying in the way of accurate measurement, rather than a phenomenon to be studied in its own right.

The assumption that effective fertility control requires modern contraceptive technologies has a certain verisimilitude, but the idea that mortality is a given is less persuasive. Bowing to the fact that we can rarely put death off while ignoring our predilection for hastening its arrival, for others if not for ourselves, it paints as necessity what is not infrequently a matter of choice. Looking to see if active decision-making and a more diverse array of population problems are involved in so-called traditional, high-fertility regimes, I begin, therefore, with death.

It is remarkable that the dominant line of analysis running through *Determinants* adheres so closely to the notion that child supply is a group characteristic, for among the papers in the second volume is one by Susan Scrimshaw (1983) that argues just the opposite. First in an essay in *Population and Development Review* (1978) and again in her contribution to *Determinants*, Scrimshaw has argued that high infant mortality might be taken as a response to high fertility. In effect, various forms of infanticide may be used to control family composition as well as family size *ex post facto*.

Thomas Smith's (1977: 59–85) elegant study of family formation in Nakahara, an eighteenth-century Japanese village, provides empirical support for Scrimshaw's contention. Here a remarkably complete run of annual population registers, listing village residents on a household-by-household basis with entries for gender, age, and household head, provides the basis for a study of demographic processes at the level of individual couples. The core of Smith's analysis is a careful study of variations in the sex ratio of registered births by birth order and previous family composition (see Table 11.1). Nakahara parents did not appear to have any discernible sex preferences for the first two births. After the second birth, however, 'couples had a marked tendency to have [that is, to permit to live and then to register] a next child of the sex underrepresented in their present [registered] family' (Smith

Table 11.1. Family Composition and the Sex of the Next Child in Completed First Marriages in Nakahara[a]

Family composition[b]	Sex of next child		Sex ratio	
	Male	Female		
Predominantly sons	30	45	67	$c^2 = 3.4$; $p < 0.07$[c]
Sons = daughters	31	21	148	$c^2 = 1.9$; $p < 0.17$[c]
Predominantly daughters	38	19	200	$c^2 = 5.7$; $p < 0.02$[c]
	$c^2 = 10.6$; $p < 0.006$[d]			

[a] Completed first marriages are those 'first marriages for both partners that lasted through the wife's age 45'.
[b] 'Includes all living siblings registered with the family at the time of birth of the next child.'
[c] Here c^2 tests the null hypothesis that the sex ratio at age 1, when births were registered, is 102, given a sex ratio at birth of 105 and Coale–Demeny model 'North' mortality.
[d] Here c^2 tests the null hypothesis that 'births are independent of each other and of the composition of the existing sibling set'.
Source: Smith (1977. 65 and 168).

1977: 65). If the majority of a couple's existing children were male, their next retained and registered child tended to be female. Male children were eliminated or 'returned' until a child of the desired female sex was born. Conversely, if the majority of a couple's existing children were female, their next child tended even more strongly to be male, with females being eliminated to achieve the desired result. Among couples with equal numbers of male and female children, the sex ratio of the next birth was more nearly equal, though here, too, there was a bias towards males.[9]

In conventional demographic usage, eighteenth-century Japan was a natural-fertility population (Smith 1977: 61–2). Nevertheless, parents in Nakahara did actively attempt to control the size of their families and the length of certain birth intervals. The mean family size of completed first marriages in Nakahara was just 5.1 children (p. 70). Smith observes, moreover, that

there was a heavy bunching around the mean, with few completed families having less than four or more than seven children. The extreme bunching of this distribution can be brought out by a comparison of Nakahara with Meulan in France, using only completed marriages that began at the wife's age 30 or less. Only ten percent of completed families in Nakahara had eight or more children, compared with 57 percent in Meulan during a period of no family limitation (1660–1739); and only 8 percent of completed families in Nakahara had two or fewer children, compared with 33 percent in Meulan during a period of family limitation (1790–1839). (Smith 1977: 71)

The relatively infrequent occurrence of large families was no doubt partly the unintended result of infanticide for sex selection. However, it also was the deliberate result of halting childbearing. Smith shows that this was so by comparing mothers who stopped childbearing early, at age 37 or less, with those who stopped late, at age greater than 37. (Among all completed first marriages in Nakahara, the mean age of mothers at the birth of the last child was 37.5) Early stoppers had an average of 4.0 children while late stoppers had an average of 6.1. That early stopping was deliberate is indicated by the fact that the last born, or last-registered, children of the early stoppers included 21 males and 8 females, a sex ratio of 2.625. Among the late stoppers, there were 19 last-born males and 16 last-born females, a sex ratio of 1.188 (Smith 1977: 72). That control of family size and sex selection are separate concerns regardless of the level of family size goals is indicated by the fact that both early and late stoppers used infanticide to select the sex of next children (p. 73).

Smith also observes that in comparison to European data these Nakahara birth intervals were both long and relatively uniform from first to last. The mean interval from marriage to first birth was 2.6 years. Subsequent birth intervals were 4.4, 3.3, 3.2, 3.2, and 3.5 years (1977: 80). The penultimate interval averaged 3.9 years and the ultimate interval averaged 4.2 years. In most cases, deliberate attempts to space birth are not detectable in the Nakahara material. However, the interval between first and second births was exceptional. Though this interval was shorter in Europe, it was longer in Nakahara. 'The first child', as Smith notes, 'had to come as soon as possible after marriage to prove the fertility of the bride.' The second child, however, might well place heavy burdens on a mother. If it came after the normal 4.4 years, its older sibling would still be 'unable to care for himself [or herself], let alone help with another child'. Reasoning that this constraint would be relaxed if there were other women in the household to help, Smith

divided all completed first marriages into families in which another adult female was present at the time of the second birth and those in which there was none, excluding families in which the first child died or departed before the birth of the second. The mean 1–2 interval was significantly different (p<0.05) in the two groups—3.5 and 5.1 years, respectively. Only 18 percent of the birth intervals in the first group were five years or more and only 5 percent were seven years or more, whereas the corresponding percentages for the second group were 47 percent and 28 percent. One suspects, therefore, some deliberate spacing for the convenience of the mother at the second birth.... (Smith 1977: 81)

Clearly, this was not a population in which the outcome of family formation was left to chance. Infanticide was used systematically to control family composition, and it also may have been a factor in the control of family size and birth intervals. Abstinence from sexual relations also may have been used to affect the latter. Even though contraception undoubtedly was difficult and uncertain in the absence of modern technology, it may not have been utterly resistant to human ingenuity.[10]

The upshot of all this is that there are good reasons to suspect that persons in seemingly natural-fertility populations not infrequently intervene in family formation processes in response to the size and gender composition of 'child stocks'. The notion that the supply of children is a function of 'exogenous' mortality and the biology of reproduction as modified by 'cultural patterns' while the demand for children is a function of deliberate choice cannot be sustained. Though it may take different forms, active decision-making occurs in high-fertility as well as low-fertility populations, before as well as after the demographic transition. Natural-fertility populations are not related to controlled-fertility populations as supply is related to demand or as culture is related to choice; the distinction between natural and controlled-fertility populations cannot be used to hold agency and culture, economics and anthropology apart. People can never be regarded as creatures of cultural constraint.

Alternatives

During the last few years, new approaches to the analysis of fertility designed to overcome the difficulties outlined above have been sketched by Eugene Hammel (1990) and Anthony Carter (1988; 1995). Neither of these proposals provides a fully elaborated theory supported by detailed empirical analysis. If nothing else, however, a brief review will clarify the kinds of difficulty that previous understandings of the relationships between agency and culture have encountered and some of the potential elements of an alternative.

Culture as 'Evaluative Conversations'

Hammel rejects economic accounts of fertility based on 'a decontextualized universal rationality'. His aim is to develop instead 'a culturally smart microeconomics' (1990: 455–6). The first part of his essay consists of a historical review of concepts of culture in anthropology, mostly within the American tradition. The second part proposes a new approach to the explanation of demographic phenomena employing the latest concept of culture in his review, 'culture as a negotiated symbolic understanding' or an 'evaluative conversation'.

Hammel's proposal has four principal elements.

1. Culture is a 'constantly modified and elaborated system of moral symbols'. It is produced and reproduced by 'the evaluative behavior of actors'. These evaluative behaviours or

symbolic expressions . . . become part of culture as guidance mechanism by entering into the social discourse. Actors respond to this discourse; their actions are guided by it, whether it is spoken in their presence, recalled from their socialization, or anticipated for their repute or their salvation. Actors move in an intensely evaluative cloud of commentary, in the presence of which they select behavioral alternatives, balancing and choosing those they think will minimize moral risk and maximize moral gain. (Hammel 1990: 467)

2. The best way to determine the manner in which culture motivates the behaviour of social actors in a particular kind of activity is through the investigation of 'communities of action' or of 'the network of social actors directly involved'. In the case of birth control, such a network might include 'a set of women, their husbands or lovers; their mothers, sisters, and closest friends, their medical and spiritual advisors; and attendants, social workers, and important figures in and representatives of organizations to which these central female actors belonged or to the policies of which they were subject' (Hammel 1990: 468).

3. Detailed ethnographic case studies of activity networks are the preferable mode of investigation. 'The value of culture for social analysis is not so much that the informants speak to the investigator, but rather that they speak to one another and can be overheard' (1990: 475).

4. Where detailed ethnographic case studies are impossible, a more macro-sociological approach may be an acceptable substitute (1990: 468–9; 472–4). This is based in part on the notion that 'the individuals who produce

[a] demographic pattern are members of a communicative system, sharing the pattern and transmitting it, one to another, in some degree'. Such communicative systems can be identified by attending to the uses of culture as identifier of social groups (1990: 458–9).

Material illustrative of Hammel's approach may be found in recent work by Susan Watkins. On or near the level of ethnographic case study, Pollak and Watkins (1993) refer to work in progress in which women report on conversations concerning fertility and contraception. They explicitly link this to Hammel's notion of culture as 'evaluative conversation' (Pollak and Watkins 1993: 485). Some substantial part of social life, they write, consists of 'conversations in which people learn from each other about opportunities and how to evaluate them in the context of their culture' (p. 491). Hammel, in turn, notes that much of his argument is 'anticipated' by Watkins's observation that 'even when the couple is literally alone in the bedroom, the echoes of conversations with kin and neighbors influence their actions' (Hammel 1990: 476, n. 5, quoting Watkins 1990: 242). Watkins's (1990, 1991) work on the aggregate data of the Princeton European Fertility Project led her to emphasize the importance of 'others', first provincial and then national, in the European fertility decline. This line of investigation illustrates Hammel's macro-sociological alternative.

Hammel's proposal has a great deal to recommend it. It should be noted, however, that the prevailing separation of agency and culture tends to reassert itself. If actors are no longer utilitarian maximizers, there remains a sense in which Hammel's theory depends on a universal, decontextualized view of rationality. Thus, he grounds his approach in the claim that all actors select 'behaviors from the cultural repertoire' so as 'to achieve a balance between competing critics and to optimize the net social morality of their position' (Hammel 1990: 474). Similarly, culture retains or recovers a degree of autonomous existence outside of action. This appears first when Hammel allows culture as identifier to stand in for culture as evaluative conversation in his macro-sociological alternative. It also appears when he spells out the aims of cultural analysis. At both the ethnographic and the macro-sociological levels, the aim of anthropological analysis of cultural material or symbolic expressions is 'to determine the native system(s) of classification of social groups, demographic events, and kinds of behavior' (p. 472). In this context, Hammel recommends the work of A. Kimball Romney on the analysis of formal interview and questionnaire data (e.g. Romney *et al.* 1986; Weller and Romney 1988). Here culture is a learned body of shared knowledge that motivates agents but is separate from their activity.

Activity-in-Setting

My own proposal (Carter 1995) draws on Anthony Giddens's (1979) theory of structuration and Jean Lave's (1988) work on cognition in practice. Two features of Giddens's work are of particular interest. First, he argues that human agency is correctly understood not as a sequence of discrete acts of choice and planning, but rather as the reflexive monitoring and rationalization of a continuous flow of conduct. Second, he suggests that cultural principles and social institutions have a virtual rather than a substantial existence, taking shape as they enter into activity. The first of these concepts enables us to detach ourselves from abstract, universal rationality. The second allows us to put aside the concept of culture, shifting our attention from enduring principles of social action to the practices in which rules that are never more than provisional are produced and reproduced.

Lave's (1988) work on the uses of arithmetic problem-solving in everyday activities adds a further important insight. Against the standard view of cognition, decision-making, or agency as intramental processes, Lave proposes the concept of 'activity-in-setting' (Lave 1988: 97). The core of this concept is the idea that agency is socially distributed. ' "Cognition" observed in everyday practice is distributed—stretched over, not divided among— mind, body, activity, and culturally organized settings (which include other actors)' (p. 1).

Demographers attempting to explain fertility using these concepts would attempt to trace all of the flows of conduct involved in family formation. This approach thus would resist the tendency of economic accounts to abstract decisions concerning fertility from issues of sexuality, the body, relations with family and friends, concepts of personhood, and so on. Particular outcomes would be explained by showing how critical problems in family formation and their solutions arise in the course of activity and how one or another activity-in-setting is structured by others.

In my earlier paper I provided two illustrations of such practice theoretical work on fertility. One is a reworking of material from *Labour Pains and Labour Power*, a study by Patricia and Roger Jeffrey and their associate Andrew Lyon (Jeffrey *et al.* 1988) of women and childbearing in two villages, one Hindu and one Muslim, in western Uttar Pradesh, India, between 1982 and 1986. This is a region in which fertility remains rather high and in which the status of women is rather low. Nevertheless, there do appear to be opportunities for women to make deliberate interventions in family formation. My reinterpretation of the Jeffrey *et al.* material focused on the role of embodiment and practices of body management in creating space for such interventions; in other words, it looks at the ways in which agency is distributed over the body and among groups of women who interact around care of the body. The other illustration is a reworking of material from *Taking Chances*, Kristen Luker's (1975) study of contraceptive risk-taking in California. Here my aim was to show how problems involved in the management of reproduction and their solutions are not given prior to action by culture but emerge or are negotiated during the course of situated activity.

The approach derived from practice theory is very close to Hammel's. Both reject the notion of abstract rationality. Both regard culture as an 'evaluative conversation'. There are, however, two critical differences. If agency is regarded as socially distributed, it is not necessary to ground analysis in any universal characteristics of abstract rationality, neither the economist's utility maximization nor Hammel's 'optimization' of 'net social morality'. Practice theory also undercuts the assumptions that permit Hammel to offer a particular kind of macro-sociological investigation as a substitute ethnographic research. Culture is never more than an evaluative conversation. It is always inextricably embedded in local interpretive practices, though these may vary in their ability to affect other activities-in-setting over space and time. Where there is a common demographic pattern over some definable region—such as a province or nation—this is more likely to be the result of hegemonic interpretive practices than of any cultural consensus. Except in those instances, rare to the point of vanishing, in which communicative systems attain the kind of intersubjective mutuality held forth as an ideal by Jürgen Habermas, claims of cultural identity are the product of some partial interest. Culture as identifier remains 'nominal and analytically trivial' (Hammel 1990: 459), if not specious.

Conclusion

I have argued that most of the social theory employed in demography is based on the separation of agency and culture. Agency is conceived of as abstract, universal rationality. Culture is regarded as a body of rules and meanings that are outside of and prior to action. In most contemporary versions of demographic theory, culture is confined to the margins. In the occasional minority viewpoint, agency is pushed aside by culture. However, the balance between agency and culture is never stable. The ambitions of each to stand alone are doomed to failure.

Theories of culture as 'evaluative conversations' and work-in-practice theory appear to provide an attractive alternative. From this perspective, both agency and culture disappear. The goals, problems, and problem-solving tools involved in human conduct are not given once and for all prior to action by either culture or agency, but are formed and reformed dialectically as action proceeds. This approach is especially attractive in connection with fertility. Where theories emphasizing abstract agency strip fertility from its social matrix, practice theories respect its situated character. Where theories that emphasize cultural norms require a kind of society-wide consistency in child supply that flies in the face of the facts, practice theories provide a basis for understanding variable fertility outcomes as skilled social accomplishments.

Those who are interested in large solutions to large population problems will be disappointed by these suggestions. I am persuaded, however, that such problems are rhetorically constructed and that they serve to underwrite an invidious distinction between 'us' and 'them' (see Greenhalgh 1995). 'We' are rational. 'They' are the source of the problem. Rather than looking for unitary solutions to global population problems, we need to 'think practically and look locally'. I borrow this motto from the title of a review of research on gender and language by Penelope Eckert and Sally McConnell-Ginet (1992). To paraphrase Eckert and McConnell-Ginet, to think practically and look locally is 'to encourage a view of [fertility] that roots [family formation] in the everyday social practices of particular local communities and sees [it] as jointly constructed in those practices' (p. 462).

Notes

1. On the separation of agency and culture in Western social theory generally, see Giddens (1979) and Ortner (1984). Voloshinov (1973/1929) is a particularly interesting critique of this split in the domain of linguistic theory.
2. For this the reader might consult Keesing (1974) or Hammel (1990).
3. This is, of course, standard demographic usage derived from the work of Henry (1961). In *Determinants* the concept and relevant data are discussed in more detail in 'The Supply of Children: A Critical Essay' by John Bongaarts and Jane Menken (1983) and in 'Natural Fertility: Age Patterns, Levels and Trends' by John Knodel (1983)
4. For critical discussions of the distinction between belief and knowledge, see Good (1994), Lave (1988), and Tambiah (1990).
5. Informed readers may doubt that LeVine and Scrimshaw's Geertzian position is representative of anthropology in the same way that *Determinants* as a whole is representative of demography. McNicoll observes that '[t]he moderate degree of consensus among social scientists that has been reached on "institutions" is not paralleled for "culture" or for how the two concepts are related. Reviews of theories of culture by anthropologists—say Keesing's (1974) or, tailored for demographers, Hammel's (1990)—set out lengthy arrays of variants. Agreement extends mainly to dismissal of the early approaches (McNicoll 1992: 408). If anything, however, LeVine and Scrimshaw underestimate the degree of theoretical consensus in the field. They are of the opinion that Geertz's concept of culture 'prevails among those [anthropologists] who put the concept of culture at the center of anthropological research, though social anthropologists may do things differently'. In this, too, their views may be traced to Geertz, who suggests that 'the British structuralists' regard culture 'as wholly derivative from the forms of social organization' (1973: 144). In support of this argument, Geertz quotes Meyer Fortes, then William Wyse Professor of Social Anthropology at Cambridge: 'social structure is not an aspect of culture but the entire culture of a given people handled in a special frame of theory' (Geertz 1973. 144, quoting Fortes 1953: 21). This is to confuse vocabulary with theoretical content. In an earlier paper, Fortes outlined his view of social structure in the following terms: 'I take "structure" to refer to a distinguishable whole which is susceptible of analysis, in the light of appropriate concepts and by suitable techniques, into parts that have an ordered arrangement in space and time. What is really important, however, is not merely the determination of the "parts" and their interrelations but the elucidation of the principles which govern structural arrangement and of the forces for which these stand. When we describe structure we are already dealing with general principles far removed from the complicated skein of behaviour, feelings, beliefs, etc., that constitute the tissue of actual social life. We are, as it were, in the realm of grammar and syntax, not of the spoken word' (Fortes 1949: 3). The implicit analogy between Fortes's concept of social structure and Saussure's concept of *langue* brings his concept of social

structure into alignment with Geertz's concept of culture and with French concepts of structure. Regardless of how the concepts are designated, all separate culture from agency.

6. Demographers certainly are aware of this sort of variation.

7. The exception is Hull (1983). Hull is well aware of the pervasive split between agency and culture: 'In some cases, the notion of individual decision making is ignored, and the focus is on societal "decisions" in the form of codes of conduct, norms, and values formulated to achieve behavior that is "functional" for the survival or growth of a group. Alternatively, the emphasis is on the individual as a decision maker carefully weighing costs and benefits, and making choices to satisfy personally defined objectives' (Hull 1983: 382). In place of these alternatives, Hull proposes that '[t]he decision-making environment is cultural, including language, belief systems, technology, social institutions, and individual environment. Decision-making is both a product and a determinant of this framework' (p. 399).

8. Demographers are well aware, of course, that this is a simplification. It derives from the fact that stable population theory, the mathematical model underlying demographic measures, is a single-sex theory.

9. Evidence supporting Scrimshaw also comes from a study of northern French peasants in the latter half of the eighteenth century by the economist Paul David and his colleagues (David *et al.* 1985; David and Mroz 1986).

10. Additional evidence of deliberate fertility regulation in a seemingly natural fertility population comes from Paul David's study of eighteenth-century France (see especially David and Mroz 1986) and Caroline Bledsoe *et al.*'s (1994) work on contemporary Gambia.

References

Alland, A. (1970), *Adaptation in Cultural Evolution: An Approach to Medical Anthropology*. New York: Columbia University Press.

Becker, G. S. (1960), 'An economic analysis of fertility', in *Demographic and Economic Change in Developed Countries*. Princeton: Princeton University Press, pp. 209–31.

Bledsoe, C., Hill, A. G., D'Alessandro, U., and Langerock, P. (1994), 'Constructing natural fertility: the use of Western contraceptive technologies in rural Gambia'. *Population and Development Review*, 20: 81–113.

Bongaarts, J. (1978), 'A framework for analyzing the proximate determinants of fertility'. *Population and Development Review*, 3: 63–102.

——and Menken, J. (1983), 'The supply of children: a critical essay', in R. A. Bulatao and R. D. Lee (eds.), *Determinants of Fertility in Developing Countries*, i. New York: Academic Press, pp. 27–60.

Bulatao, R. A. and Lee, R. D. (eds.) (1983), *Determinants of Fertility in Developing Countries*, 2 vols. New York: Academic Press.

——et al. (1983) 'A framework for the study of fertility determinants', in R. A. Bulatao and D. R. Lee (eds.), *Determinants of Fertility in Developing Countries*, i. New York: Academic Press, pp. 1–26.

Carter, A. T. (1988), 'Does culture matter? The case of the demographic transition'. *Historical Methods*, 21(4): 164–8.

——(1995), 'Agency and fertility: for an ethnography of practice', in S. Greenhalgh (ed.), *Situating Fertility*. Cambridge: Cambridge University Press, pp. 55–85.

David, P. and Mroz, T. A. (1986), 'A sequential econometric model of birth-spacing behavior among rural French villagers, 1749–1789'. Stanford Project on the History of Fertility Control, Working Paper no. 19.

——— and Wachter, K. W. (1985), 'Rational strategies of birth-spacing and fertility regulation in rural France during the Ancien Régime'. Stanford Project on the History of Fertility Control, Working Paper no. 14.

Davis, K. and Blake, J. (1956), 'Social structure and fertility: an analytical framework'. *Economic Development and Cultural Change*, 4: 211–35.

Easterlin, R. A. (1966), 'On the relation of economic factors to recent and projected fertility changes'. *Demography*, 3: 131–53.

——— (1978), 'The economics and sociology of fertility: a synthesis', in C. Tilly (ed.), *Historical Studies of Changing Fertility*, Princeton: Princeton University Press, pp. 57–133.

Eckert, P. and McConnell-Ginet, S. (1992), 'Think practically and look locally: language and gender as community-based practice'. *Annual Review of Anthropology*, 21: 461–90.

Fawcett, J. T. (1983), 'Perceptions of the value of children', in R. Bulatao and R. Lee (eds.), *Determinants of Fertility in Developing Countries*, i. New York: Academic Press, pp. 429–57.

Fortes, M. (1953), 'The structure of unilineal descent groups'. *American Anthropologist*, 55(1): 17–41.

——— (1949), 'Time and social structure: an Ashanti case study', in M. Fortes (ed.), *Social Structure: Studies Presented to A. R. Radcliffe-Brown*. Oxford: Oxford University Press, pp. 54–84.

Geertz, C. (1973), *The Interpretation of Cultures*. New York: Basic Books.

Giddens, A. (1979), *Central Problems in Social Theory*. Berkeley: University of California Press.

Good, B. J. (1994), *Medicine, Rationality and Experience: An Anthropological Experience*. Cambridge: Cambridge University Press.

Greenhalgh, S. (1990), 'Toward a political economy of fertility: anthropological contributions'. *Population and Development Review*, 16(1): 85–106.

——— (1995), 'Anthropology theorizes reproduction: integrating practice, political economic, and feminist perspectives', in S. Greenhalgh (ed.), *Situating Fertility*. Cambridge: Cambridge University Press, pp. 3–28.

Hammel, E. A. (1990), 'A theory of culture for demography'. *Population and Development Review*, 16(3): 455–85.

Henry, L. (1961), 'Some data on natural fertility'. *Eugenics Quarterly*, 8: 81–91.

Hull, T. H. (1983), 'Cultural influences on fertility decision styles', in R. A. Bulatao and R. D. Lee (eds.), *Determinants of Fertility in Developing Countries*, ii. New York: Academic Press, pp. 381–414.

Jeffrey, P., Jeffrey, R., and Lyon, A. (1988), *Labour Pains and Labour Power*. London: Zed Books.

Keesing, R. (1974), 'Theories of culture'. *Annual Review of Anthropology*, 3: 73–97.

Knodel, J. (1983), 'Natural fertility: age patterns, levels and trends', in R. A. Bulatao and R. D. Lee (eds.), *Determinants of Fertility in Developing Countries*, i. New York: Academic Press, pp. 61–102.

Lave, J. (1988), *Arithmetic Practices and Cognitive Theory: An Ethnographic Inquiry*. Cambridge: Cambridge University Press.

Lee, R. D. and Bulatao, R. A. (1983), 'The demand for children: a critical essay', in R. A. Bulatao and R. D. Lee (eds.), *Determinants of Fertility in Developing Countries*, i. New York: Academic Press, pp. 233–87.

Leibenstein, H (1981), 'Economic decision theory and fertility behavior'. *Population and Development Review*, 7(3): 381–400.

LeVine, R. A. and Scrimshaw, S. C. M. (1983), 'Effects of culture on fertility: anthropological contributions', in R. A. Bulatao and R. D. Lee (eds.), *Determinants of Fertility in Developing Countries*, ii. New York: Academic Press, pp. 666–95.

Luker, K. (1975), *Taking Chances: Abortion and the Decision Not to Contracept*. Berkeley: University of California Press.

McNicoll, G. (1980), 'Institutional determinants of fertility change'. *Population and Development Review*, 6(3): 441–62.

——(1992), 'The agenda of population studies: a commentary and complaint'. *Population and Development Review*, 18(3): 399–420.

Mueller, E. and Short, K. (1983), 'Effects of income and wealth on the demand for children', in R. A. Bulatao and R. D. Lee (eds.), *Determinants of Fertility in Developing Countries*, i. New York: Academic Press, pp. 590–642.

Newman, L. F. (1981), 'Anthropological contributions to fertility research'. Paper presented at the Annual Meeting of the American Anthropological Association, Los Angeles.

Ortner, S. (1984), 'Theory in anthropology since the sixties'. *Comparative Studies in Society and History*, 26(1): 126–66.

Pollak, R. A. and Watkins, S. C. (1993), 'Cultural and economic approaches to fertility'. *Population and Development Review*, 19: 467–96.

Romney, A. K., Weller, S. C., and Batchelder, W. (1986), 'Culture as consensus: a theory of culture and informant accuracy'. *American Anthropologist*, 88(2): 313–38.

Scrimshaw, S. C. M. (1978), 'Infant mortality and behavior in the regulation of family size'. *Population and Development Review*, 4: 385–403.

——(1983), 'Infanticide as deliberate fertility regulation', in R. A. Bulatao and R. D. Lee (eds.), *Determinants of Fertility in Developing Countries*, ii. New York: Academic Press, pp. 245–66.

Smith, T. C. (1977), *Nakahara: Family Farming and Population in a Japanese Village, 1717–1830*. Stanford, Calif.: Stanford University Press.

Stigler, G. J. and Becker, G. S. (1977), 'De gustibus non est disputandum'. *American Economic Review*, 67: 76–90.

Tambiah, S. J. (1990), *Magic, Science, Religion, and the Scope of Rationality*. Cambridge: Cambridge University Press.

Voloshinov, V. N. (1973), *Marxism and the Philosophy of Language*, trans. L. Matejka and I. R. Titunik. Cambridge, Mass.: Harvard University Press. (First published in 1929.)

Watkins, S. C. (1990), 'The transformation of demographic regimes in Western Europe, 1870–1960'. *Population and Development Review*, 16(2): 241–72.

——(1991), *From Provinces into Nations*. Princeton: Princeton University Press.

Weller, S. C. and Romney, A. K. (1988), *Systematic Data Collection*. Newbury Park, Calif.: Sage.

12 Social Norms, Natural Fertility, and the Resumption of Postpartum 'Contact' in The Gambia

CAROLINE BLEDSOE AND ALLAN G. HILL

Introduction

Social scientists have long treated normative prescriptions for behaviour as keys to maintaining social order, and departure from these norms as the root of social pathology. Even the father of demography himself, T. R. Malthus, began, after his initial prophesy of population catastrophe (1798), to place more cheerful confidence in the potentials of norms to check population increase—specifically, conjugal norms that supported premarital sexual restraint and discouraged marriage by individuals who could not yet support a family. Malthus, of course, was a minister of the Church as well as an economist and mathematician, so it is perhaps not surprising that he would find hope in normative solutions, especially those with religious backing. Since his time, demography has been adopted more by sociology than by any other field, and normative approaches familiar to sociology and anthropology have dominated many of its explanatory frameworks. Thus, fertility patterns in developing countries are commonly attributed to the influence of traditions or values that entail certain behaviour patterns, while changes in fertility are commonly attributed to the influence of new norms, often those imparted by Western education, which supplant local norms with modern cosmopolitan ones.

Yet are people everywhere, especially those who are rural and illiterate, necessarily locked into norms they must follow? We appraise this question, a very familiar one to twentieth-century social science, in the light of recent decades of anthropological and sociological reflection on theories of rules

This work was carried out with the support and encouragement of the Medical and Health Department of the Ministry of Health in The Gambia. Particular thanks go to Melville George, Reuben M'Boge, Dawda Joof, and Fatou Banja, our Field Supervisor. In addition, we thank Brian M. Greenwood, former Director of the MRC in The Gambia and his staff in Farafenni, Kabir Cham, K. O. Jaiteh, Momodou Jasseh, Mary Hill, Kim Hirschman, John Knodel, Tanya Marchant, Balla Silla, Bintou Sosu, the North Bank field workers and interviewers, and the villagers in the MRC Main Study Area. Finally, we are grateful to the Rockefeller and Mellon Foundations for their generous support of the project.

and norms.[1] Our subject is one of the most renowned patterns in the demographic literature in Africa: postpartum abstinence, or the 'postpartum sex taboo', as it was called by anthropologists in an earlier era.

Duration of postpartum abstinence is seen as a key proximate determinant of birth intervals in populations that are characterized as experiencing natural fertility. A common perception among scholars of West African demography is that Islamic normative prescriptions impose two significant obstacles to maintaining long birth intervals. One is the conviction that Islam forbids the use of contraceptives.[2] In The Gambia, for example, a national Imam project sponsored by Save the Children, the Population Council, and the Ministry of Health (Askew *et al.* 1992; Turner 1992) attempted to respond to such concerns by persuading religious leaders that the Quran permits, if not demands, birth control under certain conditions. Here, however, we will be concerned with the second religious precept that appears to pose obstacles to long birth intervals: the notion that a husband and wife should abstain from sex for forty days after a child's birth but can resume sex thereafter, a point sometimes ritualized by a cleansing ceremony (M. Ahsan, cited in Schoenmaeckers *et al.* 1981: 32).

The question of when, after a birth, spouses should resume sexual relations, or 'contact', as it is more politely referred to in rural Gambia, is a critical one in this region. Having children who survive and grow to maturity is a *sine qua non*[3] for both women and men. For a woman, bearing children steadily throughout her mature reproductive years is the most important way for her to secure her own welfare and to demonstrate her commitment to her husband and his family, thereby showing respect for her family elders who gave her in marriage. But births are not supposed to occur at random intervals or in rapid succession.[4] Most women would like to space their births at intervals of at least two or preferably two-and-a-half years in order to sustain their own health and ensure their children's survival through a long period of breastfeeding without competition for maternal nourishment from unborn siblings. In the words of a local male elder, women should give birth not like mango trees, which drop hundreds of ripe fruit in rapid, erratic spurts, but like elephants (*sama wuluwo*, 'elephant reproduction'), with long, generous spaces in between.[5] Expectations surrounding the Islamic forty day decree seem to be pitted against local norms governing child health which, though less codified, have equally strong support.

Norms governing child health are not, however, confined to the informal domestic unit. Entreaties to space births for the health and welfare of mothers and children are echoed at all levels in The Gambia, from national radio broadcasts, to local health clinics, to mothers-in-law. But inconsistencies in the normative structures are widespread. The dictum that sex can be resumed after forty days runs counter to other norms predating Islam that favour longer periods—until the child can walk or is weaned. And, although having sex around forty days after a birth is recognized locally as carrying almost no risk of pregnancy, considerable ambiguity remains concerning what should happen both on the forty-first day and as the birth interval progresses. A woman who tries to achieve long birth intervals is praised for her maternal responsibility, yet she lays herself open to accusations of spurning values of religious piety or of wifely devotion.

Despite the pressures that religious measures appear to impose, however, it is not clear that any of these norms governing the resumption of post-partum 'contact' affects behaviour in straightforward ways; important questions of interpretation and scope for manoeuvre remain unanswered. Nor is it systematically clear which norms stem from religious precepts and which from local social expectations. Data from our 1992–5 project in the North Bank area in The Gambia suggest that local people are seldom bound to norms of reproductive practice that only the importation of new norms can persuade them to change. By asking how husbands and wives in rural Gambia try to negotiate both the resumption and pace of sexual contact in the birth interval, this chapter argues that, while postpartum norms are far from irrelevant to behaviour, they are more usefully seen as means to cope with specific situations.

In the case of postpartum negotiations, the general pattern is one in which mothers of young babies try to avoid an early return to full sexuality, in contrast to male preference for a more rapid return. Caught in the dilemma of maintaining decent birth intervals versus sustaining wifely devotion, women draw upon a variety of norms as rationales or 'excuses' (in the local English translation) to avoid sexual contact with their husbands at times they believe will expose them to the risk of an early pregnancy. The goal of a long delay, however, is by no means shared only by women. Nor is the desire to resume sexuality quickly a goal espoused only by men. Men and women in different situations may have strikingly different abstinence agendas, and their respective uses of norms vary accordingly.

Rules as the Basis of Social and Demographic Order

Norms and the sanctions that bolster them have figured prominently in some of the most important schools of thought in social science. They lie, for example, at the heart of the famous structural–functional paradigm, which sought to explain why groups cohere rather than shattering into inconsequential fragments. Thus, Parsons (1949) argued that actors would maintain extant societal structures because they were socialized into common values and norms. Scholars of a more legal bent saw societal order as anchored in rules that directed or even compelled certain behaviours (e.g. Radcliffe-Brown 1950; Fortes 1969). Paradoxically, even disorder was said to reflect the workings of norms. Lineage fission in a patrilineal society, for example, was explained as a clash between the rules of affiliation to one's own lineage and 'complementary filiation', which pitted male members of descent groups against each other on the basis of their maternal ties.

Reference to norms as sources of explanation, if not as causal agents, pervades demographic works as deeply as it does those in anthropology and mainstream sociology. In mortality studies, death is often explained as an unfortunate, though unsurprising, outcome of harmful curative measures or of superstitions that inhibit the use of hospitals or oblige people to abandon disfigured infants. More cautious are authors who treat norms as social safety valves. Scheper-Hughes (1985), for example, argues that recognized norms permit a mother in Brazil to withhold care from a sickly child who is believed to have an incurable constitutional weakness.

Norms also figure prominently in fertility studies of societies on both the high and the low end of the fertility control spectrum. Seeking to mitigate views that natural fertility plays itself out through the powerful motors of biology that affect breastfeeding, sexuality, and postpartum amenorrhoea, scholars of African demography such as Caldwell, van de Walle, and Lesthaeghe have emphasized the mediating influence of culture on biology in laying out norms that guide entry into childbearing and postpartum behaviour. In many countries, for example, norms of sexual purity are said to expedite early marriage and childbearing, while lengthy postpartum bans on sexual relations are credited with creating wide birth spaces. While such qualifications throw doubt on theories of biological reductionism, it is equally easy to fall into the trap of normative reductionism. Illiterate rural people can appear to be locked into values they feel compelled to follow, and the widespread adoption of family planning can seem to be dependent on massive ideological shifts in the national cultural environment. In countries like The Gambia, where the predominance of strong Islamic doctrine is often held responsible for the collapse of lengthy postnatal abstinence periods, the conviction that national values are critical determinants of fertility behaviour has comprised a key impetus to efforts to fill national radio spots with positive family planning messages.

Alternative Views of Norms

As compelling as they can sound, norms do not necessarily dictate behaviour. Laws governing marriage are good examples. Le Roy Ladurie's (1975) description of fourteenth-century Montaillou showed that the taboo on incestuous marriages could be broken to safeguard inheritance. Conversely, laws governing marriage and legitimacy could be tightened when land resources became limited, resulting in the proliferation of bastardy in northern Spain (O'Neill 1987). As for Africa, many independent African governments have tried to outlaw polygyny and bridewealth. They also have tried to eliminate unwanted arranged marriages by establishing a minimum legal age at marriage and abolishing child marriage for girls (e.g. Brandon 1990; and Bledsoe and Cohen 1993: ch. 3). Yet reality has rarely matched legal intention. Ngondo a Pitshandenge's astute analysis (1994) points out that legislatures in francophone countries in Africa have tried to construct an ideal post-colonial order by combining the best of customary ways and new ideas. But ages at marriage remain quite low in many countries, because of the difficulty of enforcing laws when few people know their actual ages, religious pressures to protect female purity, and so on. Moreover, the laws created to govern marriage are often contradictory and incomplete; in trying to accommodate diversity, they provide further scope for manipulation.

With respect to early marriage, legal measures have suppressed most outright betrothal of small girls. Yet data compiled by the United Nations (1990; see also Brandon 1990) show that in the Ivory Coast 41% of urban women and 43% of rural women had married before the legal minimum age of 18. In Senegal, where the minimum legal age is 16, the World Fertility Survey (WFS) of 1978 revealed that 16% of urban women and 36% of rural women had married before the age of 15.

Attempts to suppress bridewealth have encountered similar failures. A bride's family may attempt to disguise bridewealth by demanding that a suitor pay her school fees or initiation expenses. Furthermore, legal polygyny continues to thrive in many countries. In the Ivory Coast, which abolished polygyny in 1954, data from the 1980–1 WFS disclosed that about 43% of currently married women aged 15–49 were in polygynous unions. In other countries, particularly in urban areas, *de facto* unions proliferate between women and already-married men (van de Walle and Kekovole 1984; Clignet 1987; Lacombe 1987). Lacking the social recognition usually accorded to civil or even customary unions, these new unions have been labelled 'outside' marriages (Baker and Bird 1959; Harrell-Bond 1975; Karanja 1987) or, in francophone countries, *le deuxième bureau* (Lacombe 1983).

Norms may sound compelling, but in reality they are slippery concepts. It is not always clear how strongly particular norms are felt or enforced. Nor is it clear which norms people should follow or how conflicts between different norms are resolved. Even in settings as small as the domestic contexts in which most demographically relevant behaviours occur, a welter of normative ambiguities and conflicts emerge almost at once. To whom should a particular norm apply? Under what circumstances should it be brought to bear? In an African society with strong expectations of brideservice from a groom, no one would think of enforcing such a norm on a polygynous chief who agrees to marry, as a token of patronage, the daughter of a humble labourer. Further, how do we know which rules people are actually following? Because a multitude of rules can apply to any given situation, 'individuals are often faced by a choice between alternative norms' (Van Velson

1967:131). Additional complications arise when we take into account the plethora of exceptions to rules. If a society stipulates that a witch child is to be killed at birth, how do people actually determine who a witch child is, and when the rule can be waived? Sargent (1988: 84) notes that Bambara women 'discussing hypothetical situations involving the threat of witch babies agreed that a woman who had no son and gave birth to one would disguise any signs of a mystically dangerous birth...'

In sum, just as individuals are not bound rigidly by rules, rules do not comprise a clear, consistent set of moral instructions, nor do they have clear referents. Action cannot be determined wholly by rules because any course of action can be made to appear as though it were following the rule; conversely, any behaviour can be construed as going against the rule (Wittgenstein 1968:82).

To declare that people do not follow norms in a straightforward way is not news to social science as a whole. Indeed, the conviction that rules are not as constraining as they might seem has spawned a corpus of literature over the last few decades that is as large as that of the normative framework itself. Scholars such as Goffman, Cicourel, Schutz, Giddens, and Simmel (in sociology) and Barth, Bailey, and Bourdieu (in anthropology) have argued against mechanistic, rule-centred explanations that present static views of culture, and against the view that norms alone can enforce compliance. Such authors have shown that, while people contest rules, they also incorporate them into minute strategies of living and coping. Rather than focusing exclusively on what the rules are, and to whom they apply, we can ask how people select among alternative rules to justify their behaviour and use these rules to persuade others that they should behave in certain ways. In this conception, rules are perceived less as rigidly binding prescriptions for conduct than as resources.

This perspective also sheds a quite different light on the notion of the individual: from an unthinking follower of rules and believer of established categories, to a strategic actor who may attempt to use rules to achieve desired outcomes. People play on ambiguity in describing themselves and their goals, seeking to construe the definition of the situation so that certain rules must then follow (Comaroff and Roberts 1981). They also draw upon outside elements to incorporate into the normative repertoire. This does not mean that people are always successful in managing rules to their own advantage. Dispute over the definition of the situation is arguably the rule rather than the exception. Yet such patterns simply reinforce the point that negotiation and innovation, rather than conformity to established rules, may be a more helpful starting point in interpreting social behaviour.

Just as people seek ways to negotiate either within normative boundaries or by circumventing them altogether, so they also regard norms as resources for negotiating pathways through demographic life: birth, death, marriage, migration. How these processes transpire in the realms of health, reproduction, and sexuality in a society that from the outside appears to have a classic natural fertility pattern is fascinating to untangle. (See also Lockwood 1995 on similar themes.) To explore them in more detail, we first outline some descriptive details and then turn to the key rules and cultural premisses that appear to govern reproduction in the context of rural Gambia. Quotes drawn from the open-ended response sections of the rounds or from separate interviews by research assistants are lightly edited.

Fertility Patterns in Rural Gambia

The demographic profile of rural Gambia is one that demographic convention would confidently label a natural-fertility population. Fertility is high and births are evenly spaced, though intervals lengthen slightly with age, a pattern considered to be the outcome of behaviours that are consistent across all birth orders. (See Hill 1991 for a general description.) As for contraception, a recent survey revealed that, although many women in the country as a whole appear to know about Western contraceptives, only about 7% of married women were using them; 5% reported using traditional contraceptives (Gambia 1993). Among those few women who do use contraceptives, many are unmarried, educated, urban adolescents, especially secondary school girls for whom pregnancy is usually problematic. But among the bulk of the female population—rural married women—very few report that they are currently using a means of contraception. In our baseline survey, only 8% of women reported that they were doing anything to avoid pregnancy at the time; 5% were using Western methods such as Depo-Provera, pills, condoms, and foaming tablets (spermicides) to avoid pregnancy; the rest were using methods such as abstinence, *juju* charms made by Islamic ritual specialists, and herbs. Finally, those few women in our survey who were using Western contraceptives were doing so in ways that seemed uninformed. They might use a contraceptive briefly and then stop after only a few months, perhaps claiming objections from religion or husbands. Some reported using pills while still amenorrhoeic, or even using methods such as pills and injections simultaneously.

Conventional family planning treatment of such users places them in categories labelled 'discontinuation', 'method switching', or 'non-compliance'. Indeed, women sometimes seem ignorant if not fearful of contraception, and men appear to be its outspoken opponents. Such apparent ignorance about birth control, and low interest in it, are often interpreted as the outcome of inevitable conflicts between the norms of fertility reduction and those of traditional or Islamic rules governing reproduction. The most commonly proposed solution is some form of education designed to change these norms, whether this be formal education, family life education in schools, or IEC media campaigns.

The data for this study came from forty rural villages surrounding the town of Farafenni, in the North Bank Division of rural Gambia. The study villages were originally surveyed in 1981 by the UK Medical Research Council, and census statistics have been kept ever since, especially for use in malaria studies. In 1993 the total population enumerated by the census was 16,714 people. The villages are quite small: seven had less than 100 inhabitants, with only three containing over 1,000 inhabitants. The people are largely Mandinka, Wolof, and Fula speakers (around 44%, 36%, and 20%, respectively), who cultivate rice, millet, and sorghum and raise cattle. All are Muslims, although patterns of religious observance vary considerably.

Our baseline fertility survey was conducted in March and April 1992. Of the women listed in the 1992 census, we found and interviewed about 80% of those aged 15–54, allowing for age misreporting, ending up with a total sample population of 2,980. Only 98 women in the entire survey (3%), and almost no one over 30, had been to school, a pattern quite typical for the area. (None of the villages had a secondary school, though a few had primary schools.) The great majority in the sample, 91%, reported that they had ever been married, and 88% were currently married. Mean age at first marriage was young: 16.3 years. One-fifth (21%) of ever-married women had been married more than once; of those currently married, 58% had one or more co-wives. Among all women, 82% had had at least one live birth (91% of ever-married women). With a mean age at first birth of 18.4 years, the total fertility rate for the five-year period before the survey was about 7.5, with no signs of major change over a longer period. Childhood mortality, high in the past, has fallen rapidly in recent years; still, some 20% of children died before their fifth birthday and infant mortality was 90 per 1,000 live births.

Analyses in this chapter draw on ethnographic field notes, open-ended interviews, and 13 months of a 15-month multi-round survey[6] conducted in 1993 and 1994 of women who had had a pregnancy in the last three years. This monthly structure was used in order to catch changes in postpartum sexual, reproductive, and contraceptive events more accurately than a one-time survey would allow. We interviewed women in eight of the 40 villages, with the major axes of difference being those of size, ethnic composition, and access to primary health care facilities.

Table 12.1, taken from one round, shows some summary demographic characteristics of the women individually. The number of interviewees varied from month to month, but ranged from 246 to 304, with a total of 3,472 responses collected (see Table 12.2). Unless otherwise stated, the analysis using the rounds data represents numbers of events, not individuals. Thus, several individuals appear only once, while a number of women are represented thirteen times.[7]

Table 12.1.   Background Means of Women Participating in the Monthly Round Survey, North Bank, The Gambia

	Means*
Age	29.1
Pregnancies	5.1
Children	0.7
Non-live births	0.6
Surviving children	3.8

* Totals reflect responses from round 12, June 1994.

Table 12.2.   Age Groups of Women Participating in the Monthly Round Survey, North Bank, The Gambia

Age group	N	%
< 20	331	9.5
20–24	786	22.6
25–29	804	23.2
30–34	663	19.1
35–39	609	17.5
40–44	247	7.1
45 +	32	0.9
Total*	3,472	100.0

* Totals reflect compiled responses from 13 months. July 1993–October 1994

Rural Norms Surrounding Postpartum Breastfeeding and Sexuality

Bans on sexuality for significant portions of marital life are one of the hallmarks of African reproductive regimes (see e.g. the contributors to Page and Lesthaeghe 1981). In rural Gambia there are several such periods. During menstruation, for example, a woman is considered unclean and therefore unavailable sexually. Moreover, a very young woman who marries may be allowed to delay full sexual relations for several months or even years so that she can mature physically. At the other end of the age continuum is the possibility of terminal abstinence, when grandmother obligations are sometimes said to override those of sexual partner. But the marital sexual ban that has drawn by far the most attention in demographic analyses of Africa has been that governing postpartum abstinence.

Rural Gambians maintain that a baby should breastfeed without nutritional competition from an unborn sibling for around 18–24 months. Because breastfeeding and pregnancy place strains on a woman, a new child should not be conceived before the previous one has finished breastfeeding. An additional local rationale for delayed entry into sexuality is a symbolic one. Because male fluids are often said to dilute, if not poison, breast milk, a woman who becomes sexually active while continuing to breastfeed puts her baby at risk, in effect exposing herself to social condemnation for unsanctioned sex, should the baby fall ill. (The two sources of rules governing such matters—Islam and more indigenous tenets—are very likely merged in many of these domains. Certainly Islamic concerns for the welfare of the family have likely been mingled with those of local origin.)

Some women, especially young ones, do not mind a small period of overlap; they often have much to gain by bearing several children quickly, to establish themselves in the compound. But if the two children overlap substantially, the one in the womb and the other nursing, then, as both babies grow bigger and their nutritional demands increase, the first may begin to consume the blood of the mother and of the unborn sibling. In such a case, the first child will likely contract life-threatening stomach ailments, the second will be born small and fragile, and the mother will become anaemic. Under such conditions, the wisest course is to wean the first child as soon as possible, once a pregnancy is detected. Indeed, if the first child becomes malnourished or sick, the mother, fearing condemnation, is even more likely to wean it quickly because people may begin to count back if an overlap is suspected. They may accuse her of being a 'jealous woman', trying to monopolize the man's attention and resources, or of being unable to control her husband. In such cases, as one woman pointed out, conception may lead to weaning, rather than the reverse:

We wean when we have breastfed for 24 months. This can be interrupted by conception, of course; for example, the conception of this child I am breastfeeding overlapped with the breastfeeding of the last child by one month. In fact, in our community, generally if one stops breastfeeding her child earlier than 24 months, it means she has conceived.

Achieving lengthy gaps between children is a goal shared increasingly by sources external to the household. Within the last two decades, public declarations that long birth intervals promote maternal and child health have become standard discourse of professionals both in The Gambia and internationally (Ross *et al.* 1992). The Gambian government tries to promote long birth intervals through both sustained breastfeeding and the use of Western contraceptives. In this context, contraception, when it is used, is viewed by women less as a device for reducing fertility than for pacing it more slowly or for gaining safer sexual access to men while their babies are still small (Bledsoe *et al.* 1994).

Although ample spaces between children are desirable on virtually all fronts, two distinct configurations of norms governing the resumption of postpartum contact lay the bases for quite different strategies for achieving long intervals. Local people identify several likely points as appropriate for the resumption of sex. The two most common seem to be (1) the Islamic forty days or, in the nearest local discourse equivalent, '[child's] neck straightened', and (2) weaning or walking. We devote most attention to the first because of its association with Islam, although patterns of contact along the entire temporal and child development span between the two points reveal equally significant patterns.

Forty Days/'Neck Straightened'

Everyone agrees that Islam allows a resumption of sexual relations after the fortieth day after birth, the time when a woman is considered to be cleansed of the blood and fluids surrounding the birth event. The question, however, is more complicated in practice. Women like this 28-year-old mother see the decree as a requirement to resume sex immediately: 'The forty days after delivery is...very important in the rule in Islam to contact your husband at that time.' But men in particular seem to have this view, as did this 30-year-old man: 'whenever the 40 days are finished the woman should go back to the husband's house...' In the case of a very young woman who has moved back to her mother's home to bear and nurse her first child, her husband might make a special visit to enact what he may see as this forty-day expectation. A few people even claim that the act itself of resuming 'contact' on precisely the fortieth day, which is ordinarily the last day of abstinence, will provide ritual protection from pregnancy until the child is weaned, though there is widespread scepticism about the efficacy of this strategy.

Most women, however, interpret the forty-day rule not as a requirement to resume contact immediately but as an obligation for the woman to make herself available any time after the fortieth day, unless the husband 'excuses' her, giving her permission to abstain longer. According to one woman, the understanding that a woman needs to make herself available is based on the need to protect the man's religious rectitude: 'To abstain forty days after delivery...is just enough so that there will not be sin for the man. If it is longer, the man can be pressed to go outside his house to have contact with others.' Many women, however, expressed a pragmatic attitude about the whole matter, as did this woman: 'It is instructed that you abstain for the first forty days after birth, but after that, it is left to one's liking. Forty days is short for some but if you feel it is short, go for what you like...' However it is interpreted, the fortieth day is clearly an important point in the post-partum cycle, comprising a focus around which conjugal skirmishes frequently occur.

The general period of forty days to two or three months after a child's birth is also referred to by a key stage of child development: 'neck straightened', a literal translation from Mandinka (*kang tilindoo*). Its symbolic connotations derive from its contrast with the very first phase of a child's life. A newborn baby is called a 'wet infant', a metaphor referring to the baby's pliability and lack of muscle tone. It refers also to the baby's proximity to the powerful, life-giving fluids that nourished and protected it for so long, accompanied it into the world, and continue to cling symbolically to it and to the mother for some weeks after birth. The phrase 'wet infant' also seems closely related to the baby's stage of feeding. A baby at this stage appears to be fed breast-milk only. Our monthly round surveys recorded only a very few exceptional wet infants (7%) being fed any supplementation. Half of these cases were those involving animal milk supplementation; almost all the others appeared to be coding or data entry errors.

Licence to traffic with the ritually powerful fluids of reproduction belongs for the most part to women. As a result, wet infants, like the postpartum fluids their mothers are expelling, are perilous for men to touch. Men display acute discomfort in the close proximity of a baby less than week old who has not yet been brought outdoors ritually and introduced to the world (Bledsoe, field notes). Male comfort with a small infant—and with its mother—increases markedly, however, as the baby progresses to the next stage of development: 'neck straightened'. By this time the neck muscles have become stronger, allowing the baby to hold up its head and to be carried in a lappa cloth on the mother's back. The baby also moves to light supplementation with a thin rice or cous pap. The association between a pliant wet child who is breastfeeding only and a firmer, neck-straight child who has moved on to a grain supplementation is both symbolically striking and quantitatively unambiguous.

For our purposes, the most important implication of the 'neck-straightened' stage of child development is that parental contact can now resume. Indeed, the phrase 'neck straightened' itself inspires endless plays on words and images bearing on this theme. In its simplest form, it connotes the rough temporal referent for this stage, the Islamic forty days. By logical extension, it also refers, as does the forty days, to the resumption of sexual contact between the parents. 'Neck straightened' can also be used to allude to the action of the man's vital organ, which, about this time, is said to replicate the action of the baby's neck. And the sight of a new baby on its mother's back for the first time, a sudden public statement of her renewed availability, is said to rekindle the husband's amorous interests.[8]

Walking/Weaning

In the past, lengthy periods of postpartum abstinence were common throughout the subcontinent (Page and Lesthaeghe 1981). Abstinence may have lasted as long as three years in Yoruba-speaking areas (Olusanya 1969); in other areas it often seemed to last simply until the child could walk or was weaned: anywhere between one and two-and-a-half years.

Rural Gambians describe several advantages of a long wait. It reduces the possibility of an overlapping pregnancy, allowing the older child to become more independent physically. It also allows a mother time to recover from the physical strains of childbearing and caring for a small baby. Finally, in a subcontinent where allegations of being an overly possessive, jealous wife are a sensitive issue in polygynous marriages, a long wait gives the other wives, if they exist, a chance to engage the husband's interest. The principal disadvantage to waiting this long, especially for a monogamous wife, is the risk that the husband will seek satisfaction 'outside' the home.

Interim Points

Everyone knows that beginning sexuality at the forty-day point itself seldom poses any risk of an early pregnancy. It is well known that fecundity usually resumes only when the menstrual period returns—often when the child is weaned, at which point most women want to get pregnant again. Far more worrisome to women is the pace of sexuality in the ensuing phases of the birth interval before the child is weaned. Indeed, these worries are not unfounded: as any reproductive biologist can affirm, changes in the child's breastfeeding patterns with the transition to supplementary foods are what most often precipitate the return of the menses.

Rules and Reproductive Behaviour

The two most salient points in the postpartum cycle—walking or weaning and the 'neck straightened' or forty days—are the most distinctive markers that people use when discussing the point when resuming contact becomes appropriate. Informal observations and conversations suggest that women prefer weaning, while men eye the forty-day target. Yet the actual time when contact begins is extremely variable. It depends on factors such as the woman's age and fecundity status as well as her past proclivity to get pregnant too early after a birth. It also depends on the man's polygynous status, the current fecundity status of his other wives, and his age.

Rural women are caught between norms of conscientious motherhood, which pressure them both to avoid an early pregnancy while they are still nursing a young baby and to fulfil the expectations of conjugal duty, which could risk the baby's health. Clearly, there are alternative pathways through this conundrum. A very young woman, who usually has little power to refuse her husband's demands, may remain with her mother for some time after the child's birth in order to maintain sexual distance. But even among those women who are staying with their husbands, sex is seldom simply 'resumed' in an all-or-nothing manner. As the following analysis shows, most of it drawing on Figure 12.1, there is an increment in sexuality through the birth interval, though the pace can adjust according to changes in the child's health and according to the mother's health and conjugal circumstances.

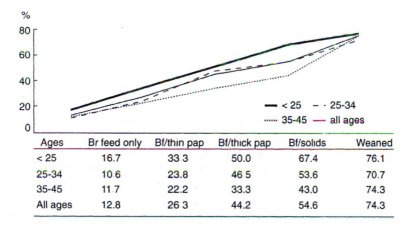

Ages	Br feed only	Bf/thin pap	Bf/thick pap	Bf/solids	Weaned
< 25	16.7	33.3	50.0	67.4	76.1
25-34	10.6	23.8	46.5	53.6	70.7
35-45	11.7	22.2	33.3	43.0	74.3
All ages	12.8	26.3	44.2	54.6	74.3

Fig. 12.1. Proportion of months when any 'contact' occurred, by woman's age and child's feeding stage: 13 rounds, 1993–1994
Note: Women in the study are those whose child from their last pregnancy is alive, and whose hubands are present

Figure 12.1 displays the percentage of months when any sexual contact was reported by women in three age groups (under 25, 25–34, and 35–45) by how the child was currently feeding: breastfeeding only, breastfeeding plus thin pap, breastfeeding plus thick pap, breastfeeding plus solid food, or weaned. (It is important to bear in mind, however, that these stages do not necessarily reflect an equivalent age progression; a child who has moved up to the thick pap phase may revert to breastfeeding alone if it becomes sick.) Included in the calculations are women whose last pregnancies had ended in live births of children who were still alive during the round in question. Excluded are women whose husbands were currently living elsewhere. The intent is to focus on husbands and wives who may be abstaining as an explicit strategy of avoiding pregnancy, although this analytical choice obviously selects against partners who temporarily live in different households as part of a larger strategy of avoiding pregnancy.

The figure shows several interesting patterns. The most obvious of these is wide disparities in contact frequencies at different points in the birth interval. Virtually all women, no matter when they resume contact, report a low pace of sexuality at the early child-feeding stages and a greater one as the birth interval progresses. Beginning, apparently, at only 13% of months during which any contact occurred for mothers of infants who are breastfeeding only, the pace of sexuality increases steadily to 55% of months just before weaning and finally to 74% among mothers of weaned children. A very similar pattern emerges when the mean number of contacts reported per month is used instead of the proportion of months of any contact. Beginning at 0.3 times per month among mothers who are breastfeeding only, the numbers of contacts increase gradually, reaching their maximum of 2.3 times per month when the child reaches the age of weaning. When the next birth occurs, sexuality will again drop off altogether, sometimes for forty days and sometimes until the child is weaned.

It is crucial to note, however, that the very slight beginning of contact appearing in the earliest feeding stage ('wet infant') is misleading. The actual number of contacts reported should be zero. The results shown in the figure are an artefact of the temporal structure of the rounds survey itself. In 20 of the total 40 contact events reported by mothers of wet infants, the new baby had been born only in the previous few days, a point that five out of the seven women involved in these 20 contacts went out of their way to explain in their open-ended commentary, unprompted by the questionnaire. In other words, the contact that appears in the responses had actually occurred *before* the baby's birth but within the previous month that our survey format specified. In all seven of these cases, the responses for the next month, when there was a subsequent round, showed the normal wet-infant pattern: no contact at all. The other 20 events in which contact was reported while breastfeeding a wet infant appeared to be either a miscode or a case of an older baby who had reverted, perhaps because of illness, to breastfeeding alone.

Looking more closely at the start of the birth interval, we can ask when, precisely, contact actually begins in order to see how often the ban on sexual relations before forty days is broken.[9] Since Figure 12.1 displays child-feeding stages as broad categories that may cover several months (wet infancy, for example, includes 11% of the interval following a live birth), the point of initial contact is impossible to ascertain. Separate calculations using individuals instead of events reveal that no one at all breaks this rule— or at least admits to doing so. But, while no one breaks the ban on contact *before* forty days, almost no one heeded the rule taken as an injunction to *begin* at this point. Out of the 100 live births in which a baby survived at least three months, data on the subsequent three rounds were available for 78 women. In only 10 of these cases (13%), if we can take reports at face value, was the forty-day expectation even *possibly* met; that is, contact was reported by the third subsequent round.

Both the pattern of a delayed entry into contact and that of a gradual increase in the pace of sexuality, once it begins, suggest that postpartum sexuality is not an all-or-nothing phenomenon, as conventional demographic understandings of 'abstinence' and 'resumption of sexuality' have implied. Thus, several women who reported that they had been 'avoiding the husband' that month as a method of avoiding pregnancy also reported one or more episodes of contact, as did this woman: 'I am not using any family planning method to keep me from getting pregnant but I do abstain from my husband sometimes.' Even more numerous were cases of women who had previously reported contacts at some point after a child's birth but later reverted to no contact for one or more months, reporting to the surveyor that they were trying to avoid pregnancy that month by 'avoiding the husband'. Because a Westerner might understand such an answer to mean '*still* abstaining from birth', the rounds structure in this case was an aid rather than a hindrance.

What about age patterns of postpartum contact? Although we might expect younger women to be under more pressure to comply with an early resumption of contact, this was not the case. Separate calculations on individual women by months following a birth showed almost no difference in the ages of the women reporting any contact during the first three post-partum months versus those reporting no contact: 27.5 and 27.2 years, respectively. Age selections are undoubtedly affecting these results: young women having their first baby may have been missed in some of the rounds, since there is a greater tendency of women giving birth the first time to move from their husband's compound for the birth and for a time thereafter. Moreover, younger women are taken out of the pool at earlier points in the birth interval, meaning that they are more likely than older women to appear as mothers with wet infants.

Although age seems to make little difference in when initial contact begins, age patterns of contact comprise one of the most striking points of difference in *subsequent* phases of the birth interval. Figure 12.1 shows a widening gap between young and old in numbers of contacts per month as time since last birth elapses. At the mid-point of the interval, when the breastfeeding child is eating thick pap, younger women are reporting twice as many sexual contacts per month as older women. By the time the breastfeeding child is eating solid foods, the gap has begun to close, even though younger women are underrepresented at this point.

It is important to refrain from drawing causal inferences too quickly from statistical patterns in postpartum behaviours and their correlates. For exam-ple, the visible increment in sexuality, especially among young women as the baby moves to thick pap, might suggest that young women have cause for worry about an early pregnancy with so many demands for sexual duty placed on them. But there is some suggestion that causation may also run the other way: young women anticipating the pressure to increase the pace of sex—or themselves desiring to begin a new pregnancy soon—may accelerate the baby's feeding progress to thick pap. The goal is to make the baby gain weight in preparation for the coming risks and the possibility of an abrupt weaning. In fact, other women sometimes claim to know that sex is imminent for a woman simply by observing what her baby is eating. A woman who begins to feed her baby pap early may be subjected to teasing insults such as 'You like men too much.' In sum, to say that moving to supplementation precipitates fecundity (and thus a pregnancy) is only part of the story; it can also happen that the prospects of a pregnancy precipitate the feeding of supplementary foods.

Other factors besides the child-feeding stage and the mother's age clearly affect the timing and pacing of sexuality during the birth interval. Among the most important is polygyny. Although the rounds data contain no direct information on polygyny, commentaries suggest that those women who resume contact around the forty-day point are most often those with no co-wives. This proportion appears to decline steadily as the number of co-wives rises. Although age very likely complicates matters (older women are more likely than younger ones to be polygynous), polygyny seems to absorb some of the pressure on women to follow the prescription to begin contact at forty days. Even more explicit is the commentary suggesting that polygyny figures strongly in subsequent postpartum sexuality, particularly when weaning or walking is seen as the goal to reach before ending abstinence. A monogamous wife with short birth intervals may actually take the initiative to acquire a new wife for her husband. One woman's statement implies relief that her husband married two more wives, since the onus of fending off the husband and of enduring short birth intervals had passed to younger women:

I am not trying to get pregnant because I am breastfeeding a child who is about one year old. Normally when I am breastfeeding I practise abstinence until after my child starts to walk. This way I always do what is called *sama wuluwo* [elephant reproduction]. Mostly when I start contacting my husband after 3–6 months, I get pregnant again. [Now, though,] my husband is not burdened by my abstinence because I have two other co-wives. We usually shift our time of delivery; one is available to him while I or the other one is breastfeeding or pregnant. I, being the first wife, have seven children with my husband but after my third child my husband married a second wife. Before I used to have some problems of children born too close to each other until I lost my second child. But now those types of mess are for the young wives, not me, because I can wait until my child is walking or completely weaned and my husband will have no cause to push me around to go to his house. He can always go to my co-wives...

In such cases (of which there were many), it is clearly a mistake to assume that polygyny solves all the problems of all the wives or that a polygynous man acts like a polygynist with respect to all domains of domestic life. His contact activity may resemble much more that of a monogamist.

Western Contraceptives and Postpartum Negotiations

As these last points have suggested, many women take active efforts to bring about desired outcomes such as long—or sometimes short—birth intervals rather than waiting for outside forces to produce them. Women who do not want to be pregnant yet may find reasons to make long visits to their mothers; others may use ritual or herbal measures to try to avoid pregnancy; still others may go out in search of a young co-wife. A number of women, however, use Western contraceptives to avoid pregnancy while resuming sex after a child's birth. Indeed, it is possible that the conflicts posed by normative expectations of long breastfeeding and wifely submission, both of which might be considered conservative, ironically may generate reactions that we might call liberal: women who faithfully observe the forty-day rule may regard this as a more compelling reason to contracept than any government exhortations to do so. Much like the function that tinned infant milk seemed to play in Sierra Leone (Bledsoe 1987), contraceptives allow a woman to adhere simultaneously to two otherwise conflictual norms: continuing to ensure that her baby is well nourished while resuming contact with her husband.[10] But in contrast to the use of tinned milk in Sierra Leone, a prestigious act, many Gambia women who show an interest in contraceptives are suspect. They are susceptible to accusations that they are trying to deprive their husband and his family of children (of 'spoiling his luck'), or trying to avoid a pregnancy that would testify to an adulterous affair: both signs of a troubled marriage.

Fears of condemnation make women intensely interested in the secrecy that various contraceptives afford. While neither abstinence nor condoms, obviously, can be hidden from a husband, most Imams and Marabouts will offer ritual protection against pregnancy only with the husband's permission. Pills are easy to hide under the bed since the husband spends little time in the wife's room, but they can be discovered by children or suspicious co-wives. An injection is the best choice of all for maintaining secrecy since there is no visible or tangible evidence of their use. One woman explained why secrecy is often desired:

I have never [previously] been using any of the *toubab* [white people's] contraceptives. I had relied on abstention . . . I decided to use a contraceptive primarily to enable me to breastfeed this child up to 24 months. I am using the injectable contraceptive for this first time. I started it two months ago. My husband is not aware of it. I hope he will never be aware of it. It might result in a divorce. It was in deep secrecy that I decided taking contraceptives because my husband is a stern man. I trust you [researchers] and hope he will not know from you people! It was a strong decision to take the injection after I have nearly failed in my strategy [abstention].

The drawback of injections, however, is the possibility of a long spillover period of infertility, a source of great worry, especially to young women, who prefer to maintain tight control over exactly when their fecundity will resume.

In the end, there is no perfect solution. Women must perpetually tinker with options, depending on their own fertility, their children's health, the availability of resources, and the pressures they feel from husbands, in-laws, and co-wives.

Women's Excuses

How should we evaluate the roles that norms play in all these pressures and decisions? While it is tempting to take norms at face value, as being if not compulsory then at least barriers that must be overcome, norms can also be used as rationales for enforcing disliked measures or permitting exceptions, or as excuses for behaviour that might otherwise meet with disapproval.

A woman who wants to use contraception or to keep her husband at bay while her child is still young must try to explain her actions in terms of norms that make the most convincing sense or carry the strongest moral weight. She may fuel her husband's fears that he will become polluted if he insists on sex at the times when she is considered unclean, according to Muslim and local ideologies. One woman admitted as much in the case of her own struggles to avoid pregnancy, which began on the fortieth day:

I have abstained completely from my husband since delivery of this child, though he had attempted to go to bed with me several times during this period. I have been refusing his attempts with excuses that I was realizing unusual menses. His first attempt was on the fortieth day after delivery. He had made other attempts and finally as my last resort, and also exhausted of excuses, I decided to consult a nearby Community Health Nurse to seek advice on contraception. He asked me several questions and recommended the injection to me.

Excuses, like contraceptives, must be chosen carefully. Once a trick is suspected, credibility is regained with difficulty. Contraceptives in particular sometimes evoke such ambivalence, and even hostility, that a woman may fabricate a sickness or exaggerate its seriousness in order to justify her use of them. Such strategies seem to be so common that, when we suggested asking about sickness as a possible variable in our survey to search for correlates of contraception, our assistants quickly pointed out that we would learn little by doing so: women commonly claim sickness as an excuse to avoid their husbands or contracept; that is, rather than sickness producing desires to contracept, the desire to contracept may precipitate claims to sickness.

Perhaps most effective in gaining access to contraceptives in a country like The Gambia, where primary health care is so strongly promoted at every level of government, are reasons relating to the health of the child. A woman who wants to contracept may have little credibility if she says she must go to town on unexplained business or even to visit relatives. People are far more likely to believe her if she draws attention to her baby's cough and announces she is going to the local health centre, where family planning services are now offered alongside antenatal and under-fives care. Even if the baby is well, she can declare that it is time for a well-baby check or inoculation. In effect, although we might assume that better health services at mother–child health (MCH) clinics lead to more use of family planning, the provision of contraceptives in MCH clinics may also generate more assiduous attention to children's health. Analogous excuses can involve a woman's declared need to go to town to visit relatives or to sell her vegetables on market day. She can also express a wish to visit her ailing mother, who happens to live near a community health nurse. (Nurses often run small private practices out of their own homes). If her detour is discovered, she can explain that she needed medicine for a backache, a common ailment in this farming society.

Parallel configurations of strategies surround the activities of the Gambia Family Planning Association (GFPA), which has expanded into activities such as providing village water and giving agricultural advice. Whatever the reasons why the GFPA took this step, one of the local distributors of contraceptives pointed out that these new functions have effectively expanded the ambiguous mix of motives that contraceptive users can try to employ. A woman who does not want her husband to know she is contracepting can hail a family planning official passing outside her house to ask for advice on her garden. Once they are inside, the private conversation can turn to contraceptives.

In many cases, institutional ambiguity is created quite deliberately. A medical supervisor reported that his centre had devised a way to provide easier access for clients such as single women and schoolgirls who normally would be reticent to come to a family planning clinic. Whereas the health centre used to maintain separate waiting rooms and hours for antenatal, under-fives, and family planning services, administrators made a conscious effort to blur the boundaries by consolidating all patient services around one large waiting room and merging the hours of service. The result was an increase in the use of family planning, especially among the groups whom the centre was targeting.

So deft are people at using norms as excuses that they may try to produce a biological condition that would demand invoking the rule they favour. A young woman who is forced to marry an older man may use contraceptives secretly, trying to create the seemingly natural precondition of sterility that might induce her husband to divorce her; she would hope that her husband, discouraged by her failure to conceive, would free her to marry the man she would have preferred.[11]

Another example of the 'unavoidable natural ailment' genre of rationales to end childbearing centres on a woman's high-parity status. The end of the reproductive years in populations such as rural Gambia has often been cast as a time when a husband is no longer justified in making sexual demands on his older wife and when she can cease childbearing, whether because of the dangers surrounding high-parity childbearing or because she is understandably 'tired', as many women express their physical state. Since everyone knows that pregnancies and deliveries at this stage of life can be dangerous, high-parity status can itself be used as an excuse either to avoid the husband or to contracept.

Some people gauge the time when terminal abstinence can begin as the time when a woman's daughter begins to produce children, and she herself may be allowed to stop childbearing and focus on being a grandmother. As one older woman put it,

I don't want to have another child again because my womb is too deep inside, for this is my tenth pregnancy. My first two girls all have their first children so I think I should stop bearing children now.

Permission to abstain permanently at this point in life, however, is not always granted automatically. Since a husband may not agree to terminal abstinence for his wife, she may try to create the condition that would give her an excuse to stop childbearing. Thus, although we might assume that older women with younger co-wives would be allowed to abstain at the end of reproductive life because their husbands have other sexual outlets, the causal direction may have been quite different. Several people indicated that older women with many living children may encourage their husbands to acquire co-wives so that they themselves can abstain.

To be sure, a woman may have quite different attitudes about abstinence, depending on her situation. A woman with few surviving children may downplay the importance of abstinence even though she may be a grand-mother because she wants to keep trying to have another child. And a woman who has been married to one man for many years and has grown increasingly resolute to stick to traditional norms of postpartum abstinence may find her ideological persuasion changing quickly if she marries again and finds herself needing to catch up with the other wives.

Whatever the excuses they use, women seem to draw upon the norms that will most convincingly legitimate their goals. This means both that they must choose norms that could apply logically to their own circumstances, and that their rationales may change in different situations. A likely example, though one on which we have little direct evidence, concerns condom use. Because condoms are seldom used by sexual partners with close personal relation-ships (Pickering et al. n.d.), a woman who fears that her husband may have AIDS may want to use condoms, but at the same time may to avoid accusing him of being infected or of suggesting that she herself is infected. Instead, she might report that she was advised to space her births for child health reasons—and the contraceptive she was advised to use was condoms.

Men's Views

In the open-ended responses to our monthly round survey, we have been struck repeatedly by the degree of religious piety that men sometimes man-ifest. Men frequently underscore the need to adhere to Islamic practice by resuming sexual duties on, or shortly after, the forty-day period. By contrast, women seem to refer to the forty-day rule more as a decree that they simply acknowledge availability after this time. They also seem to refer more often to indigenous rules that identify later points in the postpartum cycle as the time to resume sexuality. Men, if we take these responses literally, have far more passionate religious fervour than their wives, who appear to be tradi-tionalists or even backsliders.

It is true that many boys and young men in this area of the world have more formal Islamic training, on average, than do girls. Besides learning literacy and devotional skills, they learn rules governing marital life and about punishment for transgressions. Women are needed in the home for domestic work and marry soon after puberty. Their knowledge of Islam is often vague, and they tend to have a much more limited exposure to Islam's precepts. Yet it is clearly wrong to imply that all men are uniformly religious zealots while women cling to tradition. Most people agreed that men's views about postpartum abstinence vary considerably, according to:

- whether the wife in question is old or young;
- whether the union has been in existence for a long or a short time;
- where the wife is in her fertility cycle;
- whether a wife has more children of one sex or another;
- the status of the woman, e.g. an outside woman *v.* an inside one, an educated wife *v.* a less educated rural wife, etc.

Moreover, men as well as women are adept users of cultural norms. By examining some apparent exceptions, we uncover a host of other factors that strongly influence who adheres to which rule.

One such exception concerned a case of drastic social status imbalance: that of an uneducated young woman from a small rural village who managed to marry an educated man with a regular salaried job who was posted up-country as a fieldworker. The woman believed (and her mother incessantly reminded her) that her low status would put her at a clear disadvantage when the man took on another wife, as high-status men usually do. She should try to secure her tenuous position with the man by bearing a large number of children in a short period of time. To accomplish this goal, her birth intervals would have to be short. When her first child, a boy, was four months old, she began to urge the husband to resume sex, on the grounds (her mother had told her) that it was not natural to abstain any longer, that four months was appropriate for a boy and three months for a girl, a rule harkening back to a vaguely remembered pre-Islamic referent. The husband was reluctant to do so, however, because he wanted to ensure that his son was breastfed long enough. He finally agreed, on the condition that she would take birth control pills to prevent an early pregnancy. To ensure her compliance, he accompanied her to the family planning clinic and personally handed her the required pill every night and sent her off for a glass of water to drink it with. To the husband's outraged surprise, however, his wife soon became pregnant and confessed that she had been throwing away the pills. The story goes on, but the important point for our purposes is that, although men in most situations cite rules that permit an early return to sexuality, the unusually wide status difference between this particular couple produced a very different result.

While couples can be divided about when to resume contact, and while roles can shift, individuals themselves are often divided. They do not have sets of homogeneous norms that they apply uniformly to each situation. Because men are often polygynous, their differential application of different norms to different wives makes their individual disjointedness all the more visible. Such a case emerged in an interview with an older polygynist with three wives. With respect to the two older wives, especially the eldest, he voiced concern for their health and the demands of their domestic duties, and pointed to these concerns as the basis of his adherence to a long norm of postpartum abstinence with them. The youngest wife, however, was a different story. The state of her health seemed to cause him little concern, whether this concern was real or perceived, and by his own confession he frequently broke the long abstinence rule with her:

For me, I excuse my wives from sexual duties with me when they are breastfeeding until when their child is standing/starts to walk. In the case of my first wife, it is usually a longer period than the other two wives because she has a lot of work to do since she has a lot of children to take care of. She is also older and tends to give a chance to the others. The reason why I excuse them for some time is to allow them to recover from the troubles of childbirth and child care. I feel these are very tedious and demanding on the woman's general health. I sometimes break this rule with my last wife because she is more close to me than the other two. Not that I love her more than the rest, but because she is younger and is in a better shape. She has not suffered a lot like the other two.

Another vitally important case was that of a village elder, a man around 63 years of age who was currently married to four wives ranging from their mid-forties to late twenties. The two of most immediate interest are the first and the last. The first wife, apparently past the age of childbearing, had been given the freedom to leave the compound and move back to her own family. The man had spent nothing on her or her youngest child in the last month and had only a vague knowledge of her welfare or activities. The situation with respect to the fourth wife, the youngest, was entirely different. In describing her situation, he sounded like a different man. These responses were clear, specific, and worried. This wife's last birth had been three and a half years ago, far too long, and she was lagging noticeably behind the other wives in the child count. The husband badly wanted her to get pregnant:

... it is a long time now since she last delivered. We are all praying for her to conceive as soon as possible. She is my last wife and the one who has only one child. Both of us are worried about that because here we mainly marry to get kids.

These disparate responses in fertility goals and worries from one wife to the next are intensified in the cases of men with 'outside' wives. A man who confessed to having an outside woman provided an important exception that proved the rule about usual desires for high fertility. While he was anxious for his two wives to maintain uninterrupted fertility, he did not want the

outside wife to get pregnant. To prevent this outcome, he was using condoms with her.

Men's responses also vary enormously according to the child's observed
health progress. Most men reflect strong desires to ensure that the child is
progressing well before beginning to take many risks. A 33-year-old monogamist whose breastfeeding child had been sick from birth provided a good
case: 'The child is not well even since birth so I give chance to the mother
[excuse her from contact] even though she is my only wife.' The reasoning
seems to stem both from worries about dilution or contamination of the
milk, and from worries about the potential impact on the child if the mother
got pregnant at this point. The statement of another man in his early thirties
reveals careful fatherly efforts to monitor a child's progress and to recali-
brate sexuality accordingly, even if the hypothesized solution is not one that
outsiders might concur with:

When [my wife] had a child, I started to use a condom for a period of four months,
then I stopped it for the child got sick [and] I thought it was the condom I was using. I
awaited for a period until the child got well, then I continued to use the condom.

Such observations underscore in any case the fallacies of assuming either
that men are uniformly uncaring about women's and children's welfare or
that an individual's behaviour stems solely from his or her background
characteristics.

Men's Unlikely Allies

Another category of apparent exceptions further dampens any efforts to
typecast men as the sole advocates for religious piety and male sexual rights
and women as traditionalists. This category stems from the striking ideological transformation that many women seem to undergo as they finish reproduction. Not only do men seem to have different personae in their views of
sexuality within their different unions; women themselves seem to become
different people as they traverse reproductive life; so much so that men
suddenly gain key allies in their advocacy of minimal postpartum abstinence
with respect to certain wives. Men often appeal to elderly women, whether
their own relatives or the woman's, for help in persuading their defiant wives
that long periods of abstinence are unacceptable. One man, a monogamist
with a pregnant wife about 27 years old, reported that he asked the woman's
mother to intervene for him with her stubborn daughter. His pithy statement
is one of the most sobering we have collected:

I resumed sexual relations with [my wife] only after two months [after she delivered],
against her wish. I had to go and report her to her mother who talked to her to agree
to go to bed with me. What she was doing is not in line with Islam.... After two
months of her delivery I contacted my wife once a week. That is OK as far as I am
concerned. It always takes a while for her to agree to this schedule if she is breastfeeding, but after some time things become normal and more workable for both of us.

The poignant story that we sense underlying this statement is hard to surpass. If any could do so, it would be the following history of a pregnancy from a 27-year-old woman: an appeal by the husband and intervention by an older woman. It also gives hints that the intervention was heeded only grudgingly, and that further battles were to come:

I was taking the family planning pills while I was breastfeeding my last child. I weaned him at the age of 2 but still continued to use the pills because I wanted to rest. After using them for an additional eight months, after weaning my child, I was caught by my husband and he threw all the pills in a pit latrine. I never told him that I would join family planning [begin contracepting] because I know he would not agree. I took it upon myself and was doing it secretly. When my husband saw the pills he went to [tell] one old woman who is our neighbour. He told her to advise me to stop using the pills; otherwise he would divorce me. I was threatened so I decided to stop. I am now six months pregnant. [However], I have all plans [intentions] to continue using family planning again immediately after I deliver. I will continue to use the same pills because I had no problems with my fertility and health while using them. Only that I will take great care to keep them away from my husband.

My husband does not want me to use family planning pills because he said that will reduce the number of children I should have for him. He wants me to have as many kids as God gives. That is not good for my health, so I will never go by it.

Conclusion

The material discussed here hints that behind a vast number of birth intervals lie fascinating histories of negotiation over sexual contact. A woman's declaration that her daughter needs help with her own children, that she herself has a sick mother in a distant village, or that she is unclean or sick— all may be efforts to minimize the risk of pregnancy by delaying contact or minimizing its occurrences. Conversely, declarations about devotion to Islam, the need to keep a husband in the compound, or a spouse's reproductive duties may reflect efforts to hasten the resumption of contact or step up its occurrences. Evidence that a man applies different abstinence norms to different wives—and that even a woman applies different norms at different times of her life to herself or to other women—suggests that norms are vital resources in postpartum negotiations.

Observations about such apparently trivial topics as excuses have important bearing on arguments that demographic change does not occur simply through normative change or through exhortations to change behaviour. One might also point out more generally that in West Africa, Islamic norms governing at least two key fertility-relevant events, conjugal union and postpartum resumption of sex after a birth, seem to generate both early marriage and early resumption of sex. But the effects of Islam itself on precipitating early marriage may be far less powerful than local economic and political pressures recruiting young women into marriage pools. Certainly, in the rest of the Muslim world marriage is no longer early and universal (see e.g. Obermeyer 1992; Farid 1996). Nor is it clear that Islam *per se* produces fertility at young ages. Certainly Hausa women in northern Nigeria marry and often begin childbearing early. But a young woman who marries may remain at home until she is more mature. Alternatively, if she moves to her husband's home, she may remain under the watchful eye of a senior wife, who may well have 'married' her on behalf of her husband to obtain domestic labour. If sexuality does begin early, it is often initiated sparingly (like postpartum sex) until the young woman is more mature. Indeed, the fact that some people favour early fertility in certain circumstances may lead them to interpret Islamic tenets in the most conservative manner, rather than vice versa. Analogous conclusions can be drawn from cases involving the interpretation of rules governing the resumption of sex after a birth. Even if the forty-day rule is taken to require an immediate resumption of sex, the rule will probably have very little effect on fertility for some time. And, given the likelihood that a number of rules probably governed the resumption of sex even in pre-Islamic days, more would seem to depend on who has the influence to make their rule preference hold sway than on the content of the rule itself.

Local people are always casting about for ways to improve their lives. Indeed, the use of Western contraceptives is only one strategy out of a very longstanding repertoire of strategies for managing births. New public norms that promote the health and welfare of women and children or reinterpret Muslim ideology may well be affecting contraception or child spacing; but they may also be providing publicly acceptable rationales that lend an air of legitimacy to actions. (For similar observations with respect to early twentieth-century England, see Seccombe 1992.) To be sure, people would like to convince others that natural forces were at work. The reason why a woman cannot contact her husband is more credible if it sounds like a natural cause that she cannot help; nature was too strong to overcome, despite her best efforts. (See Strathern 1994 for a comprehensive anthropological critique of the nature–culture dichotomy.) Still, to point out that people use norms as excuses is not new. What seems more significant is that this realization exposes a very problematic assumption underlying the natural fertility paradigm.

There is often a tendency, when analysing what have been designated as natural fertility populations, to discount the role of volition in reproductive events. (See, however, Caldwell and Caldwell 1977 for early evidence of discomfort with this perspective.) This tendency manifests itself in analytical conventions surrounding the emphasis on biological forces and the treatment of variation and anomalies. Analyses often attempt to throw out 'unclean' data and to explain away patterns that do not seem to fit the natural fertility mould or incorporate them as facets of natural fertility; explanations of naturalism or traditionalism can then prevail. Examples include the grandmother syndrome, the use of contraception only for spacing, and the fact that younger or monogamous wives have shorter intervals. Although it is easy to default to such explanations in developing country societies, some apparently aberrant cases that are so readily discarded may comprise clues to the underlying strategies people are using in order to achieve certain demographic outcomes.

This chapter has documented a number of cases of people taking active measures to create demographic reality. One example concerned older women's efforts to acquire co-wives to escape childbearing pressures; another was the implication that the timing of weaning, an event that we interpret as an outcome of natural processes, is influenced heavily by social pressures to conform to the norm of avoiding pregnancy while breastfeeding. The data also suggest that the timing of a new pregnancy can determine breastfeeding duration, rather than the other way around. Even in cases of individual women who do have very regular intervals, these intervals may reflect more than unquestioning adherence to biological instinct or to cultural norms. The very evenness of the spacing itself is something that women try to manage, perhaps through careful strategies that vary from one birth to the next: a vision quite different from what the natural-fertility paradigm would lead us to assume.

Notes

1. We use terms like 'rule', 'norm', and 'value' somewhat interchangeably, although the terms imply, respectively, more to less formalization and codification.
2. On contraception, there is a diversity of opinions. Two other major Islamic theocratic states, Iran and Saudi Arabia, have a pronounced division of views. In Iran, a 1992 survey revealed that 45% of women aged 15–45 were using a modern contraceptive method, including sterilization (Ladier-Fouladi 1996: 1114), whereas the practice is still illegal in Saudi Arabia. Nordberg (1973) and Omran (1992) have further details on Islamic views of family planning.
3. All foreign words, including Latin tags, will be italicized. Words deriving from Gambian languages are in Mandinka.
4. Schoenmaeckers *et al.* assert that 'the postpartum taboo was a *virtually universal principle* for the whole of traditional sub-Saharan Africa' (1981: 31; emphasis in the original). However, birth interval length comes under perpetual pressure from numerous sources. Increases in female schooling, declines in polygyny, or a woman's growing need to maintain a sexual link to a supportive man may all play roles. The period of postpartum abstinence in particular may be declining; it may have lasted as long as three years in Yoruba-speaking areas (see Olusanya 1969), though in most areas it seemed to last simply until the child was weaned or could walk. Now, many African societies have quite truncated periods of abstinence.
5. We are grateful to Margaret Luck for recording this statement.
6. Two of the rounds, nos. 5 and 14, were not in a format compatible with the others for analysis.
7. The major weakness with this strategy is that the youngest women are disproportionately represented in the early parts of the birth interval: 15% of women under 25 whose last

pregnancy was alive *v.* 8% of women aged 35–45. Conversely, older women are disproportionately represented in events at the end of the birth interval: 41% of women aged 35–45 *v.* 22% of women under 25.

8. It is unclear whether the 'neck straightened' phase of child development has long been identified as a period of possible return to sexuality in indigenous practices, or whether it was transposed into a local idiom after the Islamic decree was received.

9. We asked the question of postpartum abstinence duration more directly of women in the 1992 survey. But the results were heaped in ways that strongly suggested that the question had been interpreted variously as one demanding a response of days, months, or even years. Hence we use the rounds data for these calculations.

10. Obviously, these views of contraceptives do not necessarily correspond with Western perceptions of the main purpose of contraceptives. In The Gambia, for instance, some women perceive pills as devices that allow them to (1) go to Mecca in an unpolluted state by providing them with a way to postpone their periods; (2) purge the reproductive tract of 'bad blood' that may be inhibiting their fertility—thus ultimately facilitating rather than reducing fertility; (3) abort unwanted pregnancies (pills are perceived as washing out not only blood but also any incipient foetuses each month); and (4) prevent sexually transmitted diseases—by reducing the chances that their husbands will seek sexual satisfaction outside the compound.

11. Another example concerns secondary schoolgirls in Botswana who are poor students. Many girls are under parental pressure to stay in school but recognize that their chances of getting a husband sink rapidly as they near the end of secondary school, and their chances of getting a white-collar job, because of their mediocre performances, are minimal; hence they reportedly take advantage of the fact that Botswana, like most African countries, has expectations, whether implicit or explicit, that girls who become pregnant must drop out of school. As a result, many schoolgirls who are not performing well may try to get pregnant in order to be allowed to drop out (National Institute of Development Research and Documentation, University of Botswana 1988; Dynowski-Smith 1989). That is, rather than finding themselves at the mercy of the school rules for their unintended pregnancies, such girls seem to try to create the precondition that would oblige school authorities to invoke the rule of expulsion.

References

Askew, I., Njie, S. F., and Tall, A. (1992), 'Overcoming religious barriers to family planning in rural Gambia'. Paper presented at the 19th Annual NCIH International Health Conference, Arlington, Va.

Baker, T., and Bird, M. (1959), 'Urbanization and the position of women'. *Sociological Review*, 7(1): 99–122.

Bledsoe, C. H. (1987), 'Sidestepping the postpartum sex taboo: Mende cultural perceptions of tinned milk in Sierra Leone'. Paper presented at the Rockefeller Foundation Conference on the True Determinants of Fertility. University of Ife, Nigeria.

——and Cohen, B. (eds.) (1993), *Social Dynamics of Adolescent Fertility in Sub-Saharan Africa*. Panel on Population Dynamics of Sub-Saharan Africa, Committee on Population, National Research Council. Washington, DC: National Academy Press.

——Hill, A. G., d'Alessandro, U., and Langerock, P. (1994), 'Constructing natural fertility: the use of Western contraceptive technologies in rural Gambia'. *Population and Development Review*, 20(1): 81–113.

Brandon, A. J (1990), 'Marriage dissolution, remarriage and childbearing in West Africa: a comparative study of Cote d'Ivoire, Ghana, and Nigeria'. Ph.D. dissertation, University of Pennsylvania.

Caldwell, J. C. and Caldwell, P. (1977), 'The role of marital sexual abstinence in determining fertility: a study of the Yoruba in Nigeria'. *Population Studies*, 31(2): 193–217.

Clignet, R. (1987), 'On dit que la polygamie est morte: vive la polygamie!' in D. Parkin and D. Nyamwaya (eds.), *Transformations of African Marriage*. Manchester: Manchester University Press for the International African Institute, pp. 199–209.

Comaroff, J. L. and Roberts, S. (1981), *Rules and Processes*. Chicago: University of Chicago Press.

Douglas, M. (1966), *Purity and Danger*. London: Routledge & Kegan Paul.

Dynowski-Smith, M. (1989), *Profile of Youth in Botswana*. Gabarone, Botswana: Intersectoral Committee on Family Life Education.

Farid, S. (1996), 'Transitions in demographic and health patterns in the Arab region'. *Proceedings of the Arab Regional Population Conference*, i., 1996 Arab Regional Conference, Liège: IUSSP.

Fortes, M. (1969), *Kinship and the Social Order*. Chicago: Aldine.

Gambia Medical and Health Department (1993), *Contraceptive Prevalence Survey*. Banjul: Republic of The Gambia.

Harrell-Bond, B. B. (1975), *Modern Marriage in Sierra Leone: A Study of the Professional Group*. The Hague: Mouton.

Hill, A. G. (1991), 'African demographic regimes past and present', in D. Rimmer (ed.), *Africa Thirty Years On*. London: African Society, and Portsmouth, NH: Heinemann.

Karanja, W. (1987), '"Outside wives" and "inside wives" in Nigeria: a study of changing perceptions of marriage', in D. Parkin and D. Nyamwaya (eds.), *Transformations of African Marriage*. Manchester: Manchester University Press for the International African Institute, pp. 247–61.

Lacombe, B. (1983), 'Le deuxième bureau: secteur informel de la nuptialité en milieu urbain congolais'. *Stateco*, 35: 58–78.

—— (1987), 'Les unions informelles en Afrique au Sud du Sahara: l'exemple du deuxième bureau congolais'. *Genus*, 43 (1–2): 151–64.

Ladier-Fouladi, M. (1996), 'La Transition de la fecondité en Iran'. *Population*, 51: 1101–28.

Le Roy Ladurie, E. (1975), *Montaillou: Village Occitan de 1294 à 1324*. Paris: Gallimard.

Lockwood, M. (1995), 'Structure and behavior in the demography of Africa'. *Population and Development Review*, 21: 1–32.

Malthus, T. R. (1798), *An Essay on the Principle of Population, as it affects the Future Improvement of Society, with Remarks on the Speculations of Mr. Godwin, M. Condorcet, and Other Writers*. London: J. Johnson.

National Institute of Development Research and Documentation, University of Botswana (1988), *Teenage Pregnancies in Botswana: How Big is the Problem and What are the Implications?* Gabarone: University of Botswana.

Ngondo a Pitshandenge, I. (1994), 'Les Législations sur le mariage en Afrique au sud du Sahara', in C. Bledsoe and G. Pison (eds.), *Nuptiality in sub-Saharan Africa: Current Changes and Impact on Fertility*. Oxford: Clarendon Press.

Nordberg, O. (1973), *Muslim Attitudes to Family Planning*. New York: Population Council.

Obermeyer, C. M. (1992), 'Islam, women, and politics: the demography of Arab countries'. *Population and Development Review*, 18: 33–60.

Olusanya, P. O. (1969), 'Nigeria: cultural barriers to family planning among the Yorubas'. *Studies in Family Planning*, 37: 13–16.

Omran, A. R. (1992), *Family Planning in the Legacy of Islam*. London: United Nations Population Fund.

O'Neill, B. J. (1987), *Social Inequality in a Portuguese Hamlet: Land, Late Marriage and Bastardy 1870–1978*. Cambridge: Cambridge University Press.

Page, H. J. and Lesthaeghe, R. (1981), *Child-Spacing in Tropical Africa*. London: Academic Press.

Parsons, T. (1949), *The Structure of Social Action*. Chicago: Free Press.

Pickering, H., Quigley, M., Hayes, R. J., Todd, J. and Wilkins, H. A. (n.d.), 'Determinants of condom use through analysis of over 24,000 prostitute/client contacts in the Gambia'. Unpublished paper, Medical Research Council, The Gambia.

Radcliffe-Brown, A. R. (1950), 'Introduction', in A. R. Radcliffe-Brown and D. Forde (eds.), *African Systems of Kinship and Marriage*. Oxford: Oxford University Press, pp. 1–85.

Ross, J. A., Mauldin, W. P., Green, S. R., and Cooke, E. R. (1992), *Family Planning and Child Survival Programs as Assessed in 1991*. New York: Population Council.

Sargent, C. (1988), 'Born to die: witchcraft and infanticide in Bariba culture', *Ethnology*, 27: 79–95.

Scheper-Hughes, N. (1985), 'Culture, scarcity and maternal thinking: maternal detachment and infant survival in a Brazilian shantytown'. *Ethos*, 13: 291–319.

Schoenmaeckers, R., Shah, I. H., Lesthaeghe, R., and Tambashe, O. (1981), 'The child-spacing tradition and the postpartum taboo in tropical Africa: anthropological evidence', in H. J. Page and R. Lesthaeghe (eds.), *Child-Spacing in Tropical Africa*. London and New York: Academic Press, pp. 25–71.

Seccombe, W. (1992), 'Men's "marital rights" and women's "wifely duties": changing conjugal relations in the fertility decline', in J. R. Gillis, L. A. Tilly, and D. Levine (eds.), *The European Experience of Declining Fertility, 1850–1970: The Quiet Revolution*. Cambridge, Mass.: Blackwell, pp. 66–84.

Strathern, M. (1994), 'No nature, no culture: the Hagen case', in C. P. MacCormack and M. Strathern (eds.), *Nature, Culture and Gender*, 2nd edn. Cambridge: Cambridge University Press pp. 174–222.

Turner, R. (1992), 'Gambian religious leaders teach about Islam and family planning'. *International Family Planning Perspectives*, 18(4): 150–1.

United Nations (1990), *Patterns of First Marriage: Timing and Prevalence*. New York: UN.

van de Walle, E., and Kekovole, J. (1984), 'The recent evolution of African marriage and polygyny'. Paper presented at the Annual Meeting of the Population Association of America, Minneapolis, 3–5 May.

Van Velsen, J. (1967), 'The extended-case method and situational analysis', in A. L. Epstein (ed.), *The Craft of Social Anthropology*. London: Tavistock Publications, pp. 129–49.

Wittgenstein, L. (1968), *Philosophical Investigations*. Oxford: Basil Blackwell.

13 The Limits of Diffusionism

PHILIP KREAGER

The problems that led to a revival of the concept of diffusion in population studies will be familiar to most, if not all, demographers. At the macro-level, the inability of socioeconomic postulates of 'classic' demographic transition theory to account for wide differentials in the pace and pervasiveness of fertility declines has been coupled with a recognition of the striking persistence of regional and cultural factors underlying many such differentials. At the micro-level, the difficulties encountered in reconciling models of reproductive behaviour based on individual consumer choice with observed responses have likewise pushed those involved in population studies to give more attention to how community institutions and values actually shape people's choices. A number of reviews have argued that a diffusionist approach focused particularly on ideational changes can provide the necessary corrective (Knodel and van de Walle 1979; Cleland and Wilson 1987; Watkins 1987). There are several reasons why diffusion hypotheses have seemed so appealing.

For one thing, the term and concept of diffusion was already a part of the general demographic discourse (e.g. Rogers 1973). For another, even the most programmatic early formulations of demographic transition theory were at least implicitly diffusionist, accepting that economic change is subject to the influence of varying cultural perceptions and media of communication, giving rise to lag effects, pockets of resistance, and so forth (Notestein 1945). Ideas and practices may, after all, spread faster or slower than changes in surrounding infrastructures. They can permeate the boundaries of otherwise disparate economic groups and societies. So it is inevitable that diffusion—defined broadly to include the dispersion of values, information, institutional arrangements, and products—should play a part in the international spread of fertility limitation.

Perhaps more important, the premises of post-war diffusion research coincided with some central assumptions made in fertility studies during the same period. Coale's (1973) three dicta on the preconditions necessary for sustained fertility decline remain the most convenient and oft-cited summary: (1) effective techniques of birth limitation must be available; (2) their practice must be recognized as socially and economically advantageous by potential reproductive partners; and (3) such attitudes and practices must become part of partners' everyday 'calculus' of decision-making. At the time Coale put forward these propositions, the wider field of diffusion research had an already established focus on matters of exactly these three kinds. Its usual concern was the transfer of technology and associated instrumental attitudes. It too assumed a rationalist, optimizing view of choice, and the trajectory of diffusion was assumed to lead (while being subject to possible lag effects) to an equilibrium state in which the new instrumental rationality would become normative (cf. reviews by Katz *et al.* 1963; Rogers 1962; Silverberg *et al.* 1988).

None the less, the rise of diffusion as a theoretical orientation in population studies is bound to be troubling to anyone familiar with the history of the concept. At the very founding of sociology as a discipline, Durkheim wrote a swingeing critique in which he detailed the logical flaws, imprecision, and lack of explanatory power which appeared unavoidably bound up with attempts to base explanations of social change on diffusion (Durkheim 1968: 123–42; 1982: 50–9). Such criticisms resurfaced in the writings of Malinowski (1928), whose pioneering ethnographic method failed to support the diffusion hypotheses of his contemporaries. The undoubted importance of the spread of techniques and values has, however, led to repeated attempts at reformulation, the study of diffusion itself spreading across the social sciences. It is sobering that shortcomings remarked on initially by Durkheim and Malinowski (and echoed by scholars like Kroeber 1931) are repeated again in more recent evaluations by diffusion specialists when they come to discuss the limitations of their field of study (Dosi 1991; Rogers 1976).

A Common Frontier

The striking fact about these shortcomings is that they occur at precisely those points of analysis that demographers had hoped the phenomenon of diffusion and its study would help to clarify. As Dosi remarks (1991: 185–6, 194), diffusion research has provided a multitude of case studies without arriving at an explanatory framework which can account for the wide variation in the pace at which different attitudes and technologies are adopted in a given society or societies. At the micro level, recourse to rationalist models of choice in diffusion research has proven no more satisfying than in population studies (1991: 189 *et seq.*).

The situation Dosi describes is familiar enough. On the one hand, he notes that diffusion models consistently assume that choice is explicable in terms of individual actors; that the identity of a given and potentially diffusable item, idea, or practice may be defined in terms of the instrumental factors its designers intended it to serve; and that diffusion occurs as people come to understand these instrumentalities. On the other, he reviews the results of research which suggest that decisions are the outcomes of collective processes; that even products like agricultural machinery and chainsaws require further technical and human adjustments before finding their ultimate uses; and that in this process technologies and practices acquire a range of new and culturally specific meanings. The learning process, which is the fundamental individual and collective stratum of diffusion, is bound to reflect past experience with innovations and elements of social structure like the differing status of adopters. A given innovation, as it is accommodated to such experience, sets in train other social and technical adjustments which feed back, in turn, into its meaning. The stock image of a linear trajectory to equilibrium is thus insufficient to explain such a complex and open-ended phenomenon, even when additional 'lag effects' are hypothesized. Diffusion and innovation are continuously linked; diffusing ideas and objects are essentially mutable; and multiple outcomes remain likely.

As Dosi's examples show, these problems are manifest even where consideration is restricted to commercial products disseminated within a single national culture. Turning to contexts involving more than one language and culture, we need only recall Malinowski's remarks of half a century ago: 'whenever one culture "borrows" from another, it always transforms and readapts the objects or customs borrowed.... In this process of readaptation the form and function, often the very nature, of the object or idea is deeply modified—it has to be, in short, reinvented' (1928: 37). The collection of papers assembled by Rogers (1976) severely condemns the ethnocentrism and functionalism which have kept diffusion models from addressing this process of cultural construction. Two major issues are singled out: (1) neglect of the transformation of meaning and the role of cultural symbolism in the diffusion process; and (2) the relation between inequalities in access to information and emerging economic and social inequalities. We shall return to these below. Parallel criticisms were, of course, beginning to feature in the demographic literature of the 1970s (e.g. Caldwell 1976; Kreager 1977; McNicoll 1980).

The Search for Operational Questions

It is clear, then, that population studies cannot expect to find in diffusion research a new or distinctive orientation, let alone a body of theory and method that promises ready and fruitful applications to pressing questions involving demographic change. More than a decade has passed since Knodel and van de Walle first called attention to the problem, yet approaches remain tentative. The implicitly diffusionist roots of demographic theorizing are now more likely to be acknowledged (e.g. Lesthaeghe and Surkyn 1988: 5–6). Some hints have been given about network analysis (Hammel 1990: 468–74), arguably the most sophisticated methodology for monitoring diffusion. But the main emphasis has become problem-oriented. It is argued, for instance, that if demographers are to understand how knowledge is communicated and transformed they will have to get down to rather unglamorous issues like the social functions of gossip (Watkins 1990), the impact of the spread of numeracy (van de Walle 1992), and the fact that values of children are repeatedly negotiated as part of the ordinary functioning of family and community networks (Bledsoe and Isiugo-Abanihe 1989). Topics like these suggest little willingness to follow slavishly in the path of older diffusion models. What researchers appear to be looking for is a sufficiently realistic and operational way of filling in the context or structural background in which the transmission and transformation of values and practices occur. Without this background, neither the nature of the learning process nor the comparison of its variants is really possible. The recognition that this will require new methodologies has created the space for, among other approaches, anthropological demography. The potential diversity of the topics that need attention, however, suggests that the field may be in danger of dissolving into a mere motley of interests, especially as each topic can vary from one cultural setting to another, and may be approached via a variety of methodologies.

Episodes in the History of Diffusionism

There is, however, a common denominator. A longer historical perspective, stretching back to Durkheim, can help us to appreciate this. The connecting thread is not diffusion, but the criticism of diffusion hypotheses, and the attempts to arrive at more concrete and operational approaches that have resulted from these criticisms. My account of this episode (or episodes) in the history of social science will necessarily be brief.

Diffusion debates seem to have a cyclic character, cropping up in the social sciences every thirty years or so. They follow a consistent pattern in three respects: first, sweeping generalizations indicate a need for closer scrutiny; then, special importance gradually comes to be attached to the potential contributions of ethnography, particularly as information on the form and content of people's experiences is necessary to modelling actual processes of change; finally, however, the evidence that emerges from field studies turns out either to refute the initial hypotheses or simply to bypass diffusion as too superficial a concept to account for the determinants of change.

The cycle is generally regarded as beginning in a contest between Durkheim and Tarde in the 1890s concerning the respective roles of sociology and psychology in social explanation. (For a detailed summary, see Lukes 1981: 302–13.) It resurfaced in the 1920s and 1930s as methods of social research were applied increasingly to indigenous populations in Africa, Asia, and the Americas. Up to that time, it had been common to regard traditional societies as survivals of previous and backward stages of civilization; once it was accepted that the principles of social organization in such societies were of enduring interest and value, the reasons why different groups were more or less susceptible to the spread of modern European culture and technology could become a scientific study, rather than a moral assessment of their backwardness.

These old prejudices may now seem bizarre, but they died hard. Malinowski's intervention was made in refutation of G. E. Smith's thesis (1916) that the progress of civilization in the Americas depended on elements that had diffused from ancient Egypt. Much of anthropology, including the study of 'primitive mentality' (Evans-Pritchard 1937), 'acculturation' (Redfield *et al.* 1936), and 'culture contact' (Malinowski 1938), grew up in the space created by such critiques. These were overtaken, in turn, by a third phase, beginning in the 1950s and 1960s, in which acculturation and the diffusion of agricultural innovations became topics allied to studies of economic development. This latter phase is the main object of the critiques of Dosi and Rogers, summarized in the preceding section, and need not occupy our attention further here. Since the basic issues and operational problems were raised very effectively in the first phase of this cycle, our attention may be focused there.

It was Tarde's sweeping view that social phenomena can be explained solely at the level of individual interactions: social forms arise from people's imitation of each other, and spread more widely as members of one group copy the behaviour of others. All history and social structure thus comes down to diffusion by means of the elementary mechanism of imitation. Durkheim, objecting to this reduction, initiated the line of argument we have already met in Malinowski's remarks on reinvention: what is at issue in diffusion is not simply imitation and replication, but a process by which people successively reinterpret the meaning and use of ideas, products, or practices, adapting them to their own purposes. Not only the specific nature of the disseminating ideas and objects, but the cultural logics into which they are assimilated, are altered thereby.

Durkheim and Malinowski accepted the potentially great impact of diffusion, for example where one culture takes up the superior technology of another. But they insisted, at the level of general sociological principle, on what demographers have subsequently found in their own specialized study of modern fertility declines: the Tardean hypothesis suggests that the diffusion of a certain practice (say, birth control) proceeds along pretty much the same lines in all cases. However, the diversity of historical experience (witness the record of fertility transitions), provides prima facie evidence, at least, that things cannot be so simple.

Given that the emergence of differentials appears to be the essence of the diffusion process, Durkheim reasoned that it is necessary in the first place to establish a baseline within local cultural knowledge: sound understanding of how information is ordinarily structured in a given society, together with examples of previous transformations in such structures, is needed to work out why a particular succession of meanings comes to be attached to a given practice or institution. Such knowledge also provides a framework for comparing how certain ideas and practices are altered in one way in one society, and in others elsewhere.

Durkheim emphasized two elementary properties of the way information is structured, which he called 'externality' and 'constraint'. The distinction is crude (Lukes 1981: 11–15 pinpoints its ambiguities), but it may be adopted here as it has a direct relevance to recent diffusion debates. By 'externality', Durkheim had in mind the supra-individual character of cultural systems such as language, morality, ritual, and technical specialisms. Even if we grant that a child, for example, learns much of his or her native tongue, or how to handle money, by imitation, there is more at issue in this learning process than the child's new ability to handle this or that transaction. The underlying logics of language and currency are also somehow assimilated by the child in a much deeper way, which enables him or her subsequently to understand many situations he or she has never observed, and to develop and apply this tacit or structural knowledge in ways that can create new meaningful relationships. Such underlying logics are internalized by different individuals to varying degrees, but their nature as systems transcends all individual comprehension, containing many possible patterns of behaviour.[1] The term 'constraint' is used by Durkheim to describe a diverse range of factors, including law, power relations, and ecological limits, which have the capacity to make individuals adhere to moral codes, traditional techniques, and so forth.

Durkheim intended his later writings to serve as models for analysing such information. With regard to the first set of properties, he relied on ethnographic studies of collective representations (especially aboriginal religion); for the second, he tried to devise quantitative measures that would indicate determinants of social trends (such as suicide). Despite the flaws that subsequent ethnography has revealed in his treatment of substantive issues, there remains every reason to take his two properties seriously. That, at least, would seem to be the indication of the critiques by Dosi, Rogers, and others outlined in the preceding section. For the two major lacunae in diffusion research that they cite—the construction and transformation of meaning in the course of diffusion, and the role of inequalities in the access to and control of information—fall squarely into the two fundamental contextual properties Durkheim emphasized a century ago.

The Current Round

The recent demographic interest in diffusion, having arrived in time for what should be the fourth round of diffusion theorizing (c.1980–2000), is remarkably better prepared than any of its predecessors. It is also noticeably milder.

The articles by Knodel and van de Walle and others, cited at the start of this paper, begin from a more extensive and systematically assembled body of data than any previous arguments for diffusion. Even so, they confine themselves largely to putting forward the view that diffusion processes deserve serious attention, rather than leaping directly into the reductive and sometimes wild generalizations that have characterized several past episodes.

Hypotheses of a broadly diffusionist kind have not been slow to emerge. Lesthaeghe and Surkyn (1988) have shown how Tarde's ideas on imitation can be refurbished for modern European settings as a theory of 'embourgeoisement', in which members of lower-class groups change their family values by imitating middle-class patterns. Some of Caldwell's (1980) observations on the capacity of formal education to disseminate Western family role stereotypes in Africa make a similar point. Watkins's (1990) proposal that women's gossip networks are an important media through which modern national values infiltrate family, neighbourhood, and kin relationships points to a further fruitful line of study. None of these ideas could be described as new. They differ, however, from much of what made past rounds of diffusion theorizing so debatable, in two respects.

First, they are not primarily diffusion theories. While networks and processes of dissemination may be assumed to play an active role in shaping demographic trends, this role is heavily circumscribed by wider structural limitations set, for example, by the growth of the institutions of government, market forces, and class relations. Although these papers invoke a number of externalities, to adopt Durkheim's terminology, they are concerned chiefly with patterns of constraint. The second difference is not merely coincidental to the first. Ethnographic data and methods have been an important influence on these approaches, along with cultural history, helping to shape the selection of social relationships and cultural content in terms of which hypotheses were formulated.

It is too early to say where hypotheses such as these may lead. There seems to be a good chance, however, that demography can break out of the old cycle of diffusionist debates. At the present stage, the issue appears to be less a matter of constructing a general theory of cultural diffusion for demography, than unpacking the diffusionist assumptions that have long been implicit in social and economic demography, and recasting them in a way that can be related to particular ethnographic realities. If this is to happen, however, the recent interest shown in 'constraint' factors will need to be balanced by a study of those features Durkheim referred to roundly as 'external'.

Ethnography and Theory in Anthropological Demography

As we have seen, externalities may be defined as the range of constructive capabilities people have by virtue of their everyday knowledge of the culture or cultures in which they live. While each individual is limited, he or she has access to a much larger repertoire of models of thought and behaviour than anyone could ever actually use or consciously remember. It is possession of this body of tacit knowledge that enables people to make active responses to changing circumstances as they arise, successively reinterpreting the meaning of those circumstances and the several courses of behaviour that count as a response to them. In the process, the cultural models themselves are likely to change, and further modes of behaviour may be added to the repertoire. One of the evident advantages of conceptualizing the transmission of ideas, values, and practices in these terms is that it restores an active role to persons and groups in societies undergoing major social change. Peoples and cultures cease to be essentially passive targets, receptors, or rejectors of supposedly discrete information packages, and can be studied for their capacity to create and structure meaning and modes of behaviour.

I have stated this definition in bald and non-technical terms since it can help us to show how current anthropological demography is already responding to the longstanding weaknesses of diffusionism. At this point, the focus of my paper changes. Up to now, the concern has been to review problems that writers on diffusion, as well as their critics, already acknowledge. This critical exercise is not simply a negative one, since the shortcomings of diffusionism enable us to specify the criteria that any attempt to model cultural transmission as a factor in demographic change must meet. In the remainder of this paper, I shall turn to how, in view of these criteria, this work may proceed.

Recall the conceptual problems currently recognized by diffusion specialists, as reviewed in the first section of this paper. These include the need for: (1) a way of placing individual choices realistically in community contexts, especially with regard to the processes of symbolism and meaning which local groups share to a greater or lesser degree with the wider communities (regional, ethnic, national, or international) in which they live; (2) a conceptualization of the transmission of knowledge as an open-ended process, rather than a linear one ending in a presupposed outcome; and (3) a conceptualization of the ideas, practices, and products undergoing diffusion as mutable, rather than as effectively fixed and discrete, items focused on a single instrumental identity.

Two recent seminars, devoted largely to the demography of sub-Saharan Africa and conducted under the auspices of the IUSSP Committee for Anthropological Demography, address issues of these three kinds. They are particularly useful for showing how phenomena often described in diffusionist terms arise in ethnographic data. The advantage of this ethnography, however, is that it readily enables us to see how conceptual confusions result from such descriptions. The data presented at these seminars, in short, provide explicit examples of how diffusionism narrows our awareness of cultural processes influencing demographic change, and why the information it excludes remains essential.

The first seminar, to which most attention will be given here, takes up one of the classic forerunners of the spread of fertility limitation: changes in nuptiality (Bledsoe and Pison 1994). The second is addressed to perhaps the most widely discussed of recent diffusion phenomena: HIV transmission (Dyson 1992). Neither seminar, however, approached its subject in explicitly diffusionist terms. The concern, in both cases, was characteristically anthropological. In the first, for example, insights arising from ethnography are used to identify and disentangle multiple meanings of marriage and the several sorts of partnership that coexist in African societies, especially as they relate to personal and family strategies. Clarifying and refining basic terms of reference in this way naturally precedes and accompanies attempts to build more general models.[2]

Nuptiality and Networking

The study of change in African family systems bears the characteristic stamp of diffusionist theorizing. An influential example is Goode (1963), who saw Africa as ripe for the spread of Western nuclear family values and institutions, entailing the disappearance of polygamy, the decline of economic and social reliance on extended family networks, rising age at marriage, the end of kin group control over spouse selection, and so forth. These changes are, of course, of precisely the kind that have been expected to lead to fertility control becoming a normal feature of married couples' 'calculus of conscious choice'. If Goode's prediction had been true, the linear transition to demographic equilibrium in Africa would by now have been well under way. As with the fate of past diffusion hypotheses, however, the evidence of local field studies (now combining anthropological and demographic perspectives) has shown otherwise. The survey of current trends edited and summarized by Lesthaeghe (1989) was able to give, at most, qualified support to Goode on a few variables (e.g. partner selection, modest rises in marriage age), and then only for certain regions and ethnic groups.

The paths followed by modern African family systems combine to give a very different picture from what any hypothesis based on the diffusion of Western values could have supposed. Polygamy remains at the centre: far from declining, it has diversified. While previously not a general practice, but one confined to certain ethnic groups (and often to some better-off men within them), plural marriage has become a common feature of the African urban setting. As Karanja (1988) notes, traditional forms of polygyny had been a subject of disparagement among aspiring African élites for some time before Goode prophesied their imminent demise. But this did not preclude modifications to existing practice, or the subject of plural marriage becoming a pervasive topic of town gossip and the popular media (not to mention the body of academic studies that have grown up around it). If there is an idea and practice that has been the object of general diffusion in African society, it is the real possibility of having more than one regular spouse.

Traditional forms of polygyny remain a minority practice. Pebley and Mbugua cite a range of between 15% and 50% of men currently having more than one wife in those societies traditionally practising polygyny (1989: 338). The underlying rationale of traditional forms has been recounted many times: a man with additional wives gains thereby a pool of agricultural labour, as well as improved chances of having many offspring. Both are means of increasing his wealth and prestige, not only directly, but as a continuing process. They are symbols of his strength and that of his lineage. They provide practical means of forging alliances (through his own and his children's marriages) to other kin groups. Each successive marriage and child provides avenues for extending a network of exchanges and obligations in goods, labour, and services—the visible signs through which a man's influence is made manifest. Women have had a vested interest in this system as well, especially senior wives, who can exercise day-to-day control over the labour not only of their own daughters and grandchildren, but of junior wives and their children as well.

Steady (1987) describes this system intact in a Sierra Leonian fishing village in the 1980s. She adds, however, that, while the system has proved highly productive as a labour strategy for the fish-processing industry, and has provided economic independence for men and women, they are in relative terms very underpaid: the community is a good example of how traditional cultures subsidize the world economy.

Traditional forms of polygyny need not, however, be associated with underdevelopment. In Yaounde and Douala, Cameroon, polygyny is most frequently found in the educated and civil service categories; higher salaries from the modern sector in this way are transferred directly into traditional signs of power and status (Clignet and Sween 1974). Both examples show that the system is not static. Parkin (1988) cites the Luo in East Africa and the Beti in the Ivory Coast as populations in which men keep both a village and a town wife, rotating between the two areas so that they can participate in both traditional and modern sectors. This adaptation can mean that, where marriage expenses are not prohibitive, plural spouses cease to be the prerogative of the better-off, as the costs of maintaining a village wife may be negligible (Karanja 1988). As Bledsoe (1990) notes, however, such arrangements may have another side: a successful man who, in advancing from a rural to an urban economic base, has made a sequence of ever more prestigious marriages may choose to marginalize his past by keeping his rural wives and responsibilities in the background.

These cases indicate the difficulty of saying where traditional forms of plural marriage end and modern trends begin. The Western ideal of mono-gamy formalized by a Christian or civil ceremony has, since the colonial era, provided an obvious 'modern' type, popularly contrasted with 'traditional' polygyny. However, as monogamy too remains a minority practice, research has focused on the diverse forms of union that have arisen as a kind of compromise between African and European ideals. These may be grouped under two broad and in some cases overlapping types of plural union.

The first, referred to variously as 'private polygyny', 'outside wives', or *deuxième bureau*, is defined in explicit contrast to monogamy. It describes a conjugal union in which a man maintains a woman and the children she has had by him in a separate residence from that of his formally espoused (or 'inside') wife. This arrangement, while neither publicly acknowledged nor legally sanctioned, is likely none the less to be an open secret. A man may maintain more than one 'outside' wife, either simultaneously or in sequence, but his acknowledgement of paternity enjoins his continued maintenance, even if the union ceases and this wife is bearing someone else's children. In consequence, as Guyer (1988: 19) notes, for the Yoruba, a man can be responsible for a set of children with quite varying parentage: some by his previous wives, some his current wives' children by previous husbands, others jointly born to himself and one or more current wife, and even, these days, the child of an unmarried daughter. These are situations of great complexity, giving rise to aggravations that may ultimately drive one wife to leave, or give the husband pretexts for the neglect that will make her leave.

For the most part, this kind of complexity has been seen as a male prerogative, a modern manifestation of polygyny which, like traditional forms, is a way of signifying a man's wealth and power, and manifesting his influence over an ever-widening community of people. But it is no less significant that women may see a succession of outside wifeships as a means of achieving upward mobility and, as Obbo bluntly puts it, 'a tool to defeat rival women' (1987: 277). There is good reason, as Guyer points out, for viewing women's ability to build up a set of outside relationships with different men, each of whom continues to contribute support, as a form of polyandry.

'Private polygyny' and 'polyandrous motherhood' presuppose a second and broader set of informal liaisons between men and women. As in the first variety of union, serial as well as simultaneous partnerships are possible. Each partner may or may not be already participating in formal or outside unions. The boundary between informal union and marriage/outside wifeship/polyandrous motherhood is generally crossed when the woman becomes pregnant and bears her first child to a given man. Becoming pregnant is thus a common and basic economic strategy for a woman. It removes the ambiguity of her situation, giving her a heightened claim on male resources, and signals her attainment of a new status. But there is no necessary linkage. A woman may be one of a number to whom a man has made promises. She may be able to bypass the father of the child in favour of a union with another man. But she may have to fall back on the support of her own kin, or on their plural marriages, as in Guyer's account. Women's economic vulnerability is underlined by the very fact that adroit use of their sexuality and fertility remains a basic means of survival as well as advancement. As Schoepf (1992) remarks, the support of maternal kin is not necessarily available, and women who do not work as prostitutes may none the less supplement their incomes by providing sex to casual partners. Prostitution looms very large on the East African scene, where it is at the centre of the AIDS epidemic, and where a large percentage of men who are in regular unions still frequent prostitutes (Carael 1988).

There is no fixed sequence in which childbearing, cohabitation, ritual announcement, and celebration of a union are generally ordered (van de Walle and Meekers 1988). Periods of labour migration and high bridewealth payments commonly delay nuptiality, creating periods in which informal relationships may flourish (Enel *et al.* 1988; Isiugo-Abanihe 1988). Rights and responsibilities in marriage vary, for example, between customary and Christian rites, or depending on levels of education. This will affect the willingness of some women to delay both marriage and conditions of divorce, but it does not keep a woman from childbearing, either in informal unions or in outside wifeships (Pilon 1988; Brandon and Bledsoe 1988). Informal relationships may thus exist for some time, perhaps without marital intent, or perhaps as a tentative state in which a man and a woman are, in effect, negotiating what form their potential union might take. As Obbo (1987) shows, informal unions may take the form of regular networks of wives and lovers which, despite their prevailing endogamy, provide a ready circuit for HIV transmission.

Discussion

The complexities of African nuptiality are not matters of merely local or regional concern. In addition to the pressing human problems they reveal, they have direct bearing on the several conceptual problems that have long bedevilled the diffusion hypotheses through which Western eyes have tried to see and understand demographic change. In the first place, whether the pattern observed is viewed as the widening of plural marriage or the spread of AIDS, the evidence of the mutability of ideas, institutions, and practices in the course of dissemination, and of the open-endedness of this process, emerges forcibly from the ethnography. It would plainly be inadequate to view these patterns as a linear trajectory leading to a single main outcome. The assumption that the nature of the ideas and practices 'diffusing' in a given society does not change in the process is likewise misleading.

Second, to make sense of the diversity of conjugal alternatives and the highly differential sequences in which people pass in and out of them, we are led inevitably to the need to formulate systematically the supra-individual or 'external' models—the 'polygynous templates', to use Parkin's (1988) phrase—which appear to be guiding current behaviour. Beneath people's shifting attempts, both conscious and unconscious, to control and shape the meaning of events and relationships in their lives lie the acceptable identities transmitted by their culture.

Third, in the African case, at least, it is clear that these identities are in conflict. To date, the influence of Western technology and culture appears to have done more to exacerbate this conflict than to introduce innovations whose ready diffusion can sweep problems away. Current research tends to characterize African demographic regimes in gender terms. The contrasting stereotypes are, on the one side, ambitious men multiplying (as ever) their womenfolk and their children, while seeking to limit their dependants' options; and on the other, increasingly ambitious women, seeking to use men's cupidity to their own purposes, or at least to carve out a secure and more independent niche for themselves and their children. The extent to which this picture is being influenced by the projection of conflicting male and female identities in Western societies on to the African situation is an open question.

Such alternatives could, of course, still be described in imitationist or diffusionist terms. The man described by Bledsoe (1990), who downplayed his rural wives in favour of the church-married and formally educated urban woman who became his latest spouse, may indeed be a convert to mono-gamy. However, we should like to know whether this transformation really precludes some formally educated 'outside' wives from lurking behind the scene. Diffusionist approaches tend inevitably to privilege a few avenues in a wider structure of alternatives. They isolate a few states and outcomes in a historical process, with little regard for people's past experience, and they minimize conflict. While diffusionism may be appropriate as an hypothesis in *a posteriori* theorizing (when the main influences may have become clear), as a framework for inquiry it remains an unhelpful constraint on attempts to understand transformations in the making.

Beyond the Impasse

The 'state of play' in diffusion studies, and the potential usefulness of diffusionism for explaining processes of demographic change, may be summarized in the following terms. First, our review has shown that it is useful to distinguish 'diffusionism' from the general sociological process that is its supposed object. This process consists broadly of the transmission of values, information, institutional arrangements, and products in the course of relations within and between societies. Second, this process is not adequately represented in terms of discrete products and information packages. Transmission brings with it transformations in objects, ideas, and social forms as they spread in a society or societies. These transformations in fact constitute the main interest and importance of studying diffusion, since it is here that more or less important adjustments in the structures of values and societies may occur. Diffusionism, in contrast, consists of a long series of attempts, from Tarde onwards, to describe these phenomena in terms of more or less direct imitation or adoption. The narrowness and insufficiency of diffusionist approaches has been itemized in the preceding pages, which draw on generations of criticism. Not only have diffusionists failed to resolve the shortcomings that critics have identified, but recent papers show that diffusion specialists are joining the ranks of the critics.

In the early post-war era, population studies developed their own interest in diffusion processes as an adjunct of prevailing models of socioeconomic development. According to this evolutionary and deterministic approach, demographic change was only secondarily a matter of cultural transmission; the real force underlying such changes consisted chiefly in large-scale economic development. Improvements in productivity, investment, and so forth were assumed to bring with them certain social adjustments (urban life-styles, education, etc.), and it was in the course of this wider modernization that mortality and fertility were expected to decline. As this evolutionary model effectively substituted for the history and culture of peoples, academic population studies generally found it necessary to say little or nothing about how values and products actually spread. The existence of some sort of communication process was accepted, but its role seemed to be as a kind of lubricant responsible in some cases for the speeding up or slowing down of the process. As the lines of force propelling developing societies into modernity were supposed to move at once upward (via economic growth) and downward (via declining rates of mortality and reproduction), the customary linear assumptions of diffusionism appeared entirely appropriate and unproblematic. As noted earlier, the 'calculus' of contraceptive choice took it for granted that cultural transmission consisted in all cases in the spread of unambiguous modern values and products along a trajectory to a common and relatively uniform Western-style outcome.

Diffusionism, in short, is not a new, primarily culture-oriented approach, opposed or alternative to the evolutionary postulates of socioeconomic development and modernization theories. It is part and parcel of them. Since the early 1970s, the serious neglect of the diversity of cultures inherent in this whole way of thinking has come in for a great deal of criticism. The revival of interest in cultural transmission, from Knodel and van de Walle through to Cleland, Wilson, and Watkins, is an important part of this more critical attitude. The conceptual problems that characterize diffusionism, however, indicate that a very different theory of transmission will be needed.[3] Indeed, it could be argued that one of the main legacies of stock evolutionary approaches has been not simply the devaluing of cultural transmission in favour of diffusionism: the deeper problem, still very troubling in population studies, is the impression often created that it is realistic to treat the socioeconomic determinants and the cultural aspects of society as actually separable in daily life. Their separation is, of course, a property of the models employed.

Anthropologists, meanwhile, have been encountering transmission processes in their fieldwork, which generally reflect the continuing historical encounter of European with other regional and local cultural traditions. The more recent emergence of anthropological demography has been no exception, to which the African studies cited in the preceding section amply attest. The history of anthropology, however, is littered with theoretical sketches of this wider encounter, from Malinowskian 'culture contact' to 'acculturation' and 'applied anthropology', down to Levi-Straussian *bricolage*. None of these sketches has succeeded in becoming a generally accepted paradigm in anthropology, and most remain unknown in the field of population and development studies.

Recently a senior anthropologist with established interests in demographic analysis addressed a long and stimulating article to reviewing some of these anthropological approaches (Hammel 1990). The fact that his paper has been widely cited in the demographic literature is a sign of the degree to which clarification of the anthropological background was needed. His readers, however, may well have come away disappointed (e.g. McNicoll 1992); for, despite generations of anthropological work on or around phenomena of cultural transmission, Hammel was unable to identify any existing theoretical paradigm or method that gives demographers a ready and agreed way of analysing population changes in their cultural dimensions. Demographers may well feel, paraphrasing Lord Douglas-Home, that the problem of incorporating cultural mechanisms into demographic models appears as insoluble as ever, while the reasons for anthropology's failure to rise to the occasion remain incomprehensible.[4]

This situation is likely to appear as an impasse, I suggest, only as long as we adhere to the narrow view of cultural transmission which has typified evolutionary-cum-diffusionist approaches. Taking a more realistic and subtle view of demographic change as an element in the interpenetration and transformation of cultures has, in turn, important implications for how we conceive the project of anthropological demography.

At present, a kind of 'underlabourer' thesis seems to prevail. The task of anthropological demography, in this view, is to contribute data and methods to the micro component of demographic theory and analysis. It is yet another in a seemingly endless series of sub-disciplines. This view is not without its virtues. As the African examples given above indicate, ethnography is a powerful solvent of hypotheses such as diffusionism. Much of the information that anthropological demography provides may be fed into practical efforts to improve health and related conditions in many countries. There is thus a significant positive role for anthropological demography as a sub-discipline, while its relative newness, and the sheer diversity of cultures with which it deals, provide convenient excuses for its rather inchoate appearance.

This view, however, contains a crippling flaw. As we have seen, evolutionary or deterministic development models have presupposed a concept of culture of an essentially diffusionist kind. Anthropological demography, as we have also seen, provides effective evidence to dissolve this concept. However, evolutionary models remain central to the ideals and practices of population research. Anthropological demography, if viewed simply as a sub-discipline, is in consequence put in an impossible position. On the one hand, its responsibility becomes that of constructing, as Hammel has put it, 'a theory of culture for demography', a new and better lubricant for the familiar evolutionary machine. On the other, its data and methods show that the diffusionist kind of cultural theory that fits this machine is vain.

The recent emergence of anthropological demography should be considered, rather, as part of a wider shift in the attitude of the social sciences to history. When Notestein put forward his ideas on demographic transition, he had to rely on generalized notions of socioeconomic development. At the time, there was a real paucity of comparative frameworks which gave any real appreciation of the historical context of demographic change. Nearly half a century later, the rise of new methods of social, demographic, and economic history means that we are in a different situation. This shift owes a great deal to the impressive ability of historians to weld anthropology and demography together into elements of a wider and powerful new historiography. Classic studies by Le Roy Ladurie, Ariès, Braudel, and Goubert, to cite only some better known figures, have shown how different people's identities are bound up and shaped by their historical experience of demographic events. At the level of family history, the relation between the timing of marriage and the control of status and property is probably the most familiar stock-in-trade of this literature. The issues raised, however, are not merely domestic. Family ideologies, when considered in conjunction with the demographic options and the constraints they employ, act not merely as a lubricant, but as crucial means by which classes, regional cultures, and national ideologies are actually formed and sustained. Anthropologists, by linking the study of kinship and marriage firmly to methods of historical demography, have developed important themes within this wider historical framework, including the existence of distinctive regional patterns (e.g. Segalen 1985; Viazzo 1989), and of social demographic concomitants of colonial and class structures (Kent 1977; Wolf and Huang 1980; Schneider and Schneider, Chapter 8 above). There is hardly space here to convey the range and energy of the body of research to which these works belong.

Two Descriptive Models of Demographic Change

The relation between what I have characterized roundly as evolutionary-cum-diffusionist approaches and the wider historiographical shift to which anthropological demography belongs is bound to remain contested for some time. My impression at this stage is that the two tendencies of sociological interpretation rest on fundamentally different conceptions of the nature of demographic and other wider changes in society. A brief summary of the main features and continuing difficulties inherent in each of these models provides a suitable point on which to conclude this paper.

The problem of latent demand

My task in summarizing the model of change assumed in evolutionary-cum-diffusionist approaches is greatly simplified by a recent article published by Rosero-Bixby and Casterline (1993). Their work gives an admirably clear account which is particularly informative for the following reason. In constructing a formal model of diffusion, they attempt to show that it is possible to operationalize diffusionism in a way that would make the transmission of information an independent force promoting fertility change, rather than the usual more or less invisible lubricant. Their model is given in Figure 13.1, presented here without its algebraic notation.

Demographic change is conceived in this model in terms of the movement of couples from one distinct state of contraceptive practice to another, according to the sequence non-contraception (natural fertility (N)) → desire for fertility control without the accompanying practice of it (latent demand (L)) → practice of fertility control (C). The middle term in this sequence arises principally from demand forces lying in socioeconomic determinants outside the model; the authors' main emphasis, however, is on showing how demand too is stimulated by 'diffusion interactions'. In brief, the existence of some sector of a population already in state C may become a mechanism of

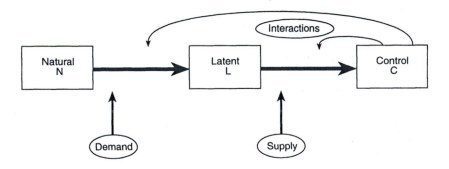

Fig. 13.1.   Interaction diffusion model of birth control adoption

fertility decline as couples in states N and L become aware of their contraceptive practice. This awareness acts as a feedback into the demand process in three related ways: via information flows, via the demonstration which members of C effectively provide of the benefits of contraception, and via the onset of normative changes accompanying such practice. The model measures all such diffusion simply in terms of contact rates, i.e. frequency of interactions. 'Adequate contact' (i.e. adequate to move a couple from one state to another) is imagined to operate in the manner of contagion; the volume of cases of an infectious disease may be a major factor in its spread in a general population.

Thus, in the model an increasing proportion of couples in state C should increase the level of latent demand, and also the conversion of this latent demand into fertility control—provided, of course, that members of these groups belong to shared communication networks. As to what actually happens in a 'contact' (that is, whatever makes it 'adequate' for diffusion to occur), and what features of a society actually structure and facilitate such contacts, the authors remain uncertain. They note that where relevant contact is minimal—say, where women are secluded, or open discussion of reproductive matters is discouraged—it seems unlikely that adequate contact can occur. In contrast, open or loosely structured societies—e.g. those with modern transportation and media networks—should facilitate diffusion.

Although the model allows a population of couples to be subdivided into social strata, the authors are aware that stratification is insufficient to specify which features of a social structure make it relatively loose. The supposed tightness or looseness of contacts raises, in turn, the question of whether cultural transmission can be understood adequately in terms of contact frequencies.[5] Not surprisingly, the authors conclude that the model remains dependent on further research into the capacity of different social structures to shape diffusion. Their dilemma is a reminder that diffusionism remains ancillary to linear evolutionary models.

Indeed, by making explicit the several premises of their model, Rosero-Bixby and Casterline provide clear instances of the three characteristic problems of diffusionism traced in earlier sections of this paper. These problems remain unsolved in their formalization. First, as they note, the model implicitly assumes isolated couples (p. 157); i.e., people are removed from the historical and cultural context in which they act. Second, diffusionist arguments presume that positive effects dominate (p. 157); in other words, the mutability of the ideas and practices presumed in the process of diffusion is not considered. Third, as the diagram shows, the model attributes a linear nature to diffusion, an evolution through successive, unambiguous states toward a limited, predetermined outcome.

In general, models that portray change as a succession of states without multiple outcomes or mutability of process show a strong tautological tendency. This feature of the diffusionist model proposed by Rosero-Bixby and Casterline is perhaps most evident in the problematic middle state or stage. As already noted, state L, like states N and C, is specified in terms of contact rates. Changes in frequency are assumed to proceed from non-existent to high levels of 'adequate contact'. Latent demand comes into being simply as the prescribed middle term in this sequence. As Knodel and his Thai colleagues have remarked, determining latent demand is admittedly a difficult task since it is an inherently hypothetical construct (Knodel *et al.* 1987: 111). Using focus groups, their research has tried to reconstruct possible past contraceptive desires via retrospective questioning, and also by assembling other pieces of information, such as awareness of traditional herbal techniques. Of course, focus groups organized for the purpose of discussing the evolution of contraceptive awareness and practice may have an effect, similar to the old KAP surveys, of predisposing participants to a certain class of answers. Knodel *et al.* understandably conclude that data pertaining to latent demand must be interpreted with caution (1987: 113).

Diffusion or transformation?

Latent demand is really a proxy for the knowledge we would need to have in order to understand the spread of fertility regulation. The knowledge in question is essentially historical, and consists in the changing significance of reproduction in a given society, or between and among several societies. A model of demographic change that approaches this problem in terms of a fixed sequence of states, as in the evolutionary assumptions of the classic demographic transition and diffusion hypotheses, in effect supplies the 'significance' at issue before inquiry has much of a chance to get underway.

   In contrast to evolutionism, there are models that conceive of change in terms of transformations. Many versions are currently on offer in the wider historical and anthropological literature, and they usually come with handy descriptive labels. Bourdieu (1977), for instance, writes of 'habitus' and 'practice'; Hobsbawm and Ranger (1983) refer to the 'invention of tradition', Anderson (1983) to 'imagined communities', and so on. A large body of writings now surrounds the notion of 'strategies' (Viazzo, forthcoming). The problems of mutability and multiplicity of outcomes are among the central issues in this literature. However, these approaches, with the exception of the study of strategies, have had relatively little impact to date on population theory and analysis, other than in anthropological contributions to regional and family history of the kind cited above. Elsewhere I have tried to show how apparently different cultural priorities may be understood as transformations of comparable sets of demographic opportunities and constraints (Kreager 1982; 1985; 1988). Since labels seem nowadays so *de rigueur*, I called these sets 'demographic regimes'.

None of these transformational approaches has concerned itself specifically with diffusion, at least as far as I am aware. The reasons for this seeming lapse are simple enough. Understanding processes of cultural transmission requires us to identify the several meanings people give to diffusing ideas, products, and practices. Only then can we begin to appreciate how their significance changes over time and space. Obviously we cannot assume that the starting point of the diffusion process is simply the instrumental and moral valuations of, say, new birth control technologies as understood in their culture of origin. What we need to understand is, rather, whether and how such instrumental and moral valuations are appropriated and modified by people in other cultures. We need, in other words, to situate them in existing structures of 'externality', to use Durkheim's terminology (see above). Diffusion, therefore, is not a special case of cultural transmission requiring its own theory: it is an ordinary part of the construction of meaning in society.

It is difficult to generalize across the several transformational approaches, such as those just cited. Three ideas that are at least implicit in all of them may perhaps be isolated. One is the notion of transformation itself. It is an historical axiom that traditional or 'old' ideas endure only in so far as they allow themselves to be reproduced in new forms; tradition is thereby reinvented in every change. 'New' ideas, in turn, can emerge only as new in relation to their antecedents. In short, it is tradition that changes; ideas and practices that cannot be related in a lasting way to an existing order become mere ephemera of a society's history.

A second guiding idea in this historiography is that transformations are manifest in several media simultaneously. By media, I refer not simply to channels of communication (newspapers, gossip, etc.), but to the several material forms in which changes in ideas and practices are manifest: acceptable expressions of sexuality; religious and political ritual; household composition; relations of production; consumption patterns; and so forth. This approach to change, in contrast to the linear trajectories of diffusionism, has more of the character of a matrix. Change is manifested in several interrelated forms of social life, more or less simultaneously. People are, so to speak, in the business of solving several problems at once. The solutions need not all proceed in the same way: there are different paths through the matrix.

Take, for example, the at first sight puzzling Catholic advocacy of birth limitation in Brittany, described by Segalen (1992). Up until the 1940s the Church forbade any form of contraception, but under Pius XII rhythm methods became permissible. Procreation was not devalued by this shift, but was reasserted as an expression of love and respect in the conjugal bond. Couples should give birth to as many children as they can raise decently; the growth of the family is a material expression of the conjugal bond, but this growth should not be allowed to put excessive strain on it. The values of marriage and abstinence were thus reaffirmed (rhythm being viewed as periodic abstinence), while sexuality within marriage was brought forward as a positive subject for discussion. At the same time, 'generous but reasonable' fertility was recognized as an aspect of how couples might resolve other material factors in their lives. Segalen notes in particular the shortage of farms to inherit, the rising cost of education, and changes in labour force requirements consequent on new agricultural techniques. The young men and women who adopted rhythm methods were the same people who organized themselves into the strong farm unions of the kind for which France has lately acquired a certain notoriety. Initially the unions, like the rhythm method, provided means of asserting positive identities of persons, couples, and extended families in a Breton context. But, like the rhythm methods, they became part of a set of linked ideas and practices capable of further transformation. Thus, the shift within Church and family which made possible the spread of birth limitation practised legitimately within the privacy of the home provided a context in which the spread of chemical contraception in the 1960s and 1970s could not be resisted effectively. The farm unions have likewise proved able to adapt effectively to new opportunities and constraints, notably as a political factor in recent debates over EC subsidies and GATT. All of this has become characteristically Breton.

An approach that sees demographic change as an element in a set of transformations thus allows us to see how changes that are related and interdependent may none the less proceed independently once a certain point is reached in the process. The fact that the several changes (some simultaneous, some not) each take a number of material forms means that our study of them needs to utilize several avenues of research, from political economy to the semiotics of the body. The linear trajectories, single outcomes, and immutability of cultural objects-in-transmission postulated by diffusionism are plainly inadequate to understand such matrices. Not until we have more of the kind of social network data advocated by Watkins (1990) and Hammel (1990) will we be in a position to assess whether recent attempts to clarify diffusionism, such as the model of Rosero-Bixby and Casterline, can prove helpful in tracking limited aspects of complex patterns of change.

The third element of transformational approaches which deserves note is that the ends to which analysis is directed can no longer be described adequately in terms of the evolutionary assumptions of socioeconomic development theory. The object to which the shift to history appears to lead is the comparative study of differing collective identities—personal, familial, communal, national, and international—and how they are constructed.

Notes

1. An account of such logics is essential, for example, to evaluating the hypothesis that a latent demand for fertility limitation has existed in certain cultures. I return to this hypothesis in the final section of the paper.

2. I should perhaps add that in what follows I have tried to stick closely to observations and implications drawn by participants at these seminars. Some reference is also made to related and supporting African research. As will be clear from the preceding critique of diffusionism, my intention is *not* to generalize in diffusionist terms on others' research (*pace* Caldwell 1993), but to take precisely the opposite approach, which shows how anthropological demography acts as a solvent.

3. In view of these conceptual problems, it may prove helpful to describe any such theory using terms other than 'diffusion'.

4. Sir Alec's epigram is much neater: 'There are two kinds of problem in life. Politics are insoluble and economics are incomprehensible' (cited in Chesnais 1992: 431).

5. The same difficulty remains in network analysis, as one of its foremost practitioners notes (Mitchell 1987). The relative looseness of social structures has not proved to be an operational concept (Evers 1969; Bunnag 1971).

References

Anderson, B. (1983), *Imagined Communities*. London: Verso.

Bledsoe, C. (1990), 'Transformations in sub-Saharan African marriage and fertility'. *Annals of the American Academy*, 510: 115–25.

——and Isiugo-Abanihe, U. (1989), 'Strategies of child-fosterage among Mende grannies in Sierra Leone', in R. J. Lesthaeghe (ed.), *Reproduction and Social Organization in Sub-Saharan Africa*. Berkeley: University of California Press, pp. 442–74.

——and Pison, G. (eds.) (1994), *Nuptiality in Sub-Saharan Africa*. Oxford: Clarendon Press.

Bourdieu, P. (1977), *Outline of a Theory of Practice*. Cambridge: Cambridge University Press.

Brandon, A. and Bledsoe, C. (1988), 'The effects of education and social stratification on marriage and the transition to parenthood in Freetown, Sierra Leone'. Paper presented to the Seminar on Nuptiality in Sub-Saharan Africa, Paris.

Bunnag, J. (1971), 'Loose structure: fact or fancy?' *The Siam Society Journal*, 59(1): 1–24.

Caldwell, J. C. (1976), 'Towards a restatement of demographic transition theory', *Population and Development Review*, 2: 321–66.

——(1980), 'Mass education as a determinant of the timing of fertility decline', *Population and Development Review*, 6(2): 225–56.

——(1993), 'Approaches to anthropological demography: an overview', in IUSSP, *International Population Conference, Montreal, 1993*, iv. Liège: IUSSP, pp. 303–12.

Carael, M. (1988), 'The impact of marriage change on the risks of exposure to sexually transmitted diseases in Africa'. Paper presented to the Seminar on Nuptiality in Sub-Saharan Africa, Paris.

Chesnais, J-C. (1992), *The Demographic Transition*. Oxford: Clarendon Press.

Cleland, J. and Wilson, C. (1987), 'Demand theories of the fertility transition: an iconoclastic view'. *Population Studies*, 41: 5–30.

Clignet, R. and Sween, J. (1974), 'Urbanization, plural marriage and family size in two African cities'. *American Ethnologist*, 1: 221–41.

Coale, A. (1973), 'The demographic transition reconsidered', in IUSSP, *International Population Conference, Liège, 1973*, i. Liège: IUSSP, pp. 53–72.

Dosi, G. (1991), 'The research on innovation diffusion: an assessment', in N. Naki-cenovic and A. Grüler (eds.), *Diffusion of Technologies and Social Behaviour*. New York: Springer-Verlag, pp. 179–208.

Durkheim, E. (1968 edn.), *Suicide: A Study in Sociology*, ed. G. Simpson, trans. J. A. Spaulding and G. Simpson. New York: Free Press. (First published in 1897.)

——(1982 edn.), *The Rules of Sociological Method*, ed. S. Lukes, trans. W. D. Halls. New York: Free Press. (First published in 1895.)

Dyson, T. (ed.) (1992), *Sexual Behaviour and Networking: Anthropological and Socio-cultural Studies on the Transmission of HIV*. Liège: Ordina Publications.

Enel, C., Pison, G., and Lefebre, M. (1988), 'Migration and marriage change: a case study of Mlomp, a Joola village in southern Senegal'. Paper presented to the Seminar on Nuptiality in Sub-Saharan Africa, Paris.

Evans-Pritchard, E. E. (1937), *Witchcraft, Oracles and Magic among the Azande*. Oxford: Clarendon Press.

Evers, H-D. (ed.) (1969), *Loosely Structured Social Systems: Thailand in Comparative Perspective*, Cultural Report Series no. 17. New Haven: Yale University Press.

Goode, W. (1963), *World Revolution and Family Patterns*. New York: Free Press.

Guyer, J. (1988), 'Polygynous motherhood: lineal identities and lateral linkages in marital change in a rural Yoruba community'. Paper presented to the Seminar on Nuptiality in Sub-Saharan Africa, Paris.

Hammel, E. A. (1990), 'A theory of culture for demography'. *Population and Development Review*, 16: 455–86.

Hobsbawm, E. and Ranger, T. (eds.) (1983), *The Invention of Tradition*. Cambridge: Cambridge University Press.

Isiugo-Abanihe, U. C. (1988), 'Consequences of bridewealth changes on nuptiality patterns among the Igbo of Nigeria'. Paper presented to the Seminar on Nuptiality in Sub-Saharan Africa, Paris.

Karanja, W. W. (1988), 'The phenomenon of "Outside wives": some reflections on its possible influence on fertility'. Paper presented to the Seminar on Nuptiality in Sub-Saharan Africa, Paris, 1988.

Katz, E., Levin, M. L., and Hamilton, H. (1963), 'Traditions of research on the diffusion of innovation', *American Sociological Review*, 28, 237–2.

Kent, F. (1977), *Household and Lineage in Renaissance Florence*. Princeton: Princeton University Press.

Knodel, J. and van de Walle, E. (1979), 'Lessons from the past: population implications of historical fertility studies'. *Population and Development Review*, 5: 217–45.

——Chamratrithirong, A., and Debavalya, N. (1987), *Thailand's Reproductive Revolution*. Madison, Wis.: University of Wisconsin Press.

Kreager, P. (1977), *Family Planning 'Drop-Outs' Reconsidered*. London: International Planned Parenthood Federation.

——(1982), 'Demography *in situ*'. *Population and Development Review*, 8(2): 237–66.

——(1985), 'Demographic regimes as cultural systems', in D. Coleman and R. Schofield (eds.), *The State of Population Theory*. Oxford: Basil Blackwell, pp. 131–55.

——(1988), 'Social and supernatural control in a Mayan demographic regime', in J. C. Caldwell *et al.* (eds.) (1988), *Micro-Approaches to Demographic Research*. London: Kegan Paul, pp. 410–28.

——(1993), 'Anthropological demography and the limits of diffusionism', in IUSSP, *International Population Conference, Montreal, 1993*, iv. Liège: IUSSP, pp. 313–26.

Kroeber, A. (1931), 'Diffusionism', in E. Seligman (ed.), *Encyclopaedia of the Social Sciences*, v. London: Macmillan, pp. 139–42.

Lesthaeghe, R. (ed.) (1989), *Reproduction and Social Organization in Sub-Saharan Africa*. Berkeley: University of California Press.

——and Surkyn, J. (1988), 'Cultural dynamics and economic theories of fertility change'. *Population and Development Review*, 14: 1–46.

Lukes, S. (1981), *Emile Durkheim, His Life and Work: A Historical and Critical Study*. London: Penguin.

McNicoll, G. (1980), 'Institutional determinants of fertility change'. *Population and Development Review*, 6: 441–62.

——(1992), 'The agenda of population studies: a commentary and complaint'. *Population and Development Review*, 18: 399–420.

Malinowski, B. (1928), 'The life of culture', in G. E. Smith *et al.* (eds.), *Culture: The Diffusion Controversy*. New York: W. N. Norton and Company, pp. 23–44.

——(1938), 'Introductory essay', in *Methods of Study of Culture Contact in Africa*. Oxford: International Institute of African Languages and Cultures, pp. vii–xxxviii.

Mitchell, J. C. (1987), *Cities, Society and Social Perception*. Oxford: Clarendon Press.

Notestein, F. (1945), 'Population: the long view', in T. W. Schultz (ed.), *Food for the World*, Chicago: University of Chicago Press, pp. 36–57.

Obbo, C. (1987), 'The old and the new in East African elite marriages', in D. Parkin and D. Nyamwaya (eds.), *Transformations of African Marriages*. Manchester: International African Institute, pp. 263–82.

——(1990), 'Sexual relations before AIDS'. Paper presented to the Seminar on Anthropological Studies Relevant to the Sexual Transmission of AIDS, Sønderborg.

Parkin, D. (1988), 'Anthropological perspectives on changes in African marriage'. Paper presented to the Seminar on Nuptiality in Sub-Saharan Africa, Paris.

Pebley, A. R. and Mbugua, W. (1989), 'Polygyny and fertility in sub-Saharan Africa', in R. J. Lesthaeghe (ed.), *Reproduction and Social Organization in Sub-Saharan Africa*. Berkeley: University of California Press, pp. 338–64.

Pilon, M. (1988), 'Types of marriage and marital stability: the case of the Moba–Gurma of North Togo'. Paper presented to the Seminar on Nuptiality in Sub-Saharan Africa, Paris.

Redfield, R. *et al.* (1936), 'Outline for the study of acculturation'. *American Anthropologist*, 38: 149–52.

Rogers, E. M. (1962), *Diffusion of Innovations*. New York: Free Press.

——(1973), *Communications Strategies for Family Planning*. New York: Free Press.

——(ed.) (1976), *Communication and Development: Critical Perspectives*. Beverly Hills, Calif.: Sage Publications.

Rosero-Bixby, L. and Casterline, J. B. (1993), 'Modelling diffusion effects in fertility transition'. *Population Studies*, 47(1): 147–67.

Schoepf, B. G. (1992), 'Sex, gender and society in Zaire', in T. Dyson, (ed.), *Sexual Behaviour and Networking: Anthropological and Sociocultural Studies on the Transmission of HIV*. Liege: Ordina Publications.

Segalen, M. (1985), *Quinze générations des bas Bretons: parenté et société dans le Bigouden Sud, 1720–1980*. Paris: Presses Universitaires de France.

—— (1992), 'Exploring a case of late French fertility decline: two contrasted Breton examples', in J. R. Gillis *et al.* (eds.), *The European Experience of Declining Fertility, 1850–1970*. Oxford: Blackwell, pp. 227–50.

Silverberg, G., Dosi, G., and Orsenigo, L. (1988), 'Innovation, diversity and diffusion: a self-organizational model'. *Economic Journal*, 98: 1032–54.

Smith, G. E. (1916), 'The influence of ancient Egyptian civilization in the East and in America'. *Bulletin of the John Rylands Library*, 13: 7–17.

Steady, F. C. (1987), 'Polygamy and the household economy in a fishing village in Sierra Leone', in D. Parkin and D. Nyamwaya (eds.), *Transformations of African Marriage*. Manchester: International African Institute, pp. 211–32.

van de Walle, E. (1992), 'Fertility transition, conscious choice and numeracy'. Presidential Address to the Population Association of America.

—— and Meekers, D. (1988), 'Marriage drinks and kola nuts'. Paper presented to the Seminar on Nuptiality in Sub-Saharan Africa, Paris.

Viazzo, P. P. (1989), *Upland Communities: Environment, Population and Social Structure in the Alps since the 16th Century*. Cambridge: Cambridge University Press.

—— (forthcoming), 'Anthropology, history and the concept of "Strategy"', in R. Wall and O. Saito (eds.), *Economic and Social Aspects of the Family Life Cycle in Europe and Japan, Traditional and Modern*. Cambridge: Cambridge University Press.

Watkins, S. C. (1987), 'The fertility transition: Europe and the Third World compared'. *Sociological Forum*, 2: 645–73.

—— (1990), 'From local to national communities: the transformation of demographic regimes in Western Europe, 1870–1960. *Population and Development Review*, 16: 241–72.

Wolf, A. P. and Huang, J.-S. (1980), *Marriage and Adoption in China 1845–1945*. Stanford, Calif.: Stanford University Press.

Index